Tribals and the Indian Constitution

Tribals and the Indian Constitution

Functioning of Fifth Schedule in the State of Orissa

N.K. BEHURA
NILAKANTHA PANIGRAHI

RAWAT PUBLICATIONS
Jaipur • New Delhi • Bangalore • Mumbai • Hyderabad

ISBN 81-316-0011-4

The publication of this book was financially supported by ICSSR and the responsibility for the facts stated, opinions expressed or conclusions reached, is entirely that of the author and that ICSSR accepts no responsibility for them.

ICSSR Consultant
Prof. Kuldeep Mathur

Published by
Prem Rawat for **Rawat Publications**
Satyam Apts., Sector 3, Jawahar Nagar, Jaipur 302 004 (India)
Phone: 0141 265 1748 / 7006 Fax: 0141 265 1748
E-mail: info@rawatbooks.com
Website: www.rawatbooks.com

New Delhi Office
4858/24, Ansari Road, Daryaganj, New Delhi 110 002
Phone: 011-23263290

Also at Bangalore, Mumbai and Hyderabad

Typeset by Rawat Computers, Jaipur
Printed at Chaman Enterprises, New Delhi

Contents

Preface

Orissa is a harmonious milieu of multi-ethnic groups. Before the formation of the State in 1936, Oriya-speaking tracts were part of the neighbouring provinces. On the face of geo-physical features the State of Orissa is broadly divided into two sub-regions, namely, the coastal belt and the interior areas. The Eastern Ghat hill range runs through the State in north-south direction. The Eastern Ghat hill range, is the abode of several tribal communities and repository of ferrous and non-ferrous ores. Compared to the coastal region and people therein, the inland region is backward for various reasons. The tribal communities inhabiting the central and western regions of the State are socio-economically backward. There are 62 Scheduled Tribes in the State of Orissa.

Realising the socio-economic backwardness of the tribal communities the founding fathers of the Constitution of India have enshrined several protective measures for their welfare and development. Apart from several Articles, Fifth and Sixth Schedules have been incorporated in the Constitution of India for appropriate administration of tribal people and tribal areas of the country.

After independence, the colonial approach towards tribals was replaced by different welfare and development approaches. During different Five-Year Plans, Government of India have formulated special schemes like Multi-Purpose Tribal Development Blocks (1968), Pilot Projects for Tribal Development (1972), Hill Area Development Programme (1975), Tribal Sub-Plan approach in

1975 so as to implement the Integrated Tribal Development Projects or ITDAs, Special Micro-Projects, MADA and cluster approaches were introduced as strategic plans for overall development of tribal communities. All these schemes basically aim to reduce the backwardness of tribal region and to develop the tribal communities. Accordingly, funds are being channelised from Central and State development plans in proportion for the development of ST population in the State.

Laws have been enacted by the State of Orissa since 1950 to safeguard the interest of tribals in respect of land, indebtedness, excise policy, protection of civil rights, reservation of vacancies in posts and services, abolition of bonded labour, tribal rights over NTFPs, etc. In spite of the existing laws, the Working Group of the Seventh Five-Year Plan (1987:11) and the Chairman National Commission for STs and SCs at various points of time have stated that the provisions of the Fifth Schedule of the Constitution have remained largely non-operational, and by and large, the Constitutional privileges for the STs have not been realised by them. The State of Orissa has started the decentralisation process by extending the Panchayati Raj Act to Scheduled Areas and thereby empowering tribal people through Gram Sabha. However, it seems to be an initial step from the scope of the Fifth Schedule of the Constitution.

The present book justifies its importance by trying to make a critical appraisal of the functioning of the Fifth Schedule of the Constitution of India in the State of Orissa. The role of various State and national level agencies for the welfare of tribal people in the State has been duly analysed and the impact of various policies has been properly assessed.

The authors are thankful to the Indian Council of Social Science Research (ICSSR), New Delhi, for providing financial support to accomplish the empirical study and to publish this book.

The study could not have been completed without the intellectual support of D.C. Mishra and B. Misra, ex-Chairman of Nabakrushna Choudhury Centre for Development Studies and L.K. Mahapatra, the present Chairman of the Centre. They are constant sources of stimulation and encouragement. We record our sincere gratitude to all of them for guidance and advice.

We very sincerely record our indebtedness to G.C. Kar, ex-Director and S. Padhi, the present Director, of Nabakrushna Choudhury Centre for Development Studies, Bhubaneswar, for their cooperation and administrative support for the successful completion.

R.K. Mohapatra, Asstt. Librarian and Mrs. S. Pani, Asstt. Computer Programmer of the Centre deserve our thanks for their untiring cooperation rendered during the work.

We thank Puskar Jena, Research Investigator for his strenuous anthropological fieldwork in different study villages.

We take this opportunity to express our gratitude to the tribal inhabitants, employees of different government departments/ agencies/institutes who have ungrudgingly extended all cooperation to us in our study.

We are solely responsible for the views expressed here or for any error therein.

NCDS
Bhubaneswar

N.K. Behura
N. Panigrahi

Abbreviations

AH&VS	Animal Husbandry and Veterinary Services
AMCS	Agriculture Marketing Cooperative Society
BALCO	Bharat Aluminium Company
BOJP	Brukshya O' Jeevara Bandhu Parishad
CBO	Community Based Organisation
CDPO	Child Development Project Officer
CD	Community Development Block
CPC	Criminal Procedure Code
CMIE	Center for Monitoring for Indian Economy
DRDA	District Rural Development Agency
DMK	Dravid Munatra Kazagam
DWCRA	Development of Women and Children in Rural Areas
DWO	District Welfare Officer
FPC	Forest Protection Committee
GoI	Government of India
GoO	Government of Orissa
GP	Gram Panchayat
HRPC	Human Rights Protection Cell
HINDALCO	Hindustan Aluminium Company
IAY	Indira Awas Yojana
ICDS	Integrated Child Development Schemes
IGP	Income-Generation Programme
IMFL	Indian Made Foreign Liquor
INGO	International Non-Government Organisation

IPC	Indian Penal Code
IPICOL	Industrial Promotion and Investment Corporation Ltd.
ITDA	Integrated Tribal Development Agency
ITDP	Integrated Tribal Development Project
IWDP	Integrated Watershed Development Project
JFM	Joint Forest Management
KBK	Kalahandi, Bolangir and Koraput
K&VI	Khadi and Village Industries
LAMPS	Large Area Multi-Purpose Societies
L&T	Lerson and Tubro
MADA	Modified Area Development Agency
ME	Middle English School
MFP	Minor Forest Produces
MLA	Member of Legislative Assembly
MML	Margin Money Loan
MNC	Multi National Company
MoU	Memorandum of Understanding
MV	Malkangiri Village
NABARD	National Agriculture Bank for Rural Development
NAC	Notified Area Council
NAFED	National Agriculture Federation
NALCO	National Alluminium Company
NCSC& ST	National Commission for Scheduled Caste and Scheduled Tribes
NGO	Non-Government Organisation
NSDP	Net State Domestic Product
NTFP	Non-Timber Forest Produce
OBC	Other Backward Communities
OFDC	Orissa Forest Development Corporation Ltd.
OLA	Orissa Legislative Assembly
OLR	Orissa Land Reform
OMLR	Orissa Money Lending Regulation
OMS	Orissa Moneylending Service
ORG	Operation Research Group
ORMAS	Orissa Rural Development Marketing Society

OS	Out Stilled
OSFDC	Orissa State Finance Development Corporation Ltd.
PHC	Public Health Centre
PRA	Participatory Rural Appraisal
PRI	Panchayati Raj Institution
PSSP	Prakrutika Sampad Surakha Parishad
PTG	Primitive Tribal Group
RI	Revenue Inspector
R&TI	Research and Training Institute
SAP	Surplus Agriculture Produces
SCA	Special Central Assistance
SCSTRTI	Scheduled Caste and Scheduled Tribe Research and Training Institute
SC	Scheduled Caste
SGSY	Swarnajayanti Gram Swarozgar Yojana
SHG	Self-Help Group
ST	Scheduled Tribe
TAC	Tribal Advisory Council
TASMAC	Tamil Nadu State Marketing Corporation Ltd.
TBA	Traditional Birth Attendants
TDCC	Tribal Development Cooperative Corporation Ltd.
THRTI	Tribal and Harijan Research-cum-Training Institute
TRIFED	Tribal Cooperative Marketing Federation India Ltd.
T&RW	Tribal and Rural Welfare
TRI	Tribal Research Institute
TSP	Tribal Sub-Plan
UAIL	Utkal Aluminium
UFPL	Utkal Forest Produces Ltd.
UN	United Nations
UT	Union Territory
VFPC	Village Forest Protection Committee
VSS	Vana Surakhya Samiti
WB	World Bank
WEO	Welfare Extension Officer
WTO	World Trade Organisation

List of Tables

1 Introduction

India is one of the nation-states of the world to have elaborate preferential arrangements for the hundreds of ethnic minorities in general and tribal communities in particular. While understanding the historical reasons for the backwardness of such tribal groups, the country has made Constitutional provisions, several special plans and programmes for their welfare and development, and has been allocating funds for this purpose in the national and state budgets.

Provision of special protective measures for the development of tribal communities was felt necessary since late 19th century and were reflected at different points of time in the form of the Scheduled District Acts of 1874, the Indian Education Commission of 1882, Government of India Act of 1919 and 1935, who paid some attention for special treatment of the communities. In post-independent period, Thakkar Bapa, Jaipal Singh and few others played a major role in reshaping the Tribal Welfare and Protective measures. As a result, series of Constitutional provisions in the form of Constitutional safeguards, Articles and Schedules have been incorporated in the Constitution of India for the welfare and development of the tribal people.

Understanding the backward features of both the tribal areas and of tribal population, the State of Orissa over the time has also taken many legislative measures (explained in Chapter 2) for tribal welfare both during pre- and post-independent era. Apart from the functioning of the Tribes Advisory Council (TAC), as regards the administration and control of Scheduled Areas and Scheduled Tribes several Constitutional provisions are also in operation in the State of Orissa.

The book justifies its importance by trying to make a critical appraisal of the functioning of the Fifth Schedule of the Constitution of India in the State of Orissa, the role of various State level agencies and the formulation of policies relating to the welfare of tribal people in the State. The present chapter has four interrelated sections. The first section, while describing in brief the physiography of Orissa, provides a brief account of tribal situation in Orissa; the second section reviews the jurisdiction of the Scheduled Areas and the list of Scheduled Tribes, the processes of inclusion and exclusion of communities in the Scheduled List; the third section describes the nature of relationship of tribal people with the natural resources, particularly land and forest, and the impact of planned development on their livelihood resources; the last section gives a brief idea about the anatomy of the study which explains the objectives, study area, methods and techniques followed, sample size, survey design, chapterisation and the limitations of the book.

I

Physiography of Orissa

The State of Orissa, located between 17 and 22.3 North Latitudes and between 51.3 to 87.5 East Longitudes, represents a State situated on the Coast of Bay of Bengal, which is surrounded by Andhra Pradesh in the south, Bay of Bengal in the east, Chhattisgarh in the west, West Bengal and Bihar in the north. The geo-physical structure of the State is divided into four major zones. Depending upon the agro-climatic features, the State is divided into various productive zones by the Department of Agriculture, Government of Orissa. These are distributed in various geographical proportions. The State presently covers 1,55,707 sq kms which accounts for 4.74 per cent of total land area of the country and geographically ranks in the 9th position among the Indian States. The administrative divisions of the State owned 13 districts during 1948, again restructured into 30 districts in 1992, which are sub-divided into 59 sub-divisions, consisting of 314 Community Development Blocks, comprising of 56,887 villages. As far as the population strength of the State is concerned, it ranks in the 11th position and shares 3.74 per cent of India's population with a growth rate of 2 per cent per annum. Since 1921, the State has experienced a progressive decline in the sex ratio of females. With regard to sex ratio while it was 1,086 females per 1,000 males in 1921, it has been reduced to 927 females during 1991.

Orissa being the heart of the Eastern Ghat hill ranges, carries major rivers like the Mahanadi, Brahmani, Baitarani, Budhabalanaga, Subarnarekha, Salandi, Kharswan, Rushikulya, Vansadhara, and Nagavali which drain into Bay of Bengal. The rivers like Indravati, Kolab, Saberi, Machakund, and Sileru are the tributaries of river Godavari which are flowing through the undivided Koraput district. The rivers like Mahanadi, Brahmani and Subarnarekha have their origin outside the Eastern Ghats, but pass through the State of Orissa. A good number of multi-purpose dam projects on the river Mahanadi, Brahmani, Subarnarekha, Indravati and Kolab have been constructed to control flood, provide irrigation and produce hydro-electric power.

According to the physical features and agro-climatic conditions, topographically, the State can be divided into four distinct zones. They are: (i) The Northern Plateau which accounts for 23 per cent of the total of the State area and includes the districts of Mayurbhanj, Keonjhar, Sundargarh, and portions of Angul, Cuttack and Sambalpur. The hills in these regions rise to an elevation of 600 to 900 m above the mean sea level. (ii) The Central Table Land consists of the districts of Bolangir, southern part of Dhenkanal and part of Phulbani. The elevation spreads maximum to the point of 300 to 800 m. (iii) The Eastern Ghat Region consists of hill ranges of the mainland of Eastern Ghats which spreads with extensive plateaus ranging from 300 to 450 m covering 36 per cent of the total land area of the State. It covers the districts of Koraput, Kalahandi (both old) Kandhamal and Gajapati. (iv) The Coastal Plain covers 18 per cent of the total land area, runs from north to south and covers the districts of Balasore, Bhadrakh, Cuttack, Kendrapada, Jagatsinghpur, part of Jajpur, Puri, part of Khurda and Ganjam.

The genesis of the soil in the State depends on the micro topographical situations and geomorphology of the different land types. Taking into account, we have various types of soil like red soil, laterite soil, black soil, mixed red and black type soil, brown soil, alluvial soil, coastal saline and sandy. The cultivable area according to the physiographic situation are generally divided into high lands producing crops like maize, millets, upland paddy and arhar; the medium lands produce medium duration paddy; and the low lands generally produce late paddy of longer duration.

As regards the forest there are two types of forest recognised by the Forest Act, i.e., reserved forest and protected forest. The protected forests are divided as cultivable and non-cultivable. All the protected forests are covered under the control of Revenue Department. As a result, the State till date, has not made proper land use planning. The second dimension of the forest issue is the coverage of forests, which varies in total area and percentage to the land area. The difference still continues. The State has three major types of forest. They are: the Northern Tropical Semi-ever Green Forest, the Northern Tropical Moist Deciduous Forests, and the Northern Tropical Dry Deciduous Forest. The major forest produces in Orissa are timber, firewood, bamboo, minor forest produces, and kenduleaf. The rich potentiality and the availability of kenduleaf and timber in Orissa has been proved from the government revenue records. The population growth in forest region, adoption of stringent forest policies by the government and expansion of mega-development projects has considerably affected the forest resources of the State.

II

Meaning of the Term 'Tribe'

To define the concept of the term 'tribe' is an old attempt. However, the attempts made by different scholars at different points of time often overlap. While defining, scholars have emphasised on universality, validity, and applicability of the term. The term 'tribe' has assumed different meanings in different historical contexts, basically refers to 'people' (Leach, 1954) or communities of people mentioned as 'Janah' in Vedic and Sanskrit literature (Choudhury, 1977: 6-12).

Since the days of extensive fieldwork carried out by Morgan among the American Indians and by Evans-Pritchard among the Nuers of East Africa, a structural definition has been drawn on this concept. However, it was basically confined to the small-scale communities. In rare cases, the neighbouring communities have been included if they figure as an integral part of the concerned community. Gradually, the demand was generated to define the tribe as a type of distinct social formation. However, it has always been a difficult task before the scholars. The conceptual understanding of the tribe by the scholars during 19th century was based on the stages of evolution and type of society and other features like relative isolation, common territory, common name and a common language, simple social formation, strong kinship bond, single social rank, distinct customs, existence of youth dormitory, common ownership over land and other natural resources and low level of technological development or combination of few such attributes.

In the Indian context, many attempts have been made to distinguish the tribe from that of non-tribal groups which help in understanding the concept of the term tribe (Mandelbum, 1956; Bailey, 1961). For the first time Ghurye (1943) brought forward a wealth of evidences from classical, medieval, and modern sources to demonstrate the interpretation of tribal and non-tribal cultural practices and social organisations. While gaining experiences through cross-cultural ethnographic studies Naroll (1964) and Moreman (1965) had attempted to define the boundaries of the tribe for cross-cultural purposes.

The necessity of making census in Indian States during British era was not simply aiming at the census of population, rather it was more of documentation of the natural resources of the localities. This became useful as a wealth for making capital, which was rightly understood by the British rulers. The first census report by Baine during 1891, the then Commissioner for Census of India included all tribal groups as 'Forest Tribes', and kept the same under the sub-heading of 'Agricultural and Pastoral Castes'. Their number was estimated at 16 million, who were again classified as 'Animists' in the Census Report of 1901 by Risley and as 'Tribal Animist' or people following 'tribal religion' in the Census Report of 1911 by Gait; as 'Hill and Forest Tribes' in the Census Report of 1931 by Hutton. These people by that time were numbering 22 million and later on came to be known as 'Backward Tribes' in the Government of India Act 1935, and as 'Tribes' in the Census Report of 1941 accounting for a total population of 2.47 crores. Similarly, over the time the term 'tribe' in Indian context, by and large, is synonymously used as *Adivasi* (original settlers), *Girijan* (hill dwellers), *Vanyajapt* (forest caste), *Adimjati* (primitive caste), *Janajati* (folk communities) and *Anusuchit Janajati* (Scheduled Tribe). Identification of the tribal groups through various fictitious names not only brought many common masses into its fold, but also imposed various new names, which the tribal people even do not recognise. Another dimension of the term tribe is that in spite of various definitions and designations given to it, during last the 10 years, anthropologists and others have come across of a new term, that is 'indigenous people' which also conceptually challenges the earlier meaning of the term for tribe. The justifications to replace all the earlier connotations of this term, tribal population basically relates to two major characteristics which have become the basis for identifying them as such, that is autochthons various later settlers. The term 'indigenous people' to a large extent are similar to that of the term 'native' used during the colonial period. Since the distinctions of physical, racial traits and religion do not show many differences as compared to the non-tribal population the question of habitat, language and dialect have been regarded as the basis of tribal identity.

Soon after independence of India, it was felt to prepare a package of special protection policies and launch development efforts for the tribal population, which were incorporated in the Constitution of India. Certain pockets in India are largely dominated by the tribal communities, then known as 'excluded area' for the outsiders, which became redesigned as Scheduled Area and the list of tribal groups, later on noted in Indian Constitution, came to be known as Scheduled Tribes as per Article 342. The number of such Scheduled Tribes in India was 212 in 1950, increased to 427 in 1971, again increased to 437 in 1981, and 612 in 1991, may be little more in recent decades, who vary in terms of population size, geographical distribution, mode of production and social organisation. The conscious attempt to change the listing of Scheduled Tribes specifically during 1956 and 1976 has never changed its number compared to the changes in the later period due to various factors like political compassion and internal divisions. Many scholars have also referred to tribe as a type of society representing stage in social evolution, signifying a set of characteristic features and specific mode of social organisation (Service, 1962; Fried, 1966; Behura, 1988-89: 195). They have explained four major sequential stages of evolution from 'band' to tribe to 'chiefdom' to the state (ibid.). Later on, some of them have denied of the existence of any difference between tribe and chiefdoms (Shalins, 1962), band and tribes (Service, 1975), who however, do not reveal a meaningful direction (Godelier, 1977: 76-87).

The logic of defining 'tribe' is easily understood if it is linked to the debates of Constituent Assembly where Jaipal Singh a member favoured the use of the term 'Adivasi' instead of 'Scheduled Tribe'. This was rejected on the ground as argued by Dr. B.R. Ambedkar, Chairman of the Drafting Committee of the Constitution that the word Adivasi is really a general term, which has no specific legal *de jure* connotations. He argued that the term 'Scheduled Tribe' has a fixed meaning because it enumerates the tribes.

Defining the concept of tribe in such a manner in India is still continuing due to the fact that very few studies have developed this issue, rather most of the scholastic studies on tribal themes are associated with tribal welfare. In this respect, Beteille concludes that anthropologists in India both before and after independence have been concerned more with the practical problems of definition (1972: 188). As a result, even after five decades of development any attempt to include or exclude a group or a part thereof became a question of benefiting or depriving them from the protective regulation and largely became a discussion for the political statecrafts. During the last couple of decades, with the promulgation of special plan and policies for the welfare of the tribal people, certain indicators concerning poverty and backwardness have influenced the scholars while defining the concept of tribe. However, it is a fact that grouping tribal communities under the banner of Scheduled Tribes of the Indian Constitution does not help much in really consolidating their positions as single ethnic, linguistic and cultural entities rather than maintain their distinct identities.

Brief Account of the Tribal Situation in Orissa

Orissa always takes an important, distinct and colourful position in the national map by harbouring various ethnic groups from time immemorial. Leaving apart the State of Nagaland, this State of Orissa carries the highest percentage of tribal population in India. Considering the development index, the President of India during 1956 declared 62 different tribal communities of Orissa as Scheduled Tribes, out of which 12 communities are considered as Primitive Tribal Group (PTG) for special treatment.

Almost 44.21 per cent of the total land area in Orissa have been declared as Scheduled Area. Except the coastal belt, many of the districts of the State have been declared either partially or fully as Scheduled Area (Map 1 and Map 2). The present Scheduled Area of the State covers six districts as fully and seven districts as partially scheduled. The districts of Mayurbhanj, Sundargarh, Koraput, Nawarangpur, Malkangiri and Rayagada are wholly Scheduled Areas. Thus, out of 314 Community Development Blocks in Orissa, 118 (37.3%) blocks are preponderantly occupied by the tribal communities which are covered under Tribal Sub-Plan (TSP). The districts dominated by tribal communities are Malkangiri (58.51%), Sundargarh (50.74%), Koraput (50.67%), whereas, the districts with a sizeable tribal population are

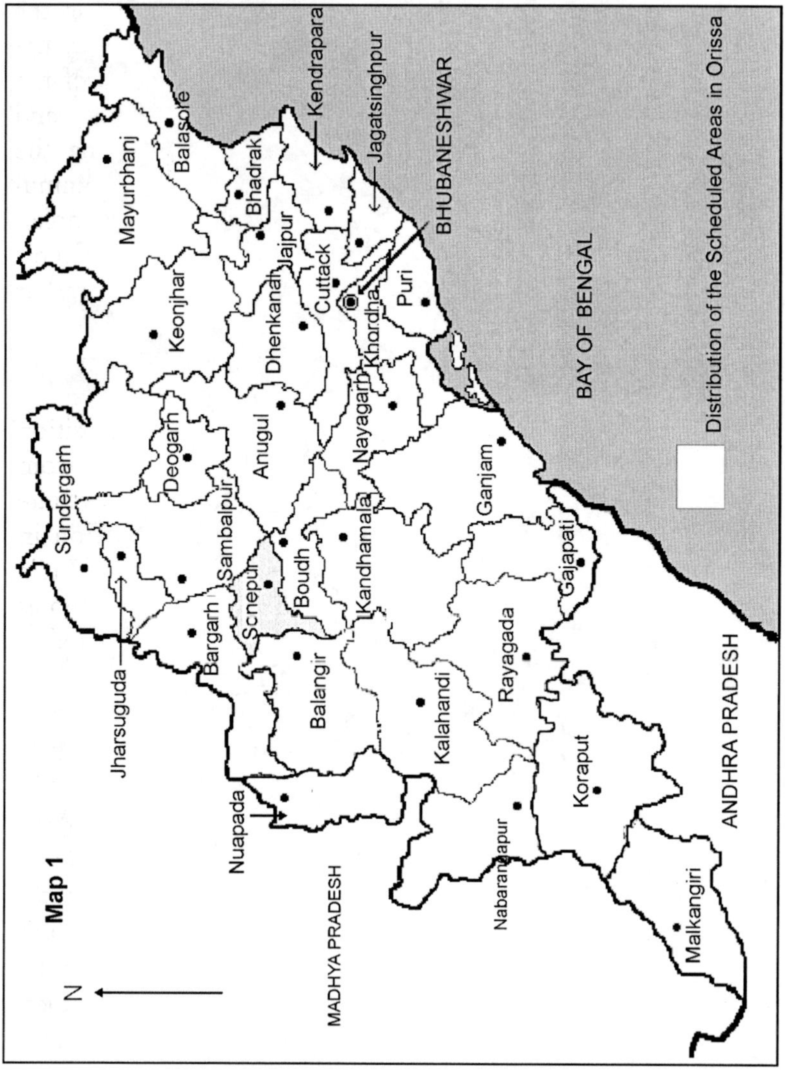
Map 1
N
MADHYA PRADESH
Nuapada
Jharsuguda
Sundergarh
Bargarh
Sambalpur
Deogarh
Scnepur
Boudh
Anugul
Keonjhar
Mayurbhanj
Balasore
Bhadrak
Jajpur
Dhenkanal
Cuttack
Kendrapara
Jagatsinghpur
BHUBANESHWAR
Khordha
Puri
Nayagarh
Kandhamala
Balangir
Kalahandi
Ganjam
Gajapati
Rayagada
Nabarangapur
Koraput
Malkangiri
BAY OF BENGAL
ANDHRA PRADESH
Distribution of the Scheduled Areas in Orissa

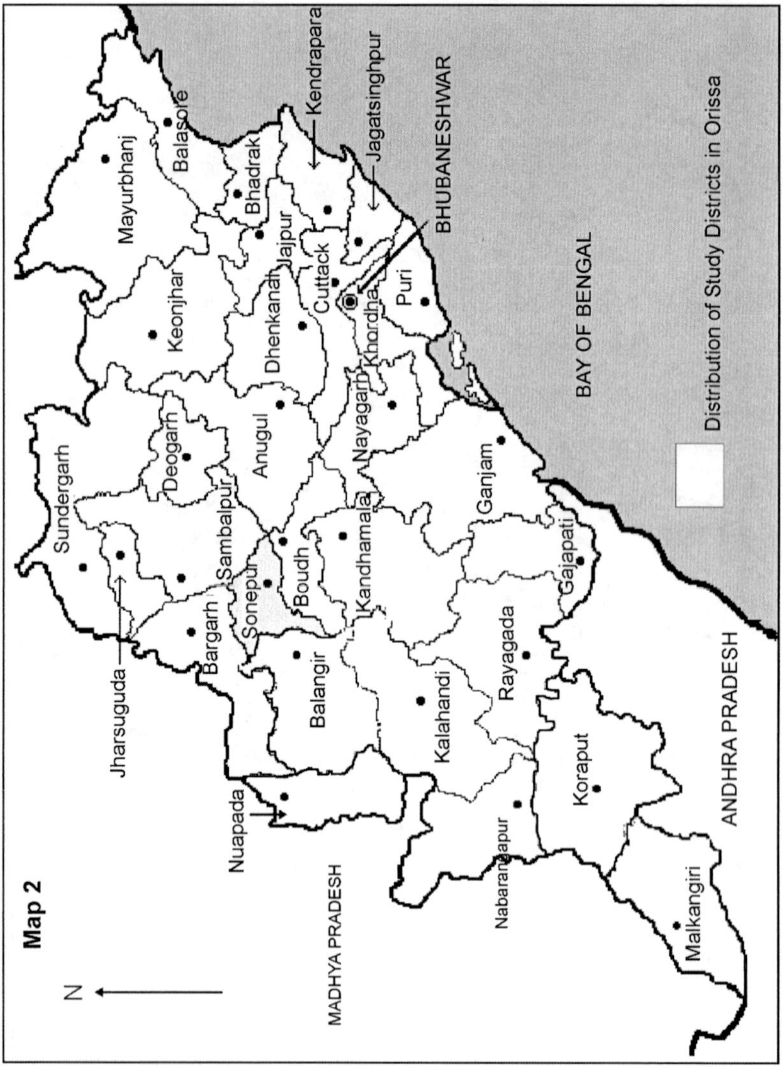

Map 2

Distribution of Study Districts in Orissa

Keonjhar (44.62%), Gajapati (47.88%), Jharsuguda (33.88%), Nuapada (35.95%), and Deogarh (33.31%). Thus, the tribal population of Orissa constitutes 22.21 per cent of the State's population. The major tribes of Orissa in terms of their numerical strength are the *Kondh, Gond, Santal, Saora, Bhuiyan, Paraja, Koya, Oraon, Gadaba, Juanga* and *Munda.* Apart from these, there are also a good number of smaller tribal communities living in Orissa. The Census Report of 2001 reflects that the *Chenchus* are the smallest tribal community representing only 28 persons. There are 15 tribal groups distributed in Orissa, each covering more than one lakh persons. When tribal communities like *Santal, Gond, Munda, Ho, Birhor, Koya, Lodha, Kondha, Bhumija, Kharia* and *Oraons* cut across the State boundaries and are found in the neighbouring states of Bihar, Chhattisgarh, Andhra Pradesh and West Bengal, the tribal communities like Juanga, Bonda and Didayee are found to be confined to the regions of origin in the districts of Keonjhar and Malkangiri (Table 1.4).

Most of the tribal communities of Orissa are of Protoaustroloid racial category. However, Mangoloid characteristics are also found among Gadabas and Saoras. The tribes of Orissa belong to three major linguistic divisions. They, by and large, maintain their linguistic identities and quite a sizeable population of them belong to Mundari group of Austric language family and South Dravidian sub-group of Dravidian language family. In recent decades, a few tribal groups like Santal, Ho, Saora, and Kui-Kandha have developed their own scripts. However, almost all these tribes have an undocumented script but well developed means of communication. A large number of tribals of Orissa speak Oriya and show various socio-cultural similarities with the neighbouring Oriyas in their way of life. Tribal societies for certain common characteristics like animism, crude technology, concentrated habitation, use of a common dialect, subsistence economy, etc., keep themselves distinguished from complex and advanced societies.

It is appropriate here to write a few lines on cultural continuity and change. It has been observed that a process of cultural and social assimilation has been going on among many tribes of Orissa. This has provided them a gradual assimilation into the Hindu peasantry at various levels like Kshatriya, agricultural clean caste groups or even caste groups (Mahapatra, 1968: 397). This process of tribe-caste integration in Orissa has become rampant as in many other pockets of India, and the process was mostly patronised by temple administrations, local kings, zamindars or influential personalities to institutionalise the achieved higher status of a tribal community (ibid., 67). However, scholars have also looked at this process of cultural assimilation and mobility along the tribe-caste continuum as bi-directional with mutual emulation of cultural traits and the way of life (Behura and Mishra, 1985: 59-69). This also proves from Bose's contemplation on the cultural absorption of the Juanga in Orissa with the neighbouring Hindu castes who quietly absorbed the subtle operation of the process of Hinduisation among them (Bose, 1974: 204). Mahapatra has given similar views while studying the Bhuyans of Bonei of Sundargarh who have adopted the style of life of the Warier caste, that is the Khandayat due to land acquisition (ibid., 68). It has so happened that the Rajas have helped to alleviate the social status of few tribal communities as reported in case of Bathudi barber, washerman and potters in Mayurbhanj who were recognised by the then Raja and conferred upon them caste status and gone under the process of Sanskritisation. They feel themselves elevated in the social hierarchy. The reverse process of bi-directional flow of cultural traits are also found due to the internalisation of the various typical tribal features by the caste communities which has generated the process of universalisation and tribalisation. The example of such a process is very much expressed in the upgradation of the Hill Bhuiyan deity 'Kanta-Kumari' from the status of a tribal deity to Hindu Goddess Samalai of Sambalpur which was claimed to be worshipped by local Sahara community and was adopted as the State deity by the king of Sambalpur (Mahapatra, op. cit.: 67-68; Sinha: 1962). Another dimension of looking at the cultural assimilation as interpreted by Roy (1972:12) and Bose (1967: 214) that superior technological, economic, political, social and cultural forces affect and influence the less powerful cultures, despite their cultural richness, because, culture flows from a politically and economically dominant group to a subservient one. The Binjhals living in the western part of Orissa are at loss of their own language, the older generation use a dialect which is not used by the young generation, while the older generation take in their native Binjhali dialect, the younger do not understand their own dialect much and talk in Oriya language. This is how their language has got almost assimilated with the neighbouring dominant Oriya language (Panda, 1982).

II

This section reviews the jurisdiction of the Scheduled Areas and the list of Scheduled Tribes of Orissa; the processes of inclusion and exclusion adopted by the State over the years. All the legislative and administrative measures adopted in Orissa for the development of the tribal people has its roots in laws and regulations enacted during pre-independent India. A review of the historical evolution of such laws and regulations reflects that prior to 1946 there were 14 number of laws which prevailed in the Scheduled Areas of the State. These regulations were either a part of Madras Presidency or Central Province regulations. Following the Scheduled District Act of 1874, the Agency Rules 1924 was made by the Government of Madras and were further amended by the Orissa Agency Rules (Orissa Amendment) Regulation, 1946 for the purpose of their application in the Agency Tracts of Ganjam and Koraput districts which were partially excluded areas of the province of Orissa.

The Orissa Regulation I of 1946: Agency (Orissa Amendment) Regulation, 1946

According to this regulation Agency Courts were established for Agency Tracts. After the annexation of Ganjam and Koraput districts on formation of the separate State of Orissa in 1936, this regulation was enforced for application for its provisions to the agency tracts of the Ganjam and Koraput districts which were declared as 'Partially Excluded Areas' of the province of Orissa. These Agency Tracts were inaccessible and unhealthy hilly areas inhabited by tribal people. Under the situation, they were provided with the benefits of establishment of Agency Courts or extension of the area of operation of the then existing Agency Courts.

Extension of Judiciary Jurisdiction to Scheduled Areas (After Promulgation of the Constitution of India)

Consequent to the repeal of the Ganjam Vizagapatam Act, 1839, the civil powers which had been originally vested in the District Magistrates (Agents), Sub-Divisional Officers (Sub-Assistant Agents), the Taluk Magistrates and the Stationary Sub-Magistrates were terminated in the Koraput, Ganjam and Phulbani districts with effect from the 1 January, 1953. Normal judicial administration was introduced in the Agency Tracts of these districts.

After enactment of Koraput and Ganjam Agency (repealing of extension of) Law Regulation, 1951, Code of Civil Procedure and Bengal, Agra and Assam Civil Courts Act were extended to Boudh-Phulbani area. As a result of this, the District Magistrate of Boudh ceased to be the Sub-Assistant Agent in respect of this area. The Deputy Commissioner, Khondmals also ceased to function as the District and Session Judge in respect of the Khondamals Sub-Division and as a result, the enactment of the Khondamals Laws (Second Amendment) Regulation, 1951, which came into force from 1954. By the aforesaid enactment, the Sub-Divisional Officer and Second Officer, Khondmal also ceased to exercise civil powers which they hitherto exercised under the Khondmals Laws and Regulations. Similarly the SDO, Balliguda and the Taluk Officers of Balliguda and G. Udayagiri also ceased to exercise their jurisdiction as Agency Sub-Judge and Munsiffs respectively, after the repeal of the Ganjam Agency Rule and Ganjam Vizagapatnam Act, 1939. The districts of Sundargarh, Mayurbhanj and Keonjhar were brought under the normal judicial administration on the model of coastal districts.

The Constitution of free, sovereign and democratic Republic of India was enforced from 26 January, 1950. The framers of the Constitution for improving the lot of the long neglected and exploited tribal population recognised the nation's responsibility. They have made special provisions for the administration and development of the Scheduled Areas and Tribal communities. The Executive has been given full direction in the Fifth Schedule to adopt the laws of the States or the Union for the purpose.

Partially Excluded Areas Enquiry Committee

In Orissa, development of Backward Classes attracted the attention of the government after receipt of recommendations of the Partially Excluded Areas Enquiry Committee appointed in 1938, i.e., two years after Orissa becoming a separate Province, but roughly one-decade prior to attainment of independence. The committee functioned under the Chairmanship of Late A.V. Thakkar (Thakkar Bapa) and gave its report to the government in 1940. No action could be taken for implementation of these recommendations due to the advent of the Second World War. However, the matter was again taken up in 1946, after cessation of the war.

Creation of a Separate Department

At the first stage, a special section called the Backward Classes Welfare Section was formed under the then Planning and Reconstruction Department of the Provincial Government in 1946 which took at examination of the report of the Partially Excluded Area Enquiry Committee for the purpose of implementation. A separate department, called the Backward Classes Welfare Department was created in 1948 and the subject 'Village Welfare' was entrusted to this department in 1949 after which the department was redesigned as the Rural Welfare Department. The Rural Welfare Department started its work with the coming into force of the Indian Constitution.

To remedy the situation prevailing in the tribal societies, a new policy between the previous two extremes of doing too little and doing too much was evolved after independence. Essentially this approach gives emphasis on looking upon the tribal themselves in a spirit of love and affection, and upon their life and culture with respect. The post-independence policy discourages thoroughly the approach of assimilation and aims at activating and developing all that is good in tribal society and culture. Late Pandit Jawaharlal Nehru, the first Prime Minister of Independent India and propounder of planning and development programmes in this country had spoken of the dangers of disintegration of tribal people. At the same time, he had insisted that the government should take suitable steps to develop them and extend all help to them to grow according to their own genius and tradition.

Special Constitutional Provision

Special provisions have been made in the Constitution of India for the development of the weaker section, particularly of the Scheduled Areas and Scheduled Tribes as have been defined in Articles 341 and 342 respectively.

Article 46 specially enjoins on the States the special responsibility of promotion with special care of the educational and economic interests of the weaker sections of the people and in particular of the Scheduled Castes and Scheduled Tribes and of protecting them from social injustice and exploitation.

Further, the provision to Article 164 lays down that there shall in the State of Orissa, Madhya Pradesh and Bihar be a Minister in the charge of tribal welfare who may, in addition be in charge of the welfare of Scheduled Castes, Backward Classes and other work. Tribal and Rural Welfare is presently included in the portfolios of a Minister of Cabinet rank and he is assisted by a Minister of State who is exclusively dealing with Tribal and Rural Welfare. Rural Welfare in practice concentrates on Harijan Welfare only. Now, there have been two separate departments one for Tribal Welfare and other for Harijan Welfare.

Pursuant to the provisions contained in the Fifth Schedule of the Constitution of India, the thickly populated tribal areas of the State have been declared as Schedule Areas. According to para 3 of the Fifth Schedule, an annual report of the Governor of Orissa on administration of Scheduled Areas is being sent to the Government of India every year. A Tribe Advisory Council has been formed in Orissa on the 24 June, 1950 to advise the government on matters pertaining to the welfare of Scheduled Tribes and development of Scheduled Areas in Orissa, in keeping with the provisions in para 4 of the Fifth Schedule and the same is being reconstituted from time to time.

According to the Scheduled Areas Order issued by Government of India in 1950, the following areas of Orissa were scheduled under the provision of the Fifth Schedule of the Constitution. They are: Koraput district excluding Kasipur Taluk; Mayurbhanj district; Sundargarh district; Ganjam Agency (Gumma, Nuagarh, R. Udayagiri, Mohana, Rayagada Block, Sorada Taluk excluding Pandakhol (Mutha); Kondhamals and Balliguda Sub-division of Phulbani district excluding Chakapad Block.

The Scheduled Areas Order, 1950 was revised and under the revised order issued during 1977 some more areas of the State were declared as Scheduled Areas. The Scheduled Areas now include the entire Tribal Sub-Plan area, which includes 118 blocks out of 314 blocks in the State. The details of Scheduled Areas in Orissa and changes over time are given in Tables 1.1 and 1.2. Similarly, the details of TSP blocks, ITDAs, MADAs, Clusters, Primitive Tribal Groups and Scheduled Tribe Communities declared from time to time is given in Tables 1.3, 1.4 and 1.5. It has been observed that the changes in the list of Scheduled Tribes and Scheduled Areas of the State are made following certain processes in which the people's representative like MLAs and MPs raise the issue both in the State Assembly and Parliament and also give representations to the government for inclusion of their community in the Scheduled list. The Department of Scheduled Tribe and Scheduled Caste of the Government of Orissa investigates the issue through different survey and by undertaking studies on the feasibility of the proposal. It also considers the backwardness of the area, and of the community by taking certain social, cultural and development indicators. The Revenue Department also plays a very important role in this process of finalising the status of the proposal. It has been observed that the people (in mass) of a particular area and of a particular community also playing an active role in sensitising the

Table 1.1

Distribution of Area, Total Population of Scheduled Areas of the State

Sl. No.	Tracts	According to 1951 Census			1961 Census			1971 Census			1981 Census		
		Area	Total Population	Tribal Population	Area	Total Population	Tribal Population	Area	Total Population	Tribal Population	Area	Total Population	Tribal Population
1	Koraput	10	1269	523	10	1498	912	25	1965	1101	25	2484	1371
2	Mayurbhanj	4	1029	505	4	1204	730	10	1435	840	10	1582	912
3	Sundargarh	4	552	313	4	759	441	10	1031	550	10	1338	686
4	Ganjam Agency including Kandhamal & excluding Chakapad, Khandam & Pandakhole Mutha of Surada Malias	4	448	182	4	490	309	4	209	144	4	309	157
5	Kandmal & Baliguda Sub-division excluding Chakapad Block	—	—	—	—	—	—	7	353	202	7	393	218
	Total	22	3298	1523	22	3951	2392	56	4992	2837	56	6106	3344

Source: Office of the Harijan and Tribal Welfare Department.
Area in sq miles, Total population in '000', Tribal population in '000'.

Table 1.2

Distribution of Scheduled Areas of Orissa according to 1991 Census

Sl. No.	District	Details of the tract declared as Scheduled Areas	Areas of the tract under Scheduled Areas (sq. km.)	Total population of the tract covered under Scheduled Areas	Population of STs in the tract covered under Scheduled Areas	Population of SCs in the tract covered under Scheduled Areas
1.	Mayurbhanj	Whole District	10,416.60	18,84,580	10,90,626	1,31,765
2.	Balasore	Nilagiri Block of Niagiri sub-division	223.60	1,06,468	53,080	10,780
3.	Keonjhar	1. Tehasils of Keonjhar sub-divisions, namely:	5,350.20	6,46,857	3,54,605	52,498
		(i) Keonjhar Tehasil				
		(ii) Telkoi Tehasil				
		2. Tehasils of Champua sub-divisions, namely:	1,585.40	3,28,437	1,52,986	32,487
		(i) Champua Tehasil				
		(ii) BarbilTehasil				
4.	Sambalpur	Kuchinda Tehasil of Kuchinda sub-divisions	2,367.30	2,25,086	1,25,741	27,263
5.	Sundargarh	Whole District	9,921.40	15,73,617	7,98,481	1,38,157
6.	Gajapati	(i) R. Udaygiri Tehasil of Parlakhemundi sub-division	2,498.80	2,87,799	1,95,497	12,525

Contd...

Contd...

		(ii) Guma Block of Khemundi Tehasil of Parlakhemundi sub-division				
		(iii) Rayagada Block of Parlakhemundi Tehasil of Parlakhemundi sub-division				
7.	Ganjam	Suruda Tehasil excluding Gazaibadi and Goshha Gram Panchayat in Ghumsur sub-division (Bhanjanagar)	912.00	1,42,649	12,852	29,076
8.	Kalahandi	2 Blocks, namely:	1,323.80	1,16,751	60,874	28,359
		(i) Th.Rampur of Bhawanipatna sub-division				
		(ii) Lanjigarh of Bhawanipatna sub-division				
9.	Koraput	Whole District	8,534.00	10,29,986	5,21,849	1,38,169
10.	Rayagada	Whole District	7,584.70	7,13,984	4,00,097	1,01,956
11.	Nawarangpur	Whole District	5,135.30	8,46,659	4,67,919	1,27,800
12.	Malkangiri	Whole District	6,115.30	4,21,917	2,46,214	84,208
13.	Phulbani	Tehasil Namely:				
		(i) Khandamal Tehasil of Khandamal sub-division				

Contd...

Contd...

	(ii) Balliguda Tehasil				
	(iii) G-Udayagiri	2,017.60	1,60,205	76,587	36,180
	Tehasil of Balliguda sub-division	5,628.10	3,86,076	2,04,799	63,319
	Total Scheduled Area	69,613.80	88,71,071	47,62,207 (53.68%)	10,14,542 (11.44%)
	State Total	1,55,707.00	3,16,59,736	70,32,214	51,29,314

Source: ST and SC Development Department, Government of Orissa, 2000.

issue of inclusion and/or exclusion of an area and/or a community under the Scheduled category. In this process, the political forces are more active and important in addition to the backwardness of the area and the community for deciding the inclusion and/or exclusion of an area and a community in the Scheduled group.

Table 1.3

Distribution of Tribal Sub-Plan Area in Orissa according to 2001 Census

Sl. No.	*District*	*No. of ITDA*	*No. of TD Blocks*	*No. of GPs*	*No. of Villages*
1.	Balasore	1	1	22	136
2.	Mayurbhanj	4	26	317	3712
3.	Keonjhar	2	10	185	1431
4.	Sambalpur	1	3	51	502
5.	Sundargarh	3	17	170	1688
6.	Gajapati	1	5	74	1257
7.	Kalahandi	1	2	24	697
8.	Koraput	2	14	197	1915
9.	Rayagada	2	11	140	2245
10.	Malkangiri	1	17	77	878
11.	Nawarangpur	1	10	148	800
12.	Phulbani	2	12	144	2336
	Total	21	118	1549	17597

Source: ST and SC Development Department, Government of Orissa.

Government of Orissa during different time periods like 1978, 1981, 1985 and 1989 has recommended to the Government of India for the inclusion and/or exclusion of certain communities. As regards the determination of caste status during 1978 almost 77 tribal groups/sub-groups were represented for inclusion in selected 16 of existing Scheduled Tribe communities. Only one tribal community was identified for new entry in the Scheduled Tribe list of the State. During 1981, similarly, there were 116 tribal groups and sub-groups represented for inclusion in the existing 22 Scheduled Tribe communities of the State. During 1985, a total number of 22 tribal groups/sub-groups were represented for inclusion in seven communities of the existing Scheduled Tribe list. Apart from, four new tribal groups and one caste group were also recommended for new entry in scheduled list. The Scheduled Caste and Scheduled Tribe Research and Training Centre, a research and training institute of the Department of ST and SC Development plays a vital role in finding out the rationality by undertaking studies and surveys to identify a community for inclusion and/or exclusion in the Scheduled List of the State.

Table 1.4

Distribution of Area, Block, Gram Panchayat, Total Population and Scheduled Tribe Population of Integrated Tribal Development Agencies of Orissa

Sl. No.	ITDA	Area in Sq. km.	No. of Blocks	No. of GPs	No. of Villages	Total Population	Scheduled Tribe Population
1	Nilagiri	223.6	1	22	136	106468	53080
2	Baripada	4191.8	10	145	1761	857884	429281
3	Kaptipada	1239.4	4	49	472	287989	188223
4	Karanjia	3077.2	5	60	728	330226	209454
5	Rairangpur	1908.2	7	62	757	408481	263668
6	Keonjhar	5350.2	7	135	1152	646857	354605
7	Champua	1585.1	3	50	409	328437	152986
8	Kuchinda	2367.3	3	51	502	225086	125741
9	Bonai	3356.7	4	35	560	243188	163142
10	Panposh	1926	4	51	374	712421	271056
11	Sundargarh	4638.7	9	84	754	618008	364283
12	Parlakhemundi	2498.8	5	74	1257	287799	195497
13	Th. Rampur	1323.5	2	24	697	116751	60874
14	Koraput	5331.7	9	113	1204	553187	294718
15	Jeypore	3202.4	5	84	711	476799	227131
16	Rayagada	3313.8	4	58	1116	356465	204779
17	Gunupur	4270.9	7	82	1329	357519	195318
18	Malkangiri	6115.3	7	77	878	421917	246214
19	Nawarangpur	5135.3	10	148	880	846659	467919
20	Balliguda	5628.1	9	101	1504	386076	204799
21	Phulbani	2017.6	3	43	832	160205	76587
	Total	68701.9	118	1548	18013	8728422	4749355

Source: Tribal Sub-Plan for Annual Plan, 2000-2001, Orissa (Draft).

Table 1.5

Distribution of Tribal Communities, their Population Range and Literacy in Orissa

Sl. No.	Tribe	Population			District	Percentage of Literacy		
		1971	1981	2001		1971	1981	2001
1	Chenchu	8	39	28	Kalahandi, Sundargarh	–	7.69	46.15
2	Baiga	92	188	539	Kalahandi, Mayurbhanj	1.1	11.17	39.28
3	Birhor	98	142	702	Sundargarh	4.1	12.68	23.30
	Less than 1,000 More than 100							
4	Bagata	262	2616	6333	Cuttack, Balasore	8.4	15.6	38.56
5	Tharua	292	1034	453	Mayurbhanj, Balasore	13.3	27.95	55.75
6	Mankidi	333	205	130	Kalahandi, Sundargarh	4.5	2.93	9.28
7	Desua Bhumij	374	183	177	Puri, Mayurbhanj	16.2	13.36	37.24
8	Ghara	548	618	275	Kalahandi, Sambalpur	10.2	12.82	53.59
9	Mankirdia	876	1005	1050	Mayurbhanj, Sambalpur	0.2	1.09	5.56
10	Media	907	1066	3017	Koraput, Dhenkanal	4.8	13.04	37.33
	Less than 10,000 More than 1,000							
11	Kol	1033	4235	13703	Keonjhar, Phulbani	6.9	10.51	32.23
12	Koli/Malhar	1504	4711	5366	Dhenkanal, Ganjam	23.7	28.72	50.69
13	Rajuar	1478	2313	2803	Mayurbhanj, Keonjhar	4.9	11.28	37.93
14	Kulia	1893	1498	11164	Ganjam, Sambalpur	32.5	36.38	70.22
15	Didayi	2164	1978	7371	Koraput	0.8	3.19	12.62
16	Gandia	2225	2263	1345	Koraput, Dhenkanal	7.9	3.8	30.00
17	Parenga	3032	9622	12646	Koraput	3.1	11.5	21.01
18	Kharuar	3234	1434	1381	Keonjhar, Mayurbhanj	11.6	24.48	57.35
19	Karua	3438	986	1280	Sambalpur, Koraput	9.6	8.42	32.83
20	Lodha	3891	5100	8905	Mayurbhanj, Cuttack	7.3	8.43	27.00
21	Kora	3961	5823	11340	Dhenkanal, Keonjhar	8.6	13.33	42.48
22	Kawar	4119	8549	7380	Sundargarh, Sambalpur	16.6	13.74	45.36
23	Bonda paroja	5338	5895	9378	Koraput	1.4	3.61	14.69
24	Holve	5728	8883	10462	Koraput, Kalahandi	9.8	14.09	35.60
25	Pentia	6266	7908	7271	Kalahandi, Sambalpur	6.7	24.77	30.69
26	Binjhia	6746	8041	9479	Sundargarh, Sambalpur	12.6	16.63	41.65
27	Bhunjia	–	7410	18504	Kalahandi, Koraput	–	8.55	29.03
28	Dharua	8791	8611	9247	Koraput, Ganjam	4.2	6.09	19.60
29	Kolah Loharas	12194	7562	9642	Sundargarh, Koraput	6.8	11.03	35.55

Contd...

Contd...

	Less than 1,00,000 More than 10,000							
30	Kotia	11050	19136	22525	Koraput, Phulbani	4.8	8.02	24.60
31	Dal	12182	18163	15404	Bolangir, Kalahandi	10.5	11.68	32.17
32	Omanatya	17671	19465	23364	Koraput, Ganjam	5.2	8.23	24.52
33	Mundari	17913	24667	23833	Sundargarh, Dhenkanal	10.8	18.12	46.94
34	Juang	24384	30876	41339	Keonjhar, Dhenkanal	5.8	7.99	25.35
35	Mirdhas	28477	28177	32279	Sambalpur, Bolangir	11.9	16.49	51.17
36	Ho	31916	44496	43113	Mayurbhanj, Keonjhar	8.1	12.75	35.18
37	Gadaba	46594	56913	72982	Koraput, Ganjam	3.3	6.54	21.22
38	Saonti	55178	67872	75556	Keonjhar, Mayurbhanj	10.5	7.92	47.65
39	Banjara	6283	10924	15868	Koraput, Mayurbhanj	11.4	16.94	46.40
40	Khond Gaud	7185	15189	31454	Phulbani, Puri	10.6	14.44	38.96
41	Jatapu	8047	18457	13804	Koraput, Ganjam	8.9	10.47	32.32
42	Matya	8648	12123	17549	Dhenkanal, Koraput	8.4	13.04	38.42
43	Khandadore	9286	17442	34160	Koraput, Ganjam	6.6	10	34.86
44	Mahali	9617	11767	17131	Mayurbhanj, Sundargarh	7.2	10.72	37.97
45	Koya	59168	87260	122535	Koraput, Puri	1.2	4.96	11.73
46	Bhumia	61900	75221	103537	Koraput, Sundargarh	4.1	6.34	20.01
47	Binjhal	83873	98631	118116	Sambalpur, Bolangir	10.5	13.86	41.49
	More than 1,00,000							
48	Kharia	120483	144178	188331	Sundargarh, Sambalpur	12.1	17.9	45.23
49	Bathudi	130792	147970	198296	Mayurbhanj, Keonjhar	13.2	20.78	49.56
50	Bhumija	146970	157613	248252	Mayurbhanj, Balasore	9.7	12.14	36.48
51	Oraon	164619	215337	308931	Sundargarh, Sambalpur	1.63	23.65	54.20
52	Kisan	180025	227992	321592	Sambalpur, Sundargarh	11.4	17.26	50.19
53	Bhuinya	188212	207793	277742	Sundargarh, Keonjhar	14.9	22.5	50.88
54	Bhottada	194842	247709	375845	Koraput, Kalahandi	4.4	7.53	24.29
55	Munda	222117	338935	480252	Sundargarh, Sambalpur	13.3	16.21	39.69
56	Paroja	206699	267184	317301	Koraput, Kalahandi	2.5	4.76	17.96
57	Sabar Lodha	240344	329209	442537	Kalahandi, Koraput	8.6	12.96	35.40
58	Kolha	309586	326523	512919	Mayurbhanj, Keonjhar	5.8	8.79	27.04
59	Saora	342757	370060	473233	Ganjam, Sambalpur	10.1	14.48	41.13
60	Santal	452953	530776	777460	Mayurbhanj, Balasore	9.1	14.34	40.43
61	Gond	499267	602749	782347	Kalahandi, Sambalpur	13.5	18.73	46.96
62	Khond	869965	989342	1395643	Koraput, Phulbani	—	12.38	31.87
63	Unspecified	—	42332	48080			1.29	44.42
	Grand Total		5915067	8145081			13.96	37.37

Sources: Census of India, 1971 complied in 'Tribal Development and Welfare Legislation', by G.K. Srichandan, Pratibha Prakashan, New Delhi.

Census of India, 1981, Series-16, Orissa, Part-IX (iii), Special Tables for Scheduled Tribes.

Census of India, 2001, referred in *Land and People, Orissa*, Vol. 21, (eds.) S. Bhat and Gopal K. Bhargava, Kalpez Publications, Delhi.

III

Tribal Livelihood Resources

The survival of tribal communities has a vital stake on land and forest resources. For historical reasons, most of the tribal people inhabit in the forest and hilly regions of Orissa. The social structure and day to day living of tribal people reflect their intimate relationship with land and forest surrounding their habitat. In Orissan context, it has been observed that different tribal communities inhabited in specific locations, in the past, particularly till the advent of the British. In early days, there was hardly any population movement in tribal areas due to lack of road communication. The inflow of non-tribal population started on a large scale into the tribal areas when the British started their contact with these regions. This process also facilitated inter-territorial movement between neighbouring tribes for acquiring natural resources for livelihood. In this process, the original settlers in a particular territory asserted their rights over all the surrounding natural resources, and the neighbouring tribes never questioned this. However, subjugation over tribal groups and control over their resources by colonial government and native Rajas at different points of time has been questioned, and the agony of the tribal people has been reflected through resistances and rebellions, but the tribal people were always subdued and made subservient by the non-tribals.

The present section tries to focus on the symbiotic relationship of tribal people with the natural resources particularly land and forest which are in fact their major sources of livelihood and the impact of planned development on their livelihood resources. First, it describes the landholding and land use pattern among the tribal people of Orissa. Second, it explains the relation of tribal people with forest resources and its management with special reference to Minor Forest Produces/Non-Timber Forest Produces and Joint Forest Management in Orissa. Third, it explains the Extension of Panchayati Raj Act, 1997 to the Scheduled Area of Orissa with regard to the management of natural resources.

Tribal Livelihood and Land

Prior to the intervention of the outside agencies, tribal people had free access into the land owned by their respective communities. Individual ownership of land was unknown in their customary rule. Right to use land in conformity with the decisions of community leader was in practice. The land-men-forest-nature and super natural complex of the tribal people had offered them a living in harmony with the nature. The unplanned loss of natural resources due to imbalances created on land and land-based resources around their natural environment have become a severe threat to tribal subsistence. Earlier rudimentary technologies and techniques of production innovated and developed by the tribal people, may be less productive in the perception of the non-tribal people, but continued to keep the socio-economic harmony within the tribal community.

Tribal economy is something more than what economists view in terms of production, distribution and consumption through transaction of goods and services. Therefore, local subsistence economies need to be understood in terms of the concerned community's man-material resources in the context of its culture. Again an investigation of tribal economy at operational level needs a thorough understanding of the concept of common property resources which centres around land and forests and the role of non-tribal groups, particularly the Scheduled Castes, like *Pano* and *Doma* for use, ownership and control of land. Most of the social scientists have treated land as an object for agriculture and house construction purely from a capitalistic or materialistic viewpoint. However, for the anthropologist land of tribal communities assumes some value beyond a tangible asset. The land is the pivotal property and the tribal people attach strong emotions. It has also been found in practice that many tribal communities, by and large, do not enjoy legal proprietorship over the land they are in occupation for generations. In Orissa, the cultivable land came to acquire the status of a commodity during the British administration. Among tribal communities, it could not change the status so easily due to socio-cultural factors. The corporate and the joint rights over land did not allow the land to be a saleable commodity. For example, the Kutia Kondha and others believe that their ancestors have given land to them and they have no right to sell it.

In spite of the efforts made to survey agricultural lands and to settle the proprietorship with individual rights over land so far, the government in certain cases has not yet become successful. The customary corporate rights of the tribal communities on land and land-based resources are still in practice. The government has not properly taken care of such a vital issue. This at certain level reflects the uncritical adoption of the colonial concept of land ownership and the treatment towards natural properties even in the post-independent India. Going back to the British period, one sees that due to the absence of private/legal ownership the *Muthadars, Pirha Sardars,* and *Zamindars* with the help of village headman were collecting land revenue through annual payment in the form of crops at the time of harvest. Apart from this, the obligatory contributions of the tribal people rendered in the form of various kinds like special crops, animals and labour to the Rajas during festive occasions and/or during the visit of officials to the villages of the tribals. Delay in or deviations in payment of the tax were leading to confiscation of cattle, other properties and imposition of strict punishment by the *Muthadar*-the headmen of the *Mutha.*

Tribal land question is not just how much land they have lost at present and how much land has been alienated into the hands of non-tribal households, and or to the State in the name of development projects. The way the tribal people are losing their land and have been deprived of it is a serious issue before the social anthropologists in particular and development workers in general, who are more concerned for tribal development. In Indian society, more particularly among the tribal communities, loss of land seems to be the loss of social identity not only for the present generation but even for the future generations.

The new form of land-man relation introduced among the tribal people was in practice even with the interference of outside forces, but it was constrained during early 20th century due to the introduction of survey and settlement of land. Though many social scientists have treated land as an object for agriculture and house construction, anthropologists normally treat land not simply as a tangible asset, as understood by many; they have highlighted the emotional attachment between the land and the users and the reserve value it carries for them. Ghurye categorically observed that tribals are agrarian people (1943). The problems of the tribals are therefore seen to be agrarian in nature. Beteille termed tribals as peasant (1972). Many of the tribals by and large do not enjoy legal proprietorship over land, due to the fact that land is understood as common property among tribal communities of Orissa. Perhaps, that is one of the major reasons as to why the attempt to survey agricultural lands in certain tribal regions of Orissa is still incomplete. As a result, the statistics on tribal landholding patterns are either not available or available with lot of lapses. Perhaps due to the absence of data on tribal landholding, it has become necessary for the government to frequently change the definitions of worker, cultivator and non-worker during census operations.

Tribal Landholding and Land Use Pattern

Here an attempt has been made to highlight the status of tribal landholding and land-use pattern in the State of Orissa as reflected in the secondary data available in the State. The findings of the Socio-Economic Bench Mark Survey undertaken during 1978-80 by the Scheduled Castes and Scheduled Tribes Research and Training Institute of Bhubaneswar (now known as SCSTRTI), in the entire Tribal Sub-Plan regions of Orissa reveals that out of 7,31,403 tribal households, almost 22.84 per cent had no land and 40.46 per cent households were the owners of an average of 2.5 acres by each household. The study also reflects that more than 30 per cent of households among different tribal communities like *Lodhas* (37.14%) *Kandhas* (30.49%), *Saoras* (31.11%), *Parajas* (36.65%) *Mundas* (25.32%), *Bhumijas* (25.18%), and the *Kharias* (25.97%) were found to be landless. The tribal communities of Southern Orissa had higher percentage of landless households than tribal communities of other parts of the State. The average landholding among the tribal communities of Orissa ranges from

1.55 acres among the *Oraons* (highest) to 1.15 acres among the Bhumija (lowest). The data also reflect that farmers holding more than 5.1 acres are less among the tribal communities like *Kandha, Gond, Munda, Paraja, Kharia and Kisan*. Apart from the landless households who claim one-fifth of the total population strength, the marginal and small farmers share 81.12 per cent of the total land-owning classes (Mohanty et al., 1993).

Table 1.6

Distribution of Number, Area and Average Size of Operational Holding in Broad Size Group for Scheduled Tribes in Orissa

(No. in Lakhs, Area in Lakhs Ha.)

Category	*1980-81*			*1985-86*			*1990-91*		
	No.	*Area*	*Av. size (hect.)*	*No.*	*Area*	*Av. size (hect.)*	*No.*	*Area*	*Av. size (hect.)*
Marginal (Below 1.0 hect.)	3.0	2.1	0.6	4.5	2.4	0.5	5.1	2.8	0.5
Small (1.0 to 2.0 hect.)	2.6	3.6	1.4	2.7	3.8	1.4	3.0	4.1	1.4
Semi-Medium (2.0 to 4.0 hect.)	1.9	5.0	2.6	1.8	5.0	2.7	1.8	4.8	2.7
Medium (4.0 to 10.0 hect.)	0.8	4.1	5.5	0.6	3.6	5.8	0.6	3.0	5.0
Large (10.0 hect. & above)	0.1	0.9	13.2	0.05	0.7	14.4	0.03	0.5	16.7
All Categories.	9.2	15.7	1.7	9.6	15.5	1.6	10.5	15.2	1.4

Source: Report on Number and Area of Operational Holding in Orissa 1990-91. Agricultural Census Commissioner, Orissa.

The average size of landholding among STs as gathered from the Agriculture Census Reports for the years from 1980-81, 1985-86 to 1990-91 suggests a fall in the size of tribal landholding for all categories. More specifically, the average size of ST landholding among the marginal and small farmers, when compared during the decade from (1980-81 to 1990-91), shows a declining trend both in terms of absolute number of tribal households and coverage of land areas. The details of number, area and average size of operational holding in large size category for Scheduled Tribes in Orissa can be seen from Table 1.6.

The Board of Revenue conducted another study during 1990-91 to survey the operational holdings of tribal people in Orissa with special reference to different social groups. Of the study of 3,948,000 holdings, small and marginal farmers account 79.86 per cent which includes 20.49 per cent among STs. It is assumed that the number of small and marginal farmers must have been reduced due to distribution of ceiling surplus land and agricultural land by the State. The study also shows that out of the total of 21,18,800 marginal holdings of the State who occupy an area of 1,045,000 hectares, 5,14,000 (24.25%) ST households control 2,75,000 hectares (26.31%). Similarly, out of the total of 1,035,000 of small holders who account for 1,426,000 hectares of land, there were 2,95,000 (28.5%) ST households holding 4,14,000 hectares (29.03%) of land (Report of Revenue Department, 1997).

A recent empirical survey in tribal dominated hill tracts of Orissa shows that on an average a tribal household possess 0.5 acres of land which is less productive and susceptible to the damages caused by wild animals, pests, and non-tribal exploitation. The tribal land is normally located on the hill slopes or on hilltops. In addition, whatever quantity of land tribals cultivate, a negligible percentage of land is recorded against their names because land above 9 degrees slope from the sea level is normally declared as government land. Tribal people use land patches for shifting cultivation and for terrace cultivation which are normally above 9 degrees elevation. Only recently Government of Orissa (2000) has conformed the ownership rights to persons cultivating land in the hill slopes within 30 degrees in scheduled areas. Government has realised that the non-conferment of rayati rights to persons cultivating land in the hill slopes within 30 degrees is one among other reasons for their unrest of the tribal community. Government as a matter of conscious policy, decided to carry out a special survey of unsurveyed hill slopes in Scheduled Areas (except Kashipur Tehasil of Koraput and Kalahandi district in the past) which are in cultivation either in form of Podu or Kudki up to 30 degrees hill slopes (ibid.).

Shifting Cultivation

It will be lopsided to understand tribal livelihood system and land use pattern unless we explain briefly tribal agricultural activities. Most of the tribal inhabited areas are located in hilly and forest areas. In such geo-physical locations shifting cultivation largely influences the land use pattern of the tribal people. Shifting cultivation is a primitive farming technique known by different names in Orissa like *Dangar, Bagad, Pahad, Toila, Rama, Dabi, Biringa,* etc. In Orissa, shifting cultivation is being practised by about eleven tribal communities in Phulbani, Keonjhar, Sundargarh, Rayagada, Gajapati, Koraput, Kalahandi and Ganjam districts. The tribal communities practising shifting cultivation are: Bonda, Didayi, Koya, Gadaba, Paraja of Koraput; Kutia Kandha of Kamdhamal; Dongaria Kandha of Rayagada; Lanjia Saoras, Malua Kandha, Pengo Kandha of trajapati; the Juanga and Pauri Bhuyan of Keonjhar district. Increased population pressure has not discouraged such practitioners much mainly because of the non-suitability of better farming land. In fact, the traditional practice of multi-cropping on shifting land has proved to be more productive and agriculturally viable for the tribal people compared to the mono-cropping with modern agro- technologies. The crop cycle, crop quality and quantity depends on the cyclic distance of time as well as on the land, which is being used for the purposes. The age old ascribed status of the village chief to distribute the patches for cultivation is still practiced on the kinship lines. The authority for distribution of shifting patches are vested on the village elders with no property right on Sweden land, except in those areas where royatwari tenure was imposed by the local chiefs on the tribal people with taxes and/or tributes (Mohapatra, 1968: 403; Pathy, 1987). It is no doubt that the growth of population, restricted government forest policies, commercial plantation, deforestation, land alienation, non-availability of suitable hill slopes and availability of viable livelihood alternatives have reduced the cycle of shifting cultivation from 10-15 years cycle to a short period of 2 to 5 years gap. This has direct bearing on reducing the cycle of shifting cultivation in Orissa. The status of land changes depending upon the yield and years of cultivation. For example, among the Bhuiyans the first year crop is known as *buda* which assumes the name *pori* after extraction of stones from their land in the second year. The extent of land covered under shifting cultivation as surveyed by different agencies at various points of time is given in Table 1.7. The table explains that more than eleven different tribal communities are practising shifting cultivation in Orissa. As regards the tribal population depending on shifting cultivation various reports state that an average of 30 per cent tribal people of the State are depending on shifting cultivation. Similarly, the total forest area under shifting cultivation in Orissa is quite large in size. The figures with regard to the number of tribal communities practising shifting cultivation and total area of forestland covered under such cultivation varies from study to study. However, it has been established that quite a good number of tribal communities are practising shifting cultivation, covering a sizeable amount of land of the State.

Table 1.7

Distribution of Different Estimates of Shifting Cultivation in Orissa

Estimate Years	*Source of Estimation*	*No. of Tribal communities practicing*	*No. of Tribal depending on shifting cultivation and % to tribal population*	*Total area of forest land affected and % to total forest area (in acres)*
1951	F.H. Mooney	12	9,33,500 (31.46%)	81,72,800 (53.57%)
1956	ICAR	20	10,00,000 (33.70%)	4,00,000 (2.64%)
1960-61	Commissioner for ST & SC Government of Orissa	11	9,35,700 (31.53%)	4,00,000 (2.64%)
1971-72	DFO, Forest Resource Survey, Government of Orissa	—	10,00,000 (19.71%)	34,59,400 (20.75%)
1972-73	THRTI Survey Government of Orissa	11	2,40,000 (4.73%)	46,500 (0.29%)
1975	Directorate of Agriculture, Orissa Erts-I, Satellite Imagery	—	—	81,72,800 (49.70%)

Source: Various sources as mentioned above.

Tribal people practise shifting cultivation for multiple reasons. Their long experience and knowledge help them a lot to adhere to such a practice. Because of the gradient landscape, which erodes the fertility of topsoil, the tribal people normally do not plough their hill land and make contour bunds to reduce erosion of the soil. While chopping the trees and burning them the tribal people even today preserve fruit bearing trees like mangoes (*mangifera indica)*, jack fruits (*artocarpus intergi folia*), mahua (*basia letifolia*), tamarind, tendu, guava, kaith (*foronia acida*) cashew, jamun, (*Eugenia Jambolana*), Amla (*Emblica offcinalis*), Ber (*Aegle mormoles*) Bamboos etc.

Shifting cultivation is essentially a mixed cropping where 10 to 20 varieties of cereals, millet, like ragi (*elucine corocema*), kodo (*paspalam scrobiculatum*), swnua *(Echinochloa frummenta cea*), Bajara (*pennisetum typhoidessno*) jawar (*sorghum vulgara*), maize (*zea mays*), etc., pulses, oilseeds, vegetables, perennial crops like ginger, turmeric, tapioca, etc., are grown. This type of crop diversities ensure conservation of minerals of the soil, checks damage of pests and diseases, ensures food grains for couple of months, conserves the soil nutrients and act as an insurance against total crop failure as observed under mono-culture system (Guillet, 1983; Pathy, 1987).

Many scholars interpret shifting cultivation as a subsistence economy. This seems to be ridiculous because these scholars while saying this compares tribal economy with that of capitalist-economy where the productive inputs are supplied as per the demand and outputs are measured as per investment. While looking at the strength, opportunities of the tribal societies in general and non-availability of infrastructure facilities, it is very difficult to say shifting cultivation is a subsistence economy. Pathy (ibid.) says that cash crop is more or less of equal importance to staple crops because in tribal societies in many cases crops are found mortgaged even before its harvest. It has been observed that the shifting land is a community land where the individual households are given usufrucatory right over a patch of land. However, over the time due to the pressure on land a tendency of heritable rights in shifting land is also found. As a result, tribal people have developed the shifting patches to permanent patches. Though they have been cultivating the same patches for years together with back-up social support, the Revenue Department of the State Government still considers them as encroachers of forest land where there is no forest for the last couple of decades. The social division of labour among the shifting cultivators is largely based on extended and regular reciprocal cooperation among members of the village. This provides strength to the tribal community.

Understanding the potentiality of forests to accumulate natural resources, the Britishers for the first time restricted the customary rights of the tribal communities since 1855. In 1878, the Britishers enacted Indian Forest Act classifying all forests into three major categories. The Indian Forest Act of 1927 and Government of India Act of 1935, consolidated the power of the government on forest, emphasised on the revenue yield aspect and resource requirements of British industry, commerce and military sectors. Therefore, during the 200 years of colonial rule, the British brought changes in land use pattern; exploited forest resources, mineral ores, and introduced cash crops, established communication networks and thus distorted the land structure, ecology, forest resources, flora and fauna of the land which kept the tribal communities at the receiving end.

In spite of the debate on the desirability and/or undesirability of the shifting cultivation, one can say that good chunks of tribal population still practise shifting cultivation. It is a fact that because of the capitalistic notion adopted towards land and land-based resources the planners, development workers and State at large have started looking emphatically towards shifting cultivation. However, it has been proved that whatever reformatory welfare services have been provided by the government during last five decades to abstain tribal people from practising shifting cultivation, all seem to have not proved fully worthy. In other words, one can say that shifting cultivation has its strength within it which is sustainable for the livelihood of the tribal people.

Tribal Livelihood and Forest Resources

The relationship of tribal people and forest resources is symbiotic by nature and seems to be as old as human civilisation and will continue till human survival. The tribal people maintain a close relationship with the forest resources available around their habitat. The life-way processes of the tribal people reflected in their economy, religion, polity and social institutions cannot be understood without understanding various aspects of forests surrounding them (Roy, 1935; Roy Burman, 1961; Dube, 1977; Mohapatra, 1983; Fernandes, 1988; Behura, 1990; Mallik and Panigrahi, 1998). The intimacy of tribal people with forest resources have been expressed through their adoption of natural species of plants/animals/birds as totem and performance of rituals both in day-to-day life and in special ritual occasions. The use of various forest produces in the form of leaves, fruits, flowers and other forest biproducts are mainly guided by natural laws, various festive occasions and their traditions. In other words, the functional aspects of the totems and taboos among the tribal communities guide their intimate interdependence with nature.

Until the intervention of the Britishers the tribal people believed that they were the owners of the forest and forest resources that surrounds them. The attitude of the tribal people towards forest resources was not changed much till the independence of the country. Looking at their traditional use of forest resources one can say that they were more forest friendly and were not exploiting forest resources randomly. Almost all the tribal communities of Orissa observe various forms of social sanctions to undertake or not to undertake certain forest related activities; to eat or not to eat certain forest produces, when to eat, how to eat these forest produces, and while performing rituals on community basis before first intake of food items. The customary laws of various tribal communities have become the guiding force for binding them closely with the forest. This partially justifies, when one examines the folk taxonomies given by tribal communities for flora and fauna, and from their classification of plants as more useful and less useful, edible and non-edible, hygienic and poisonous, ritualistic and non-ritualistic, medicinal and non-medicinal (Behura, 1982). Even today, since the tribal people live within the forest coverage and/or near the forest and hills, their dependence on forest still prevails. Forest influences their livelihood, personality, worldview and ideology (ibid.).

In post-independence era, serious damage came to forest resources through the establishment of development projects basically in tribal inhabited inland areas. These development projects might be multi-purpose irrigation dams, mines, roads, railways, new townships, refugee settlements and big industries. To mention a few of such development projects in Orissa so far established in tribal inhabited forest areas, which have tremendous impact on the forest resources and tribal life are hydroelectric-cum-irrigation projects like Hirakud, Balimela, Machakund, Sileru, Upper Kolab, Upper Indrabati, Mandira, Rengali; mineral based industries, like Rourkela Steel Plant, National Aluminium Company, Hindustan Aeronautics Limited; and mining projects on cement, iron, dolomite and limestone. A detailed estimate on the deforestation for various purposes like irrigation, mines, roads and housing, railways, defense, industry, etc., shows that there are 190 projects which were established in Orissa till 1999, and 24124 hectares of land have been deforested.

The impact of massive deforestation has been observed in the life-way processes of the tribal people, which can be categorised as environment effects, social effects and economic effects. The social effects of deforestation restrict the access of tribal people into the forest and limit the availability of forest produces. It affects the religious activities, life cycle rituals, customs, practices and the habits of the tribal people. Similarly, the economic effects of deforestation, due to development projects as observed, have drastically influenced the traditional livelihood resources of the tribal people, which were produces of the forest. Many people allege that the tribal people are responsible for the destruction of natural resources and massive deforestation of the forest resources. In fact, tribal people for their survival largely depend on forest resources. Since the tribal people more or less live in the forest which are terrained with hills and mountains, under this situation for agricultural purpose they clean the land patches on the slopes of the hills and practise shifting cultivation, which of course is pernicious because it causes deforestation. Tribal people do not have much alternative sources of livelihood. Government provisions for them to earn their livelihood and to make their day-to-day survival by and large, depend on hill slopes, foothills and forest produces. However, few people attribute multiple reasons for forest degradation and some people blame the innocent tribals for total degradation of forest resources. In this regard, Forest Department and Government employees are the first group of people to blame poor tribal people for deforestation.

Forest Management Policy

The policies adopted overtime for the management of forest resources is the product of long history of political administration of the State. All the regional forest laws which so far existed were declared to be included under Indian Forest (Orissa Amendment) Act 1952 only after the merger of princely States. The essence of Forest Policy of 1952 was the reiteration of bureaucratic management of forest and promotion of State capitalism in the forest sector (Behura, 1990). Roy Burman (1982) viewed that much of the uneasy political situation that have prevailed in the hills in the post-independence period are related to this policy (1982). During 1970s the National Commission on Agriculture (NCA) highlighted the livelihood interest of the tribal people over the forest resources. The cultural importance of the forest resources for the forest dwellers was hardly given importance by this commission.

The subsequent debates at national and international levels on various new dimensions of forest ecology, environment, resource sustainability and forest revenue forced the government to formulate a new forest policy in 1988, basically with an aim to ensure environmental stability and maintenance of ecological balance. It was proposed that the derivations of direct economic benefits must be subordinated to this principal aim while meeting the requirement of fuel-wood, fodder, minor forest produces and small timber of the rural and tribal population (Lok Sabha Secretariat, 1985).

Joint Forest Management in Orissa

The National Forest Policy of 1988 provides 100 per cent share on Non-Timber Forest Produce (NTFPs) and 50 per cent share of the people on major forest produces, whereas, under the new Joint Forest Management (JFM) Policy the forest inhabitants are made partners in the management, utilisation and protection of forest around the villages. In Orissan context, studies have shown that the tribal people have shown remarkable performance in managing their land-based resources (Saxena, 1995). Another study shows that the people of Orissa have protected 1.5 to 2 lakh hectares of forest land in 3,000 villages (Kant et al., 1990). This at certain level reflects the long functioning of various formal and informal village level organisations protecting their forest resources. In addition to the protection of village forests such local level organisations have also been playing constructive roles in maintaining common resources, organising the community and establishing social harmony by resolving community conflicts. Forest Department of Government of Orissa much later tapped these resources and formed Village Forest Protection Committee (VFPC) which by and large include the traditional authority structure of tribal villages. In this regard, the role of few apex/ regional bodies like Brukshya O' Jeevara Bandhu Parishad (BOJBP) in Kesharpur of Nayagarh district and Budhikhamari Joint Protection Party (BJPP) at Baripada of Mayurbhanj district, Budatika Anchalik Committee at Negipalli in Bolangir district are remarkable (Pati and Panda, 1993). Similar practices are also found in their study by Raju and others (1993) in Gania forest of Dhenkanal district where people have their own rules and regulations for use and imposing restriction on the appropriation of forest resources.

In fact, Orissa is the first State to introduce Joint Forest Management (JFM) during 1988, which was much later adopted as a policy by Government of India (in 1990). In 1990, Government of Orissa passed another resolution to include all the Reserved Forests for protection by the villagers and recognised the role of VFPC in the management of both reserved and protected forests.

Again during 1993, Government of Orissa provided 50 per cent share over any major harvest of produces in addition to meeting all intermediate requirement of the protecting communities. Distribution of Forest Protection Committees (FPCs) in different Forest Divisions of Orissa reflects that there are certain Forest Divisions like Koraput, Sundargarh, Kalahandi, Rayagada, which have suffered in forest protection when compared with other Forest Divisions of Orissa. The details of functioning of Vana Surakhya Samiti (VSS) and FPC, in the scheduled and non-scheduled districts are presented in Table 1.8.

Table 1.8

Functioning of Organisational Set-ups for Forest Management in Orissa

Sl. No.	*Indicators*	*Organisational set-ups*						
		Forest Division in Tribal Areas			*Forest Division in Non-Tribal Areas*			
		VSS	*FPC*	*Un-Registered Groups*	*VSS*	*FPC*	*Un-Registered Groups*	*Total FPC in Social Forestry*
1	Total number of groups working	648	3087	243	412	2348	397	9055
2	No. of GPs involved	311	718	53	288	532	129	3649
3	No. of Forest Blocks Covered	438	831	141	282	638	148	–
4	Forest Area Covered (hect.)	44264	603897	39107	49631	355504	50757	121460
5	Organisation signed MOU	412	–	–	333	–	–	–
6	No. of Micro Plans made	74	–	–	47	–	–	–
7	Active Organisations working	–	700	–	–	527	–	5683
8	Forest covered under active organisations (hect.)	–	96247	–	–	84658	–	78,646

Source: Forest Department, Government of Orissa, 1997.

The discussion indicates that the practice of forest management involving the community at certain level reflects the constructive contribution of village communities both in the form of formal and informal structures. The State has felt the importance of village communities and their role in managing the forest resources, has helped tribal people in meeting their livelihood requirements.

Minor Forest Produces and Tribal Livelihood

In spite of the rich availability of Minor Forest Produces (MFPs) in Orissa the attempt to collect, process, and market and thereby to generate income out of it by the State as well as by the tribal people are inadequate. Owing to the fact of uncertain agricultural yields the tribal people largely depend on MFPs for their food security as well as for household medicines. As a result, in the recent past the policy makers, environmentalists, researchers and government have been highlighting the multiple significance of MFPs in the life and livelihood of the tribal people. Though MFPs are the sustainable sources of livelihood for the poor tribal, but these sources have very badly been affected largely due to their random exploitation by the middlemen, traders and forest contractors.

Forest and tribal people maintain a symbiotic relation with each other which plays an important role in the economy, culture and livelihood of such people. Forest supplies fuel-wood, feed, fibre, medicinal plants, timber, etc. The income generated from this sector while comparing this income with the Net State Domestic Product (NSDP) of 1960 it was 1 per cent, whereas, it had increased to 1.4 per cent in 1970s, decreased to 1.1 per cent in 1980s, again increased to 1.2 per cent during the period of 1989-90 and 1.9 per cent in 1994-95. Timber and bamboo are the major forest produces, constituting 76, 87 and 75 per cent of the total forest revenue of our State, earned during 1991-92, 1992-93 and 1995-96 respectively. Since the forest area of the State during last three decades of 1971, 1981 and 1991 has reduced from 43.5, to 38 and to 35.24 per cent respectively (Economic Survey, 1996-97), the contribution of revenue from forest resources to the State exchequer does not give a definite positive trend. This, when compared from 1993-94 to 1998-99 reflects that forest still plays an important role in the State economy. Coming to the fact of revenue which is generated from NTFPs in Orissa when compared with the total revenue from the forest resources one finds that it was only 3.50 per cent during 1993-94 which has been reduced to 2.46 per cent in 1998-99. This is largely due to the deforestation caused owing to multiple reasons. On an average, an extent of 154.521 hectares of forest land per year has been converted into non-forest use between 1952-1980 mostly for the purposes of constructing multi-purpose irrigation dams and other development projects (Shyam Sundar, 1998). This has no doubt adversely affected the livelihood sustenance of a large number of poor tribal households. For the first time, Roy Burman Committee set up by Planning Commission highlighted the commercial value of almost 300 MFPs (1982). The Committee has highlighted the importance of MFPs in the livelihood processes of the tribal people. However, the tribal people have been either cheated or denied fair price and most often they receive a price lower than that of the prevailing market price (Mohapatra, 1982; Mallik, 1997).

Government of Orissa from time to time has formulated and implemented a host of policies and enacted laws with regard to collection, processing and marketing of NTFPs. The trade of kenduleaf, sal seed and bamboo has been nationalised in different periods, that is in 1973, 1983 and 1988 respectively. The objectives behind the nationalisation were partly to enable the primary collectors to get remunerative price. In spite of various policies formulated by the State at different points of time regarding the optimal collection, fixation of fair prices and processing of NTFPs, there still exists rampant corrupt practices, exploitation of tribal, State monopoly over forest resources, lack of management skill and non-responsive attitudes of the government agencies are reflected in the procurement, processing and marketing of NTFPs. All these have paved the ways to encourage illegal trading of forest produces both within and outside the State.

While the forest dwellers, particularly the tribal people treat forest resources as their sources of livelihood, the government has always treated it as a source of generating revenue for the State. Over the years, the government has formed/established various organisational networks for procurement and marketing of MFPs. A few of them established over the time are: (a) Tikabali Agency Marketing Cooperative Society (AMCS) in 1950s; (b) The Orissa Forest Development Corporation Ltd. (OFDC) in 1962; (c) Tribal Development Cooperative Corporation Ltd. (TDCC) in 1973; (d) Large Area Multi-Purpose Societies (LAMPS) in 1977; (e) Tribal Cooperative Marketing Federation India Ltd. (TRIFED) in 1989; (f) Utkal Forest Produces Ltd. (UFPL) in 1989; and (g) Orissa Rural Development Marketing Society (ORMAS) in 1989.

All the organisations mentioned above have been established basically to deal with minor forest produces (MFP) collection, its storage, processing, and marketing which have different objectives, organisational structure and operational guidelines. For example, TDCC which is an apex cooperative organisation is engaged in collection of MFPs and Surplus Agricultural Produces (SAP) in tribal regions. The business achievements of TDCC for last couple of years, when analysed, do not reflect a definite trend in harvesting a good business (TDCC Records, 1996). TDCC has sustained a net loss due to various factors. They are viz. heavy interest on the borrowing, high establishment costs, market fluctuation, irregular tapping of NTFPs, heavy royalty given and scarcity of working capital (Patnaik, 1998). A detailed structural and financial analysis of the functioning of TDCC is given in Chapter 5. Thus, the objective of having such organisational structures to upgrade the socio-economic condition of the tribal people by procuring and processing of NTFPs and in providing soft loans to the poor tribal could not be achieved to the desired extent.

In Orissa practically almost 90 per cent of Large Area Multi-purpose Societies (LAMPS) are defunct due to their large operational areas, heavy expenditure due to transport of products, poor financial base, low payment to the primary collectors, irregular supply of agricultural inputs, lack of dynamic management, poor co-ordination among TDCC, AMCS, ORMAS, NAFED, and poor staffing structure (Patnaik, 1996;

CPSW, 1996; Mallik, 1991; Mallik and Panigrahi, 1998). Such arrangements basically could not solve the basic purpose of protecting tribal interests and also of State interests.

Even the attempt of Government of Orissa to go for joint venture between IPICOL and M/S J.P. Latt & Associates which gave birth to Utkal Forest Products during 1989 was severely criticised by NGOs, Activists and Planners due to the monopoly over 29 MFPs in Orissa. During 1989, the Department of Panchayati Raj, Government of Orissa created an autonomous organisation called as Orissa Rural Development and Marketing Society (ORMAS) to procure, process, add value and market few MFPs in Orissa by organising the unorganised people through DWCRA. As observed, ORMAS also suffers from weak management, poor accounting, lack of market-oriented planning and lack of efforts for product development. However, all these formal bodies built up over the time to deal with MFPs while experimenting in tribal areas have, more or less, not achieved their desired goal. As a result, the poor tribal people suffer in the hands of the non-tribal.

Extension of Panchayati Raj Act to the Scheduled Area & Tribal Livelihood

With the 73rd Constitutional Amendment, Government of Orissa has enacted the Orissa Gram Panchayat (Amendment) Act 1996 for operation in the Scheduled Areas of Orissa. Since its inception the Government of Orissa has been trying to make various structural arrangements for the economic development of the tribal communities. The following paragraph analyses the issue of decentralisation of powers among various tiers of Panchayati Raj with special reference to the policy on procurement of non-timber forest produces in the tribal regions of the State.

Structurally all the tiers starting from Gram Sabha (Palli Sabha) at the bottom level, Panchayat Samiti at middle level and Zilla Parishad at higher level have been formed in Orissa. Only recently a lot of changes have been initiated in the decentralisation of power and mode of operation in some departments of the Government of Orissa.

The NTFPs for tribal people have traditionally been perceived as one of the important sources of livelihood. However, the approach of government towards NTFP resources has always been to maximise the State revenue out of it. Only recently the Government of Orissa has realised that the NTFP items have been an important source of livelihood for the tribal and rural people but the prevailing system does not provide scope to the tribal people to get a fair price over these produces (Government of Orissa, 2000).

In Clause 3A of new policy of Government of Orissa, in respect of the Scheduled Areas of the State, the power for issuing license to procure and market seventy items of NTFPs has been given to Gram Panchayats. However, this policy also empowers the government to modify the list from time to time depending upon various factors not linked up with people's interest. The Gram Panchayat/Gram Sabha in the Scheduled Area will have the ownership over any of these seventy NTFP items available within the territory, i.e., in the forest of a revenue village under the said Gram Panchayat.

Clause 3 of the new Forest Policy, 2000 explains that no Gram Panchayat within and outside the Scheduled Area will have ownership over NTFP items produced in the reserve forest, wild life sanctuaries and national parks, which are outside the jurisdiction of the revenue villages. Thus, the Gram Panchayat is not entitled to grant lease or license to any individual or agency for collection of NTFP items from these restricted areas. However, members of Vana Surakhya Samitis and tribal artisans as a part of their customary rights will be free to collect NTFP items from forest areas including sanctuaries and national parks. The Gram Panchayats who enjoy the power to regulate procurement and trading of the NTFP items will control once these items brought into the jurisdiction of the Gram Panchayats. Since a good chunk of the forestland in the tribal regions is in the reserve forest and sanctuaries, the right for collection of MFPs from these areas should also be given to Gram Panchayats.

As per Clause 3C of the policy any person desirous of purchasing NTFP items from primary gatherers or trading in such items has to register in specific Gram Panchayat for every session *between 1 October and 30 September* on payment of the registration fees to the concerned Range Officer along with royalty of 10 per cent. However, it is a fact that in the Scheduled Areas the Scheduled Caste groups like Pano, Dom and Ganda have played a dominant role in appropriating the resources of the tribal people over generations together. Under the context of new Forest Policy, 2000 of the State, the tribal people in Scheduled Area may not come forward to adopt the cumbersome process of registration, etc., required for trading of NTFPs. Again, Clause 3 while making open for collection of MFPs allows the government agencies like OFDC and TDCC to register themselves to procure one or more NTFPs in the same region. During the fieldwork, it was observed in Lanjigarh block of Kalahandi and Daringibadi block of Kandhamal districts that this has already created problems for tribal people to struggle in the process with these agencies. As a result, the tribal people have become dumb license holders in the hands of the non-tribal traders who trade in NTFPs in the region. The tribal people not only avoid the cumbersome process of registration and are unable to compete in the open market along with the non-tribal people. As regards the minimum price support for the NTFPs, involvement of Zilla Parishad in deciding pricing of value added NTFPs and restricting its inter-State illicit trade, clear cut policies should be spelt out by the government by handing over powers to the Gram Panchayats.

The foregoing discussion reflects that the livelihood of the tribal people centres around land and land based forest resources particularly NTFPs. In Orissan context, it has been observed that because of the reserve value, tribal land was precious for the non-tribals, particularly for the Scheduled Caste groups. They had adopted various social and economic measures to exercise control over tribal land during the post-independence period, especially from 1950s to 1970s. The State in the name of development projects has acquired quite a lot of land which had not only displaced tribal people from their age-old ancestral land and land-based resources but also from their sustainable livelihood sources. The influx of outsiders along with the construction of so-called development projects in the tribal areas, which caused loss of their valuable productive lands. Of late from 1980s and 1990s, the multinational companies in the name of development again could manage to enter into the tribal areas. This provided opportunities to the plantation companies, big landholders of coastal districts of Orissa and from neighbouring States, particularly from Andhra Pradesh to grab land in tribal areas by influencing the government functionaries. Similarly, as regards the NTFPs are concerned, much late the State understood the economic values of these produces for the tribals. Over the time, the State has experimented with various State controlled corporations and societies to trade over NTFPs basically to enhance the State revenue. In spite of all these attempts, the parallel trade by the private agencies is more intense in tribal areas. However, with the extension of Panchayati Raj Act (Amendment) 1996 to the Scheduled Areas of the State and with the handing over of seventy NTFP/MFP items to the Gram Panchayats a new chapter has been opened in the history of MFP business in Orissa. Finally, we can say that land and land-based forest resources have been still playing a major role in the life and livelihood of the tribal people of Orissa. If the State administration is streamlined as per the provisions of the Fifth Schedule of the Constitution of India a lot of problems of tribal communities could be eliminated. Rapid development of tribal communities could be assured if action is taken as per the Fifth Schedule.

IV

Research Design

In the context of tribal society social scientists, particularly social anthropologists play a crucial role in understanding the processes of social formation, their social institutions and the pattern of development carried out by different State level agencies. Studies of tribal societies by the social scientists vary in terms of their objectives and interpretations. Variations are also observed with regard to the adoption of inductive and deductive reasoning, subjective and objective approaches, and quantitative and qualitative methods of data collection and also as regards the duration of field investigation. Since humans as socio-cultural beings, live within interrelated social and cultural institutions which influence their way of life, it is required that collection and interpretation of data in tribal societies should be more holistic by nature. This reflects the peculiarities in the subjective concepts, cultural practices, and community notions of different tribal communities which help the researchers to understand their responses to the state mechanisms in both subjective and objectives ways.

Objectives

- Review of the jurisdiction of Scheduled Areas and the list of Scheduled Tribes, the processes of inclusion and exclusion therein over the years in Orissa.
- To find out the impact of State policies and the extent of problems pertaining to prohibition, indebtedness, and land alienation observed among the tribal people of the State. In other words, it tries to analyse the status of States action, relation to the prohibition or restriction on the transfer of land, regulation of allotment of land, regulation of moneylending business by private persons and agencies in tribal areas of Orissa and assessing the excise policy of Government of Orissa in tribal regions of the State.
- Review of the functioning of various State level agencies meant for the welfare of the tribal communities in the context of the provisions of Fifth Schedule with special reference to the functioning of Tribes Advisory Council (TAC) the Department of Welfare, Government of Orissa; Tribal Development Cooperative Corporation (TDCC), Bhubaneswar; Scheduled Castes and Scheduled Tribe Research and Training Institute, Bhubaneswar (SCSTRTI) and National Commission for Scheduled Castes and Scheduled Tribes, Bhubaneswar, (NCSC&ST); Panchayati Raj Institutions.

Study Area

In order to understand various aspects of the functioning of the State level agencies in respect of the Fifth Schedule of the Indian Constitution a multistage sampling was designed to select the districts at higher level and the villages at lower level. At first, four Scheduled Districts in Tribal Sub-Plan area were identified basing on concentration of tribal population, backward indicators and geographical representation. Thus, for the study the districts selected are: Malkangiri on the south, Keonjhar on the north, Kalahandi on the west and Phulbani on the east-central region of the TSP area.

At the second stage, one Community Development Block from each selected district was chosen considering the factors of tribal concentration, backwardness, development indicators and inaccessible/accessible location of the block. Thus, the study has covered Padia block in Malkangiri district, Telkoi block in Keonjhar district, Lanjigarh block in Kalahandi district and Daringibadi block in Kandhamal district of Orissa.

Since the primary focus of this study was the village, it was felt very important to select representative villages in each identified C.D. Block. After discussion with the government and non-government organisations and institutions, few villages were surveyed and finally after a pilot survey one village in each identified block of different district was selected for intensive fieldwork. The indicators adopted for selection of the villages were: the total number of households, size of tribal households in the village, location of the village and some other relevant indicators. Thus, the villages finally covered under the study are Lachipeta in Malkangiri district, Tungurubahal in Keonjhar district, Kendubardihi in Kalahandi district and Penaposi Pangara in Kandhamal district.

The justification for selecting four different villages in four districts seems to be sound because of the variations in the impact of the functioning of Fifth Schedule of the Indian Constitution, and the response of the State level development agencies in implementing various welfare programmes, and the receptiveness of the tribal people are supposed to be different due to various factors.

The State departments are approaching tribal people of different districts and different tribal communities in a similar manner, but the tribal communities in different districts respond differently because of their regional variations. This resulted in differential impact of the provisions of Fifth Schedule of the Indian Constitution on the tribal people. To speak precisely, these are the reasons which influenced to undertake the study in four villages located in different districts covering different tribal communities.

Data Source

Unlike other anthropological studies the authors spent on an average of 15 days in each of the selected villages of different districts. The study had adopted both primary and secondary sources for data collection. While staying in the villages the study encompassed household survey for unraveling various aspects of their socio-economic life-way processes. Special care was taken to get data on land alienation, land leased-in and land leased-out; moneylending practices; production, consumption, exchange of goods and sale of various types of liquor by the tribal people. Special case histories were also documented on various issues so as to understand different mechanisms and processes adhered to by the tribal communities. Those apart, issue-based discussions were also carried out with the tribal men in general and tribal women in particular.

To understand the functioning of various agencies at grass-root level the primary data were collected from 10 to 15 office bearers such as Ward members, Sarpanch and Naib Sarpanch of the local Gram Panchayati Raj Institutions covering the study village in each district.

In order to know the functioning of programme implementing agencies in the tribal areas and keeping the study villages at the centre, personnel of various government departments, institutions and agencies were personally interviewed. Few of them: Panchayat Samiti Office, Revenue Inspector's office, branch offices of Tribal Development Cooperative Corporation, (TDCC); LAMPS, Nationalised Banks, Rural Banks and Ashram Schools, and non-government organisations operating in the area.

At the State level, data have been collected from secondary sources like published reports, records, registers, proceedings of meetings of various government departments. They are viz: the Scheduled Tribe and Scheduled Caste Development Department, Directorate of Scheduled Caste and Scheduled Tribe Training and Research Institute, Tribal Development Cooperative Corporation, State Office of National Commission for Scheduled Castes and Scheduled Tribes. Their officers were interviewed to understand their responsibilities regarding effective implementation of welfare programmes over the years, specifically, in the context of the Fifth Schedule of the Indian Constitution.

Tools for Data Collection

Keeping in view the objectives of the study four different structured interview schedules were prepared to document primary data from each household, members of Gram Panchayat, Scheduled Tribe members of Orissa Legislative Assembly, etc. Apart from this, few research guidelines were specially prepared on different issues like land alienation, moneylending, prohibition, etc., for data collection.

The village schedule contain data on village social demography; land, forest, water and, agricultural resources and infrastructure facilities available in the village. Apart from the use of different techniques, Participatory Rural Appraisal (PRA) was used to get data on the positions of different natural resources and the changes in them which have taken place over the time.

The second Schedule used for household survey, documented demographic structure of the household, resource position of the household, income from agriculture, animal husbandry, forest resources, wage labour, and land leased-in and leased-out, sale and purchase of land; production, consumption, distribution and sale of liquor; practices of moneylending, bonded labour, if any, by the households.

The third Schedule was adopted to interview the members of local Panchayati Raj Institutions. It covers their family particulars, their knowledge on tribal population in their block, implementation of special Constitutional provisions for the Scheduled

Tribes in respect of prohibition, land alienation, practice of bonded labour, status of women, and lastly their view on the trends of development operative for the tribal population.

The fourth Schedule used to interview the selected members of the Orissa Legislative Assembly to explore their knowledge on the Scheduled Tribe situation in Orissa and specifically Constitutional arrangements in respect of land issues, the practice of prohibition and bonded labour, and implementation of development programmes for the tribal people in their areas. In addition to the interview schedules, detailed interview guidelines were prepared for use on various aspects like landholding, land transfer, land alienation, indebtedness, etc.

Chapterisation

The report has eight chapters covering various dimensions of the present study.

First chapter while providing a brief account of tribal situation in Orissa describes the changes in the jurisdiction of Scheduled Areas and the list of Scheduled Tribes of Orissa. It explains the changing symbiotic relationships the tribal people maintained with the natural resources like forest and land. It also elaborates the anatomy of the study.

Second chapter explains the concept of Fifth Schedule, the provisions therein for the development of Scheduled Tribes in India and various Constitutional safeguards enshrined in various parts of the Indian Constitution through different Articles, Clauses, and Sub-Clauses.

Third chapter provides a brief idea on the profile of the study villages in different selected districts of the State. It describes the social and physical resources of the villages and their influence on tribal people.

Fourth chapter deals with the problems of alcoholism and excise policy, the impact of State made regulations in controlling the problem of alcoholism in the society.

Fifth chapter deals with the problems of tribal indebtedness and the impact of State regulations on regulating the money-lending by private persons and agencies in tribal areas of Orissa.

Sixth chapter deals with the problems of land transfer and/or alienation by or among the members of Scheduled Tribes, regulation of allotment of land among the members of the Scheduled Tribes. The chapter specially highlights the impact of globalisation on the life and livelihood of the tribal people of the State and the organised resistance of the tribal people against the State.

Seventh chapter describes the role of government agencies in the welfare of the tribal communities of Orissa. Here, special emphasis has been given to understand the role played by them in implementing various tribal development programmes. It also highlights the possible potentialities of these agencies for the purpose.

Last chapter provides a concluding remark on the overall finding of the study and on the functioning of Fifth Schedule in the State of Orissa.

2 Constitutional Safeguards for Tribal Communities

This chapter has three sections. The first section deals with the state sponsored provisions for the Scheduled Tribes during pre- and post-Independence periods. The second section deals with the concept of Fifth Schedule and provisions thereof for the development of the Scheduled Tribes of India. The third section explains Constitutional safeguards elaborated in various parts of the Constitution through different Articles, Clauses and Sub-Clauses for the development of tribals.

I

Pre-Independence Period

Promotion of planned efforts for the development of backward communities particularly for the tribal groups had its foundation in pre-independence India. More or less in pre-independent era, the tribal communities were self-governed with their own political structures, which were headed, by hereditary chieftains and kings. Some of the kings and chieftains were independent while others showed allegiance to the powerful kings of their states and formed parts of bigger states (Government of India, 1981). The entry of British into India and bringing tribal dominated areas under their hegemony was strongly opposed in some regions of the country. Revolts and rebellions by the tribals against the British expansionistic approach were a regular phenomenon. Orissa was also not free from these processes; for instance, the Ghumusara uprising of Kondhs (1835-37), Sambalpur uprisings (1857-64 AD), the anti-feudal Bhuiyan and Juanga movement (1867-68 and 1891-93), Nayagarh uprising (1849-52 and 1893-94), Nilgiri peasant uprising (1930), Kol Rebellion (1821), Santhal Rebellion of 1855, the Kandha Revolt of 1869, the Koya Movement of 1879, the Sardari Agitation of 1887, the Rampha Rebellion of 1911, the Bastar Uprising of 1911, Gond and Kolan Movement of 1941-42. They were crushed by police, killing several people, burning crop fields and huts, and imposing punitive fines in the villages (Bailey, 1960). This led the British to formulate special administrative arrangements and special programmes for the tribal people and for the development of tribal dominated regions.

The Scheduled District Act of 1874 bestowed a special status for the tribal dominated areas of old Madras Presidency and restricted the application of general rules in these areas. It formulated the concept of 'Scheduled Districts' with special civil and judicial administration. Realising the backwardness of these areas the Indian Education Commission of 1882 had made few suggestions for preferential treatment of tribal children through: non-payment of school fees and provision of additional grants for schools located in tribal areas. The first half of the 20th century had the impact of Government of India Act 1919 and Government of India Act 1935, which created a good number of partial and fully excluded areas. The Government of India Act 1919 empowered the Governor General with more powers to modify the acts applicable to the backward tracts according to his discretion. Similarly, he was also authorised to issue directions, so far, as, the acts of the provincial legislatures were concerned. Soon-after the declaration of the Communal Award on 17 August, 1932 by the then British Prime Minister Ramsay McDonald under which the depressed classes for the first time were recognised as 'minority community' and were granted assured representation with separate electorate for a period of twenty years. Mahatma Gandhi, the father of the nation went on fast unto death over this decision. Looking at the gravity of this crisis, B.R. Ambedkar after long discourse made them agree upon the principle of proportional representation of 147 seats in the Provincial Legislatures and 18 per cent seats in the Central Legislature of India. This agreement was popularly known as Poona Pact and was made functional on 24 September, 1932. The Government of India Act 1935 went a step further and classified the areas inhabited by tribals as Excluded Areas and Partially Excluded Areas for smooth administration. This act delegated more power to the Governor General in the sense that without his prior approval through public notification, none of Dominion Legislatures would be applicable to 'Excluded' and 'Partially Excluded Areas'. The Governor General was also vested with powers of amending or repealing any existing law that were in operation in those areas if he considered it essential for the sake of administration.

Post-Independence Period

During the post-independence period, members of the Constituent Assembly while framing the Indian Constitution made a critical review of such privileges and formulated prescriptive benefits for the tribal people. The Indian nationalists during that time had also pointed out the divisive political intentions of the colonial administration for conferring distinct statuses on different ethnic groups. While looking at the spirit of such preferential privileges it was probably felt by the British to grant such statuses not merely to alleviate the plight of the tribal communities, but rather to suppress the revolts and protests. Later on, understanding the requirements for protective measures even today we realise that a major portion of the safeguards contained in the Indian Constitution has been drawn from the Government of India Act, 1933 and Indian Independence Act of 1947 which were largely developed after the Second World War. It also carries enormous influence from Cripps Mission of 1942 and the Cabinet Mission of 1946. As per the specific recommendations of the Cabinet Mission of 1946, a Constituent Assembly was formed in 1948 under the chairmanship of Dr. Rajendra Prasad to prepare the draft Constitution and to present it before the Constituent Assembly and the task was completed by 1949. The Government of India Act 1935 helped a lot as a stepping stone (Saxena, 1995). However, not being too critical the framers of Indian Constitution adopted a two-way strategy of tribal development: providing protection against exploitation and simultaneously assisting them through economic activities, to rise above the level of poverty. In this regard, Thakkar Bapa and Jaipal Singh two Indian proponents of tribal interests contributed enormously to the shape of the Indian Constitution. It seems that protective discriminations are the prerequisite for the development of tribal communities.

Considering the difference on the qualitative and quantitative bases of both the Scheduled Castes and Scheduled Tribes, Constitutional experts preferred to make different footings for the minorities, which are known as Constitutional Safeguards. The basic thrust behind such safeguards was to destigmatise the Scheduled Castes from certain cultural derogation long been imposed on them and simultaneously favouring them under positive discriminations. For the Scheduled Tribes, the basic thrust was to maintain their command and access into the natural resources endowed to them and assuring the tribal people to take advantage of the benefits of sponsored development.

Thus, there are almost twenty Articles and two Special Schedules in the Constitution of India which elaborately explain the protective privileges meant for the tribal people. These provisions were embodied in the Constitution of India and came into force on 26 January, 1950. The Special provisions incorporated in the Constitution under different sections are: Part-III on Fundamental Rights, Part-IV on Directive Principles of State Policy, Part-X on Scheduled and Tribal Areas, Part-XII on Finance, Property, etc., Part-XVI on Special Provisions relating to certain classes, and lastly the Fifth and Sixth Schedule of the Indian Constitution. Specifically the protective provisions contained in the Constitution are the Articles of 14, 15 (I, II), 15 (4), 16 (I) 16 (4), 16 (4 A), 17, 19 (5), 23, 24, 25, 29, 46, 164, (II), 244, 275, 330, 332, 334, 335, and 338, 339 (1), 340, 341, 342, 366, 371 (A, B, C) Fifth Schedule and Sixth Schedule. The Directive Principles of State

Policy explains privileges for the tribal communities through different Articles of 38,39,39A, 41, 43, 46, 47, 48 and 48 A. For a clear understanding, here an attempt has been made to highlight each of these provisions meant to benefit the tribal communities.

These Constitutional provisions when classified into certain broad categories reflect that under social category the safeguards have been described under Articles of the Constitution, namely, 14, 15 (I, II), 17, 23 and 25. These pertain to social problems, like abolition of untouchability, prohibition of discrimination on grounds of caste, race, sex, access to public places, use of public wells, tanks, hotels, restaurants, etc., prohibition of forced labour and throwing open Hindu religious institutions, etc. Secondly, the Educational and Economic provisions are included under Articles of the Constitution, namely, 15 (4), 16(1), 16(4), 14(4) A, 29, 46 and 335, which describe the safeguards/measures, such as: reservation for admission, employment, claims in appointments and in the services, promotions of educational and economic interests and protection against social injustice and all forms of exploitation. Thirdly, the political category includes the Articles of the Constitution, like 164 (II), 330, 332, and 334 which explain the safeguards/measures pertaining to reservation of seats in Lok Sabha and State Assemblies and period of reservation, Minister in charge of tribal welfare in the States of Bihar, Madhya Pradesh and Orissa. Fourthly, there are some other safeguards which have been incorporated under the Articles of the Constitution like 244, 275, 338, 339, 340, 341, 342, 366, 371, Fifth and Sixth Schedules provide guidelines for the administration of Scheduled Areas, flow of grants-in-aid out of the Consolidated Fund of India to the States for Scheduled Areas for promoting welfare of Scheduled Tribes, functions of the National Commission for SCs and STs, Commission on the administration of Scheduled Tribes, Executive Power of Union in giving direction to the States for Scheduled Tribes, appointment of Backward Classes Commission, specifications of SCs and STs, definitions, special provisions with regard to the States of Nagaland, Assam, Manipur, Mizoram, and Arunachal Pradesh.

II

Fifth Schedule

Article 244 of the Constitution of India provides various provisions for the administration and control of Scheduled Areas and Scheduled Tribes within the jurisdiction of the Fifth Schedule, Proviso (2) of this Article relates to the formation of an Autonomous State in the Sixth Schedule Areas of Part-1. Article 244 (1) deals with the provision of the Fifth Schedule, which shall be applied to the administration, and control of the Scheduled Areas and Scheduled Tribes in any State other than the States of Assam, Meghalaya, Tripura, Manipur, Nagaland, Arunachal Pradesh and Mizoram. Similarly, Article 244 (2) deals with the provisions of the Sixth Schedule, which shall be applied to the administration of the tribal areas in States of Assam, Meghalaya, Tripura, Manipur, Nagaland, Arunachal Pradesh and Mizoram. The Fifth Schedule of the Indian Constitution is divided into four parts – Part-A provides a general picture, while Part-B describes the administration and control of Scheduled Areas and Scheduled Tribes, Part-C deals with the creation of Scheduled Areas, whereas, Part-D deals with the amendment of the Schedule.

Part-A

The scope of this Schedule does not include States such as Assam, Meghalaya, Manipur, Nagaland, Arunachal Pradesh, Mizoram and Tripura. As per the provisions of Fifth Schedule the executive powers of a State extends to the Scheduled Areas. The States annually, or whenever required submit a report to the President regarding the administration of the Scheduled Areas. The executive power of the Union shall extend in giving directions to the States as regards the administration of the said areas.

Part-B

Administration and Control of Scheduled Areas and Scheduled Tribes

Tribes Advisory Council (TAC)

- There shall be a Tribes Advisory Council (TAC) established in each State having Scheduled Areas therein and, if the

President of India so directs, also in any state having Scheduled Tribes but not Scheduled Areas therein. The TAC is consisting of not more than twenty members, of whom, as nearly as may be, three-fourths shall be the representatives of the Scheduled Tribes in the Legislative Assembly of the State provided that if the number of representatives of the Scheduled Tribes in the Legislative Assembly of the State is less than the number of seats in the TAC to be filled by such representatives, the remaining seats shall be filled by other members of those tribes.

- It shall be the duty of the TAC to advise on such matters pertaining to the welfare and advancement of the Scheduled Tribes in the State as may be referred to them by the Governor of the State.
- The Governor of the State may make rules prescribing or regulation as the case may be regarding: (a) the number of members of the Council, the mode of their appointment and the appointment of the chairman of the Council and of the officers and servants thereof; (b) the conduct of its meetings and its procedure in general; and (c) all other incidental matters.

Law Applicable to Scheduled Areas

- Notwithstanding anything in the Constitution, the Governor may by public notification direct that any particular Act of Parliament or of the Legislature of the State shall not apply to a Scheduled Area or any part thereof in the State subject to such exceptions and modifications as he may specify in the notification and direction given under this sub-paragraph may be given so as to have retrospective effect.
- The Governor may make regulations for the peace and good governance of any area in a State, which is for the time being a Scheduled Area. In particular and without prejudice to the generality of the foregoing, such regulations may: (a) prohibit or restrict the transfer of land by or among members of the Scheduled Tribes in such area; (b) regulate the allotment of land among members of the Scheduled Tribes in such area; (c) regulate carrying on of business on moneylending by persons

who lend money to members of the Scheduled Tribes in such area.

- In making any such regulation as if referred to in Sub-paragraph (2) of this paragraph, the Governor may repeal or amend any Act of Parliament or of the Legislature of the State or any existing law, which is for the time being applicable to the area in question.
- All regulation made under this paragraph shall be submitted forthwith to the President of India and, until assented to by him, shall have no effect.
- No regulation shall be made under this paragraph unless the Governor making the regulation has in the cases where there is a Tribes Advisory Council for the State consulted such council.

Part-C

Scheduled Areas

In the Constitution, Part C of the Article 244 (1) provides that the expression "Scheduled Areas" means such areas as the President of India may by order of 1950, 1975 and 1977 declare to be Scheduled Areas.

The President may at any time by order: (a) direct that the whole or any specified part of a Scheduled Area shall cease to be a Scheduled Area or a part of such an area; (b) increase the size of any Scheduled area in a State after consultation with the Governor of that State; (c) alter, but only by way of rectification of boundaries of any Schedule Area; (d) on any alternation of the boundaries of a State or on the admission into the Union or the establishment of a new State, declare any territory not previously included in any State to be or to form part of a Scheduled Area; (e) rescind in relation to any State or States, any order or orders made under this paragraph, and in consultation with the Governor of the State concerned, make fresh orders redefining the areas, which are to be Scheduled Areas; and any such order may contain such incidental and consequential provisions as appear to the President to be necessary and proper, but same as aforesaid, the order made Under-paragraph (1) shall not be changed by any subsequent order.

The Scheduled Areas have been declared in the State of Andhra Pradesh, Bihar (undivided), Gujarat, Himachal Pradesh, Madhya Pradesh (undivided), Maharashtra, Orissa and Rajasthan. These Scheduled Areas have been constituted with two major objectives. First, to assist the tribals in enjoying their existing rights unhindered or unobstructed by others through summary process. Second, to develop the Scheduled Areas and promote the economic, educational, and social progress of the Scheduled Tribes.

The Fifth Schedule of the Constitution of India empowers the President to declare by an order the Scheduled Areas, but it does not empower him to declare any part of the Scheduled Areas to be an agency tract or agency area. That power is conferred under Para 5 on the Governor to make Regulations for the peaceful and good governance of any Scheduled Area in the State or to extend any law with such exceptions and modifications as he deems fit for the Scheduled Areas. In fact, Para 5 and 6 do not contemplate any agency area or tract. It is for the Governor while administering the Scheduled Areas to declare any agency area either as a whole or in part and make necessary laws and put them under the administration of the agent.

The government has full power to make regulations, which are laws to the same extent as Parliament can enact that certain legislation will apply to a particular State. The Governor under Para 5 of the Fifth Schedule can apply specified laws to a Schedule Area. The Bihar Regulation of 1951 is an instance of a valid legislation emanating from a legislative authority; it is not delegated or conditional legislation (AIR 1970 SC 1951). The word land in Para 5 (2) (a) of the Fifth Schedule is not to be interpreted in a restricted sense but in its legal sense. Land in legal sense is comprehensive and wide enough to include structures, if any, revised thereon.

The power to make laws included the power to make laws prospectively as well as retrospectively. From the fact that Para 5 (1) vests the power on the Governor to issue notifications with retrospective effect; but as Para 5 (2) is silent with regard to such power and no inference can be drawn that in the matter of making regulations, the Constitution makers did not want the government to promulgate the regulations with retrospective operations. So far as the notifications are concerned, the Constitution makers thought that specific powers should be given under Para 5 (1) to the Governor to issue notifications with retrospective effect. But, so far as law making is concerned, it stands on a footing different from the issue of notification on the ground of considering the importance of Legislatures to enact laws with retrospective operation. If the Regulation is for peace and good governance of a Scheduled Area, it is immaterial if the Preamble does not indicate that it is for the peace and good governance of the area.

The phrase "peace and good governance" has a connotation wide enough to justify even prohibition of any business provided it is for the protection and promotion of welfare of the Scheduled Tribes on the grounds that the provisions though made ostensibly for regulating moneylending business they are so wide as to come under the purpose for maintenance of peace and good government.

As per Para 6 of the Fifth Schedule is not a basic feature of the Constitution; rather it is a temporary feature and will continue so long as Scheduled Areas need protection. Thus, insertion of Clause (a) and (d) in its Para 6 (2) by the Fifth Schedule to the Constitution (Amendment) Act, 1976 is not *ultra vires* as distracter of basic features. The Amendment does not include any area in or exclude from the Scheduled Areas; that remains within discretion of the President.

The Constitutional guidelines indicate that the areas included in Scheduled Area should have tribal concentration and presumed backward which needs special protection.

Part-D

Amendment of the Schedule

Parliament may from time to time by law amend by way of addition, variation or repeal any of the provisions of this Schedule and when the Schedule is so amended, any reference to this

Schedule in this Constitution shall be constructed as a reference to such Schedule as so amended.

No such law as is mentioned in Sub-paragraph (1) of this paragraph shall be deemed to be an amendment of this Constitution for the purposes of Article 368.

III
Protective Provisions

Article 15 (4) prohibits any form of discrimination on grounds of religion, race, caste, sex, place of birth maintained by State or dedicated for the use of the general public. Clause 4 of this Article empowers the State to make any special provision for the advancement of socially and educationally backward classes or for the scheduled communities. Through amendment the State has reserved seats for SCs and STs in educational institutions including technical, engineering and medical colleges, and in scientific and specialised courses.

Article 16 (4) under Fundamental Rights is another exception to the right of equality of opportunity in the matters of public employment. The term "Backward Classes" is used as a generic term and comprises various categories of backward classes, viz.; Scheduled Castes, Scheduled Tribes, Other Backward Classes, Denotified Communities, and Nomadic and semi-Nomadic Communities. The Scheduled Tribes who are specifically mentioned in Article 15 (4) are not specified in 16 (4) but are covered under backward classes. The State can make provisions for the reservation of seats and appointment in favour of backward classes if not represented adequately. Though the State cannot reserve unreasonable percentage of the posts for the backward classes, a member of a backward class can be appointed to non-reserved posts if found eligible after such competition.

As per Article 17, all citizens shall have the right to freedom of speech and expression, to assemble peacefully and without arm, to form associations or unions, to move freely throughout the territory of India, to reside and settle in any part of the territory of India, to acquire, hold and dispose of property, and to practise any profession, or to carry on any occupation, trade or business. However, important exceptions have been made to some of the fundamental rights for protection of the interest of the members of the Scheduled Tribes.

Under Proviso (s) of the Article 17, the State has been authorised to make reasonable restrictions on the exercise on any of the rights relating to movement, acquisition of land, and settlement for the protection of the interest of the Scheduled Tribes. In fact, the problem of alienation of tribal land in Assam has very close relations arising out of the restrictions exercised mainly on two fundamental rights, namely, (1) to reside and to settle in any part of the territory of India, and (2) to acquire, hold and dispose of property.

In effect of this Article, Parliament of India has made an enactment viz.; Untouchability (Offences) Act 1955. In later period, the Protection of Civil Rights Act, 1955 was enacted in 1976 to rename and amend the Untouchability (Offences) Act, 1955, making the punishments under this Act more stringent by setting up of special cells, special courts, mobile squads, provision of legal aid, etc. In spite of this, prevalence of untouchability has not been abolished, rather has taken different shapes and sizes. The cases registered under the Act have been declining as observed that there were 3,148 cases registered during 1992 which has been reduced to 778 registered during 1998. (Annual Report of Ministry of Social Justice and Empowerment, 1999-2000). One of the major reasons for non-registration of such cases as observed in the tribal areas is largely due to delay in investigation, low conviction and low acquittals (Acharya et al., 2000).

Parliament passed another important Act in 1989 for taking measures to prevent the atrocities. This Act known as the Scheduled Castes and Scheduled Tribes (Prevention of Atrocities) Act 1989, became effective from 30 January, 1990.

Article 19 (5) while it provides free movements, residence and acquisition or sale of property to all its citizens in the Indian territory, however, it reserves the right to protect the interests of the members of Scheduled Tribes by arresting the transfer of property particularly from tribal communities to non-tribal, except under special conditions. In order to check the alienation of tribals from their age-old land and land-based resources, the State has formulated various regulations like Regulation 2 of 1956 and OLR Act 1960. The details of achievements of these regulations both in controlling land alienation and restoring alienated land has been discussed in chapter four.

Article 23 eliminates the system of serfdom, bondage and other forms of forced labour and provides that any contravention of this provision shall be an offence. Though the Act does not mention SCs and STs but since the majority of the bonded labour belong to SCs and STs this Article has a special significance for these communities. Following this provision, the Bonded Labour System (Abolition) Act 1976 was enacted after a lapse of 26 years in 1976, with a view to abolish this evil practice by making this offence punishable. Under centrally sponsored programmes launched in 1978-79 grant-in-aid was provided to the State Governments and UTs for the administration on 50/50 basis for identification, liberation, and rehabilitation of the bonded labourers. The achievement of three State Governments including Orissa in this respect seems to be tardy and lack proper implementation.

Article 29 (2) that provides for Cultural and Educational Rights, is controlled by clause 4 of Article 15, incorporated in the Constitution by the First Amendment Act, 1951. This has also brought Articles 15 and 29 in line with Articles 16 (4), 46 and 140 and made it Constitutional for the States to reserve seats for the backward classes of citizens in public educational institutions. This ensures the minority groups to preserve their language, dialect and cultures. The State would not by law enforce upon it any other culture or language. All the educational institutions under direct control or receiving grant-in-aid follow the reservation policy of 15 per cent for SCs and STs in matter of admission. The Government of India also initiated a number of centrally sponsored Schemes/Non-Plan Schemes for the benefit of these students. In spite of this, the literacy rate of the members in these communities have not changed remarkably as compared to the general communities. The poor educational achievements of these groups also indicate large number of drop-outs who leave the schools at different levels of their education, particularly at primary level.

Article 30 (1) guarantees the minorities the right to establish educational institutions of their choice and to continue with them.

Article 39 says that the State shall, in particular, direct its policy towards securing adequate means of livelihood for all; and the operation of the economic system does not result in the concentration of wealth and means of production to the common detriment.

Article 45 notes that the State shall endeavour to provide for free and compulsory education for all children until they complete the age of fourteen years. At the beginning of this protective measure, it has been indicated that it should be for a period of ten years from the commencement of the Constitution.

Article 46 looks at the promotion of educational and economic interests of weaker sections of the people and, in particular, of the Scheduled Castes and Scheduled Tribes, and shall specially protect them from social injustice and various forms of exploitation. In order to give effect to this Article, the Constitution Act of 1951 has amended Article 15 and 29 on Fundamental Rights. However, the fact is that it also envisages the tribals be protected from all forms of exploitation which seems to have been given due importance over the years. N.K. Bose, one of the most knowledgeable anthropologist and close associate of Mahatma Gandhi, has rightly mentioned this fact.

Bose viewed that this (protection from all forms of exploitation) has unfortunately not taken place so far. The reason is simple. Exploitation arises out of a system, or the social arrangement in the productive organisation under which people live in. If we have to end the exploitation of one class by another, it cannot be done separately for either the Scheduled Castes or Scheduled Tribes, so long as the productive organisation itself continues to remain in its old condition, and so long the society itself is divided into those who provide labour and produce wealth, but do not enjoy the full fruits of their labour and another class which enjoys privileges in excess of what they contribute by means of their own labour. One particular section among the people cannot be freed from all forms of exploitation as long as their co-workers who do not belong to their caste or tribe continue in their old condition (Bose 1972a: 95).

The Directive Principles of State Policy lays down the policy guidelines for the State to work under the Constitution. However, the State's action is limited by provisions such as maintenance of efficiency of the administration or the maintenance of a minimum standard in educational institutions.

Article 164 provides for the provision of a Minister of Tribal Welfare in Orissa, Madhya Pradesh (undivided) and Bihar (undivided) to look after the tribal welfare which points to the concern of the Constitution for safeguarding the interest of Scheduled Tribes.

Article 275 (1) provides grants from the Union to certain States for tribal development. The creation of Sixth Schedule for the formation of autonomous regions and regional councils as regards the management of resources according to the customs also receives directions under this Article. Thus, the entire welfare programme for the Scheduled Tribes is based on Article 46, whereas, the required funds are provided under Article 275 (i). This Article also envisages provisions for grant-in-aid for meeting the cost of such schemes of development as may be undertaken by a State with the approval of Government of India for the purpose of promoting welfare of tribal people or for raising the level of administration in the Scheduled Areas. Provisions of Special Central Assistance (SCA) have been made to the States having Scheduled Tribes population against specific schemes for their welfare. During the Eighth Five-Year Plan, an amount of Rs. 54,000 lakh was released to the State Governments under this provision. The amount released during 1997-98, 1998-99 and 1999-2000 was Rs. 25,000 lakh. A similar provision exists in the Article for paying special grants to the North-East States under Sixth Schedule out of the Consolidated Fund of India.

Article 320 (4) provides that Public Service Commission need not be consulted in respect of the manner in which any provisions referred to in Clause 4 of Article 16 may be made or as regards the manner in which effect may be given to the provisions of Article 335.

Articles 330, 332, 334, and 335 ensure reservation of seats for the Scheduled Castes and Scheduled Tribes in the Lok Sabha (Article 330) and State Legislative Assemblies (Article 332). Though such reservations were to be ceased but on the expiry of a period of 40 years from the commencement of the Constitution, i.e., in 1990 (Article 334) it has been repeatedly amended and the duration has been extended. The original provisions were for a period of 10 years. However, it has been amended for 30 years up till 1990 and again amended for ten years that is up to 2000 AD and for another ten years, that is up to 2010 AD.

Article 335 on the limits of reservation explains that the claims of the members belonging to Scheduled Castes and Scheduled Tribes as regards reservation to the posts and services of the Union and states as far as may be consistent with the maintenance of efficiency of administration. The quota was fixed keeping in mind the population size of the two groups at the rate of 15 per cent for the SCs and 7.5 per cent for the STs. Though a change in population size has been observed in both the groups, the reservation share of these groups have not changed over time. With this provision, filling up of the quota of SCs and STs as fixed by the government and semi-government services is a problem even today. The problem is far more in case of upper levels of the government. The reasons put forward range from apathy and indifference of the government to the unavailability of suitable candidates from the SC and ST categories, on account of their social, economic, and educational backgrounds. However, this provision empowers both Union and State Government to take steps to ensure that the claims of the SCs and STs are duly considered in making the appointments to services and posts under the central as well as the State Governments with relaxation of age limits, reduction in examination fees, lowering down of educational and other qualifications and in providing pre-examination coaching. It is a fact that due to the reservation policy there has been a considerable increase in the representation of SCs and STs in various posts and services under the Central Government and State Government. In spite of this, there have been significant distortions in the implementation of the reservation policy and the progress in this regard has not been made very satisfactory. It is largely because a large section of this population is much below the educational level even required for a post of peon. Another dimension of poor achievements of these provisions is that by and large only few ethnic communities known as creamy layer have always been representing. For example, in Orissa, not even a dozen persons from the tribal communities like Juanga, Bonda, Didayi, Khadia, Mankiridia, etc., have passed high school education to be appointed as a clerk in the government jobs, whereas, the members of few tribal groups like Santhal, Munda, Oraon, Khond have been well represented in government services. In such a situation, it has been proposed that the facilities of reservation should only be confined to the members of first generation of the family. However, State attempt for the spread of education in tribal areas should be made qualitative than quantitative and it is the duty of the State to ensure quality education to this section of population.

Article 338 explains about the appointment of Special Officer, which clearly spells out, that the President of India will appoint a Special Officer for the Scheduled Castes and Scheduled Tribes to assess their welfare activities. The primary responsibilities of the Special Officer are to investigate all matters relating to the implementation of safeguards provided for them in the Constitution. He is expected to report to the President of India on the working of these safeguards to be laid before each House of the Parliament. This institution was renamed in 1996 as National Commission for Scheduled Castes and Scheduled Tribes. The details of the functioning of this institution are explained in Chapter 5.

Article 339 (1) provides for the appointment of a Commission by the President of India at any time after the expiration of 10 years from the commencement of the Constitution, to report on the administration of the Scheduled Areas and welfare of the Scheduled Tribes of the State. Details of ST and SC Commission have been explained in chapter five of the book.

Article 339 (2) further empowers the Union Executive to issue directives to a State as to the drawing up and execution of schemes specified in the directives to be essential for the welfare of the Scheduled Tribes in the States.

Article 340 envisages that the President of India by order may appoint a Commission consisting of such persons as he thinks fit to investigate the conditions of socially and educationally backward classes within the territory of India and the difficulties under which they labour and to make recommendations as to the steps that should be taken by the Union or any State to remove such difficulties and to improve their conditions. Clause 2 of the Article explains about the duties of the Commission to investigate the matters referred to them and present to the President a report setting out the facts as found by them and making such recommendations as they think proper. The first Backward Class Commission known as Kaka Kalekar Commission was appointed in 1953 which submitted its report in 1955. The second Backward Class Commission was appointed in 1979 under the chairmanship of Shri B.P. Mandal. The National Commission for Backward Classes Act 1993 was enacted on the direction of the Supreme Court to set up a permanent body for entertaining, examining and recommending upon requests for inclusion and complaints of over or/and under-inclusion in the list of OBCs of citizens. The Commission was constituted on 14 August, 1993 and the GoI have so far specified more than 3,000 communities as OBCs in various States and UTs.

The Indian Constitution has never defined the terms Scheduled Tribe and Scheduled Caste in any part of the Constitution, The Article 341 simply says that the President may with respect to any State or Union Territory and where it is a State after consultation with the Governor, thereof, by public notification, specify the castes races of tribes or parts of or groups within castes, races or tribes which shall for the purposes of this Constitution be deemed to be SCs in relation to the State or Union Territory, as the case may be ... While Article 342 specifies that the President of India may with regard to any State or Union Territory after consultation with the Governor by public notification specify the tribes or tribal communities or parts of or groups within tribes or tribal communities which shall for the purposes of this

Constitution be deemed to be Scheduled Tribes in relation to the State. Clause 2 of this Article explains that Parliament may by law include or exclude from the list of Scheduled Tribes specified in a notification issued under clause (1) any tribe or tribal community or part of or group within any tribe or tribal community, but save as aforesaid a notification issued under the said clause shall not be varied by any subsequent notification. Even Article 366 which deals with the definition does not go beyond what has been stated in Article 341 and 342 about these terms. Since the Constitution (ST) Order 1950 was notified, there are nine Presidential Orders that have so far been issued specifying the list of 640 ST communities in different States and UTs. The criteria followed for specifying STs in 1950 was primitiveness distinct culture, geographical isolation, shyness of contact with the community at large, social, education and economic backwardness.

Article 350 B makes the provision of a Special Officer for linguistic minorities. President of India can appoint a Special Officer to investigate all matters relating to the safeguards provided for linguistic minorities under this Constitution and report to the President upon those matters as the President may direct and the President shall cause all such reports to be placed before each House of Parliament and sent to the Government of the States concerned. Most of the tribal communities have their own language or dialects, which usually belong to different family of languages.

Article 336 (25) defines the term Scheduled Tribe, which means such tribes or tribal communities or parts of groups within such tribes or tribal communities as are deemed under 342 designated as to be Scheduled Tribes for the purposes of the Constitution.

The impact of Constitutional privileges on the Schedule Tribes highlights the uneven impact of such privileges on the tribal communities, which is basically due to the variations in the levels of development between one tribal region and another, and between different tribal communities. Consequent upon this, there has emerged a small elite class among the tribes, who have been benefited from the protective discrimination, while majority of the tribals faced more hardship or have remained where they were before the formulation of these policies. This has been evident in the life-way processes of the tribal communities, be it education (Ahmed, 1972: 69-72; Behura, 1993, 1996) or politics (Pathy, 1987a) or economy (Pathy, 1976; Mohanty, 1984). The fact is that these vested groups are capable of articulating their interests in ethnic lines instead of making an effort to marshal the progressive forces in India in the common task of ending all forms of exploitation (Bose, 1974:95); rather small sections of tribal elites have become internal exploiters.

Five decades of experience on tribal development in India reflect that the goal of all-round development of the tribal communities as conceived in the Indian Constitution has raised certain basic issues before the nation. These issues may be recognition of rights of the tribal people over natural resources like land, water, forests and mineral resources, crisis in tribal identify, etc. However, it is very difficult to say that since independence and from the formulation of Indian Constitution, the social-economic conditions of these communities have not changed much. It is a fact that as long as the disparity between the tribal groups on one side and non-tribal on the other prevails, the Constitutional goal of building one socio-economic order remains a daydream. Under the situation, the government policy should be more focussed towards bridging the prevailing disparities both within and outside the tribal communities.

3 Profile of the Study Villages

Physiography of the Study Villages

The study covers four villages in four different Scheduled districts of Orissa. These districts are Kalahandi, Keonjhar, Kandhamal and Malkangiri. A brief comparative profile of certain indicators on the backwardness and development of these districts is given in Table 3.1. This at certain level justifies the rationale for selecting these districts for study. The first village covered in the study was Kendubaradihi, a hamlet of the revenue village of Jagannathpur under Lanjigarh Gram Panchayat in Lanjigarh block of Kalahandi district. The total geographical area of the revenue village of Jagannathpur is 1269.129 hectares, which consists of reserve forest, wasteland, etc. The homestead land and *raiti* land in total account for 162.468 hectares. The second village of the study is Tungurubahal, a revenue village of Jagamohanpur Gram Panchayat in Telkoi block of Keonjhar district. The third village of the study is Penaposi Pangara a revenue village in Bhramarbadi Gram Panchayat under Daringibadi block of Kandhamal district. Lachipetta one of the revenue villages of Tandbai Gram Panchayat of Padia block in Malkangiri district is the fourth village of the study. The total geographical area of this village is 1806.179 hectares of which reserve land accounts for 762.987 hectares, community land covers an area of 36.669 hectares, wasteland covers 554.891 hectares, agriculture and homestead and *raiti* land covers only 75.218 hectares. As per 1992 land settlement records, there were 93 holders in the village who owned 75.218 hectares of *raiti* land. The total geographical area of Tungurubahal village is 266.216 hectares. The forestland in the village covers 156.740 hectares; *gochar* land covers 4.550 hectares, encroached land accounts for 0.510 hectares, while agricultural land of the village in total is 31.621 hectares as per 1992 land settlement records. The study villages are situated on an average distance of 2 kms to 4 kms from Gram Panchayat headquarters. In case of Malkangiri district, the village Lachipetta is situated at a distance of 57 kms from the Panchayat Samiti headquarters, while in case of all other study villages the average distance of the Panchayat Samiti headquarters ranges from 13 to 18 km. Similarly, the nearest urban centre in case of Kendubaradihi of Kalahandi district and Lachipetta of Malkangiri district is 2 to 3 kms, while Tungrubahal village of Keonjhar district and Penaposi Pangara village of Kandhamal district are situated about 13 kms away from the nearest urban centre that is, from their respective block headquarters. The naming of the villages carries a definite religious meaning and/or linked to certain factors like copious availability of natural resources. For example, the name of the village Kendubaradihi refers to sufficient availability of Kendu in earlier days. Similarly, the village Penaposi Pangara carries the religious meaning that is, the name of the local deity of the Kandhas. All the villages are surrounded by forest. The forest surroundings are thick only in case of Penaposi Pangara village of Kandhamal district, whereas, in all other study villages the forest coverage is thin due to large-scale deforestation. This has highly affected the animal resources of the region. During annual *paridhi* or hunting the villagers have to travel more than 10 to 15 kms from their village. The flow of natural *nalas* (streams) once perennial by nature now have become seasonal. This was observed in case of Kendubaradihi of Kalahandi district, and Tungurubahal village of Keonjhar district. During the discussion, it was found that the villagers are able to correlate the deforestation with the loss of perennialty of these natural *nalas*.

Table 3.1

A Comparison of Selected Development Indicators of Study Districts

Development Indicators	*Unit*	*Kalahandi*	*Keonjhar*	*Kandhamal*	*Malkangiri*
Administrative Divisions					
Geographical Area	Sq. kms.	8,364	8,303	7,650	6,190
Sub-Division	Nos.	2	3	2	1
Tehasil	"	7	8	4	3
C.D. Blocks	"	13	13	12	7
Villages (inhabited)	"	2,068	2,067	2,336	878
Demography					
Total District Population	000	421	1,337	546	113
District Population to State Population	000	357	422	173	133
Sex Ratio (per 1000)	Nos.	999	974	999	985
SC Population to District Total Population (1991)	%	17.1	11.49	18.21	19.96
ST Population to District Total Population (1991)	%	28.88	44.52	51.51	58.36
ST Population to States Total Population (1991)	%	4.61	8.46	4.00	3.50
Literacy					
All Communities Total	%	31.08	44.73	37.23	20.04
SC Total	%	28.20	43.67	34.51	33.76
ST Total	%	18.54	24.89	27.49	6.77
Primary Schools (1994-95)	Nos.	1452	1543	1329	813
Primary Schools Teacher (1994-95)	Nos.	2,962	4,091	2,499	1,557
Middle School (1994-95)	"	316	579	209	80
Middle School Teacher (1994-95)	"	1,317	1,953	888	275
Secondary School (1994-95)	"	187	368	73	36

Contd...

Contd...

Secondary School Teacher (1994-95)	Nos.	1,465	3,026	749	331
Colleges General Education (1994-95)	"	24	42	12	6
College Teacher (1994-95)	"	325	683	189	59
Health					
Homeopathic Hospitals (1994-95)	Nos.	7	12	9	6
Dispensary (1994-95)	"	2	4	6	3
PHC Adl PHC	"	29	41	21	12
Health Centres	"	7	8	3	2
First Aid Centre	"	—	—	7	—
Medical Aid Centre	"	1	2	1	—
Socio-Economic Indicators					
Average size of Operational Holding (1990-91)	Hect.	1.94	1.28	1.38	1.81
Per Capita Availability of Food Grains (1994-95)	In kg	245	176	164	264
Villages Electrified (1995-96)	%	53.92	79.05	38.18	32.35
Population Served by Bank (1996)	Nos.	15,762	16,712	24,336	15,143
Persons per Hospital Beds (1995-96)	"	2,514	2,864	1,960	1,597
Per Capita Availability of Milk per Day (1994-95)	Grams	29	41	22	27
Per Capita Availability of Eggs per Year (1994-95)	Nos.	13	10	17	16
Area Covered under Paddy Cultivation (1995-96)	000 Hect.	233	2,19	57	77
Yield rate of Paddy per Hect. (1995-96)	Qntls	17.71	15.93	18.59	18.30
Production of Rice (1995-96)	(0000) Qntls	2,730	2,451	707	936

Flora and Fauna

The role of flora and fauna in a tribal village is very important. It influences their economy, social and religious life-way processes. It is a fact that due to the intervention of outside agencies and development projects, flora and fauna in the tribal regions have been highly affected. This has been found in all the study villages. For example, in Lachhipetta village of Malkangiri district, settlement of refugee Bengalis under Dandakaranya Resettlement Project has affected the flora and fauna of the village to a large extent. This has occurred due to high deforestation caused through both planned and non-planned development. Similarly, in Penaposi Pangara, a study village in Kandhamal district, the influx of non-tribal households has destroyed natural resources of the village, and by and large affected the animal world of the region. This was found to be true when the study team during its stay found that a pup of wild boar was killed by the villagers in Tungurubahal of Keonjhar district, for community feast.

The dominant tree species still available in the study villages by and large include Sal *(Sorua robusta)*, Asan (*Terminalia tomentosa*), Kusum (*Scheleichera oleosa*), Mahua *(Basia letifolia)*, mango (*Mangifera indica*), Anala (*Phymanthus emblica*), jackfruit (*Artocarpus intergi foila*), Bahada (*Terminalia bellerica*), Harida (*Terminalia chebula*), Jamu (*Mangifera indica*), Kusum (*Syzygium cumuni*), Siali (*Bauhinia vahli*), and Dumuri (*Ficus glo merata*). In spite of large-scale deforestation and degradation of flora and fauna in the tribal dominated study villages the tribal people still maintain symbiotic relationship with the available natural resources. The natural and super-natural forces still determine the life-way processes of the tribal people. The ritualistic attitude of the tribal communities towards plants and other natural phenomena is reflected when one observes that their first eating of new crops (mango, jackfruit, varieties of roots, beans, etc.) is preceded by certain rituals. Collection of bamboo shoots as food item by leaving few strong shoots for future growth or leaving a piece of tuber inside the pit when they collect tubers and roots as food items are some of the examples of their symbiotic relationship with the nature and natural objects. This reflects their conservative attitude towards nature (Behura, 1982). It was observed that the tribal people while cleaning forests for shifting cultivation still do not cut the trees like sal, bahada, harida, kusum, mahua, tentuli, mango, etc., with the premise that these trees have been providing food to them for generations.

Settlement Pattern

Settlement pattern influences the social status of a village. The villages in four different districts representing different regions of the State, obviously find distinct settlement patterns. Except the Kalahandi district, where the houses are ordered in a linear pattern, in almost all other villages the houses are distributed in clusters. With the change of time tribal people have also started thinking that *pucca* and semi-*pucca* houses symbolises one's higher economic status (though found in few cases only). Traditional tribal housing pattern consists of only one single composite room having multiple functions. In this study, an attempt has been made to find out the structure of tribal housing. It is observed that in Kendubardihi of Kalahandi district all the houses are made up of *Kutchha* (mud) wall and roofed with baked mud tiles. Houses fulfil multiple functions. In Tungurubahal of Keonjhar district only 1.51 per cent (2 ST households) have semi-*pucca* houses and others have *Kutchha* houses. In Penaposi Pangara village of Kandhamal district, almost 20 ST HHs (40%) have semi-*pucca* houses with asbestos roof. In Lachipetta village of Malkangiri district only one ST household (0.57) has semi-*pucca* house. In total, in all the study villages, while 23 ST households (5.51%) have semi-*pucca* houses for accommodation, all other households are staying in *Kutchha* houses. The introduction of semi-pucca houses in tribal villages not necessarily relates to the higher economic strength of the villagers. It is observed that the government has provided the single room asbestos house with brick wall under Indira Awas Yojana (IAY) scheme to the poor tribal households. It is also observed that some well-to-do tribal households are having mud house constructed on traditional plan. The beneficiaries of Indira Awas Yojana admitted that they have paid bribes in advance to the authorities of Panchayat Samiti and members of Gram Panchayats, which varies from Rs. 500 to Rs. 1,000 per beneficiary. Since this scheme is meant for the poor tribals, several tribal households were deprived of the benefit who could not pay the bribe, as a result, the scheme was diverted to other persons.

During the construction of a new house in the tribal villages religious leaders still play an important role in performing certain rituals. Performance of rituals is a basic requirement to start the construction work. Juanga settlements in Keonjhar are located in separate hamlets which are away from Bhuinya settlements, while Munda and Gond households are in clusters which are adjacent to each other. In all other study villages the ethnic groups maintain their social boundaries in settlement. This helps them also to maintain their socio-cultural boundaries. The study reflects that in Penaposi Pangara village of Kandhamal district the Kandha habitations are normally located in isolated clusters and separated from the non-tribal houses. The relation between Kandha and Sundhi a Hindu caste group is symbolic and parasitic by nature, where the Sundhi people exploit the poor Kandhas. The Kandha houses are mainly located away from Sundhi households. This proves that the Kandha households do not want the Sundhis as neighbours because of various socio-economic reasons. Similarly, in Lachipetta village of Malkangiri it was observed that the relation between Koya tribal people and Bengalis are of similar type. The Bengalis always try to exploit the resources of the poor Koya persons. The village is only inhabited by the Koyas. In none of the Koya villages, which the study team visited to interview PRI members, found that a Bengali household is staying. This may be for two reasons: one is that Koya people always try to maintain their settlement solidarity, and secondly, the Bengalis always like to stay away from the Koya villages so as to maintain their exploitative relation.

Ethnic Composition

Most of the villages are multi-ethnic in composition and dominated by tribal households belonging to different Scheduled

Tribes (ST). In Kendubaradihi the habitation of Jagannathpur village is fully inhabited by Kutia Kandha (69) households. The Tungurubahal village is inhabited by 132 (76.74%) ST households who belong to different ST groups, like Bhuinyan (46 HH), Gond (45HH), Juanga (26 HH), Munda (14 HH) and one Saora household. There are also 40 HHs (23.25%) in the village who belong to caste groups. Penaposi Pangara village is inhabited by 50 (66.66%) Kutia Kandha households, 20 (26.66%) Scheduled Caste HHs and 5 (6.66%) HHs belonging to Hindu caste groups. Lachhipetta village is inhabited by 166 (99.39%) ST HHs.

Table 3.2

Distribution of Households according to Ethnic Categories in the Study Villages of Different Districts

Sl. No.	*Caste/ Communities*	*HHs in the Study Villages*				
		Kendubara-dihi (Kalahandi)	*Tunguru-bahal (Keonjhar)*	*Penaposi Pangara (Kandhamal)*	*Lachipetta (Malkangiri)*	*Total*
A.	*Scheduled Tribe*					
1	Koya	–	–	–	165	165
2	Kutia Kandha	69	–	50	–	119
3	Saora	–	1	–	–	1
4	Bhuinyan	–	46	–	–	46
5	Juanga	–	26	–	–	26
6	Gond	–	45	–	–	45
7	Munda	–	14	–	–	14
	Sub Total	69(100)	132(76.74)	50(66.66)	166(99.39)	471(86.33)
B.	*Scheduled Caste*	–	–	20(26.66)	–	20 (4.14)
C.	*Other Groups*	–	40(23.25)	5(6.66)	1(0.59)	46(9.52)
	Grand Total	69(100)	172(100)	75(100)	167(100)	483(100)

Note: Figures in the brackets are percentage to the total.

Out of the total 483 HHs, the study covers 417 (86.33%) tribal households who belong to different Scheduled Tribes, 20 (4.14%) households belong to Scheduled Caste groups and 46 (9.52%) households belong to Hindu Caste groups. The major Scheduled

Tribe Communities covered in the study villages are Koya (165 HH), Kutia Kandha (119 HH), Bhuinyan (46 HH), Gond (45 HH), Juanga (26 HH) and Munda (14 HH) (Table 3.2). During the discussion in all the villages, it was found that SC and other Hindu Caste households by and large had entered into these villages only 30 to 50 years back. The villagers said that these households basically entered their villages with business interest, and, are more or less, still continuing with same trades. Many of them have acquired landed properties from the ST households of the villages at different points of time.

Demography

Sex Composition

Data on the sex composition of a village is very important. The sex composition at certain level may influence the economy of the village. Therefore, an attempt has been made to highlight the sex and age composition of the population in each village. In order to understand sex composition, an analysis has been made according to different ethnic categories. While discussing the field situation in different districts it is observed that in Kendubaradihi village of Kalahandi district the proportion of female is marginally more, whereas, in all other study villages the male population is more in the sex composition. In total, the study reflects very little difference in the sex distribution of the study-population.

Age Group Classification

Distribution of population by ethnic categories according to age reflects that almost 43.34 per cent of the total male population are below the age of 14 years, whereas, 46.46 per cent male are within the age group of 15-45 years. More specifically among the ST population 42.5 per cent of male are under the age of 14 years, while 47.24 per cent of ST male are within the age group of 15-45 years. While comparing to ST male and female population above the age of 45 years, one finds ST female population to be predominant (12.26%), over the ST male (10.37%).

Marital Status

Knowledge of marital status of an ethnic group and/or of a village helps researchers to understand the status of productive age group in the population and the productive harmony maintained in the village demographic structure. It has been observed that the strength of widows and widowers in total accounts for 6.5 per cent in the Kendubaradihi village of Kalahandi district (is highest), whereas, it is 2.1 per cent in Tungurubahal village of Keonjhar district, 3 per cent in case of Penaposi Pangara village of Kandhamal district, and 4.1 per cent in case of Lachipetta village of Malkangiri district. From an analysis, it is found that in total there are 4 per cent households having widows or widowers among Scheduled Tribe ethnic groups, whereas, it is 3.9 per cent among the SC groups. While comparing the status of married and unmarried population in each village it is observed that quite a sizeable portion of the total population are unmarried.

Normally, tribal adolescents marry at an early age and, by and large, they select their life partners. With the intervention of development programmes and due to the influx of non-tribal households into the tribal areas a lot of changes have been observed in the mate acquiring processes of the tribal people. This has negatively affected the functional need of youth dormitories that in earlier days were playing a major role in the selection of life partners. However, now-a-days dormitories have been abolished and/or restructured in many tribal communities. For example, the migration of Bhuiyans and Mundas of Keonjhar district to outside areas to earn their livelihood has not only dismantled the social institutions of these groups, but also increased the age of marriage for both the sexes. While comparing this with the Koya youths of Malkangiri district, where adolescent boys and girls always prefer to go on seasonal migration to Andhra Pradesh in search of work, at the destination they maintain their social boundaries. This is strengthened by the social institutions, which they have at their native places. Among the Kutia Kandha of Kandhamal district one can say that more or less tribal youths still maintain their norms for selecting their mates. The influence of traditional institutions in some tribal groups of Orissa is still observed largely because of their confinement to traditional village environment and social boundaries. The study shows that the tribal people follow monogamous form of marriage. None of the household head found adopting polygynous form of marriage. There were five households in total who have undergone second marriage primarily due to the lack of productive capacity of their first wives and two tribals have married for the second time, because their first wives left them.

Family Size

As regards the size of the family of the tribal households an attempt has been made to classify the size into certain categories. In case of Tungurubahal village of Keonjhar district, it was observed that there were only six households having more than seven persons in the family. Largely the houses are small in size and the average size of tribal household in the district carries four persons, while it is 4.18 persons in Kendubaradihi village of Kalahandi district and 4.98 persons in Penaposi Pangara village of Kandhamal district and 4.22 persons in case of Lachipetta village of Malkangiri district. The study shows that the average household size of the tribals is 4.23 in Orissa.

Literacy

The distribution of population according to ethnic categories and their educational achievements (Table 3.3) reflects that among the Scheduled Tribe population, rate of illiteracy is highest with women (95%) as compared to men (85%). In Kendubaradihi of Kalahandi district, literacy rate among women is almost 0.95 per cent, whereas, among men it is 14.67 per cent. In Tungurubahal of Keonjhar district, literacy among women is 6.49 per cent while among men it is 9.31 per cent. In the study villages of Kalahandi, Keonjhar, and Kandhamal districts not a single tribal male or female has gone beyond the primary level of education, whereas, in case of Lachipetta of Malkangiri district only 1 per cent of tribal youths have gone beyond the primary level of education.

When one looks at the educational institutions available in and around the study villages it is observed that in Tungurubahal of Keonjhar district, the village has one Primary School, one M.E. School and one High School operating in the area which are adjacent to the village. In the study villages of Kandhamal, Kalahandi and Malkangiri districts both M.E. School and High School are located at a distance of 3 to 4 kms. Except Lachipetta in Malkangiri district where a college is situated 3 kms away from the village (located at MV-79), in all other study villages the colleges are situated at a distance of 13 to 18 kms from the villages (Table 3.8).

Here an attempt has been made to analyse the data on the educational achievements specifically of the Scheduled Tribes so as to review the impact of education on the tribal people. In case of Kendubaradihi of Kalahandi district, 85.32 per cent male and 99.05 per cent female are reported as illiterate, while 6.42 per cent of male have education up to the primary level. It is surprising to know that only one per cent tribal women were reported as literate. Perhaps, this is the reason that after 50 years of independence, tribal women in this village did not come forward to share their problems with the research team. In case of Tungurubahal village of Keonjhar, illiteracy among the tribal population is still conspicuous, while illiteracy among male has been reported, as 90.69 per cent, it is 93.51 per cent among the female. Similarly, only 1.96 per cent of tribal male have been educated up to primary level. In case of Penaposi Pangara village of Kandhamal district, 85.57 per cent male and 81 per cent of female have been reported as illiterate. Compared to other villages, illiteracy in this village is less because the village has a primary school located inside the village. Lachipetta village of Malkangiri district also witnesses high illiteracy ratio, which has been 80.85 per cent among male population and 99.31 per cent among the female population. Only in case of Malkangiri, 0.33 per cent and 0.66 per cent tribal people have acquired HSC and higher degrees respectively. The data reflect that among the tribal people 85 per cent male and 95 per cent female are reported as illiterate.

Table 3.3

Distribution of Study Population according to Educational Status by Ethnic Categories

Districts and Ethnic Groups	Total Population*			Educational Standard														
				Illiterate			Only Literate			Up to Primary			Up to HSC			Above		
	Male	Female	Total	Male	Female	Total	Male	Female	Total	Male	Female	Total	Male	Female	Total	Male	Female	Total
Kalahandi																		
Total	109	105	214	93	104	197	9	1	10	7	—	7	—	—	—	—	—	—
	(100)	(100)	(100)	(85.32)	(99.05)	(92.06)	(8.26)	(0.95)	(4.67)	(6.422)	—	(6.42)			—			—
ST	109	105	214	93	104	197	9	1	10	7	—	7	—	—	—	—	—	—
	(100)	(100)	(100)	(85.32)	(99.05)	(92.06)	(8.25)	(0.95)	(4.67)	(6.42)		(6.42)			—			—
SC	—	—	—	—	—		—	—		—	—		—	—	—	—	—	—
OC	—	—	—	—	—		—	—		—	—		—	—	—	—	—	—
Keonjhar																		
Total	292	258	550	213	242	455	42	14	56	16	2	18	4	—	4	17	—	17
	(100)	(100)	(100)	(72.95)	(93.80)	(82.73)	(14.38)	(5.43)	(10.18)	(5.48)	(0.78)	(3.27)	(1.36)	—	(0.72)	(5.82)		(3.09)
ST	204	185	389	185	173	358	15	12	27	4	—	4	—	—		—	—	
	(100)	(100)	(100)	(90.69)	(93.51)	(92.03)	(7.353)	(6.48)	(6.94)	(1.96)	—	(1.02)						
SC	—	—	—	—	—		—	—		—	—		—	—		—	—	
OC	88	73	161	28	69	97	27	2	29	12	2	14	4	—	4	17	—	17
	(100)	(100)	(100)	(31.88)	(94.52)	(60.24)	(30.68)	(2.73)	(18.01)	(13.63)	(2.73)	(8.70)	(4.54)	—	(2.46)	(19.31)	—	(10.55)

* Children below 6 years have not been included in total population

Contd...

Contd...

Kandhamal																		
Total	150	141	291	91	98	189	30	32	62	19	8	27	5	3	8	5	—	5
	(100)	(100)	(100)	(60.66)	69.50	64.95	(20.0)	(22.69)	(21.30)	(12.66)	(5.67)	(9.27)	(3.33)	(2.12)	(2.74)	(3.33)		(1.71)
ST	104	100	204	89	81	170	10	19	29	5	—	5	—	—	—	—	—	—
	(100)	(100)	(100)	(85.57)	(81.0)	(83.33)	(9.61)	(18.26)	(14.21)	(4.8)	—	(2.45)						
SC	32	29	61	2	14	16	18	12	30	12	3	15	—	—		—	—	
	(100)	(100)	(100)	(6.25)	(48.27)	(36.22)	(56.25)	(41.37)	(49.18)	(37.5)	(10.34)	(24.59)						
OC	14	12	26	—	3	3	2	1	3	2	5	7	5	3	8	5	—	5
	(100)	(100)	(100)	—	(25.0)	(11.53)	(14.26)	(8.33)	(11.53)	(14.28)	(41.66)	(26.92)	(35.71)	(25.0)	(30.76)	(35.71)	—	(19.23)
Malkangiri																		
Total	306	293	599	245	289	534	19	2	21	39	2	41	1	—	1	2	—	2
	(100)	(100)	(100)	(80.06)	(98.63)	(89.14)	(6.02)	(0.68)	(3.5)	(12.74)	(0.68)	(6.84)	(0.32)	—	(0.16)	(0.65)	—	(0.33)
ST	303	291	594	245	289	534	19	2	21	36	—	36	1	—	1	2	—	2
	(100)	(100)	(100)	(80.85)	(99.31)	(89.89)	(6.27)	(0.68)	(3.53)	(11.88)	—	(6.06)	(0.33)	—	(0.16)	(0.66)	—	(0.33)
SC	—	—	—	—	—		—	—		—	—		—	—		—	—	
OC	3	2	5	—	—	—	—	—	—	3	2	5	—	—	—	—	—	—
	(100)	(100)	(100)							(100)	(100)	(100)						
Grand Total	857	797	1654	642	733	1375	100	49	149	81	12	93	10	3	13	24	—	24
	(100)	(100)	(100)	(74.91)	(91.96)	(83.13)	(11.66)	(6.14)	(9.0)	(9.45)	(1.5)	(5.62)	(1.16)	(0.37)	(0.78)	(2.8)	—	(1.54)
ST	720	681	1401	612	647	1259	53	34	87	52	—	52	1	—	1	2	—	2
	(100)	(100)	(100)	(85.0)	95.0	(89.86)	(7.36)	(4.99)	(6.20)	(7.22)	—	(3.71)	(0.13)	—	(0.07)	(0.27)	—	(0.14)
SC	32	29	61	2	14	16	18	12	30	12	3	15	—	—	—	—	—	—
	(100)	(100)	(100)	(6.25)	(48.27)	(26.22)	(56.25)	(41.37)	(49.18)	(37.5)	(9.37)	(24.59)	—	—	—	—	—	—
OC	105	87	192	28	72	100	29	3	32	17	9	26	9	3	12	22	—	22
	(100)	(100)	(100)	(26.66)	(82.75)	(0.52)	(27.61)	(3.45)	(16.67)	(16.19)	(10.34)	(13.54)	(8.57)	(3.44)	(6.25)	(20.95)	—	(11.45)

Household Assets

Possession of different household assets reflects one's economic status. Understanding this, an attempt has been made to list out the assets possessed by the households in the study villages. Accounting of these has been restricted to the possession of major assets like gold, sliver, bicycle, radio, watch, *pucca* and semi-*pucca* houses. The study shows that of the total tribal households only 14.14 per cent households have possessed gold, while 51.55 per cent have sliver, about 16.78 per cent have bicycles, 19.9 per cent have radios and only 4.79 per cent have wrist watch. Almost all the households belonging to SC and other high caste categories possess several, types of assets. While looking at this phenomenon in different districts it is found that 48 per cent Kutia Kandha possess gold in Penaposi Pangara village of Kandhamal district, but in other districts possession of gold by households varies from 6.28 per cent in Lachipetta of Malkangiri district, to 7.25 per cent in case of Kendubaradihi village of Kalahandi district, and 14.39 per cent in case of Tungurubahal in Keonjhar district. The details of asset possession by different ethnic categories are given in Table 3.4.

Livestock Possession

Livestock resources play a very important role in the economy of the tribal people of Orissa. Not only the tribal people directly depend on animal resources for food, but also to collect manure for their agriculture. It is observed that tribal people keep livestock as an insurance to meet their future exigencies. It so happens that the livestock resources determine the economic strength of the tribal people. Here an attempt has been made to understand the contribution of animal resources to the household economy of tribal people. During the survey possession of different varieties of livestock like cow, bullock, pig, poultry, goat, sheep and buffalo have been documented. The purpose is to find out which variety of livestock in the study villages is more cared for by tribal people. As a whole, the data in all the villages reflect that poultry is more preferred, which shares 33.3 per cent of their total livestock possession, followed by cattle (30.27%) and goatery (18.3%). In the

Table 3.4

Distribution of Households by Ethnic Categories according to Possession of Household Assets in the Study Villages of Different Districts

Districts	*Total HH*	*Households Possessing Assets*						
		Gold	*Silver*	*Bicycle*	*Radio*	*Watch*	*Pucca House (RCC Roof)*	*Semi Pucca House Tile Roof with Brick Wall*
Kalahandi								
Total	69 (100.0)	5 (7.25)	32 (46.38)	10 (14.49)	5 (7.25)	1 (1.45)	—	—
ST	69 (100.0)	5 (7.25)	32 (46.38)	10 (14.49)	5 (7.25)	1 (1.45)	—	—
SC	—	—	—	—	—	—	—	—
OC	—	—	—	—	—	—	—	—
Keonjhar								
Total	172 (100.0)	57 (33.13)	91 (52.90)	49 (28.48)	22 (12.79)	53 (30.81)	2 (1.16)	19 (11.04)
ST	132 (100.0)	19 (14.39)	51 (38.13)	9 (6.81)	8 (6.06)	13 (9.84)	—	2 (1.51)
SC	—	—	—	—	—	—	—	—
OC	40 (100.0)	38 (95.00)	40 (100.0)	40 (100.0)	14 (35.00)	40 (100.0)	2 (5.00)	17 (42.50)

Contd...

Contd...

Kandhamal								
Total	75	41	69	25	30	27	—	43
	(100.0)	(54.66)	(92.0)	(33.33)	(40.0)	(36.0)	—	(57.33)
ST	50	24	44	2	5	2	—	20
	(100.0)	(48.0)	(88.0)	(4.0)	(10.0)	(4.0)	—	(40.0)
SC	20	12	20	18	20	20		
	(100.0)	(60.0)	(100.0)	(90.0)	(100.0)	(100.0)		
OC	5	5	5	5	5	5	—	18
	(100.0)	(100.0)	(100.0)	(100.0)	(100.0)	(100.0)	—	(90.0)
Malkangiri								
Total	176	12	89	50	66	5	—	2
	(100.0)	(6.81)	(50.56)	(28.40)	(37.5)	(2.84)	—	(1.36)
ST	175	11	88	49	65	4	—	1
	(100.0)	(6.28)	(50.28)	(28.0)	(37.14)	(2.28)	—	(0.57)
SC	—	—	—	—	—	—	—	—
	—	—	—	—	—	—	—	—
OC	1	1	1	1	1	1	—	1
	(100.0)	(100.0)	(100.0)	(100.0)	(100.0)	(100.0)	—	(100.0)
Grand Total	483	115	281	134	123	86	2	64
	(100.0)	(23.80)	(58.17)	(27.74)	(25.46)	(17.8)	(0.41)	(13.25)
ST	417	59	215	70	83	20	—	23
	(100.0)	(14.14)	(51.55)	(16.78)	(19.9)	(4.79)	—	(5.51)
SC	20	12	20	18	20	20	—	18
	(100.0)	(60.0)	(100.0)	(90.0)	(100.0)	(100.0)	—	(90.0)
OC	46	44	46	46	20	46	2	23
	(100.0)	(95.96)	(100.0)	(100.0)	(43.47)	(100.0)	(4.34)	(50.0)

Note: Figures in the brackets refer to the percentage of HHs possessing various type of assets.

study villages of Malkangiri and Kandhamal districts possession of cattle by the tribal households is equally important. Tribal households by and large do not milk their cows, neither for their own consumption nor for sale. They allow the calf to drink all milk with a belief that the calf in future will be stronger and can be useful for ploughing on the terrain hill slopes. Even after five decades of planned development, in animal husbandry sector, tribal people follow primitive methods of rearing. As a result, it has been observed that tribal people are yet to take up animal husbandry as a major source of income. However, livestock resources are one of the sustainable sources, which have been contributing partly to the livelihood of the tribal people.

Landholding

In order to know the landholding situation in the study villages an attempt has been made to find out the distribution of average landholding of the households by ethnic categories, which includes the possession of both the varieties of *patta* and non-*patta* land. Of the total households, almost 20.49 per cent do not have any *patta* land, while 17.5 per cent ST HHs and 70 per cent SC HHs also do not have *patta* land. Data show that the households having *patta* land in all the districts is 82.49 per cent. Scheduled Tribe households together own 469.5 acres of land with an average landholding of 1.36 acres per household. The average landholding of *patta* land among the ST HHs in different study villages is that the tribal households in Kendubardihi of Kalahandi district own 3.15 acres of *patta* land, whereas, it is 0.75 acres in case of Tungurubahal of Keonjhar district, and 1.78 acres in case of Penaposi Pangara of Kandhamal district and 1.04 acres in case of Lachhipetta of Malkangiri district.

Similarly, an attempt has been made to highlight the holding of non-*patta*/encroached land by the tribal households. Almost 41.24 per cent tribal households do not posses encroached land. While the tribal households who have encroached land is quite less in case of Keonjhar district (15.15%), but it is more in case of Lachipetta village of Malkangiri district (84.93%) and Kandhamal district (78%). The average land encroached by the tribal households in the study villages of different districts varies from 0.78 acres in case of Keonjhar to 1.99 acres in case of Kandhamal district. The details of landholding across different study districts and ethnic groups are given in Table 3.5. Here an attempt has been made to find out the distribution of operational holding of ST HHs who own both *patta* and non-*patta* land. The distribution has been made according to size of the operational holdings. It is observed that there are almost 36.53 per cent of ST households who own 12.63 per cent of the total land accounting to less than 1 acre of land. Similarly, 26.37 per cent of households own 18.78 per cent of the total land, belonging to the marginal category (1-2 acres) and 20.87 per cent of tribal households own over 28.31 per cent of land who belong to small land-holding category (2-4 acres of land). The operational holding in different districts according to different size categories are given in Table 3.6. The details of land leased-in and leased-out, sale and purchase, and the extent of land alienation is explained in Chapter 6.

Household Income

The household annual income of the tribal people has been calculated taking into account the income raised from the major livelihood sources. These major livelihood sources are agriculture, Minor Forest Produces (MFPs), livestock and livestock produces, and wage earnings. It has been a fact that availability of different agricultural and forest produces are region-specific. The income from agriculture accounts for 52 per cent, while MFP shares 18.48 per cent, livestock and livestock produces a share of 12 per cent and wage-labour accounts for 18.11 per cent (Table 3.7). A district-wise look into the annual income of the tribal households from various sources shows that agriculture contributes the highest proportion in Penaposi Pangara village of Kandhamal district, while MFP contributes 30.07 per cent (highest) in case of Tungurabahal of Keonjhar district and livestock contributes more in Lachipetta village of Malkangiri district. Production of turmeric is the major agricultural produce in Kandhamal district. However, paddy cultivation still continues to be the major agricultural produce in the tribal regions of the State. As regards the minor

Table 3.5

Distribution of Households by Ethnic Categories and Average Landholding (Both Patta and Non-Patta Land) in the Study Villages of Different Districts

Districts	*Total HH*	*Land Type*							
		No. of HH with Patta land				*No.of HH with Non-Patta/Encroached land*			
		Not Having Patta Land	*Having Patta Land*	*Total Land Possessed*	*Average Land Holding*	*Not Having Non-Patta Land*	*Having Non-Patta Land*	*Total Land Possessed*	*Average Land Holding*
Kalahandi									
Total	69 (100.0)	18 (26.08)	51 (73.91)	161.0	3.15	24 (34.78)	45 (65.21)	55.5	1.23
ST	69 (100.0)	18 (26.08)	51 (73.91)	161.0	3.15	24 (34.78)	45 (65.21)	55.5	1.23
SC	—	—	—	—	—	—	—	—	—
OC	—	—	—	—	—	—	—	—	—
Keonjhar									
Total	172 (100.0)	31 (20.93)	136 (79.06)	131.0	0.97	150 (87.20)	22 (12.79)	16.5	0.75
ST	132 (100.0)	28 (21.21)	104 (78.78)	78.0	0.75	112 (84.84)	20 (15.15)	15.5	0.78
SC	—	—	—	—	—	—	—	—	—
OC	40 (100.0)	8 (20)	32 (80.0)	53.0	1.66	38 (95.0)	2 (5.0)	1.0	0.5

Contd...

Contd...

Kandhamal									
Total	75 (100.0)	23 (30.66)	52 (69.33)	94.0	1.8	15 (20.0)	60 (80.0)	141.0	2.35
ST	50 (100.0)	5 (10.0)	45 (90.0)	80.0	1.78	11 (22.0)	39 (78.0)	77.5	1.99
SC	20 (100.0)	14 (70.0)	6 (30.0)	5.0	0.84	4 (20.0)	16 (80.0)	57.5	3.6
OC	5 (100.0)	4 (80.0)	1 (20.0)	9.0	9.0	— —	5 (100.0)	6.0	1.2
Malkangiri									
Total	167 (100.0)	22 (13.17)	145 (86.82)	151.0	1.04	25 (14.97)	142 (85.02)	274.5	1.94
ST	166 (100.0)	22 (13.25)	144 (86.74)	150.0	1.04	25 (15.06)	141 (84.93)	269.0	1.9
SC	—	—	—	—	—	—	—	—	—
OC	1 (100.0)	— —	1 (100.0)	0.5	0.5	— —	1	5.5	5.5
Grand Total	483 (100.0)	99 (20.49)	384 (79.50)	537.0	1.39	214 (44.3)	269 (55.69)	487.5	1.81
ST	417 (100.0)	73 (17.5)	344 (82.49)	469.5	1.36	172 (41.24)	245 (58.75)	417.5	1.7
SC	20 (100.0)	14 (70.0)	6 (30.0)	5.0	0.84	4 (20.0)	16 (80.0)	57.5	3.6
OC	46 (100.0)	12 (26.08)	34 (73.91)	62.5	1.84	38 (82.6)	8 (17.39)	12.5	1.57

Note: Figures in the brackets are percentage to the total households.

Table 3.6

Distribution of Total Operational Holding of ST Households (Owning Both Patta and Non-Patta Land) in the Study Villages of Different Districts

Districts	ST Households		Total Extent	Distribution of Operation Holding (In Acres)								
				Below 1 Ac			Marginal (1-2)			Small (2-4)		
	Total	Land Holding HH		No. of HH	Extent of Land	Average	No. of HH	Extent of Land	Average	No. of HH	Extent of Land	Average
1	2	3	4	5	6	7	8	9	10	11	12	13
Kalahandi	69	51	216.5	9	8.5	0.94	23	42	1.82	7	26.5	3.78
		(100.0)	(100.0)	(17.64)	(3.92)		(45.09)	(19.39)		(13.72)	(12.24)	
Keonjhar	132	104	93.5	83	64.5	0.77	18	21	1.16	3	8.0	2.66
		(100.0)	(100.0)	(79.8)	(68.98)		(17.3)	(22.45)		(2.88)	(8.55)	
Kandhamal	50	45	157.5	9	9.5	1.05	17	34.5	2.02	14	49.5	3.53
		(100.0)	(100.0)	(20.0)	(6.03)		(37.77)	(21.9)		(31.11)	(31.42)	
Malkangiri	166	144	419.0	32	29.5	0.92	38	69	1.81	52	167	3.21
		(100.0)	(100.0)	(22.22)	(7.04)		(26.38)	(16.46)		(36.11)	(39.85)	
All Total	417	364	886.5	133	112.0	0.84	96	166.5	1.73	76	251.0	3.3
		(100.0)	(100.0)	(36.53)	(12.63)		(26.37)	(18.78)		(20.87)	(28.31)	

Districts	*Distribution of Operation Holding (in Ac)*								
	Semi Medium (4-10)			*Medium (10-20)*			*Above 20 +*		
	No. of HH	*Extent of Land*	*Average*	*No. of HH*	*Extent of Land*	*Average*	*No. of HH*	*Extent of Land*	*Average*
1	*14*	*15*	*16*	*17*	*18*	*19*	*20*	*21*	*22*
Kalahandi	9	81.5	9.05	2	37	18.5	1	21	21.0
	(17.64)	(37.14)		(3.92)	(17.09)		(1.96)	(9.69)	
Keonjhar	—	—	—	—	—	—	—	—	
Kandhamal	3	28.0	9.33	2	36.0	18.0	—	—	
	(6.66)	(17.77)		(4.44)	(22.85)				
Malkangiri	18	102.5	5.69	4	51	12.8	—	—	
	(12.5)	(24.46)		(2.77)	(12.17)				
All Total	30	212.0	7.06	8	124.0	15.5	1	21	21.0
	(8.24)	(23.91)		(2.19)	(13.98)		(0.27)		(2.36)

Note: Figures in the brackets are percentage to the total.

forest produces, there exists regional variation in the availability of MFP, which is prominently reflected in the study. Among the important minor forest produces one finds unlimited availability of siali leaves (29.10%) followed by mahua flower (24.98%). The data when analysed in respect of each study village, to find out the important MFP varieties which contribute more to the total income from forest sources, it is found that siali leaf contributes more in Kendubaradihi village of Kalahandi district (72.24%) and Penaposi Pangara of Kandhamal district (66.49%), while muhua flower contributes more in Tungurubahal village of Keonjhar (39.92%) and kenduleaf in Lachipetta village of Malkangiri (60.16%) district.

Table 3.7

Distribution of Average Annual Income Per ST Household from Various Sources in the Study Villages of Different Districts

Districts	*No. of Households*	*Income from Major Sources (in Rs.)*				
		Agriculture	*MFP*	*Livestock*	*Wage Labour*	*All Total*
Kalahandi	69	3305	1052	688	975	6020
		(55.0)	(17.47)	(11.42)	(16.19)	(100.00)
Keonjhar	132	1585	1623	395	1793	5396
		(29.37)	(30.07)	(7.32)	(33.23)	(100.00)
Kandhamal	50	6574	1355	642	943	9514
		(69.09)	(14.24)	(6.74)	(9.91)	(100.00)
Malkangiri	166	2138	826	1422	1048	5454
		(39.20)	(15.14)	(26.07)	(19.21)	(100.00)
All Total	417	3400	1214	788	1190	6596
		(52.0)	(18.48)	(12.0)	(18.11)	(100.00)

Note: Figures in the brackets are percentage to the total.

Livestock and livestock-produces provide a regular support income to the tribal households. Among various livestock species, poultry seems to be the major income category in all study villages of Kalahandi (59.01%), Keonjhar (33.16%) and Kandhamal (41.74%) who raise their income, whereas, in Malkangiri cow produces generate more income (42.40%).

Earning through wage-labour by tribal households has been documented separately according to various government and private sources. Further, the income from wage-labour has also been measured according to average days of engagement and average income earned per annum. The data show that private sources provide frequent engagement and it comprises a major share in the total annual income raised from wage-earning. In some cases, there is regular seasonal migration. This has been observed in Lachipetta village of Malkangiri district where the youths every year migrate to the neighbouring Andhra Pradesh for wage-labour. In Tungurubahal village of Keonjhar district, it is also observed that the tribal people migrate to Talcher, Angul, Badabil and Bhubaneswar for wage-labour. It has been observed that migration to outside regions for wage-earning in the study villages is more or less a common practice, which generates handsome income for tribal households. The average earning for unskilled labour is Rs. 30 per day, whereas, for the labourers engaged in the local area it varies from Rs. 20 to 25 per day. Another factor for going to outside area is the influence of labour contractors or *dalal* who pays some advance money and ensures engagement for a minimum period and also provides temporary accommodation at the destination.

Infrastructure Development

A look into the infrastructure available in the study villages (Table 3.8) indicates that all the villages are linked up by *kutchha* road and located at a distance of 1 to 3 kms from the nearest pucca road. In all the villages, tube-wells have been provided to solve drinking water problem. Except Kendubaradihi village of Kalahandi, 'dug wells' are available in all the study villages. Similarly, except Penaposi Pangara village of Kandhamal district, ponds are available in all other villages, which were used for day-to-day living. The river streams found in all the villages, except Lachipetta of Malkangiri, are seasonally used for all purposes except agriculture. These natural water bodies like ponds, nalas, rivers are found to be badly managed.

Table 3.8

Distribution of Infrastructural Facilities Available and Distance from the Study Villages in Different Districts

Infrastructure/Services Available	*Distance from the Studied Villages in District (in km)*			
	Kalahandi	*Keonjhar*	*Kandhamal*	*Malkangiri*
Location				
Nearest Urban Centre	3	13	13	2.5
GP Headquarters	3	2	4	2.5
Police Station	3	13	13	2.5
Forest Guard Office	3	1	2	2.5
Post Office	3	1	4	2.5
Block Headquarters	18	13	13	57
Market				
Daily	3	1	—	2.5
Weekly	3	1	13	2.5
Bi-weekly	3	1	13	2.5
Communication				
Bus Stop	3	3	1	2.5
Railway Station	19	65	200	2.5
Telephone Facility	3	3	13	2.5
Road Communication	3	3	1	2.5
Health Care Service				
Health Centre	3	1	13	2.5
Dispensary	3	3	13	2.5
Primary Health Centre	3	*	4	2.5
Community Health Centre	3	*	4	2.5
Sub-Centre	3	3	13	2.5
Maternity and Child Welfare Centre	3	1	13	2.5
Untrained TBA	1	*	*	*
Trained TBA	3	1	*	2.5
Medicine Shop	3	3	13	2.5
Anganwadi Centre	*	*	*	*
Non-Government Organisation	3	3	*	2.5

Contd...

Contd...

Educational Institutions				
Primary School	*	*	*	*
M.E. School	3	*	4	3
High School	3	*	4	3
Colleges	18	13	13	3
Training Institute	NA	2.8	90	80
Water Sources				
Tube-wells	*	*	*	*
Sanitary Dug Wells	NA	*	*	*
Million Wells	NA	*	NA	*
Pond	*	*	NA	*
River/Stream	*	*	*	NA

* Available within the village; NA: Not Available; TBA: Traditional Birth Attendants.

As regards the repair and maintenance of hand pumps, specific questions were asked about the frequency of breakdown, time gap between breakdown and repair, quality of water, maintenance responsibility, etc. In all, the study villages except Kendubaradihi of Kalahandi district, the tube-wells are used for all purposes. However, the tribal people basically use tube-well water for cooking and other household purposes. In all the villages though the frequency of breakdown of the hand pump is comparatively less but breakdown period was reported as very high which makes the hand pump idle even for a period of 10 to 15 days. The quality of water of the tube-wells as reported was good and acceptable. However, on testing the tube-well water in Tungurubahal village of Keonjhar district, the team member observed that the water carries more iron content than the normal level. The maintenance system adopted by the government is still centralised in the Government Panchayat Samiti Offices, i.e., Block Office. However, in Biswanathpur block of Kalahandi district, one decentralised hand pump maintenance system introduced by IWDP was reported to be under operation for the last couple of years. This system develops the capabilities of the local artisans/youths to take up hand pump maintenance activities, now operational, at Gram Panchayat level of the entire block.

In all the study villages, there are primary schools for educating the children. Except Tungurubahal in Keonjahar district, in none of the villages other educational institutions are available within the vicinity of the village. The M.E. and High Schools in all the study villages are located at a distance of 3 to 4 kms from the respective village settlements, while the colleges are located at a distance of 13 to 18 kms, except in Lachipetta where it is located in MV-79, which is about 3 kms from the village. It has been observed that all the schools are running regularly, but the results are said to be poor, even below the minimum standard. This is largely due to low receptivity of the tribal children, irregular and stereotype teaching and poor monitoring by higher authorities.

As regards the availability of health care services in every study village, there are untrained Traditional Birth Attendants (TBA) and Anganwadi centres. The Anganwadi centres in all the villages do not fully cater to the needs of the target groups in the villages. In case of Kendubaradihi, a tribal cluster, the Anganwadi centre is located in the village proper, so the tribal children normally do not attend the feeding programme. The major reason behind this seems to be the domination of non-tribal households in the village. In all the villages while discussing with the authorities of the ICDS centres it is found that in the feeding programme there is a wide gap in the record and attendance of children (0-6 years) in the Anganwadi centre. In all the study villages, the PHCs are situated within a distance of 4 kms, but the services from such centres seem to be a daydream for the poor tribal households particularly in Tungurubahal village of Keonjhar district and Penaposi Pangara village of Kandhamal district. Though Kendubardihi village of Lanjigarh block in Kalahandi district is covered under the Additional PHC at Lanjigarh and is quite old to have specialists, but practically the dispensary was always closed, which is observed even during the 15 days stay of the research team in the area. During the time of fieldwork, it was observed that a bear attacked one person of Rangapalli village and he died in the hospital due to the want of basic medical services in the dispensary. In other words, health services available from the government health institutions are poor and these do not provide the minimum level of services to the tribal people. As a result, the tribal people always prefer either private clinics or local quacks.

The aforesaid discussion highlights certain development and backward indices of the tribal dominated regions of the State. The backward situation of tribal area when compared with other parts of Orissa, in general, and coastal districts in particular, clearly reflects that the tribal regions and/or the tribal people are still suffering from getting adequate basic services, which are required for a human life. Automatically the question arises whether the State has given due importance to the tribal region on equal terms with the coastal districts or not; quantity of resources supplied to the tribal regions were inadequate and whether a major share of the supplied resources which was meant for the development of the tribal people and the region have been diverted and pocketed by the nexus consisting of bureaucrats and contractor-politicians.

4 Alcoholism and Excise Policy

Alcohol and excise policies have been a matter of great importance to the world population. From ancient times to the present age, this has become the source of pleasure and pain. In *pauranic* period, consumption of alcohol, i.e., *somarasa* (the best type) was the right of Gods, while in later period the rulers more or less continued to control over the production and consumption of liquor. In subsequent periods, liquor has taken an important position in the socio-cultural and politico-economic life of the people. Nobody including saints like Maharshi, Manu, Gautam Buddha, Chanakya, Sankaracharya, Mahatma Gandhi could stop the use of liquor. It has always been highly placed and patronised by the ruling class. In tribal societies, liquor is consumed as a means of relaxation, which also carries ritual importance. In all other societies, this has been considered as a source of entertainment and acquisition of pleasure. In the modern age, liquor has contributed a lot to controlling the State political system, State economy, and social degeneration. And further, the statecraft, in order to increase control as well as State revenue, has attempted to regulate liquor circulation in the society. In the new liberal economy, the importance of liquor for State exchequer has increased manifold. Perhaps taking the opportunity of public psychology towards the consumption of liquor, the State authorities have always felt this as a source of easy revenue income. While highlighting the revenue factor of liquor, the educated bureaucrats and elites have overlooked the socio-cultural and health loss of the society.

Theories of alcoholism suggest that biological, genetic, psychological, and socio-cultural factors help in the promotion of alcoholism (Encyclopedia American, 1981:518). While the biological theories postulate that alcoholism results from an inherited metabolic defect that causes the need for certain dietary substances in excess, the genetic theories justify that alcoholism is much higher among relatives of alcoholics than general population. The psychoanalytical explanation rests on three major theoretical propositions. First, it relates to factors such as repressed urges, oral dependency, need for security, self-punishment and parental hatred. The second view is that alcoholism represents striving for power that compensates for pervasive feelings of inferiority. The behaviour model (Bandura, 1969), based on the learning theories explains alcoholism as a conditional behavioural response. The socio-cultural theories of alcoholism claim that appropriate use of intoxicants, attitude towards alcohol, regulation of drinking practices, environmental support for drinking, etc., are largely determined by cultural settings (Pitner and Capell, 1974:412-415).

The cultural perceptions of alcohol consumption in India are typical in many respects. It classified the typology of behaviour towards alcohol as per cultural settings, which includes abstinent cultures, ambivalent cultures, and permissive cultures. The Hindu religion has always stressed abstinence from alcohol. However, drinking *soma* to be transcendentally blissful, stimulating both body and mind. The Great Ramayana depicts alcohol consumption in a bad-good dichotomy, which continued even in post-Vedic age. Buddhism prohibited drinking by monks, but in the *Sukrantisara*, fermentation of wine is described as an art. During mediaeval period, alcohol was a part of court life.

With this in mind, the present chapter has four sections to explain, the status of alcoholism and excise policy in the State of Orissa and more particularly in the Scheduled Areas where tribal communities determine the socio-cultural and politico-economic life of the region. The first section explains the growth of excise policies in pre-independence and post-independence period of the country. The second section elaborates the growth of excise policy in the State of Orissa, and more particularly, in the Scheduled Areas of the State. The third section while explaining the newly established Liquor Corporation in Orissa tries to foresee its possible impact on the life and livelihood of the tribal people of the State. Fourthly and finally, the data collected during field-study in four villages of different districts covering various dimensions of alcoholism and excise policies of the State have been explained. It also provides certain recommendations for effective implementation of the excise policy and the newly formed 'Liquor Corporation' while focusing on its primary objective of revenue maximisation.

I

Historical Background of Excise Policy

Pre-Independence Period

The excise policy of early British period in India was linked with twin principles of maximising revenue collection and minimising over consumption of liquor. During 1905, the British brought an excise policy to minimise the temptation of those who do not drink, to discourage excess drinking among those who do, and to a furtherance of this policy and all considerations of revenue must be absolutely subordinated. This came in conflict with the moral of the peasants, especially the adivasis or the tribals who take liquor as an integral part of their social life. In other words, the collective domain of liquor making and drinking, and the resistance by these communities against the State was not considered adequately by the British. This is justified when one analyses the implementation of two important legislations, the Bombay Abakari Act of 1878 and the Mhowra Act of 1892. Both the policies did not take into account the possible impact on the customary drinking practices of the adivasis (Saldanha, 1995). These two legislations blocked the major sources of liquor toddy, the fermented/distilled juice of palm tree and *mahua* drinks made from the flowers of *Bassia latifolia* by taxing the former beyond the means of the poor and banning the latter. This became a source of revenue for the government. It was the second important source of revenue and gave rise to a class of capitalists for whom manufacturer of liquor became an extremely lucrative business (ibid.).

In this way, the policy of regulation and discouraging the use of alcoholic drinks in excess continued up to 1921 till the State legislature passed bills for prohibition. Gokhale in 1912 asked the government to enforce prohibition instead of using liquor as a source of revenue. Even 30,000 women sent their signatures to the Viceroy in January 1925 pleading for prohibition and the matter was also taken up in the Council and other legislative bodies. As a part of the civil disobedience the volunteers of Indian Congress gave *dharanas* before the liquor shops and toddy booths. This led to the demand for the enforcement of total prohibition as the first item on agenda put forth by Gandhiji, the Father of Nation, before the British Government in 1931. In *Young India* during 1931, Gandhiji wrote "If I was appointed as dictator for one hour for India, the first thing I would do would be to close without compensation all liquor shops, destroy all toddy plants such as I know in Gujarat, compel factory owners to produce human conditions for their workmen and open refreshment and recreation rooms where these workmen could get innocent drinks and equally innocent amusements.... For the loss of revenue from drinks, I would straightway cut down the military expenditure...." In Gandhi-Irwin Pact of 1932, Gandhiji managed to insert a clause declaring the peaceful pickting of liquor shops as legal (*Young India*, 1929). After the declaration of provincial autonomy in 1937, the Congress party when it came to power in 10 States expressed its anguish over the soft British policy with regard to prohibition. Subsequently, many provincial States like Bombay and Madras started their programme for complete prohibition. Many times the question of prohibition revolved between the state of complete *laissez-faire* and/or complete prohibition. In the United Provinces, the government, received revenue of Rs. 1.75 crore from liquor in 1936-37 and was loathe to give it up. But on 1 April, 1938, the Congress Ministry declared six districts as dry, but in 1939 when Congress resigned, the prohibition was lifted.

The onset of Second World War indirectly affected Indian States. It demanded generation of more revenue to meet national and international requirements. Collection of revenue from imposing more excise tax became the single largest source of income, was left with the government. In Bombay State, the revenue raised from liquor excise was Rs. 2.8 crore in 1938-39, to Rs. 9.7 crore during 1947-48. Similarly, in Madras State the revenue from liquor excise was Rs. 3.8 crore in 1938-39, and was raised to Rs. 16.8 crore in 1945-46. In spite of the growing revenue, both the States in post-Second World War period adopted prohibition through opening up of new Ministries/Department in the Government in 1946. The policies of gradual prohibition adopted by both the States were reflected through closure of liquor shops for two days in a week in 1947-48, three days in a week in 1948-49, and five days in a week in 1949-50; progressive reduction in the total number of liquor shops; and reduction in the strength of liquor in case of country liquor (Reddy and Patnaik, 1993).

Post-Independence Period

In the post-independent India, the makers of Indian Constitution included prohibition as an important State policy both in Directive Principles of State Policy and Article 47 of the Constitution of India. The Article 47 of the Indian Constitution directs that the State shall endeavour to bring about prohibition of consumption except for medical purposes of intoxicating drinks and of drugs, which are injurious to health. The founding fathers of Indian Constitution and the makers of modern India were expecting the government to consider Prohibition as a national policy.

During 1954, the appointment of the Prohibition Enquiry Committee popularly known as Sriman Narayan Committee was very optimistic to adopt prohibition as a national policy in the Second Five-Year Plan. Some of the important recommendations of the Committee are: (i) that prohibition should be regarded as an integral part of the Second Five-Year Plan, (ii) that the target date for completing nationwide prohibition should be 1 April, 1958, (iii) that in States which were yet to make a beginning and in the wet areas in partial prohibition States from 1 April, 1956, there should be total closure of drinking in hotels, bars, restaurants, messes, clubs, cinemas, in parties and functions, (iv) that there should be prohibition committee in each district and at the village and *mohalla* level, (v) that the excise duties on narcotics and intoxicants collected in the States are highly iniquitous, regressive and anti-social and this kind of levy has no justification to exist in a progressive tax system and should be wiped out at the earliest, (vi) that the Union Government would give adequate assistance to those States which depend on excise for a considerable part of their revenue to introduce prohibition in their areas, and (vii) that a clear-cut statement may be issued by the Union Government to the effect that prohibition has become a national policy (Prohibition Enquiry Committee, 1954). The policy of prohibition was discussed as non-official resolution by the Lok Sabha which passed the following resolution on 31 March, 1956: "The House is of the opinion that prohibition should be regarded as an integral part of the Second Five-Year Plan and recommended that the Planning Commission should formulate the necessary programme to bring about nationwide prohibition speedily and effectively."

The Government of India in the Second Five-Year Plan included prohibition as a part of its social policy. It suggested the following steps to be taken by the State Government in wet or partially wet areas: (i) discontinuance of advertisements and public inducements relating to drink, (ii) stoppage of drinking in public premises (hotels, hostels, restaurants, clubs) and public receptions, (iii) setting up of technical committees to draw up phased programmes with the object of: (a) reducing progressively the number of liquor shops both in rural and urban areas; (b) closing liquor shops for an increasing number of days during the week; (c) reducing quantities supplied to liquor shops; (d) progressively reducing the strength of distilled liquor produced by distilleries in India; (e) closing of shops in and near specified industrial and other development project areas; and (f) removal of liquor shops to places away from main streets and living quarters in towns and villages; (iv) taking active steps to encourage and promote the production of cheap and healthy soft drinks; (v) assisting voluntary agencies in organising recreation centres; and (vi) including prohibition as an item of constructive work in national extension and community development project areas and social welfare extension projects. Nothing more was done than the appointment of a Technical Prohibition Committee to draw up a phased programme to achieve complete prohibition and the appointment of a Central Prohibition Committee to oversee and review the policy during the Second Five-Year Plan (Sarojini, 1987: 341).

The Third Five-Year Plan gave emphasis on the creation of public opinion through social and educational programmes. It emphasised prohibition as a part of the social welfare movement and recognised that if prohibition were to rest primarily on police and excise staff, not much progress would be made. Therefore, importance was given on the following aspects: (i) creation of a growing public opinion in favour of prohibition conceived as a social welfare measure in the interest of the general mass of the people; (ii) voluntary organisations should be given the necessary support and assistance by the government for carrying out social and educational programmes; (iii) implementation of various development programmes undertaken by government agencies in education, health, social education, etc., with due emphasis on the significance of the prohibition; (iv) availability in canteens of cheap and nutritious food and non-alcoholic beverages and encouragements of sports and recreational activities on a group and community basis; and (v) fixing a minimum age for purchase and/or consumption of liquor (Table 4.1).

The Planning Commission under the chairmanship of Justice Tek Chand appointed a committee to study the problem of liquor in 1963. The Committee submitted two voluminous reports consisting of 1,265 pages which covers almost all aspects like liquor manufacturing, trade, consumption, consequences, the history of the movement against liquor in India, the problems and failures of prohibition law, and recommended a couple of liquor laws, mass education, role of NGOs and suggested four-fold programme culminating in total prohibition by January 1970 (Government of India, 1964). The State Governments did not look into the

Table 4.1

Distribution of Legal Minimum Age for Consumption and Purchase of Liquor and Excise Acts Applicable in Different States

States	*Legal Minimum Age for Purchase/ Consumption (in years)*	*Act Under Which Applicable*
Andhra Pradesh	21	Andhra Excise Act, 1968
Assam	18	Assam Excise Act, 1910
Bihar	21	Bihar and Orissa Excise Act, 1915
Gujarat	Blanket Prohibition	Bombay Prohibition Act, 1949
Haryana	25	Punjab Excise Act, 1914
Himachal Pradesh	25	Punjab Excise Act, 1914
Karnataka	18	Karnataka Excise Act, 65
Kerala	18	Abakari Act (Year unknown)
Maharashtra	Minor	Bombay Prohibition Act, 1949
Madhya Pradesh	21	Madhya Pradesh Excise Act, 1915
Punjab	25	Punjab Excise Act, 1914
Rajasthan	18	Rajasthan Excise Act, 1950
Orissa	21	Bihar and Orissa Excise Act, 1916
Tamil Nadu	21	Tamil Nadu Prohibition Act, 1937
Uttar Pradesh	21	Uttar Pradesh Excise Act, 1910
West Bengal	21	Bengal Excise Act, 1909

Notes: Includes amendments to the various mentioned acts. Legal Minimum Age for consumption of alcohol in Delhi is 25 years (under the Punjab Excise Act, 1914).

Source: Centre for Monitoring the Indian Economy (CMIE) 1999.

Tek Chand report rather they gave a very decent burial to the report. Different State Governments like Uttar Pradesh (1964), Haryana (1967), Mysore (1964), Orissa (1969), Assam (1970), Andhra Pradesh (1969), and Tamil Nadu (1971) started searching for withdrawing the prohibition laws in different forms, except the State of Gujarat, which continued with the total prohibition policy (Reddy and Pattnaik, 1993). In Andhra Pradesh with the formation of popular ministries in the State in 1946, prohibition as a State policy was accepted. Madras State had adopted its prohibition policy in the Andhra region, but the neighbouring Hyderabad State (Telengana region which became a part of

Andhra Pradesh later) remained untouched by it, as it was under the rule of Nizam. With the formation of Andhra Pradesh as a new State in 1956, instead of making new policy for prohibition the State scraped prohibition policy in 1969 (ibid.).

The State Governments pressed the Central Government to bear the revenue loss in case they implemented prohibition, but Government of India did not show any interest to press State Governments to adhere to total prohibition policy. Even the Planning Commission, which included prohibition as a part of the welfare programmes of the Second and Third Five-Year Plans, seems to have turned a cold attitude. There is no mention of prohibition in the Fourth Five-Year Plan document or Annual Plan documents in the subsequent periods. The reasons for such a complete reversal to the 'prohibition policy' are not far to seek, rather these were closely linked with the economic and political changes and due to the changes in the nature of ruling classes in the State power structure.

During the last couple of decades, production, sale and consumption of alcohol have been a volatile political issue. The liquor lobby wielded tremendous political clout by providing funds to political parties. Liquor barons have made sure that money was not a problem for parties, especially during election times. In the last decades, they have generated capital out of the consignments taken from distilleries and breweries on permits already issued in collusion with excise officials, without paying official duty. Vijay Mallya of UB Groups and his rival Srihari Khoday, Magunta Subbarama Reddi and NPV Ramaswamy Udayar have been significant contributors to different political parties (Arun, et al., 2004). They vary in their mechanisms adopted in providing support. From the inception of Tamil Nadu State Marketing Corporation (TASMAC) in the year of 1986 by M.G. Ramachandran and Karnatak Beverages Corporation (KBC) in 1999 by S.M. Krishna as the sole wholesaler of liquor, the nature of support by the liquor barons has been changed, who thought of taking an active part in Indian politics by making their active representation in the Parliament and/or State Assembly, and influencing the political system in their favour by financing political parties. In this permutation and combination processes, Mallay could represent himself in the Rajya Sabha through Subramaniyam Swamy of Janata Party, while Khoday founded a political party as Urs Samukta Paksha (named after Devaraj Urs) but failed. But it has run out of steam or has had its wings effectively clipped by the various brands of prohibition policies followed by the governments in southern States.

The prohibition situation in Tamil Nadu is slightly different than other south Indian States. It was the first State to introduce total prohibition in 1937, which continued till 1960s. However, the cheap rice policy of the DMK in the State shattered the State economy. In a later period during 1972, M. Karunanidhi lifted total prohibition with a famous quote "can camphor remain unaffected inside a circle of flames?". During that time this was gambling for the political parties to exercise or not to exercise control over liquor trading. During the reign of Ms Jayalalitha though the TASMAC enjoyed the absolute right over the retail liquor trade, but unlike Andhra Pradesh and Karnataka, the liquor barons of Tamil Nadu have enjoyed their presence in the background.

In Andhra Pradesh, the liquor lobby was quite strong in all the periods of Congress and NTR rule. The introduction of total prohibition by NTR in 1995, got a major setback immediately after two years. It was N. Chandrababu Naidu who while taking into account the massive financial crisis of the State, diluted prohibition policies of the State. In recent election, a few liquor barons could manipulate the political parties to get elected in the TDP ticket for Parliamentary election in the State.

The State of Kerala has witnessed the presence of liquor barons and their liquor lobby both in the State Excise as well as in the Malayalam movies. The hooch tragedy in 2000, during the Left Democratic Front Government and the follow-up report of Justice V.P. Mohankumar Commission reflected the nexus and the flow of funds between the *abakari* contractors and political parties. Knowing this, later on Left Front Government punished the *abakari* mafias and handed over toddy shops to toddy tappers cooperatives, which was again reverted back when the Congress led United Democratic Front came to power, but A.K. Antony later on cut down the size of the *abakari* lobby and handed over the business to a large number of State Government owned liquor shops. As a result, in Kerala quite a good number of liquor mafias have converted their business to the real estate which seems to be a temporary arrangement for them. What does it mean for the once powerful liquor lobby? Are they failing to cut ice with politics or is the trend just a temporary bottleneck? Well, at the moment, the bottle seems to be half-empty (ibid.).

This has raised two issues, first, imposition of outright total prohibition as a matter of State Policy, i.e., a ban on the production, sale and consumption of liquor. Support for prohibition has provided a basis for periodical bouts of anti-colonial agitation spearheaded by women in Indian States (Illaiah, 1992; Pathak, 1985; Reddy and Patnaik, 1993; Saldanha, 1995). The second issue in favour of alcohol is the individual's right for liquor consumption as happens in many tribal communities to consume as a part of cultural requirements. However, in all this a key element is the increase in excise and sales tax rates on alcohol, so as to raise its market price (Saldanha, ibid.). An increase in its price would simply increase the response of alcohol consumers aggravating the economic hardship of their family members without necessarily reducing any of the other negative impacts (Reddy and Patnaik, 1993). In other words, prohibition may be counter productive and may increase corruption, crime and the production and consumption of illegal liquor with even more adverse health impact (Saldanha, ibid.). Experiments with prohibition policy have failed in India and elsewhere in the World and it made no sense to move to an obviously inferior policy regime (Vyasulu, 1998). Here the question that comes to our mind is whether prohibition experimented in India has failed? Its experiment during mid-1990s in the States of Haryana and Andhra Pradesh shows that it could not be effective due to multiple reasons; as a result, both the governments later on repealed the anti-alcohol policy. To mention one reason for this failure is that in Andhra Pradesh and Haryana consideration of excise tax revenue and declining land values (in Haryana) are likely to have played an important role in the repeal of prohibition (Mahal, 2000).The data on the distribution of State Excise Revenue as a share of own Tax Revenue in different 15 States of India when analysed from 1992-93 to 1998-99 reflect a declining and fluctuating trend in almost all the States. In many States like Andhra Pradesh, Himachal Pradesh, Haryana, Punjab, Rajasthan, Tamil Nadu, and Uttar Pradesh, the State Excise Revenue share a substantial portion to their own tax revenue (Table 4.2). Since alcohol policy is a part of the legislative power of individual States and not of the Central Federal Government, the inter-State variation of policies with regard to price, age of consumption and imposition of tax affects the prohibition policy of a State. The data as regards the reported, proportion, of IPC cases, arrest under Narcotics Act, reflect that among the 16 States, Orissa has reported a substantial number of

Table 4.2

Distribution of State Excise Revenue as a Share of Own Tax Revenue, by States

States	*1992-93*	*1994-95*	*1996-97*	*1998-99*
Andhra Pradesh	27.2	10.5	1.3	12.3
Bihar	3.4	3.5	3.5	3.7
Gujarat	0.4	0.4	0.4	0.4
Haryana	27.2	28.0	3.0	21.6
Himachal Pradesh	34.1	31.7	32.3	29.4
Karnataka	16.6	16.6	14.6	13.7
Kerala	11.8	12.6	10.7	10.8
Maharashtra	10.5	10.0	9.1	10.8
Madhya Pradesh	19.0	19.3	18.1	17.1
Punjab	33.7	34.0	36.6	36.8
Rajasthan	23.9	24.2	25.1	24.7
Orissa	8.2	6.4	6.8	7.7
Tamil Nadu	13.6	10.5	13.3	15.0
Uttar Pradesh	22.8	22.7	21.0	18.1
West Bengal	7.8	6.2	7.7	6.9

Note: Share is expressed as a percentage of own revenue.

Source: Various State Excise and Prohibition Acts.

cases. The State is the third highest in the number of arrests made under Prohibition Act being followed by Tamil Nadu and Gujarat. The details of these reported cases in different States are reported in Table 4.3.

Table 4.3

Distribution of Selected Statistics on Crime Enforcement in India, by States (1996-97)

States	*Reported IPC cases per 1,000 population*	*Proportion of IPC cases charge sheeted*	*Arrest under Narcotics Act (per 100,000)*	*Arrests under Excise Act (per 100,000)*	*Arrest under Prohibition Act (per 100,000)*
Andhra Pradesh	157	0.62	1.2	42.0	20.2
Bihar	123	0.45	0.4	3.6	0.0
Gujarat	254	0.68	1.0	0.0	406.0
Haryana	268	0.63	7.7	99.7	0.0
Himachal Pradesh	164	0.69	2.0	90.2	0.0
Karnataka	228	0.59	0.6	5.0	0.0
Kerala	294	0.72	1.2	0.8	3.0
Madhya Pradesh	270	0.78	1.5	28.9	0.0
Maharashtra	210	0.56	2.1	0.0	13.0
Orissa	147	0.70	0.6	6.2	0.1
Punjab	66	0.56	7.7	61.7	0.0
Rajasthan	324	0.77	2.1	8.8	0.0
Tamil Nadu	235	0.69	4.0	0.0	619.2
Uttar Pradesh	95	0.60	6.5	17.0	0.0
West Bengal	86	0.36	0.8	2.5	0.0
NE Region	145	0.27	1.8	3.6	0.3

Note: IPC - Indian Penal Code.

Source: NCRB (National Crime Records Bureau), 1997, Government of India (2000a).

II

Excise Policy of Orissa

Consumption of various toxic items by the people of Orissa is one of the causes of poverty. A few of common intoxicants consumed by them are ganja, opium, country liquor, *handia*, foreign liquor, etc. The common intoxicants consumed by the tribal people of Orissa are country-liquor made out of *mahua* flower, juice of palm tree, *salap* or sago palm and rice beer. It is popularly said that poor Adivasis usually become a pray to this evil habit. Even they go for borrowing to meet community feasts where liquor would flow like water. Until the late 60s, very few caste communities were mostly carrying out brewing of liquor in Orissa. Production of liquor and its trading was considered as a 'social stigma'. In earlier days, liquor produced in a village was consumed within the village or partly supplied to the kith and kins of the nearby villages.

A historical look into the evolution of prohibition policy in the State of Orissa shows that Biswanath Das, the Prime Minister of Orissa, in 1938, proposed to amend the first ever policy on prohibition, i.e., the Bihar and Orissa Act on Prohibition. In order to have a critical assessment of Assam Prohibition Act, Raj Krishna Bose the Parliamentary Secretary and a senior member of the Excise Department was sent for its in-depth study prior to its implementation in Orissa (Orissa Legislative Assembly, 1938: 963). During that time since Orissa was not financially sound to bear the loss of Rs. 34 lakh, which was generated by the Excise Department, introduction of this policy was strongly objected to; however, it was experimentally started in certain pockets of the State.

There were two legislative measures taken up in Orissa during this period. They were: Opium (Orissa Amendment) Bill 1939 and Orissa Prohibition Bill 1939. These bills were formulated with an aim to bring total prohibition in the entire province. Subsequently the Bihar and Orissa Excise (Orissa Amendment) Bill of 1947 was introduced and adopted on 2 July, 1947 which empowered the government to prohibit any or all kinds of selling intoxicating materials either in the whole province or in any part of it (OLA, 1947: 37-50). During this period, a good number of liquor traders from Bihar entered into the State and engaged themselves in liquor business of the State. They were distributed in almost all the inland areas of the State.

The integration of various Oriya tracts into Orissa forced the State to bring an uniform excise policy through Excise

Department, which was raised during 1947-48. This led to a detailed survey of excise administration in the State. Imposition of total prohibition in the State although was a daydream, the government made unfailing attempts for achieving partial prohibition.

Strong condemnation of this policy by the Scheduled Areas and Scheduled Tribes Commission in no uncertain terms was ignored by the system until 1975 when the excise policy in the tribal areas was reviewed afresh (Sharma, 1994: 85). In subsequent periods in order to check exploitation of tribal people, it was thought that the existing rules and regulations are not sufficient. Understanding the contextual conditions of the tribal regions and requirements of the tribal people, Government of Orissa on 1 April, 1974 had decided to close down the vending of liquor in the entire tribal inhabited areas of the State. Again, Government of Orissa from 1 April, 1977 more specifically had abolished the contract system of vending liquor in Koraput, Mayurbhanj and Sundargarh districts except at the district, sub-division, and tehasil headquarters, industrial areas, NACs and municipal areas having urban characteristics. More specifically according to the National Policy of Prohibition, Government of Orissa had closed down almost 419 country liquor shops during the period 1974-1980 in tribal areas of Koraput, Mayurbhanj, Sundargarh, Kalahandi, Keonjhar and Balasore. Apart from this, 42 country liquor shops had also been closed down in ITDA areas of undivided Koraput district. In this connection, the State Government had adopted the policy of progressive closure of liquor shops in the tribal concentrated areas. To this effect, the end of 1978-79 witnessed the closure of around 366 main liquor shops and 53 branch liquor shops. Apart from this, 42 country spirit shops in the ITDA areas during 1988-89 had also been closed down. In order to bring about a complete prohibition, quite a good number of actions have been taken up by Government of Orissa. Those are: the restriction on the issue of license, increase the number of dry days and closure of liquor shops in tribal areas. Quite a good number of shops have been closed in peripheral areas, whereas, it was decided that severe actions would be taken at district headquarters and mining areas if there was any deviation of this rule.

It was further envisaged for community empowerment for implementation and to make further regulations for self-management. Much later during 1992, Government of India, Tribal Division, made effective the excise policy in Scheduled Areas of India. Government of India asked the Government of Orissa to adopt two basic principles of National Excise Policy: first, the commercial vending of alcohol beverages should be discontinued in tribal areas; second, Scheduled Tribes may be permitted to brew their traditional beverages for consumption at home and on religious and social occasions.

The country liquor may be prepared out of rice or mahua flower, is an ingredient required at the time of all the festivals and religious celebrations. Apart from this, the nutrition received from rice beer locally known, as handia, seems to be more than simple boiled rice. Understanding its ritual importance and nutritious value, Government of Orissa had granted specific privileges to different regions and communities of Scheduled Areas for brewing rice beer for festive occasions and for home consumption on normal days. However, during 1995-96 Government of Orissa made comparatively an uniform policy providing concession to the tribal people by allowing them to brew liquor for their festive consumption but not for sale. They were allowed to possess liquor up to a limit of 1.5 litres for individual consumption and 5 litres for family consumption. As regards the possession of *pachwai* the tribal people can have it to the extent of 18 kgs of diluted one and 7 kgs of pure *pachwai* individually.

The issue of prohibition was also discussed in the Tribal Advisory Council Meeting on 8 October, 1991 and 28 December, 1992 as regards the proposal for amendment of the excise policy of the State. The Parliamentary Committee on welfare of SCs and STs in their meeting on 21 and 22, September, 1992 and 12 October, 1992 while examining the works of the officers of the State has repeatedly accused the State Government for violating the Central Excise Policy in the Scheduled Areas of the State. The committee recommended that there should be complete ban on distillation and vending of liquor in Scheduled Areas. It was also observed that Excise Act should be amended to give power to the

Executive Magistrates for trial and quick disposal of cases. A committee headed by Law Department examined this proposal. It was observed that permission for such trials will require the approval of the High Court and may give rise to legal complications. The Law Department, while going through this, suggested that cases booked under the Bihar and Orissa Excise Act are to be tried by the Executive Magistrates by summary procedure considering Article 21 and 50 of Indian Constitution and provisions of Criminal Procedure Code (CrPC). The committee felt that the trial of offence by the Executive Magistrates might lead to Constitutional difficulties of deviation of the rule of trials by Judicial Magistrates. Under Section 13 of the CrPC, the High Court if requested by the State Government can confer on any person to hold any part under the government or any of the powers conferred or conformable under the code on a Judicial Magistrate of First Class or Second Class. However, this power can only be converged by High Court as a person (not by designation) who possess such qualifications and experiences on legal matters for one year only. Even if an Executive Magistrate satisfying the qualifications is conferred with this power, there is every likelihood that after one year the consequent gap in power may create considerable gap in trial of these cases. Again the court will be the supervisory authority. Hence, the committee felt that it might not serve the purpose of expediting the disposal of pending excise cases. Regarding the unconditional withdrawal of excise case against STs as proposed in TAC meeting held on 8 October, 1991, government viewed that these rules are uniformly implemented in all areas of the State. Under the situation, the excise cases booked under the excise law against the adivasis if withdrawn it will not only increase the illicit trade, but will also create administrative and legal complications.

While few argue that the local community should be empowered to decide whether the State should go for total prohibition, and it is the country that should control it, whereas, many argue that National Government is to decide and the State Government is only to implement. The whole history of prohibition during both colonial and post-colonial era of India is perhaps the outcome of the uprisings, along with brutal suppression of the minority ethnic groups including tribal people. After a long gap, it seems that the government has realised that empowerment of local panchayats is the only solution for implementing any law for their (tribes) development.

Out-still (OS) was in force in four undivided districts of Orissa, viz., Sambalpur, Bolangir, Kalahandi, and Phulbani (Boudh Sub-division). But with effect from 1 April, 1994 sale of both out-still and country spirit was discontinued. With a view to exploit the abundance of mahua flowers in the tribal areas of the State and to provide an avenue of income for the tribal people, who mostly earn their livelihood by collection of mahua flowers during the harvesting season, and finally to check the illicit distillation, out-still based on mahua flower has been reintroduced in 9 (nine) districts of the State viz., Sambalpur, Bargarh, Jharsuguda, Deogarh, Bolangir, Sonepur, Kalahandi, Nuapada and Boudh with effect from 1 July, 1996.

In order to extend the benefit of participatory management to the tribals in Scheduled Areas, the Bihar and Orissa Excise Act, 1915 has been further amended by the insertion of a new Section 26 (A). The amended provision aims at restriction of grant of license for manufacture, possession or sale, or any exclusive privilege for manufacture or sale, of any intoxicant, except with the prior approval of the concerned Gram Panchayat and no license or exclusive privilege which is granted in contravention of the above shall have any effect for the purpose of this Act.

For effective implementation of the above, the authority competent to grant license for manufacture, possession or sale or exclusive privilege of manufacture or sale, of any intoxicant shall, before granting any license or exclusive privilege, refer every proposal thereof to the concerned Gram Panchayat for its decision within a period of thirty days from the date of its receipt of such reference; and if the Gram Panchayat fails to communicate its decision within the period referred to in Clause (1) it shall be deemed that the concerned Gram Panchayat has accorded the required approval. Thus, Gram Sabhas have been effectively empowered to regulate sale of liquor and other intoxicants in the Scheduled Areas (ST and SC Development Department, 1999-2000).

The rampant preparation and sale of contraband liquor has made certain tribal dominated districts heaven for anti-socials, pushing tribals on to the brink of socio-economic vulnerability. Illegal trading of country liquor has become a flourishing business in every nook and corner of the district. In many tribal areas taking the advantage of the relaxation due to the cultural need of the tribal people, tribals and many others in their name are preparing contraband liquor, mohua and other intoxicating drinks. For example, in Koraput district while the illegal liquor trade is high, the Excise Department is unable to collect its targeted revenue. In Koraput district around Rs. 3,39,230.31 was collected as revenue in 1997-98 against the target of Rs. 5,78,890. In 1999, Rs. 1,63,19,104 only was collected and 1,529 cases were filed. It is commonly complained that the police and the Excise Department have no or little control over the widespread preparation and sale of contraband liquor. In bordering districts, in many cases, tribals are involved in transporting or smuggling the illegal liquor with the neighbouring States. In some parts of undivided Koraput district, production of liquor has in fact now become a cottage industry. The places of Luhaba of Nandapur block, Dumuripadar of Koraput block, Dudhari and Ranikona of Semiliguda block and many other places are becoming principal centres for the production of contraband liquor (Satapathy, 2000).

III

Functioning of Orissa State Beverages Corporation

This section deals with the newly established Orissa State Beverages Corporation which has started functioning since April, 2001. It is a part of the growth of Excise Policy of the State. While describing the operational areas of the newly formed Beverages Corporation and certain prospective achievements proposed by the government, the analysis also deals with the potential effects of the corporation on the tribal people of Orissa.

Following the Cuttack hooch tragedy, which claimed more than 100 lives in Cuttack district during 1993, a special ban was imposed on the circulation of country spirit. Again during 1994, mahuli liquor sale was also banned in tribal areas by the then Chief Minister of Orissa, Late Biju Pattnaik. Although there was a "demand from various quarters to lift the ban on the sale of country spirit during subsequent periods", the Congress Government in between 1995 to 2000 did not venture to take such a decision. In spite of this, during the month of February 2001 another hooch tragedy took place, which claimed 24 lives in Puri district. The repetition of such incidences only reflect the insensitiveness of State administration to the spread of illicit liquor trade, which flourishes under the connivance of Excise Department, despite the ban on the manufacture and sale of spirit based country-liquor. Such incidences always question the loopholes in the Bihar-Orissa Excise Act, which is still in implementation in Orissa even after more than six decades of the formation of separate Orissa State. The Excise law itself always comes to the rescue of the culprits. Understanding the failure of Orissa-Bihar Excise Act to catch hold of illicit trade in country and Indian Made Foreign Liquor (IMFL) during 1999, the then Chief Minister of Orissa thought to bring an amendment in the Act.

In 2001, the government led by Biju Janata Dal decided to withdraw the ban on the production and distribution of country liquor which was imposed in various parts of the State. In spite of the opposition from various quarters regarding the lifting of ban a special bill came into effect on 1 April, 2001. The operational area of the newly formed Beverages Corporation is extended to 16 districts in which Country-Spirit (CS) is reintroduced. These districts are; Ganjam, Gajapati, Nayagarh, Khurda, Puri, Cuttack, Jagatsinghpur, Kendrapara, Jajpur, Bhadrak, Balasore, Mayurbhanj, Keonjhar, Dhenkanal, Angul and Kandhamal. The Government of Orissa also decided to introduce out-stilled (OS) liquor (mahuli) in five more districts: Rayagada, Koraput, Nawarangpur, Malkangiri, and Sundargarh, i.e., the tribal dominated Scheduled areas of the State. Earlier the selling of OS was prevalent in Sambalpur, Jharsuguda, Bargarh, Deogarh,

Bolangir, Nuapada, Sonepur, Kalahandi and Boudh. However, the government has decided that sale of country spirit will be introduced only in those pockets of the Scheduled Areas where the Gram Sabha will permit it. This will help the tribals to earn their livelihood by collecting muhua flowers and check illicit distillation. An individual or family can possess up to 15 quintals of mahua flowers for retail sale. According to 73rd amendment of the Indian Constitution, elected PRI members have been given powers to control the sale of liquor in their areas. The amended provision aims at imposing restrictions of grant of license for manufacture, possession or sale or any exclusive privilege for manufacture or sale of any intoxicant except with the prior approval of the concerned Gram Panchayat and no license or exclusive privilege, which is granted in contravention of the above shall have any effect for the purpose of the Act. For effective implementation of the above, the authority competent to grant the license for manufacture, possession of any intoxicant shall before granting any license or exclusive privilege refer every proposal thereof, to the concerned Gram Panchayat, which if it fails to communicate its decision within the period then it shall be deemed that the concerned Gram Panchayat has accorded the required approval. Thus, Gram Sabha has been effectively empowered to regulate sale of liquor and other intoxicants in the Scheduled Areas (SC and ST Development Department, Government of Orissa, 1997-98). In the previous Orissa-Bihar Excise Act, the deviation of the Act was a non-cognisable offence and the bailable provisions helped offenders to get bail in no time. In the new law though the amendment Act compounded punishment up-to five years of imprisonment, the bailable provision remained intact. Even though the amendment made the offence cognisable, it forces the police to register the FIRs. This repeats the same paperwork at police station, but at the end the culprit roams freely in no time, because the offence is bailable. Because of this there has been a fall of 30 to 40 per cent of the registration of excise cases.

Again taking the advantage of the outdated excise laws and laxity in the excise administration, all the bottling plants including the famous United Breweries Group and Shaw Wallace are allegedly not maturing their liquor for sale in Orissa. This gives rise to bad taste, headache and other problems. A premier club located in capital city of Bhubaneswar complained receiving an old stock beer from a reputed company, which could not be sold in West Bengal. This shows that in the absence of any monitoring mechanism by the Excise Department and complaint from any quarter of retailer or consumer, the liquor companies have a field day. The manufacturers in the State are even not using caps or seals supplied by Larsen and Toubro or by other reputed companies. They purchase them from unregistered companies, which gives maximum scope for adulteration (*New Indian Express*, 23 December, 2000).

This proves that hooch lobbies, undoubtedly generate tremendous clout; a figure of Rs. 300 crore has been cited if the illicit operation is taken to be true. The manipulations in the Indian Made Foreign Liquor (IMFL) segment in the State would nearly run into another Rs. 100 crores by way of tax evasion. Again with the support of Excise Department in lieu of *'hafta'*, country liquor trade has almost become a cottage industry in Orissa. (Minister Excise Department quoted by Kar, S., in *New Indian Express*, 25 February, 2001). The plea for the situation as raised by the Minister is due to the shortage of manpower, seems to be ridiculous; but the truth is that the nexus between the hooch barons and the authorities is lucrative to both sides. Response of the State Government always had been reflected through arresting few vendors, giving judicial inquiry order, but always leaves the real culprit. Establishing another judicial inquiry committee during every incidence seems to be like playing hide and seek with the law. This is borne by the fact, when one sees that the suggestions given by B.K. Behera Commission in 1995 on the Cuttack hooch tragedy of 1993 are yet to be implemented. This also proves that the government has given lowest value to the people and somehow or the other succeeded in maintaining good governance. Such lip services of the State only dictate the corrupt practices in the system, which affect the tribal dominated regions and the tribal people to a greater extent.

Another example can be given of corrupt practices in the liquor lobby in Koraput district, where the District Collector mobilised the *Madamukti abhiyan*, which led to the closure of 1,100 illegal liquor outlets in different blocks of the district. The District Collector was transferred from the district probably for this action. The rumour is that the liquor mafia played a major role in the transfer of the District Collector but the government claims that there is no such reason behind this transfer (*New Indian Express*, 10 September, 2000). During the month of July 2001, the government decided to handover the police power to the workers of *Madamukti Abhiyan* in Koraput district. This at a certain level proves that the State is trying to understand the strength of the people and is convinced that many such social problems can be solved or minimised if people are empowered.

The Orissa State Beverage Corporation (OSBC) has been appointed as the wholesale dealer for country-spirit. It has been decided that retail outlets will be determined on auction basis. Country liquor and beer bottles will be sold in certified pouches and sealed bottles. This will enable consumers to differentiate between the liquor, i.e., traded through OSBC and the duplicate one, which will increase collection of sales tax and excise tax. It is expected that the nexus between the manufacturer and wholesalers would be restricted. The first Chairman-cum-Managing Director, Prafulla Kumar Mishra (who in later period was suspended and sent to jail due to his controversial role in the Corporation), while explaining the profit, prospect of the new OSBC informed that in the last one decade, manufacturers and retailers must have cheated the State Government of more than Rs. 2,000 crores. While States like Tamil Nadu and Andhra Pradesh have earned Rs. 2,400 crores each as tax from liquor trade every year, the excise revenue of Orissa is only Rs. 75 crores and sales tax on liquor is a meagre amount of Rs. 20 crores (*New Indian Express*, 15 February, 2001). The collection of revenue from excise in the State of Orissa since 1976-77 till 1993-94 reflect an increasing trend. Though the increase is much higher in comparison to the previous years, but in none of the years the increase is significant. The distribution of

State Excise Revenue as a share of own Tax Revenue reflect from Table 4.4.

Table 4.4

Details of Excise Revenue Collected in the State of Orissa

(In Crores)

Years	*Total Revenue Collected*
1976-77	8.37
1977-78	3.97
1978-79	4.15
1979-80	4.37
1980-81	7.51
1981-82	10.37
1982-83	12.13
1983-84	15.15
1984-85	20.65
1985-86	—
1986-87	21.73
1987-88	24.06
1988-89	26.72
1989-90	38.30
1990-91	45.60
1991-92	55.10
1992-93	62.80
1993-94	76.20
1994-95	44.9 (part)

Sources: Statistical Abstracts of Orissa, Different Years.
Directorate of Economics and Statistics, Orissa, Government of Orissa.

It is normally alleged that people of Orissa are timid, lazy and are not receptive. A good number of people's movement have emerged in Orissa during the past opposing the mega-development projects including against the newly formed OSBC. This accusation about the people of Orissa seems to be baseless. While the bill for new liquor corporation was not finalised a couple of NGOs, and women organisations have expressed their protest through meetings, blockade, etc. The political parties in the State Assembly either supported or took a neutral stand or timidly opposed the bill. The Chairman of the National Commission for Scheduled Castes and Scheduled Tribes, Dillip Singh Bhuria during his visit to Orissa while reacting to government's move to form a liquor corporation asked the Chief Minister of the State on 10 August, 2001 to ensure total prohibition in the Scheduled Areas, as free flow of liquor would affect the welfare of the SCs and STs. He suggested that total prohibition would save SCs and STs from exploitation in the hands of liquor mafias. While lamenting, he expressed that the tribals of Orissa have not been given their due rights over drinking water, education and electricity even after five decades of independence.

Liquor has a significant role in the social life of tribal people. To meet the cultural necessities it was prepared by them through various indigenous methods. But now the availability of liquor from shops located in their areas tempted them not to prepare liquor at their homes during festive occasions. For the vendors, to dupe the tribals became an easy task. The tribal people by and large do not know the use of money for their betterment. Taking the advantage of their cultural necessity of liquor and innocence, liquor vendors exploited them through various means. Ready availability of liquor made the evening gossip groups casual, and changed the contents. The village elders, normally who were related to each other through their kinship bond or otherwise could get no scope to maintain harmony. It made the attitude of many tribal people indifferent towards each other in their social behaviour and reflected the sudden abrogation of community life.

IV

The fourth and final section describes the data collected during the field-study carried out in four villages of different districts in respect of alcoholism and excise policy. The study focuses on the consumption of liquor, sources of liquor availability, sale of liquor, income raised from the sale of different types of liquor, increase and/or decrease of liquor consumption. Here, an attempt has also been made to highlight the mechanisms adopted by non-tribal people, particularly the Scheduled Castes who sell liquor to the tribal people, and in this connection the mechanisms adopted by the non-tribals to grab the physical assets of the tribal people. An attempt was also made to understand the attitude of the tribal people about the harassment, if any, made by the Police, Excise Department personnel towards them for production and consumption of liquor, which they do as a part of their traditional way of life. A few police personnel and about 10 to 15 Panchayati Raj Institution functionaries in each district were also interviewed and their views on the problem of alcoholism in tribal areas have been collected and analysed.

Liquor Producing Households

The field data reflect that availability of various types of liquor depends on the availability of liquor preparing ingredients in the region, like mahua flower for the preparation of mahuli and Mushakani root which is used in the preparation of handia or rice beer. The type of raw materials available in an area influences the quantity and quality of liquor prepared by the tribal people. While looking at the type of liquor available in different villages one finds that in Kendubaradihi village of Kalahandi, villagers do not produce liquor at all. They purchase mahua liquor from the Scheduled Caste households (Pana) of the neighbouring villages. The study shows that all the tribal households in the study villages consume liquor. As regards the type of country liquor available in the study villages one finds that except Tungurabahal village of Keonjhar district, in none of the villages the tribal households produce handia or rice beer. In Keonjhar, the households belonging to Munda, Bhulyan and Kissan tribal communities (31.81%) prepare handia for self-consumption, while 19.69 per cent tribal households in this village prepare mahua liquor on commercial basis. In Penaposi Pangara of Kandhamal district, similarly the Kandha tribal households do not produce any type of liquor but they purchase from the households belonging to caste Sundhis of the village. Of the total, Koya tribal households in village Lachhipetta of Malkangiri district, about 55.42 per cent produce mahua liquor on commercial basis. Thus, the study in all the four villages of four different districts shows that out of total 417 tribal households, 118 (28.29%) prepare mahua liquor and 42 (10.17%) prepare handia on commercial basis.

Quantity of Liquor Produced

Except Kendubaradihi of Kalahandi district and Penaposi Pangara of Kandhamal district, in two other villages the tribal households produce mahua liquor by themselves. An attempt has been made to quantify the total production of both mahua and handia at household level. The following section tries to present a quantitative picture of the total liquor production in the study villages. It is found that during the previous year in Tungurubahal village of Keonjhar district, 26 tribal households produced 3,120 litres of mahuli liquor and 26,880 litres of handia. On an average, each tribal household produces 120 litres of mahuli and 640 litres of handia per annum. The liquor is prepared during the peak seasons of summer and winter. However, if sufficient mahua flowers are available then very few households prepare mahua liquor on commercial basis even during lean seasons. In Penaposi Pangara of Kandhamal district, there are five households belonging to Sundhi (distiller) Caste group who are fully engaged in the preparation of mahua liquor. During the year 1999, those households produced 7,200 litres of mahuli with an average production of 1,440 litres by each household. In Lachhipetta village of Malkangiri district, similarly, 92 (55.42%) Koya households are engaged in the production of mahuli who had produced 18,400 litres of mahua liquor during the previous year. The average liquor produced by each household in this village is 200 litres. In total, the study has found out that 118 (28.29%) tribal households in all the four study villages have produced 21,250 litres of mahuli and 42 Scheduled Tribe households have produced 26,800 litres of handia. The average mahuli produced per household is 182 litres while the average handia produced per household is 638 litres. The study shows that in total 28.29 per cent (118) tribal households are producing mahua liquor on commercial basis and 10.17 per cent (42) tribal households produce handia on commercial basis.

Tribal people keep account on the production of mahuli and handia on regular basis. The Bhulyans and Mundas in Kendubardihi village of Keonjhar prepare handia on commercial basis. They sell handia in weekly *haat* days. There is a seasonal variation in the sale of handia. Handia is sold more in summer followed by winter season and comparatively less in rainy season. During summer, the tribal people from their experience know about the quantity of sale in a market day. Since all households do not brew handia on commercial basis and few households sell in the market, so it is very easy for them to keep a calculation on the production of handia on the basis of total rice boiled. Similarly, among Koyas who produce mahuli for direct selling to liquor vendors (of whom many are belonging to Bengali community), also keep an estimation of the quantity of liquor they produce. The calculation is based on the quantity of mahua flower (*pocha*) used. During specific season mahua flowers are available in plenty, the production and sale of mahuli at that time touch the peak. However, during off-seasons, except few tribal households, who store mahua flower, all others purchase from the local shops or belong to Bengali community. It also happens that few non-tribal people hoard mahua flower, supply the raw materials to the tribal people in advance with a condition to return them the produces in the form of liquor. From this, one can infer that a group of non-tribal people, who are in liquor business, directly making tribal people as a medium to produce liquor. Another dimension of the liquor production is the importance of gender in the process of preparation of liquor. Handia is produced by women folk and sold in the weekly *haat* by them. The male members of Kissan tribe also sell handia. In case of mahuli preparation, both male and female are involved in the process. There are certain activities, like bringing water to prepare clay to cover the earthen pot, etc., which are mainly carried out by women. The male members enjoy the rights over collection and distribution of *salap*, another form of local beverage collected from a type of palm tree.

Apart from normal consumption, liquor has ritual importance in the life of the tribal people. Though its importance varies from community to community, there are certain rituals when the tribal people offer mahuli liquor to their spirits, deities and divinities. The Kondhs of Penaposi Pangara village of Kandhamal offer liquor to their divinities for overcoming the unusual curse of God and Goddesses. Regarding the use of handia for ritual purposes, it is observed that Mundas and Bhuinyas, in Keonjhar district offer handia on various festive occasions and religious ceremonies, which are observed both at family level as well at community level.

Compared to the tribal communities of northern Orissa, the tribal communities of southern Orissa use mahuli liquor as one of the ritual ingredients. The study has found out that the Koyas of Malkangiri and Kondhas of Kandhamal use more mahuli during these occasions. In Penaposi Pangara village, the tribal people said that they are not producing mahua liquor – rather are purchasing from the non-tribals of the neighbouring villages and also using that liquor on all ritual occasions. Tribal people consider liquor as a form of pure liquid which is not polluted even if purchased from Hindu caste groups like Sundhi, Gauda and Chasa communities.

Income Accrual from Sale of Liquor

It is observed that income from sale of liquor is substantial for 28.29 per cent of tribal households. Taking into account the sale price of both handia and mahuli an attempt has been made to find out the total income raised during the preceding year. The data have been analysed ethnic group-wise and the type of liquor sold by the households. A district-wise calculation of income accrual reflects that in Tungurubahal village of Keonjhar district Rs. 31,200 and Rs. 1,34,490 were generated from the sale of mahuli and handia respectively during the last year. The average income raised by each tribal household per annum from the sale of mahuli was Rs. 1,200, whereas, from that of handia the income was Rs. 3,201. In Penaposi Pangara of Kandhamal, Sundhi households had raised an amount of Rs. 86,400 from the sale of mahuli liquor. The average income raised by each Sundhi household was Rs. 17,280 per annum which justifies that the Sundhi households have adopted liquor sale as their principal source of income.

On discussion, few Sundhi informants told that due to restrictions imposed on liquor production the quantum of liquor production by them has been reduced over time. In Lachhipetta of Malkangiri district, 55.42 per cent of Koya tribal households have sold mahuli liquor to the tune of Rs. 1,84,000 which when divided accounts for an amount of Rs. 2,000 per household. Data of all the four villages and the income raised from the sale of liquor reflect that there are 118 (28.29%) tribal households who have been engaged in production of liquor on commercial basis. They have sold handia and mahuli amounting to Rs. 2,15,200 and Rs. 1,34,490 respectively during the previous year of the study.

The average income raised by each household from the sale of handia was Rs. 3,202 and mahuli was Rs. 1,823. While discussing with the villagers it transpired that production of mahuli is linked with the total production of mahua flower in the village as well as in the region. In all the villages, it is reported that on an average 30 to 40 per cent of the total liquor produced is normally consumed by the household members.

Regarding the place of sale it is observed that in Keonjhar district mahuli is often sold in the houses, whereas, handia is sold in the weekly *haats*. In Kandhamal district, the Sundhis sell mahuli at their doorsteps in a secret manner. Though everybody in the locality knows about the availability of liquor in a Sundhi house it is difficult to get the information from local people about the availability of liquor.

During data collection, an attempt was made to find out the number of liquor non-consuming households in each of the study villages. Surprisingly it has been found that all 417 tribal households of four study villages in different districts consume liquor. The Scheduled Caste households admitted without hesitation that they too regularly consume liquor. The same question was also asked to the general caste group households in all the study villages who flatly denied consumption of liquor. They admitted that occasionally some might be consuming but they are not habitual takers.

As regards liquor consumption habit of men, women and children, special questions were asked to the villagers through group discussions. The villagers said that women consume liquor only during festive occasions while the male members consume liquor as and when available and affordable from their own sources and even by taking loan from others. In tribal society, women play a vital role in carrying over family responsibilities. The girls before their marriage do not take mahuli, however, in rare occasions they consume salap if it is brought to their house or friends' house. During the season when mahua flower is available in plenty consumption of mahuli in many villages among the tribal people becomes frequent. It is true to say that liquor flows like water in many tribal villages during the mahua season. Except the festive occasions liquor consumption (mahuli) is very rare among the tribal women. However, consumption of handia is a common practice among both male and female belonging to Munda and Bhuinya tribal communities and also among other tribal communities of northern Orissa like Santal, Ho, Juanga, Oraon and Bhuinya.

As regards consumption of liquor by tribal children, the villagers commented that in early days tribal children after their admission to youth dormitory start consuming salap and handia (not mahuli), but now-a-days a new group of children with little education have started consuming liquor (mahuli). This has been rightly observed among the Kondhas of Puttasing region of Rayagada district (Acharya, et al., 2001). While undertaking the evaluation of the functioning of a Special Micro-Project, he found that easy availability of money earned due to the sale of horticulture produces along with availability of communication facilities into the area, which linked to nearby urban centres and even with district headquarters, the younger generation adopted changes more quickly by visiting cinema halls, putting on new dresses, consumption of liquor, etc. Among the Koyas of Lachipetta village of Malkangiri district, it is observed that Koya adolescents (particularly the male) due to their seasonal migration to different urban centres of Andhra Pradesh have also picked up certain urban characteristics, which are reflected in their dress pattern, hairstyle, personal habits and adherence to consumption of liquor.

Tribal people believe more on the presence of ancestral spirits and their rebirth through the offsprings. While consuming liquor in the family normally they offer a drop of liquor on the earth aiming at their forefathers. As soon as a child is born in a family the parents regard the child (of either sex) as a representative of their ancestors. So, instead of putting a drop of liquor on the floor many tribal communities just touch a tip of liquor on the child for similar purpose.

All the households were also asked about the source of liquor availability. It was found that out of 417 ST households, 348 (83.45%) said that they brew different types of country liquor at their houses, whereas, all the 20 (100%) households belonging to SC category said that they brew liquor in their houses and 5 households belonging to other caste categories also gave the same view. Not a single tribal household in the village of Kendubaradihi brew liquor in the village. They all purchase liquor from outside the village.

Apart from home brewing many households also purchase liquor from outside the village. Those who brew in the village for consumption have an understanding that they would not prepare liquor on the same day rather on rotational basis. It was observed that during ceremonial occasions and during the harvest, liquor flows like water in the village. In general, the tribals lose their control over them by excessive drinking during the peak seasons as well as in festive occasions. That is the major problem, as well as the weakness with the tribal communities. Apart from home brewing, almost all the tribal communities purchase liquor from outside the village. The major sources of purchase of liquor for the tribal people are the nearby weekly markets. The weekly markets in the tribal economy and tribal way of life play a very important role. It is an arena for economic transaction, merrymaking, and social networking with the neighbouring villages and many other socio-economic purposes. Availability of salap juice and palm juice in the study villages are found to be getting scarce day by day. Unlike earlier days the tribal people are not giving much importance to the plantation of salap trees. The most important reason, as put forth by the villagers, is the long gestation period of the salap trees. Again, during the production period the police and excise staff harasses them by demanding more salap juice as and when they need. The concepts of planting salap trees for the children are no more prevalent in the minds of the tribal people (excepting a few tribal people) as observed in the study villages. Another dimension of not giving importance to the salap trees is the easy availability of mahua liquor even at short distances. The Scheduled Caste communities and the Sundhi Caste group people are commercially engaged in producing and marketing mahuli that is available at walking distances in their own village or in neighbouring villages.

Effects of Alcoholism on Tribal Livelihood

Tribal livelihood system centres around forest produces and partly around agriculture, which are not sufficient throughout the year. Many of them live on hand-to-mouth state of living. The wage labour available in tribal areas under different employment schemes does not reach all households. Due to the attachment of tribal people to their cultural practices very few go beyond village boundaries or beyond the region to earn their livelihood in nearby urban centres. Under this situation various market forces operate in tribal areas to exploit them by collecting various forest and agricultural produces during the harvest seasons in cheaper prices. Tribal people are very fond of taking liquor both during festive occasions and also during normal days. Taking this opportunity the non-tribal people particularly Hindu-caste groups like Sundhis, Goudas, and Pradhans in many inaccessible tribal areas sell liquor (mahuli) to them at their door-steps. The study found that in Penaposi Pangara village of Kandhamal district, there are five Sundhi caste households who prepare and sell mahuli to tribal people.

Though the liquor is not available within the study village of Kendubardihi of Kalahandi district, the tribal people purchase liquor from the neighbouring villages and from shops selling at Lanjigarh, the Panchayat headquarters. On discussion with the tribal people, it was observed that tribal people in spite of having a lot of awareness still follow certain age-old practices while purchasing liquor from non-tribals. If the tribal people do not have ready-made cash to purchase liquor they assure the liquor vendors (who is virtually a non-tribal pushes sale of liquor by maintaining an account), which is normally collected during harvest time. He sells liquor at a higher price, but purchased commodities during harvesting period normally at lesser price. By paying in the form of grains during the harvest the tribal households normally face food shortage throughout the year which affects the entire family. Secondly, due to excess drinking the tribal people, particularly male members, suffer from certain diseases, which ruins their family life and harmonic relation within the village. When liquor vendor does not agree to provide liquor on credit, the tribal people are tempted to sell and/or mortgage their tangible assets like watch, bicycle, etc., but unable to recover those assets after a period. The most important plight of a drunken tribal is the misery he causes to his children and wife. Wife beating cases, due to such reason, are not few as discussed with villagers. Due to this the children become the first victims of drop-outs from primary level. This affects their education and health condition.

Opinion of PRI Members on Liquor Consumption

In order to assess the extent of liquor consumption in the tribal society, members of Panchayati Raj Institutions (PRIs) have been interviewed in and around the study villages located in different districts. A total of 49 PRI members have been interviewed in order to assess the consumption of liquor. The assessment has been done on a three-point scale, like 'increased', 'decreased' and 'no view'. Questions have been asked to know whether there is any change in the liquor production and consumption among the tribals. The opinion has been collected separately on the use of handia, mahuli, juice of salap and palm, mango and jackfruits. The study findings reflect that out of 49 PRI members 45 (91.83%) persons have commented that consumption of mahuli has increased over the years, while out of 39 PRI members only 29 (74.35%) per cent have viewed that consumption of salap, and palm juice has increased over the years.

As regards the exercise of control by the tribal people over production, distribution and consumption of liquor, out of 49 PRI members 40 (81.63%) have opined that their control has been decreased. To substantiate their view they put forth a couple of justifications. First, there is a marginal positive impact of the development programmes on the tribal people, which has made them refrain from preparing liquor. It is clear when one compares the present situation, with that of the 1950s and 1960s. Second, the NGOs operating in tribal areas have influenced the minds of the tribal people against consumption of liquor. Third, the tribal people are unable to cope with the increasing harassment of the police and excise personnel, and hence to avoid it they try to give up their practice of liquor production and consumption. Fourth, excepting the mahua collection season tribal people are poverty-stricken, that at other times they are unable to invest in home brewing and prefer to purchase liquor as and when they can afford.

Another objective of this section is to present a review of the secondary sources of information on the effects of liquor on the tribal people as well as on the government revenue. Since uniform data could not be available, here an attempt has been made to highlight this aspect with specific reference to Kalahandi and Nuapada districts. From a cursory estimate, it is calculated that during the last 40 years (1960-2000) more than 40,000 people in both the districts have died which has an effect on female population of the districts who belong to the age bracket of 25 to 35 years. Around 3 lakh daily-wage labourers of the district are the victims of consumption of liquor who spent almost 90 per cent of their daily income for purchase of liquor and other related items. As a result of this, almost 75 per cent of the people of these districts are in debt trap.

During 1982-83, there were 114 liquor production centres in Kalahandi district (undivided). Since the withdrawal of liquor shops in the Scheduled Areas of the district (Lanjigarh and Thuamal Rampur blocks) now there are 69 government liquor shops still operating in Kalahandi and Nuapada districts. During

1992-93 in Kalahandi district around 1,00,04,748 LP litres of mahua liquor was produced.

Since April 1994, the production of mahua liquor in such centres have been banned. In spite of this, since 1996-97 (from July) the production of liquor has started and the total production has been to the tune of 37,69,995 litres of LP natural liquor while the production of LP mahua has increased to 99,68,80,865 litres. As regards foreign liquor, there are 18 such shops in undivided Kalahandi district. The official data with regard to collection of revenue when compared from 1995-96 to 1999-2000 reflect that there is a sharp fall in the revenue collection in the undivided Kalahandi district. Compared to 1995-96 collection of revenue from the sale of foreign liquor, the growth rate during 1996-97 was 100 per cent. Since then in every subsequent year the revenue collection, when compared with the previous years has fallen sharply. The number of cases filed by the Excise Department against the deviants also does not show a specific trend – rather provides a fluctuating figure when compared with the previous year.

Similarly, in Koraput district, sale of liquor has touched the sky because of rampant preparation and sale of contraband liquor. This has made the district a heaven for the anti-socials, pushing tribal people onto the brink of socio-economic degradation; illegal trading of country liquor has become a flourishing business in every nook and corner of the district (*The Utkal Age*, 2000). Though State Government has banned (up to March 2001) the preparation and sale of locally brewed liquor, but the business of liquor transaction is open like the flow of water.

Considering the passion for liquor of the tribal people a government order permits tribal people to produce five litres for their own consumption; and commercial production and sale have been banned in the entire tribal region (Scheduled area) of the State until the recent days of March 2001. Different sources say that while illegal liquor trade is high in Koraput district the personnel of Excise and Police Department are unable to control the illegal trade; and realise the targeted revenue of the district out of this business. For example, an amount of Rs. 3,39,23,031 revenue has been collected during 1997-98 against the targeted amount of Rs. 1,63,19,104 and 1,529 cases have been filed. Many people have complained that the Police and Excise Department have no control over the widespread preparation and sale of contraband liquor. While working from 1993 to 1997 in four blocks of Koraput, Jeypore, Lakhmipur and Kundra of Koraput district, the author has seen tribal women selling liquor in the weekly market and quite a good number of tribal people are involved in smuggling of liquor, to nearby areas including Andhra Pradesh in polythene packs, rubber tubes, etc. In other words, one can say that with the assistance of local suppliers in villages like Luhaba of Nandapur block, Dumuruipadar of Koraput Block, Dudhari, Ranikona, Charangul, Bhairaguda of Semiliguda Block and many other places are becoming principal centres for the production of contraband liquor. One can say that it has largely taken the shape of cottage industry in certain pockets of the district.

Conclusion

The above discussion on alcoholism and excise policy in the context of Orissa reflects the following observations:

- The State of Orissa in post-independent period has largely followed the Bihar and Orissa Excise Act, 1915. Much later some amendments have been incorporated into it. The concept of revenue maximisation has always influenced the State approach towards this. In spite of this, in Orissa the State Excise Revenue as a share of its Own Tax Revenue is much less compared to many other States.
- Understanding the importance of liquor in the life and livelihood of tribal people, the State Government at various points of time has imposed restriction on the production, distribution and trading of liquor in Scheduled Areas as well as in non-Scheduled Areas of the State.
- After the 73rd amendment of the Constitution of India and its Extension to the Scheduled Areas of the State, Government of Orissa has decentralised the Excise Act and handed over the power to the Gram Panchayat so as to give license for production and trading of liquor.

- In addition to this, the State Government should reduce the number of days and timing of liquor sale in a week. This in spite of all problems will reduce the quantity of liquor consumption. The State Government should reduce the number of liquor shops in Orissa and more particularly in tribal areas of the State.
- The State Government should reduce the quantity of liquor production. Gram Panchayats should regulate the demand and supply of liquor to a particular area.

5 Indebtedness

This chapter is divided into three sections. First section while reviewing the secondary data gives an overview of the magnitude of the problem of indebtedness. Second section provides a review of the existing policies with regard to moneylending in the State, their amendments to meet time requirements. Third section provides the data collected during field-study as regards the extent of moneylending practised in villages and the impact of the policies on the poor tribal people.

I

Magnitude of the Problem

The problem of indebtedness in rural areas in general, and in tribal areas in particular, seems to be the root cause and product of poverty. Tribal people are living in an economy, which provides them livelihood only for a couple of months. Habits of liquor consumption marginalise the tribal people. Not finding the existing livelihood sources as sufficient and with limited alternatives, tribal people quickly and easily go to non-tribal whoever available within their access seeking help from them both in cash and kind. Since education and awareness status of tribal people in tribal regions is much below the average level, taking this opportunity the moneylenders (mostly unregistered) exploit them to their level of satisfaction and ask for mortgage of their land and standing crops. As a last resort, the poor tribal people finding no way out agree to the proposal and give their agricultural land in lieu of the loan. On several occasions, tribal people not being able to repay the loan as per the terms and conditions of the *Sahukars,* finally handover the land to the moneylender who enjoys the occupancy rights over the land. The terms and conditions imposed during such transactions normally vary from region to region and also from community to community. On many occasions, it has been found that tribal people not able to repay the loan as per the terms and conditions of the Sahukars finally hand over land to the moneylender who enjoys the use-rights over his agricultural land. These conditions are normally imposed during such transactions and vary from region to region and maybe from community to community.

Understanding the acuteness of tribal indebtedness and the problem of moneylending in tribal areas, State authorities in order to minimise exploitation, have formulated various rules and regulations from time to time. Needs for such legislations were felt to give relief to tribal people, who were being compelled to pay exorbitant rate of interests. Such legislations were intended to ensure that the moneylenders register themselves, maintain proper accounts and charge only reasonable rates of interests.

Due to chronic indebtedness tribal people of Orissa continue to be the victims of exploitation in the hands of moneylenders, who are mainly non-tribal people. Data on the volume of ongoing moneylending in the tribal regions of the State are not available. However, it is a fact that imbalances between income and consumption expenditure of tribal people make them an easy prey in the hands of the non-tribal moneylenders (Behura and Panigrahi, 2001). The Pana, Sundhi, Komiti, Mohanta and Gouda, caste groups are in moneylending business for a long time. Development of communication system linked the inaccessible tribal areas with the outer world, which has facilitated the inflow and outflow of labourers, raw materials and the produces from and to the tribal areas. This has increased the inter-regional movement of non-tribal population to tribal areas (Jha, 1977; Mohanty, 1997). For example, in Koraput district (undivided) immigrants especially the Telugu Komites, the Oriya Sundhis and the Doms exploited tribals through unscrupulous trade and moneylending business (Patnaik, 1972:12). This later on led to the practice of Gothi (bonded labour) system in the district (ibid). In fact moneylending system was the major route of large-scale land transfer from tribal people to non-tribals (Sabu, 1942:136). In this context, Nabakrushna Choudhury one of the members of the Partially Excluded Areas Inquiry Committee of Orissa, during 1940 and also the Chief Minister of Orissa, in early fifties stated that "...the backward tribes of the tracts under our inquiry had been left completely at the mercy of the non-aboriginal Maharajas, hill chiefs, *Bissoyees, Patros,* etc...." (ibid.).

As per the sample survey carried out by the Planning Commission of Government of India, the incidence of indebtedness among the tribal people had increased from 14.47 per cent in 1975-76 to 33.77 per cent in 1982-83. The study also reflects that the debt liability per household has also increased from Rs. 419 in 1975-76 to Rs. 819 in 1982-83 (Verma, 1998:101). The survey on the indebtedness of rural and urban households of India carried out by NSSO in its 48th round shows that indebtedness of rural households was marginally lower at 62.8 per cent in 1962 over that of 1951 (63.3%) which decreased significantly to 41.3 per cent in 1971 and further to 19.4 per cent in 1981. In India, this has increased to 32 per cent and 26.9 per cent for rural and urban households respectively in 1991 with an average amount of Rs. 2,116 and Rs. 3,976 per household respectively. Reduction in the reporting of the rural indebtedness in recent years has raised many debates (Rao and Tripathi, 2001). Seetha Prabhu et al., (1988) examined the reasons for substantial decrease in the registration of indebtedness, which relates to the methods of accounting, rise in household income, expansion of institutional credit network in rural areas and demand of credit from outside market. In Orissan context, the proportion of rural household reporting debt (includes cash loans and current liabilities) during 1971, 1981 and 1991 was 29.6, 19.2 and 28 per cent respectively. Average amount of debt in Orissa during the above period was Rs. 163, Rs. 346 and Rs. 1,158 respectively. However, the data do not specify variations across ethnic groups. Proportion of households reporting outstanding cash loans and current liabilities and corresponding average amount per household in Orissa reflects 23.3 per cent with an average loan amount of Rs. 1,054, and proportion of current liabilities was 8.2 per cent with an average loan amount of Rs. 104 (1991). Decline in debt share of institutional agencies of rural households showed that the non-institutional sources like moneylenders, traders, relatives and friends, played a dominant role in rural areas, but to a lesser extent in urban areas even in 1990. The organised sectors like cooperatives and nationalised banks have also started leaving a mark in the process.

Though data on tribal indebtedness are scanty still the process of tribal indebtedness is established due to various causes that can be categorised under social, economic and political reasons. Loss of tribal rights over land and land-based resources, shortage of food grains, observance of expensive socio-cultural rituals (compared to their income), ignorance and poor accessibility to the opportunities available in organised sectors, inability to follow up complicated procedures of formal financial institutions, etc., are some of the specific factors responsible for the precarious state of tribal indebtedness.

SCSTRTI carried out a study on 'indebtedness among the Scheduled Tribes of Paralakhemundi Sub-division (undivided) of Ganjam District', in October 1971. Basic objective of the study was to collect information on indebtedness among the STs living in rural Orissa. The study has covered 1,539 HHs in 64 tribal villages distributed in five police stations of Paralkhemundi Sub-division. The study found that tribal people exclusively dominate almost 54.3 per cent of the 1,208 inhabited villages. Major tribal groups in the area are Saora and Kandha. The study reflects that almost 66.7 per cent of the total 1,539 households were indebted. Of them around 91.4 per cent of the loan were borrowed in the form of cash, which comes to an average of Rs. 135 per household. As regards the purpose of loan, almost 37.8 per cent households had taken loan for the purpose of purchasing cattle and reclamation of land, development of agriculture; and 23.1 per cent for home consumption and to meet the social and religious obligations and 23.7 per cent had taken loan for treatment of diseases.

Rate of interests varied from a minimum of 25 per cent to 100 per cent per annum. The survey found out that almost 30 per cent of the total loans were old loans and were 3 years old, while 11 per cent cases were 5 years old. The study also explains that tribal people take loan mainly during the months of March to October. Repayment style of these loans varies according to different conditions. However, the tribal people more or less follow the payment in kind. Nature of payment is normally decided at the time of taking loans. To get loan from unorganised sector no written agreements are made except in few cases where moneylenders keep few lines of writing about the amount, rate of interest and date of loan. It is widely accepted that the tribal people are trustworthy as they are peace loving and truthful. The moneylenders keep moveable assets as properties as mortgage against their loan. The study finds that compared to the non-tribal in the study villages the tribal people are highly indebted. Non-tribal people of the village or of the neighbouring villages are the major moneylender. Still they are the best friends of good tribal people because of the personal relationship that they maintain.

Due to the chronic indebtedness, tribal people of Orissa continue to be the victims of exploitation in the hands of moneylenders. It is a fact that due to the imbalances between the income and consumption expenditure, tribal people became easy prey in the hands of the non-tribals, namely, Pana, Sundhi, Mohanta and Gouda. As per the sample survey carried out by the Planning Commission of Government of India, the incidence of indebtedness among the tribal people had increased from 14.47 per cent in 1975-76 to 33.77 per cent in 1982-83. This study also reflects that the debt liability per household has also increased from Rs. 419 in 1975-76 to Rs. 819 in 1982-83 (Verma, 1998:101). These barrowings are made basically from non-institutional and unorganised sectors. However, the organised sectors like cooperatives and nationalised banks have also started leaving a mark in the process. The problem of indebtedness not only creates economic suffering but also brings on social and psychological stress.

Understanding the acuteness of the problem of moneylending in tribal areas, State authorities from time to time have formulated various rules and regulations. Need of a legislation was felt to give relief to the tribal people who were compelled to pay exorbitant rates of interest. Such legislation was intended to ensure that the moneylenders to register themselves maintain proper accounts and charge only reasonable rates of interest. Objective of that legislation was designed to give relief to the debtors.

II

Origin of indebtedness among the tribal people goes back to the beginning of penetration of non-tribal people into the tribal regions and introduction of money economy, which later on replaced the barter form of transactions. The process of tribal indebtedness linked to various causes experienced over the years can be categorised under social, economic, political reasons. A few specific causes which resulted in this type of situations are: loss of tribal rights over land and forest resources, deficit supply of food grains due to the backward character of their economy, adherence to expensive socio-cultural rituals, ignorance of opportunities available in organised sector, inability to follow up the complicated procedures of organised sectors to get loan, non-availability and their inaccessibility to alternative modern opportunities, etc. Understanding the acuteness of this situation and to save the small landholders from becoming a victim in the hands of moneylenders, during 1938, the then government passed an act which was known as Orissa Small Holders Relief Act. Objective behind this was that "owing to continued economic depression there were indications that the condition of the small peasant proprietors and small agricultural tenants was deteriorating. However, government was desirous of preventing the eviction of small holders from their lands". At a later period during the Congress Ministry in Orissa headed by Biswanath Das the first attempt was made to amend the Agriculturists' Loan Act 1884 by the Orissa Act VI of 1937 which provided that indebtedness of agriculturists should be a valid ground for obtaining loans. During that time this had not only encouraged the poor *royat* to cling to his land, but also largely checked the migration of Oriya peasants to Calcutta (Kolkata), Assam and Burma to earn their livelihood.

The Scheduled Areas and Scheduled Tribes Commission under the chairmanship of U.N. Dheber enquiring into the working of the existing moneylending regulations or legislations, have revealed the following practices which were common in India:

- There is evasion of the regulations and legislation, moneylenders taking little notice of the restrictions imposed on their operations.
- Transactions between the tribals and the moneylenders are generally oral. Even when they resorted to writing, the amount for which pro-notes were given included the usurious portion.
- Sometimes the usurious portion of interest, much higher than that prescribed in the regulations of legislation is deducted in advance from the money advanced.
- In many tribal areas as in Madhya Pradesh, Orissa and Tripura, the crop is invariably mortgaged in advance. In Tripura and part of West Bengal, according to the '*Dadan*' system, it is a condition for the advancement of a loan that the crop has to be sold to the moneylender at harvesting time.
- In several tribal areas, although the title to the land is nominally with the tribal debtor, it is under usufructory mortgage to the moneylender, who reaps full benefit out of it.
- The worst manifestation of moneylending is in the form of bonded labour.

Having considered the problem and the extent of indebtedness the Commission has arrived at the following broad conclusions:

- State governments have not made adequate use of the protective provisions of the Fifth Schedule to lend protection to tribal people against bonded labour and moneylenders.
- State governments have not been able to utilise the protective provisions of the Fifth Schedule to lend protection to the tribal people against usurious practices, partly because the State governments have been unable to find funds for alternative credit.

- State governments have not been able to make effective use of the penal provisions in their existing legislation against evasion of moneylenders.

The moneylender's position is impregnable on account of the absence of an alternative source of credit. Until alternative credit becomes available to the tribal people at reasonable rates of interests, the moneylender will continue to hold to his present position.

In order to provide loan to the poor villagers at easy rate of interest Government of Orissa introduced the Orissa Money Lenders Bill 1938. This bill had four objectives. First, the moneylenders were required to register themselves for legalising the practices; second, the principle of '*Damdu Pat*' was introduced with the right to open up old accounts from 1 April, 1936; third, the Bill introduced the principle of simple interest of 9 per cent in case of a secured land and 12 per cent in case of an unsecured land; and fourthly, it provided for some penalties including the cancellation of registration certificates granted to moneylenders for illegal extortions (OLA, 1938:167).

Finding the provision of moneylenders as not the permanent solution for the loan requirements or indebtedness of the poor people, the then government considered cooperative Banks and Societies as the viable solution. Thus, the Orissa Cooperative Land Mortgage Bank Bill was introduced on 24 January, 1938 which aimed for providing low interest-based loans for agricultural purposes for mortgaging land (OLA, 1938: 44).

The Second Moneylenders (Second Amendment) Bill 1947 was passed on 29 August, 1947. Earlier, license for doing moneylending was given for a period of ten years. However, this new amendment considered neither fair to the government nor to the person taking up moneylending as a business. In the new bill, it included that the license should remain so long during which the person might have dropped the business and the government might have also an opportunity to judge whether the person was fit enough to carry on the profession, (OLA, 1947: 93) and hence the license was limited to a period of five years.

Government of Orissa while undertaking the problem of the tribal people felt the necessity of special attention to the Partial Excluded Areas of the State. Government appointed a committee in December 1938 under the chairmanship of Sri A.V. Thakkar of Harijan Sevak Sangha. The Committee was also asked to examine the extent of implementation of general rules and regulations in the Partially Excluded Areas and to make suggestions for their modifications in the interest of these tracts (1940). Thakkar Committee often reviewing the situation suggested for special policies for the tribal people who are residing in Partially Excluded Areas. Thus, the Orissa (Scheduled Area) Moneylenders Regulation 1967 (Regulation 2 of 1968) is in operation since 15 November, 1968. The basic objectives of this Act are to monitor and review for preventing exploitation of Scheduled Tribes in the Scheduled Area.

Planning Commission Report of the Study Team on Tribal Development Programme in 1969 admitted the acuteness of this problem and viewed that no programme of economic development is likely to have any impact on the tribal economy unless vigorous measures are taken to rescue the tribal people from the clutches of the moneylenders. Apart from this, the Sub-Committee on Excluded and Partially Excluded Area (other than Assam) had gone into the details of this problem and justified the need for prevention of exploitation of tribal people by the moneylenders. They observed that in Scheduled Area moneylending should not be permitted and at any rate they should be allowed to operate only with license and stringent control system. Even the Constitutional experts made special provisions in the Fifth Schedule of the Constitution which empowers the Governor of a State to make regulations to control the business of moneylending by private persons. A probe into the Protective Legislations Regarding Money Lending/Debt Redemption in different States and Union Territories of India (Table 5.1) reflects that the State Governments from time to time have formulated different regulations for protecting the interests of the tribal people from exploitation by non-tribals.

Table 5.1

Protective Legislation's Regarding Money Lending/Debt Redemption In Different States and Union Territories in India

State/Union Territories	*Act/Regulation*
Andhra Pradesh	1. The Andhra Pradesh (Scheduled Tribe) Debt Relief Regulation, 1960, and Amendment, 1970.
	2. The Andhra Pradesh (Scheduled Areas) Money Lenders Regulation, 1960.
	3. The Hyderabad Money Lenders Act, 1938.
	4. The Agency Debt Bondage Abolition Regulation, 1964.
Assam	1. The Assam Money Lenders Act, 1934.
	2. The Assam Debt Conciliation Act, 1936.
	3. The Assam Rural Indebtedness Relief Act, 1975.
	4. The Mikir Hills District (Money Lending by Non-Tribals) Regulation, 1953.
Bihar and Jharkhand	1. Bihar Scheduled Areas Regulation, 1969.
	2. Bihar Money Lenders Act, 1938.
	3. Bihar Money Lenders Act, (Regulation of Transaction) Act, 1939.
Gujarat and Maharashtra	1. The Mumbai Money Lenders Act, 1946.
	2. The Mumbai Agricultural Debtor's Relief Act, 1958.
	3. The Maharashtra Tribals Economic Condition (Improvement) Act, 1976.
Kerala	1. The Kerala Agricultural Money Lenders Act, 1958.
	2. The Kerala Agricultural Debt Relief Act, 1958.
Himachal Pradesh	1. The Himachal Pradesh Debt Redumption Act, 1953.
	2. The Spiti and Lahaul (Relief and Indebtedness Laws Application and Amendment) Regulation, 1962.
Madhya Pradesh	1. The Madhya Pradesh Scheduled Tribes Debt Relief Regulation, 1965.
	2. The Madhya Pradesh Usurious Loans Act, 1938.
	3. The Madhya Pradesh Anusuchit Janajati Rini Sahayata Ordinance, 1966.
	4. The Madhya Pradesh Anusuchit Janajati Sahukar Viniyam, 1972.
Karnataka	1. The Mysore Money Lenders Act, 1939.
	2. The Coorg Money Lenders Act, 1939.
	3. The Mysore Agricultural Relief Act, 1937.
	4. The Mysore Debt Reconciliation Act, 1937.

Contd...

Contd...

Orissa	1. The Orissa (Scheduled Area) Money Lender's Regulation, 1967 (Regulation 2/1968) as amended in 1976 (Regulation 2 of 1976).
	2. The Orissa Money Lender's Act, 1939.
	3. The Orissa Debt Bondage Abolition Regulation, 1948.
	4. The Bonded Labour System (Abolition) Act, 1976.
	5. The Orissa Debt Relief Act, 1980.
	6 The Orissa State Legal Aid and Advice Scheme, 1981.
Rajasthan	1. The Rajasthan Sagri System Abolition Act, 1961.
	2. The Rajasthan Relief of Agricultural Indebtedness (Amendment) Act, 1962.
	3. The Rajasthan Money Lender's Act, 1963.
Tamil Nadu	1. The Madras Money Lender's Act, 1937.
	2. The Madras Debt Conciliation Act, 1936.
	3. The Madras Indebted Agriculturalists (Repayment of Debts) Act, 1955.
	4. Tamil Nadu Debt Relief Act, 1976, 1980.
Tripura	1. Tripura Agricultural Indebtness Relief Act, 1979.
Utttar Pradesh	1. Uttar Pradesh Money Lenders Act, 1976.
	2. Uttar Pradesh Debt Relief Act, 1976.
West Bengal	1. The Bengal Money Lenders Act, 1940.
	2. The Bengal Agricultural Debtors Act, 1936.
Andaman and Nicobar Island	1. The Andaman and Nicobar Island (Protection of Aboriginal Tribes) Rules, 1956.
	2. The Andaman and Nicobar Island Rules, 1957.
	3. The Andaman and Nicobar Island (Protection of Aboriginal Tribes) Money Lenders Regulation, 1956.
Lakshadweep	1. The Laccadives, Minority and Administrative Islands (Debt Conciliation and Grant of Loans) Regulation, 1964.

Source: Various Sources.

The Orissa (Scheduled Area) Money Lenders' Regulation, 1967- Orissa Regulation 2 of 1968

The Regulation as a legislative measure was promulgated by the Governor of Orissa to control and regulate the business of money-lending in the Scheduled Area of the State of Orissa in 1968. It is provided in this Regulation that an application for a license shall be filed before the prescribed licensing authority and shall be accompanied by such fee, not exceeding twenty-five rupees, as the government may, from time to time, by notification, determine. It is also provided that no moneylender shall change his place of business without previous notice to the licensing authority. Every moneylender shall keep exhibited over the outer door of his shop or place of business a board containing in Oriya language the equivalents of the words 'Licensed Money Lender' and the name of the debt collector, if any, authorised under Section 14 of the Regulation.

Interest and Charges Allowed to Moneylenders

It is provided in the Regulation that no moneylender shall charge interest on any loan advanced by him at a rate exceeding:

(a) Nine per cent per annum simple interest, where the loan is secured, and

(b) Twelve per cent per annum simple interest, where the loan is not secured.

Duties of Moneylender to Keep Accounts and Furnish Copies of the Document

- Every moneylender shall keep and maintain a cashbook and a ledger in such form and in such manner as may be prescribed under the legislation.
- Every moneylender shall deliver or cause to deliver to the debtor and to the authority prescribed in that behalf within thirty days from the date on which a loan is made, a statement in the Oriya language showing in clear and distinct terms the amount and date of the loan and the date of its maturity, the nature of the security, if any, for the loan, the name and address of the debtor and of the moneylender and the rate of interest charged. It is further provided that no such statement shall be required to be delivered to a debtor, if he is supplied by the moneylender with a passbook in the prescribed form containing an up-to-date account of the transaction with the debtor and,
- Upon repayment of a loan in full, mark indelibly every document signed by the debtor with words indicating payment or cancellation and discharge every mortgage,

restore every pledge, return every note and cancel or reassign every assignment given by the debtor as security for the loan.

- A moneylender shall grant a receipt containing the prescribed particulars to the debtor for every payment made by him on account of the loan.
- Restrictions have been imposed that no moneylender shall accept from a debtor any article as a pawn, pledge or security for a loan without giving him a receipt for the same with its description, estimated value, the amount of loan advanced against the article and such other particulars as may be prescribed.

Delivery of Statement of Amounts and Copies thereof by Moneylenders

Under this Regulation, every moneylender shall deliver or cause to be delivered every year to each of this debtors and to the authority prescribed in this behalf a statement of such debtors' accounts signed by him or by his agent showing therein:

- The amount of principal and the amount of interest due to the moneylender.
- The amount of every payment received by the moneylender in respect of the loan during the year together with the date on which each payment was made.
- All payments credited in the account of interest and the residue, if any, payment more than sufficient to discharge the balance of interest due to the time is made, credit to the debtor in the account of principal or in the alternative such of the payments credited first in the accounts of principal as the moneylender may determine and the remaining payments credited in the account of interest calculated on the basis of the decreased balance of principal and when the balance of interest is fully discharged the residue of the payments, if any, further credited in the account of principal, and
- The amount of principal and interest remaining unpaid. It is further provided that no such statement shall be required to be delivered to a debtor if the moneylender supplies him with

a passbook in the prescribed form containing an up-to-date account of the transactions with the debtor.

A moneylender shall on demand in writing being made by the debtor at any time during the subsistence of any loan advanced by him whether before or after the appointed date and on payment of the prescribed fee, supply to the debtor or to any other person specified in that behalf in the notice of demand, a statement in respect of such loan signed by the moneylender or his agent, and containing the particulars specified in Sub-section (1) of the Regulation.

A moneylender shall on demand in writing made by the debtor and on payment of the prescribed sum on account of expenses, supply to the debtor or to any other person specified in that behalf in the notice of demand, a copy of any document relating to any loan advanced by him to such debtor or relating to any security therefor.

Debtor not Bound to Admit Correctness of Accounts

A debtor to whom a statement of accounts or a passbook has been furnished shall not be bound to acknowledge or deny its correctness and his failure to do so shall not by itself be deemed to be an admission of the correctness of the accounts.

Procedure in Suits Regarding Loans

- If any suit is filed in the court, the court shall, before deciding the claim on merits, frame and decide the issues whether the moneylender has complied with all the provisions regarding duties of moneylender to keep accounts and furnish copies and delivery of statements of accounts and copies thereof by him.
- If the court finds that the aforesaid provisions have not been complied with by the moneylender, it may, in case the plaintiff's claim is established in whole or in part, disallow the whole or any portion or the interest found due, as may seem reasonable to it in the circumstances of the case and may disallow cost.

Maximum Amount of Interest which may be Decreed

No court shall, in respect of any loan whether advanced before or after the appointed date, pass a decree, on account of interest, a sum greater than the principal of the loan due on the date of the decree. This is, of course, to be done without detriment to anything contained in any agreement or any law for the time being in force.

Employment of Debt Collectors

Any moneylender for the purpose of demanding or recovering any loan due to him shall employ no person unless such person is in possession of a certificate authorising him to act as a debt collector granted under the law. This is a provision to prevent use of muscle men to collect dues with threat or force.

Appointment of Inspectors and their Powers

Government or any authority or officer empowered by them may, by notification, appoint one or more persons to be inspectors for the purpose of this Regulation and may specify in such notification the local limits of their jurisdiction. An Inspector may, at any time, with such assistance as he thinks necessary, enter any premises within his jurisdiction in which any person carries on business as a licensed moneylender and inspect the books, accounts, records, files, documents, safes, vaults and pledges in such premises.

A Magistrate of the First Class on receiving a report from an Inspector that he has reason to believe that a person is carrying on the business of moneylending without a license at any place within the jurisdiction of such magistrate, may issue a warrant empowering inspector to enter such place with such assistance as such magistrate considers it necessary to inspect the books, accounts, records, files, documents, safes, vaults and pledges in such a place.

Power to Suspend of Cancel Licenses

It is provided that the licensing authority may, by an order in writing at any time during the term of a license suspend it for such a period as he may deem fit or cancel it if the license contrivances any of the provisions of this Regulation or the rules made there-under or the conditions of the license.

Law provides for punishment for charging higher interest and advancing loan of a lessor amount than that shown in the papers. Any moneylender whether licensed or not can be punished if he actually advances an amount less than the amount shown in this accounts, registers, pawn tickets or other documents relating to the loan and if receives interest or other charges at a rate higher than the rate mentioned in Section 7 of the Regulation. Punishment prescribed under the Regulation is imprisonment for a term, which may extend to one year or with fine, which may extend to five hundred rupees or with both.

Penalty for Carrying on Business without License

There is provision of punishment for carrying on business without license. Doing business of moneylending without obtaining a license or otherwise, in conformity with the terms and conditions of a license, shall be punishable with imprisonment, which may extend to six months, or with fine, which may extend to one thousand rupees or with both.

In TAC meeting held on 24 October, 1983, it was proposed that the Orissa Money Lending Act 1939 has been comprehensively amended by Revenue Department and made more progressive in some respect with a view to protecting the interest of the indigenous debater with a view to maintaining uniformity between Orissa Money Lending Act and Orissa Money Lending Regulation. The Revenue Department has advised that the amendment is necessary for proper implementation of the Orissa Scheduled Area Moneylenders Regulation 1967.

The implementation of the Orissa (Scheduled Area) Money Lenders Act (Regulation 2 of 1967) experienced the need of certain modifications. Accordingly, in order to make this law more effective a few recommendations were made in the Tribal Advisory Committee meeting held on 24 October, 1983, and were sent to the Revenue and Excise Department and Law Department. Firstly, Section 19 of the Orissa Moneylending (OML) Act 39 the penalty for carrying moneylending without license was one year and this period was again referred to six months in the Section 21 of the OML Regulation of 1967. Both Revenue and Law Department also felt the amendment of making it uniform to a period of one year. Secondly, Section 20 (C) speaks that every offence under the Act shall be cognisable and bailable. Section 23 (i) of the OML Regulation of 1967 provides that no Act shall take cognisance of an offence punishable under this Regulation except on a compliant in writing made by the Inspector appointed. Thus, it was proposed to delete the above provision with the justification that sufficient provision under Section 23 (2) that not withstanding anything contained in the CPC 1973, 2 of 1974, all offices are punishable under the Regulation excepting those punishable under Section 20(A) shall be cognisable and bailable. Responding to it, the Law Department opined that it cannot be ruled out, but due to the simple nature of tribal people, crafty people may motivate them to file complaints against competing moneylenders.

Since this is a check with the Inspector for not allowing simple tribal people for not investing in malafied work, the omission of Sub-section (1) of Section 23 of the said Regulation may be detrimental to the interest of the members of the Scheduled Tribes. Government of Orissa later on enacted the Orissa Debt Relief Act, 1980 which became effective from 13 March, 1981. The objective of this Act is to provide relief from indebtedness to small farmers, rural artisans and agricultural labourers. With the promulgation of this law any debt incurred by the scheduled debtor before time, including the amount of interest payable on such debt shall be deemed to have been wholly discharged and will not be recovered from him or his heirs. If any property pledged by the debtor, will immediately be released to him, which became binding on the creditor. Even any verbal agreement between the scheduled debtors to provide labour to the creditor will also be made null and void. Regarding this, no civil court will entertain any suit against the scheduled debtor. In order to make this law more effective at ground level, various responsible functionaries like Sub-Collectors, Tehasildars have been empowered with judicial powers of Judicial Magistrate and the trial will be of summary by nature (Annual Administration Report in Scheduled Areas of Orissa 1995-96).

Functioning of Credit Institutions

The Bawa Committee (1971) recommended that tribal people require a package of services, which includes production, and consumption credit, supply of agricultural inputs and consumer goods in a more integrated manner. This will divert the tribal people from falling into the clutches of moneylenders. Thus, the Large Area Multi-Purpose Societies (LAMPS) are formed for operation at block level with its branches. The Central Cooperative Banks and Regional Cooperative Marketing Society and Tribal Development Cooperative Society (1972) have become the part of large organisational network for operation in tribal pockets to replace moneylenders and to boost tribal economy. The first experiment of having LAMPS started in Bonei sub-division of Sundargarh district of Orissa. Presently, there are 240 LAMPS and other Primary Societies, 47 Panchayat Samitis, and three individuals as members of TDCC functioning in Scheduled Areas of the State of Orissa. It has 130 procurement centres, 69 fair-price shops, and 66 godowns. Apart from these, 47 Panchayat Samitis have invested their share capital in TDCC. However, since 1985-86 very few numbers of LAMPS are procuring minor forest produces for TDCC (TDCC Office, 1998). Incurring of losses by TDCC are basically due to low turnover, low working capital, high overhead cost, heavy interest burden, payment of royalty, etc.

Piecemeal studies have been carried out to assess the impact of these organisations on the tribal life. Though a number of credit cooperative societies have come up with a view to provide credit facilities to the tribal people in need, both in cash and kind, but practically the tribal people have been helped very little. The local merchants who did not want to lose their grip on the tribal people dominated the management of these cooperative societies. The evaluation study by SCSTRTI (1995-96) on the working of LAMPS at Gunupur of Rayagada district has observed that the primary objectives of LAMPS are to provide short-term loans to the tribals for seasonal agriculture, and medium-term loans for creation of farm assets seems not to have been not fulfilled. It is due to various structural, functional, managerial and financial bottlenecks. The study suggests financial assistance for tribal beneficiaries, infrastructure development and to activate LAMPS by supplying both controlled and non-controlled commodities. Similarly, the study of Das (1996-97) on the functioning of Tribal Development Cooperative Corporation of Orissa Ltd. (TDCCOL) of Balliguda branch found that the operational areas of the branch is too big to address to the objective of the organisation. The sales and procurement centres of TDCCOL suffer from shortage of working capital. As a result, the organisation is unable to provide consumption loans to the tribals during lean seasons regularly. The study of Mallik and Panigrahi (1998) found that TDCCOL in Bhuiyan and Juanga Pirha of Keonjhar district though entitled to procure 19 minor forest produces against available 27 items, but practically they collect only two items. This has led to the functioning of de-facto agents of TDCCOL collecting more varieties of forest produces. When compared with its objectives TDCCOL in Orissa seems to be handicapped. It needs a revamping from various facets but it must first uphold the interest of the tribal people.

III

Study Findings

During the fieldwork in four villages of different districts, an attempt was made to find out impact of the Orissa Scheduled Area Moneylenders Regulation, 1967 and the Orissa Regulation 2 of 1968. The purpose was to find out the extent of loan tribal households taken from private sources which maybe from within the community and/or outside the community, and the type of loan circulated maybe in the form of cash, kind or in both, the purpose of loan received, and the loan repayment status.

Loan Received from Private Sources

In order to collect the households who have taken loans from private sources an attempt was made to find out the loan status for a period of two years, i.e., from 1999 to 2000. The findings have been explained in different districts according to various ethnic categories. The study also reflects the source of loan, which has been broadly divided into two types, i.e., from own community members and from other community members. It has been observed that in Kendubaradihi village of Kalahandi district almost 20.28 per cent households have taken loan from private sources of which around 64.28 per cent households have taken loan from the members of other communities. In Keonjhar district, it has been observed that 24.24 per cent of the tribal people have taken loan from private sources in which more than 62.50 per cent have taken loan from the members of other communities. In Penaposi Pangara of Kandhamal district, all the 50 (100%) tribal households are regularly taking loan from the Sundhi households who have grocery shops in the village. These Sundhi households supply loans to the tribal households for their normal day-to-day living. The basic aim behind their debt is to harvest the turmeric crop. The Sundhi households never close their loan account and keep the poor tribal people in loan status by encouraging them to mortgage their standing crops. Normally, the transactions made by Sundhi households with a tribal household never surpass the value of average turmeric production of the Kandha. This, at certain level justifies that the Sundhis who are informal moneylenders creating an environment on the need of lending in the village. In Lachipetta village of Malkangiri district, of the total tribal households, only 14.45 per cent have taken loan of which quite a majority of households, i.e., 79.16 per cent have taken loan from within the community, whereas, only 20.83 per cent households have taken loan from the Bengalis the dominant non-tribal community in the region who have migrated into the region.

The study shows that almost 28.57 per cent of the total households (HHs) have taken loan from private unregistered sources of which around 68.11 per cent households have taken loans from other communities. Among the Scheduled Tribe communities, there are 28.77 per cent households who have taken loans from private sources of which 71.66 per cent loan is from other communities. Among the Scheduled Caste communities out of 20 HHs, or 60 per cent have taken loan from private sources are belonging to other community members. In general, except in Kandhamal the loan providers are not necessarily Scheduled Castes but belong to the general caste categories of whom few are in government service who also carry on the business of illegal money lending. At Lanjigarh of Kalahandi district while interacting with the selected government employees it was found that few teachers and one Revenue Inspector because of their long adherence to such practices have acquired landed property and are quite rich and enjoy higher social status in the locality. The study also reflects that those who lend money to the tribal people during their need are not the registered moneylenders. This at certain level justifies that though three decades have passed on, the impact of the policy of Orissa (Scheduled Area Moneylenders Policy of 1967, Orissa Regulation 2 of 1968) is yet to be seen in the rural villages. The data show that around 97.36 per cent tribal households have not heard of such a law framed by the State to help the tribal people to protect them from exploitative moneylenders.

Types of Loan Incurred

Data as regards the type of loan have been collected at two levels. The first one was to know the form of loan paid, i.e., in cash, kind or in both cash and kind; second, the terms and conditions of the loan, i.e., whether any mortgage kept against the payment of loan, rate of interest, etc. As regards the terms and conditions used while taking loan, the practices vary from district to district. In Penaposi Pangara village of Kandhamal district, mortgage of turmeric crop is preferred over land mortgage. Since turmeric has lasting (comparatively) market value and often fetches good profit, the Sundhi households who normally provide loans to the Kandha tribal households, prefer to keep crop mortgage against the loans paid throughout the year both in the form of cash and kind. In all other study villages, the terms and conditions for loan transactions always centres around the mortgage of agricultural land. It is a common practice that the loan amount is decided depending on the annual productive value of the land. The creditors normally take the agricultural produces during the mortgage period. Till the debtors do not return the principal the moneylender cultivates the land and takes the produces. Since the tribal people are unable to pay the interest in the from of cash to produce a guarantor before the moneylender, they have no other way out except putting their valuable agricultural land under mortgage. By this, the tribal households again lose their principal source of livelihood. Since tribal people are unable to repay the loan amount within the stipulated time period they become more marginalised with the passage of time. The interest rate in all the study villages varies. However, annually it varies from 35 to 50 per cent per hundred rupees per annum. Apart from cash loans, the loans are also paid in the form of kind in all the study villages. In Keonjhar district for a loan of 20 kgs of paddy seeds one has to pay 10 kgs of paddy per annum, whereas, paddy loan for consumption purposes carries 50 per cent less interest than the previous loan. However, loans in the form of kind should be repaid only in the form of kinds.

There are two typical system a of land mortgage found in Keudubaradihi village of Kalahandi district. They are known as *Uden* and *Buden* system. According to Uden system, the debtor has to give a land (best type) for 10 year periods and @ 10 per cent the amount will be deducted from the principal loan every year. In this way, the moneylender will enjoy the mortgaged land. Under Buden system if within the mortgaged period the debtor is unable to repay back the principal along with the interest then he loses the use right over the mortgaged land for another two consecutive years. In Lachipetta village of Malkangiri district, the practice of loan repayment is different. If the debtor is unable to repay the loan within the stipulated time then he has to pay back the amount by rendering free labour throughout the year till the loan money along with the interest is cleared.

The Baidyanath Commission has rightly pointed out that up to 1961, the lands were in the hands of 40 per cent population, which now has been concentrated with 20 per cent people.

Perhaps the change in the concentration of landholding in tribal areas has been largely due to moneylending process pertinently observed during the village study in this project. In Tungurubahal village of Keonjhar district, there are two systems of land mortgage. They are *Tankali* system in which the tribal people mortgage their best land for a period. During that period, the moneylender (who are normally general caste people) by using fertilisers, insecticides and pesticides tries to produce maximum yield. If the debtor does not return the principal within the stipulated period then the release of mortgaged land fully depends on the wish of the moneylender. In such a situation, conflict often arises between both the parties and the issue is normally decided in the village meeting. However, the matter is always solved within the village and never goes outside the boundary of the village. The villagers know well the weak base of such cases before the court of law. However, such practices are very rare. The second form of land mortgage against moneylending is known as *Karati Bandhak*. This practice now-a-days is rarely prevalent. In this form, one villager has to again act as the guarantor along with mortgaging his land. Because of the awareness and self-consciousness the villagers during lending do not feel the necessity of bringing a person as a guarantor when they give their land under mortgage. Thus, it can be concluded that land is mortgaged under certain conditions. The important terms of reference in the process of moneylending is that land remains under the control of the creditor. In this process, tribal people always lose their valuable land, which marginalises them to a greater extent.

Purpose of Loan

It is normally concluded by many that tribal people mortgage their land even for consumption of liquor. In order to find out the major reasons, for which tribal people go to the private moneylenders rather than to the scheduled banks, it is considered necessary to document the major purposes of their loan. Accordingly, the purposes are categorised as health reasons, family maintenance, social obligations, and other reasons. Analysis of the data reflect that in Keundubaradihi village of Kalahandi district health related reasons (42.85%) were followed by the social obligations (35.71%) and family maintenance which compels the tribal people to go for borrowing money; while in Tungurubahal village of Keonjhar district family maintenance (65.62%) is followed by health related reasons (25%) which forces the tribal people to go for barrowings. Similarly, in Penaposi Pangara village of Kandhamal, social obligations (28%) and treatment of sick family members (12%) followed by family maintenance (60%). In total one can say that the tribal people under the pressure of family maintenance (52.50%) go for private borrowing, which is again followed, by their social obligations (21.66%) and health related requirement (20.83%). The details of the different reasons for which the tribal people take loan are given in Table 5.2. This at one level justifies that tribal people always live in marginalised conditions, and unable to meet their basic requirements which forces them to go for private barrowings even at the cost of mortgaging their land – the only assured source of livelihood. In the process so as to repay, either they migrate outside for wage labour (regular source for a period) or force their children again to work as bonded labour in others' houses. The study shows that there were 60 cases of bonded labour.

Repayment Status of Loan

The study wanted to find out the repayment status of the loans incurred by the villagers taken during two consecutive years like 1999 and 2000. The data on the repayment of loans have been collected as fully paid, partly paid and not yet paid. The form of payment has also been documented. The data have been analysed according to ethnic groups in different districts. The analysis of the data reflects that in Kendubaradihi village of Kalahandi district, the payment of loan has been basically made through cash, and around 14.28 tribal households have not paid their loan dues. In Tungurubahal village of the Keonjhar district, almost 18.75 per cent tribal households had also paid their loan through kind, and 53.12 per cent of ST HHs have not repaid their loan at all. The tribal people have very small holdings and do not have much alternative sources of livelihood for repayment. In case of Penaposi

Table 5.2

Distribution of Households By Ethnicity according to the Purpose of Loan Taken From Private Sources During 1999-2000

District/Ethnic Group	*Total HHs Taken Loan*	*Household Distribution as per the Purpose of Loan*							
		Disease Treatment	*Per cent*	*Family Maintenance*	*Per cent*	*Social Obligation*	*Per cent*	*Other Purpose*	*Per cent*
Kalahandi									
Total	14 (100)	6	(42.85)	2	(14.28)	5	(35.71)	1	(7.14)
ST	14 (100)	6	(42.85)	2	(14.28)	5	(35.71)	1	(7.14)
SC	—	—	—	—	—	—	—		
OC	—	—	—	—	—	—	—		
Keonjhar									
Total	38 (100)	10	(26.31)	21	(55.26)	7	(18.42)	—	—
ST	32 (100)	8	(25.0)	21	(65.62)	3	(9.37)	—	—
SC	—	—	—	—	—	—	—	—	—
OC	6 (100)	2	(33.33)	—	—	4	(66.66)	—	—
Kandhamal									
Total	62 (100)	9	(14.51)	33	(53.22)	19	(30.64)	—	—
ST	50 (100)	6	(12.0)	30	(60.0)	14	(28.0)	—	—
SC	12 (100)	3	(25.00)	3	(25.00)	5	(41.66)	—	—
OC	—	—	—	—	—	—	—	—	—

Contd...

Contd...

Malkangiri									
Total	24 (100)	5	(20.83)	10	(41.66)	4	(16.66)	5	(20.83)
ST	24 (100)	5	(20.83)	10	(41.66)	4	(16.66)	5	(20.83)
SC	—	—	—	—	—	—	—	—	—
OC	—	—	—	—	—	—	—	—	—
Grand Total	138 (100)	30	(21.73)	66	(47.82)	35	(25.36)	6	(4.34)
ST	120 (100)	25	(20.83)	63	(52.50)	26	(21.66)	6	(5.0)
SC	12 (100)	3	(25.0)	3	(25.0)	5	(41.66)	—	—
OC	6 (100)	2	(33.33)	—	—	4	(66.66)	—	—

Pengara village of Kandhamal district, the tribal people as per the loan condition are paying their loans in the form of kind and there were 74 per cent households who had partly paid their loans. As per the conditions, outstanding loan is attached to their prospective turmeric produces. In Lachipetta village of Malkangiri district again the repayment of loans were made in the form of cash. Of the total debtor, almost 20.83 per cent tribal households in the village had not paid back their loan amount. In total, the analysis reflects that 46 borrowers in general had paid back the loans, whereas 62 households had partly paid their loans during the survey and 30 households had not paid back their loan at all. Coming to the tribal borrowers we found that out of 120 HHs 40 (33.33%) had paid their loan while 50 (41.66%) tribal HHs had partly paid back and there were 30 (25%) HHs who had not paid their loan at all.

Loan Received from Nationalised Banks and LAMPS

The study has also tried to find out the number of households who had received loans from the nationalised banks and LAMPS during the last five years from the period of 1994-95 to 1999-2000. Attempt was made to analyse the data according to the purposes of loan, total loan amount received and the status of loan repayment. Since the data regarding these were collected from secondary sources from concerned banks in Penaposi Pangara village of Kandhamal district, the bank authorities did not render timely help to provide data on the loan provided in the study village. In all other three study villages, the data were collected from the concerned banks. The analysis of the data reflect that 14.49 per cent ST households in Kendubaradihi village had received loan from Indian Overseas Bank for the purpose of agriculture (40%), livestock (40%) and land development (20%). The total amount given to the village was Rs. 76,870. In Tungurubahal village of Keonjhor district, of the total tribal households, only 21.96 per cent had received bank loan, which were basically invested in business (31.03%) and land development (41.37%). The villagers from State Bank of India at Jagamohanpur had received a total amount Rs. 6,33,506. Similarly in Lachipetta village of Malkangiri

Table 5.3

Distribution of Households by Ethnicity according to the Purpose of Loan Taken from Nationalised Banks During 1994-95 to 1999-2000

Districts/Ethnic Group	Total HHs	Purpose of Loan									
		Agriculture		Land Development		Livestock		Business		Any Others	
		No. of HH	Amount Received	No. of HH	Amount Received	No. of HH	Amount Received	No. of HH	Amount Received	No. of HH	Amount Received
Kalahandi											
Total	10	4	20000	2	18100	4	38770	—	—	—	—
	(100)	(40.0)		(20.00)		(40.00)					
ST	10	4	20000	2	18100	4	38770	—	—	—	—
	(100)	(40.0)		(20.00)		(40.00)					
SC	—	—	—	—	—	—	—	—	—	—	—
OC	—	—	—	—	—	—	—	—	—	—	—
Keonjhar											
Total	46	5	43532	17	235183	1	20000	16	231891	7	102900
	(100)	(10.86)		(36.95)		(2.17)		(34.78)		(15.21)	
ST	29	—	—	12	151708	1	20000	9	84216	7	102900
	(100)	—	—	(41.37)		(3.44)		(31.03)		(24.13)	
SC	—	—	—	—	—	—	—	—	—	—	—
OC	17	5	4332	5	83475	—	—	7	147675	—	—
	(100)	(29.41)		(29.41)				(41.17)			

Contd...

Contd...

Kandhamal											
Total	75	—	—	—	—	—	—	—	—	—	—
ST	50	—	—	—	—	—	—	—	—	—	—
		Data	Data not available	—	—	—	—	—	—	—	—
SC	20	—	—	—	—		—	—	—	—	—
OC	5	—	—	—	—	—	—	—	—	—	—
Malkangiri											
Total	110	110	1,24,153	—	—	—	—	—	—	—	—
	(100)	(100.00)		—	—	—	—	—	—	—	—
ST	110	110	1,24,153	—	—	—	—	—	—	—	—
	(100)	(100.00)		—	—	—	—	—	—	—	—
SC	—	—	—	—	—	—	—	—	—	—	—
OC	—	—	—	—	—	—	—	—	—	—	—
Grand Total	166	119	187685	19	253283	5	58770	16	231891	7	102900
	(100)	(72.12)		(11.51)		(3.03)		(9.69)		(4.24)	
ST	148	114	144153	14	169808	5	58770	9	84216	7	102900
	(100)	(77.02)		(9.45)		(3.37)		(6.08)		(4.72)	
SC	—	—	—	—	—	—	—	—	—	—	—
OC	17	5	43532	5	83475	—	—	7	147675	—	—
	(36.95)	(29.41)		(29.41)		—	—	(41.17)		—	—

Note: * Figure in parentheses are percentage of total.

district, all the tribal households had received bank loan from Panchabati Gramya Bank situated at MV 79 which were basically invested in agricultural development.

In total, the data reflect that out of the total tribal households covered in the study, 35.49 per cent households had received bank loan. These households had primarily taken loan for development of agriculture (77.02%), followed by land development (9.45%) and for taking up petty business (6.08%). The details of data on bank loan according to different ethnic groups are given in Table 5.3.

Repayment of Bank Loan

Data have also been collected from the concerned households as regards the repayment of loan amount to the banks. It has been observed that at the beginning the loan disbursement procedures were not free from personal factors. While discussing with the bank employees it was found that in many cases the loan amounts were not used for the purposes as it was provided. Secondly, lack of adequate staff in the bank results in poor monitoring of the implementation activities. As a result, the poor tribal people get scope to divert the money for day-to-day livelihood purposes. Thirdly, the tribal people take it for granted that the loan money will be declared non-refundable by the ruling government. So, they do not like to repay the loan amount. The details of household-wise distribution by ethnicity as regards repayment of loan taken from nationalised banks are explained in the Table 5.4.

Wage Labour (Loan Ties)

The tribal people are exploited through 'wage labour' and/or loan-tie-*Goti* system (Kulkarni, 1979; Roth, 1979). In both the systems, the poor tribal is given loan in the form of cash and kind basically to meet the social obligations and/or to maintain regular livelihood with a condition to repay the advance by rendering free labour (in several cases). Keeping this in view, the Orissa Debt Bondage Abolition Regulation Act 1948 (Orissa Regulation 1 of 1948) was promulgated with a view to abolishing the system of debt bondage. This regulation had provisioned for certain kinds of labour in the Ganjam Agency Tracts, the district of Koraput

Table 5.4

Distribution of Households by Ethnicity according to Repayment of Loan Taken from Nationalised Banks During 1994-95 to 1999-2000

District/ Ethnic Group	Loan Taken		Household Distribution as per Loan Repayment Status			
	No. of HH	Amount (Rs.)	No. of HH	Per cent	Amount Paid	Per cent
Kalahandi						
Total	10 (100)	76,870 (100)	2	20.00	6806	8.85
ST	10 (100)	76,870 (100)	2	20.00	6806	8.85
SC	—	—	—	—	—	—
OC	—	—	—	—	—	—
Keonjhar						
Total	46 (100)	6,33,506 (100)	10	21.73	26,243	4.14
ST	29 (100)	3,58,824 (100)	6	20.68	3,625	1.01
SC	—	—	—	—	—	—
OC	17 (100)	2,74,682 (100)	4	23.52	22,618	8.23
Kandhamal						
Total	NA	NA	NA	NA	NA	NA
ST	NA	NA	NA	NA	NA	NA
SC	NA	NA	NA	NA	NA	NA
OC	NA	NA	NA	NA	NA	NA
Malkangiri						
Total	110 (100)	1,24,153 (100)	—	—	—	0
ST	110 (100)	1,24,153 (100)	—	—	—	0
SC	—	—	—	—	—	—
OC	—	—	—	—	—	—
Grand Total	165 (100)	8,34,529 (100)	12	7.27	33,049	3.96
ST	148 (100)	5,59,847 (100)	8	5.4	10,431	1.86
SC	—	—	—	—	—	—
OC	17 (100)	2,74,682 (100)	4	23.52	22618	8.23

N.A.: Not Available.

(undivided) and Nuapara sub-division which are Partially Excluded Areas of the province which later on covered under the Scheduled Area of the State. Likewise, the Bonded Labour System (Abolition) Act 1976 (Act 19 of 1976), a Central Act has its operational jurisdiction over the entire State. Under this Act, no person shall make any advance under, or in pursuance of the bonded labour system, and compel any person to render any bonded labour or other forms of forced labour.

The data collected from different study villages reflect that the problem of bonded labour still exists in various forms in almost all the villages of different districts. These cases among the tribal households vary from 11.59 per cent (the minimum) as observed in Kalahandi district to a maximum of 22 per cent (as observed) in Kandhamal district. All these cases of bonded labour are linked to their indebtedness, which have been paid back through labour and partly through cash. Since the moneylending transactions between the tribal people and the moneylenders (who are virtually non-tribals) is made through undocumented manner, it is very difficult to trace back the linkages between indebtedness and tribal wage-labour. Basically, it is the poor tribal households who repay their debt through physical labour.

An attempt has been made to find out the ethnic background of the creditor who later on became the bonded labour-recruiting households. Except Malkangiri where the Scheduled Castes resettler Bengali households (63.15%) engage the debtors as bonded labourers, in all other districts the creditor households belong to general caste categories who play a major role both in moneylending and recruiting the debtors as bonded labour. In total, the study shows that households belonging to SC categories recruiting tribal debtors as bonded labour are less (20) compared to the households belonging to general caste categories.

The study also attempted to find out the age status of such labourers. In Kendubaradihi village of Kalahandi district, it has been found that children comprise 37.5 per cent and youths constitute 62.5 per cent. This at certain level justifies that the children and youths are forced into this practice against the loan taken by their respective families. Similar situation has been found out in case of Penaposi Pangara of Kandhamal and Lachipetta village of Malkangiri. However, in case of Tungurubahal, the adult and old members of the family along with others repay the loan through free labour. In total, the study found out that 89.99 per cent bonded labour are children and youths who are the easy haunt of the process of indebtedness. This correlates when one observes the poor literacy achievement among these groups. Examples of such attack on children and youths for forceful bonded labour are many and goes unrecorded in the government, even if such cases are highlighted through news media. In Telkoi block of Keonjhar district, 9 ST children within the age group of 10-12 years have been working as child labour outside the State (*Sambad*, an Oriya daily dated 2 April, 2001). Such cases of supplying tribal girls and boys to outside agencies are more frequent in the districts of Sundargarh, Kandhamal, Nuapara and Nawarangpur. The exploitative role of mediators, who are normally non-tribal, is the key factor in such processes.

The terms and conditions for recruiting these bonded labourers vary. In Tungurubahal of Keonjhar district, it is observed that these labourers are preferred for engagement during agricultural season, particularly during the months of June and July and again during the harvest period of September and October of the year. The landowner knows that work can be extracted from these people only during peak agricultural periods. The wage (in local rate) supposed to be paid to them is deducted from the loan. However, the landowner provides them a major meal and one light meal every day free of cost. Since they are engaged for short periods (at a stretch) twice a year and payments are calculated through local rates, it is obvious that an indebted labour is engaged for a period of 3 to 4 years for repayment of the loan amount. In all the study villages, the young boys are preferred for engagement for a year or two through local terms and conditions. The amount settled for their annual payment is either deducted totally or partially from the loan advanced to their family. However, the landowners provide one major meal and two light meals per day to the loan-tied labour. Such practices are popular in the tribal areas. It is very difficult for an outsider to understand the dynamics of labour-tie with indebtedness.

Conclusion

In spite of the legislations made by the State to curb the problem of moneylending in the tribal societies, the ground realities have been changed to a lesser extent. Even the rule to issue licenses to the moneylender has not been implemented as desired. The practice of moneylending has inflated the rate of interest and encouraged bonded labour in the tribal area. The policies in this regard are also not complete by themselves. For example, the Bihar Money Lending Act recognised that a moneylender can have business of rupees five hundred only, which seems to be deficient because very few moneylenders will come forward to present their business accounting over and above Rs. 500 to the government. Moneylending in our State is so intertwined during the time of urgency that it is very difficult to root it out through various laws.

Enactment of laws will not solve the invisible problem of moneylending where a majority of the tribal people (in tribal area) faces difficulties to eke out their two square meals a day. The proposal of providing various time-bound loans through local cooperatives has not been implemented satisfactorily. Although this measure has been implemented by the State, it has failed to meet their timely requirements. In case of Orissa, the establishment of LAMPS, TDCCOL and their poor achievements over the years are the examples before the State and statecrafts. The functioning of these credit institutions does not have organic linkages with the tribal marketing networks, which has not been attuned to the needs of the tribal economy. In fact, consumer credit is a misnomer and unless it is accepted as one of the most primary forms of production credit, the reluctance of the system to accord the importance of the so-called consumption credit is crucial for the poor men's economy (Sharma, 1994:88). The report of the Scheduled Area and Scheduled Tribes Commission, and Planning Commission's report of the study team on Tribal Development programmes find the causes of this situation. It seems the State Government has not made adequate use of the protective provisions of the Fifth Schedule to provide protection to the tribal people against these problems. The State Government has not been able to make effective use of the penal provisions in their existing legislation against evasion by moneylenders. Lack of will-power and commitment by the agencies involved in the process are largely responsible for the continued exploitation of the tribal people by the greedy moneylenders. It is a fact that unless the tribal people are provided with long-term support to increase their purchasing capacity and to enhance their income level, it is fruitless to expect to free the tribal people from the clutches of the moneylenders.

Suggestions

- The case of indebtedness accompanied by oral or under customary arrangements or written agreements for bonded labour legislation should be passed forthwith treating the agreements as void, arrangements as offences, the debt as discharged and the labour as released. The tribal will not be in a position to stand up against the creditor so long as the burden of debt survives. An agreement of this nature should be declared not only illegal but an offence punishable severely.
- The Scheduled Areas and Scheduled Tribe Commission have considered the question of total abolition for old debts and the question of reconciliation. The Commission felt that a practical programme would have to be worked out so as not to destroy the credit which the tribals possess today until it is possible for the Government or the cooperatives to take up the responsibility to provide effective alternative credit to a reasonable extent.
- It is suggested that the non-official agencies should undertake the responsibility of educating the tribals that too much borrowing does harm not only to themselves, but also to their

future generation. There should be proper educative propaganda about the new legislation as and when undertaken (U.N. Dhebar, 1963).

- It was alleged that the moneylenders charge exorbitant rates of interest for the loans given to them as a result of which they always remain indebted to the moneylenders. It is suggested that the State Government should take necessary action to arrange for the sanction of consumption loans to the tribals through the LAMPS, so that the tribals do not have to depend on moneylenders for their urgent need. The role of cooperatives in the tribal areas is still insignificant. Attempts should be made to develop and function those societies in large areas. Those societies will collect the various agricultural produces and cottage industry products of the tribals and arrange for their marketing. It will also finance and issue loans to them on easy and simplified procedure and will generally strengthen the economy of the tribal people.
- Self-Help Women Groups (SHGs) promoted by NABARD and under different programmes of both State and Central Government have been playing a crucial role in ensuring the livelihood of the tribal people. This has immense impact in minimising the extent of indebtedness of the tribals. Such like women empowerment process should be made and strengthened in tribal areas.
- Tribals are largely earning their livelihood from agriculture and minor forest produces. Due to distress sale they do not fetch a good price. The value addition of surplus agriculture produces and minor forest produces can increase the market price of these produces and fetch more money for them. The value addition processes of these produces have been experimented by many NGOs and NABARD in certain tribal regions. This has to be widely propagated.
- More importance should be given for the creation of immovable and durable assets like horticulture, sericulture, irrigation wells, check dams, rehabilitation of shifting cultivators, etc.

- Special assistance schemes should be implemented centring livelihood issues of the tribals in a more integrated and holistic manner.
- The protective regulations so far available have to be suitably amended and more stringent regulations to be made relating to livelihood issues.

6 Tribal Land Alienation

India, the largest country in South Asia, covers an area of 3,288 thousand square kilometres, and has a population of 1,016 million (World Development Report, 2002). This country, while accounting for 2.42 per cent of the total world area, accommodates nearly 35 per cent households who are living below the poverty line (BPL) and are deprived of the basic amenities of living (ibid.). Till the end of 1990-91, the bottom 58.99 per cent marginal farmers, operated only 14.87 per cent of the total cropped area, while the top 1.59 per cent of large farmers operated as much as 17.45 per cent (CMIE, 1998) of land. In spite of this, land is the primary necessity of ruralites. Though 60.1 per cent of the total work force is dependent on agriculture, this segment, however, contributes to only 27.4 per cent of the GDP (GoI, 1999). The reasons for low productivity may be inadequate irrigation facility, inefficient cropping patterns, lack of appropriate distribution system of seeds and fertilisers, low levels of mechanisation, natural calamities and outdated agrarian policies. In addition to the large landholdings, unregulated tenancy and fragmented holdings cause poverty (GoI, ibid.). The equity dimension of land distribution is equally important like that of the productivity. The average size of holding for marginal farmers is 0.40 hectare, while the large landholders own an average of 17.30 hectares. The marked disparities of landholding in a society not only yields economic, social, politico and cultural disabilities, but also, reflects poor access to health care services, education, and to the rural power structure.

This is the reason for the low ranking of human development in India, which can be directly traced back to the distorted distribution of landholding in the country.

Land gives a sense of belonging to humans and provides life support system to the people. Land has very significant impact on the life and livelihood of tribal people. Understanding the reserve value of land, people always try to possess it as much as possible. In this process of land grabbing, the poor tribals have been affected more. Because of their acute poverty, super natural beliefs and backwardness, the tribal people fell easy prey to moneylenders, traders and exploiters. With the opening of tribal areas to the non-tribals and to the State, the processes in the name of development thereupon adopted in tribal economy have resulted in large-scale land alienation from tribal land to non-tribals or to the State. The fact is that alienating tribals from their age-old land is largely due to their inability to discharge the loan liabilities incurred by them, or due to the policy inadequacies, which could not retain land with the tribals. This may also has been due to State interventions in tribal areas in the name of development.

In order to understand these processes and the state of affairs, the first section of this chapter describes the land reform measures, so far taken, in general and in tribal area of the State in particular. The second section describes the major legislations and the provisions therein, which have been undertaken by the State in the post-independence period to restrict alienation of tribal land and to restore the alienated land of tribal people. The third section deals with the empirical study and analyses the impact of these policies on tribal people in tribal regions. Analysis of the problem is based on collection of both quantitative and qualitative data, which tries to explain the role of the State in safeguarding the interest of the tribals.

The objective here is to answer certain basic questions constantly raised by several scholars from time to time. What changes one observe in the extent, nature and mechanisms adopted by non-tribal and different agencies to alienate tribal people from their land resources? Whether the safeguards so far we have designed to protect the interests of the tribal people on land are sufficient enough? What are the major changes that is required in the existing policies so far we have in our State?

I

Historical Overview

British rule in India has strongly influenced the land management and revenue policies, which were basically exploitative in nature. The long exploitation and suppression of the tribals and poor had resulted rebellions one after another. A few such movements were the Chota Nagpur Tribal Revolt (1807-08), Munda Rebellion (1832, 1867-08), Kol Rebellion (1831-32), Santal Rebellion (1885-86), Rampha Rebellion (1879-90) and Madri Kalo Revolt (1898) had not only challenged the British Rule in India, but also became the major threat to them. The British understood the strength of these movements and later on enacted certain rules and regulations to pacify the rebellions. A few of them are the Chotanagpur Tenancy Act 1908, Central Provinces Land Alienation Act 1916, Bihar Tenancy Act 1885, and Bombay Land Revenue Code (Section 73A). These regulations did not get sufficient attention from the British, rather helped the upper caste elites, who were landlords, moneylenders, zamindars, and other intermediaries, who were the agents of the British in India. Similarly, a couple of tribal movements, which took place during the early 20th century, were mostly agrarian by nature. All these movements generated pressure on the State to protect and promote the land rights of the poor tribals and lower caste peasants (Ekka and Danda, 1979; Das, 1983; Dhanagare, 1983). Each of the movements was followed by some legislative or ameliorative measures (Dhanagare, 1983). There were a couple of social reform movements that took place in India with anti-brahminical overtones, which provided the lower castes with a distinct identity and awakened the government to recognise the rights of these deprived groups and to undertake measures for the removal of social injustice and exploitation (Patankar and Omvedt, 1979; Ranadive, 1979; Ram, 1979).

In the post-independence period, land reform being the State subject under the Constitution of India falls under Entry 18 of the State List. The Directive Principles of State Policy (DPSP) also refers to the objectives contained in the programme for land reforms, though it does so indirectly. Clause (a) of DPSP is evident that citizen, men and women equally have the right to an adequate means of livelihood. Clause (b) makes it evident that the ownership and control of the resources of the community are distributed to serve the common good. As per Clause (c) of the DPSP, the operation of economic system does not result in the concentration of wealth and means of production to the common detriment.

The premise behind the land reform in India has always been to do away with the inequities prevalent in the system of landholding, and to increase productivity. Enactment of legislations has been the basis of action through which the government has tried to redress the problems of intermediaries, tenants, ceilings, and consolidation, etc. The Kumarappa Committee (1949) has enormous influence on the formulation of land reform policies in India. The major recommendation made by this committee includes complete elimination of all intermediaries between the State and the tillers. The tiller must enjoy the right of ownership over the land. The personal cultivation should be clearly spelt out basing on the inclusion of physical labour and participation in agricultural activities. The need for reforming the laws for regulating the ownership and operation of landholdings as well as providing security to the tenants has been the focus. In India, in total, there are 82 land reform legislations, 10 ceiling, 70 tenancy, 4 abolition of intermediaries, 3 on consolidation and 4 others, passed by different State Governments at various times (Table 6.1). All these laws have helped in land acquisition and redistribution of land to the landless, aims to abolish the intermediaries and in reducing the absentee landlords, provided ownership rights and security of tenure to tenants, and in consolidating the holdings for better management of land.

Table 6.1

Distribution of Important Legislatures on Land Alienation in Different States and Union Territories of India

States/Union Territories	*Act/Regulations*
Andhra Pradesh	1. The Andhra Pradesh (Scheduled Areas) Land Transfer Regulation, 1959.
	2. The Andhra Pradesh (Scheduled Areas) Land Transfer (Amendment) Regulation, 1970, 1971 and 1978.
Assam	The Assam Land and Revenue Regulation, 1886.
Bihar and Jharkhand	1. Chota Nagpur Tenancy Act, 1908.
	2. Santhal Pragana Tenancy (Supplementary Provisions) Act, 1949.
	3. Bihar Scheduled Area Regulations, 1969.
Gujarat	1. Mumbai Land Revenue Code, 1879.
	2. Mumbai Land Revenue (Gujarat Section Amendment) Act, 1980.
Himachal Pradesh	The Himachal Pradesh Transfer of Land (Regulation) Act, 1968.
Karnataka	1. Land Revenue (Amendment) Rule, 1960.
	2. The Karnataka Scheduled Castes and Scheduled Tribes (Prohibition of Transfer of Certain Lands) Act, 1978.
Kerala	1. Kerala Land Assignment Rules, 1964.
	2. The Kerala Scheduled Tribes (Restoration of Transfer of Land and Restoration of Alienated Lands) Act, 1978.
Madhya Pradesh (undivided)	Madhya Pradesh Land Revenue Code, 1959.
Maharashtra	1. Maharashtra Land Revenue Code and Amendment Act, 1974.
	2. The Maharashtra (Restoration of Lands to Scheduled Tribes) Act, 1974.
Manipur	Manipur Land Revenue and Land Reforms Act, 1960.
Orissa	1. The Orissa Scheduled Areas Transfer of Immovable Property Property in the Scheduled Areas Regulation, 1956 (Regulation 2 of 1956).
	2. The Orissa Scheduled Areas Transfer of Immovable Property (Scheduled Tribes Regulations) Amendment, 1965.
Rajasthan	1. Rajasthan Tenancy Act, 1955 (Sections 42,43, 46A and 49A).
	2. The Registration (Rajasthan Amendment) Act, 1976.

Contd...

Contd...

Tamil Nadu		The Revenue Boards Order (A 10 years Binding for Land Alienation in Tamil Nadu).
Tripura	1.	Tripura Land Revenue and Land Reforms Act, 1968 (Section 187).
	2.	Tripura Land Revenue and Land Reforms Act, 1974.
Uttar Pradesh	1.	Uttar Pradesh Jamindari Vinash and Bhumi Vyavastha (Sansodhan) Adhiniyan, 1969 (Section 157).
	2.	Uttar Pradesh Alienation of Land Reforms Act, 1950 as amended by the U.P. Land Laws (Amendment and Ordinance, 1981).
West Bengal	1.	West Bengal Land Reforms Act, 1955.
	2.	West Bengal Land Reforms (Amendment) Act, 1955.
Arunachal Pradesh		Bengal Eastern Frontier Regulation, 1873.
Nagaland	1.	Bengal Eastern Frontier Regulation, 1873 and 1886.
	2.	Nagaland Revenue Regulation (Amendment) Act, 1971.
Meghalaya		Meghalaya Transfer of Land (Regulation) Act, 1971.
Andaman and Nicobar Islands		Andaman and Nicobar Islands (Protection of Aboriginal Tribes) Regulation, 1956.
Lakshadweep		Lakshsdweep (Protection of Scheduled Tribes) Regulation, 1964.
Dadra and Nagar Haveli		Dadra and Nagar Haveli Land Reforms Regulations, 1971.

Source: Collected from various sources.

The abolition of intermediaries has been ensured through the formulation of laws in almost all the States. While analysing all these laws, it is established that all laws brought the principal tenants on lands outside the intermediaries hoe-farm into a direct relationship with the State. Except West Bengal, Assam, Hyderabad, and Jammu and Kashmir, no limit was imposed on the area of the home farm; and all laws provided provisions for compensation to the ex-intermediaries. In spite of these measures, the results are not encouraging and have varied impact in different States. In later periods, millions of tenants became landowners. In India, around 36.6 per cent of the total land reform related legislations have devoted to tenancy issues. Various States and Union Territories have enacted 82 legislations concludes the following observations. They are as follows:

- The State laws passed for the eradication of intermediaries and with regard to ceiling vary in provisions.
- The inheritable rights of the tenants have been protected through these laws except in few situations.
- The redistribution of land by different States in principle has more or less protected the interests of the Scheduled Tribes and Scheduled Castes.
- Special provisions have been made in all States having a sizeable tribal population to protect them from alienation of their land.

In spite of these provisions, the country has witnessed a couple of peasant movements even in post-independence India. Telangana Movement, one of the most politically effective movements of the century, fought for the rights over the land. Naxalbari movement in West Bengal, Bihar, Andhra Pradesh started during the years of 1967-70 still demands for the land to the tiller through forced redistribution and share in produces. The land struggle in Bodh Gaya in the year 1978 also focussed on secure land rights. The peasants demanded that the land be legally registered in the names of the tillers, and also that women be given these rights. The Bhoodan and Gramdan Movement from 1952 to 1969 has execrated the process of land reform in the country.

Land Reform in Orissa

In the first half of the 19th century, after the confiscation of few States like Banki (1840), Kandhamal (1840), Angul (1947), the British had introduced revenue system like *muthadari* in Orissa (Pathy, 1987). In Ganjam district of Madras Presidency, about 40 per cent land were under inamdari tenure system. In Sambalpur region, apart from 17 Zamindars, the Malguzari tenure system was also introduced in 1867. The proprietorship interest in Sambalpur region were of five types: Gauntia, Malguzari, Bhogara Bhogis, Malik Makbuzas and Brahmotar.

About 90 per cent of the tenants in Sambalpur were occupancy tenants who were put to great difficulty on account of statutory restrictions on the transfer of their property (Mishra, 1962:24). The undivided Koraput district had two types of land administration system like *reyatwari* and *mustajhari* system (OLA, 1937). In Dhenkanal district, since there was no Zamindari the tenure holders were known as Debottar, Brahmottar and Zagir. Similarly, in Phulbani (undivided) district apart from the systems, which were practised in Dhenkanal district, the additional systems in practice were khorak *posak* or maintenance and Jhupapan (spittle). In Bolangir district, the land tenure system was based on Gauntia, Umrah, Maufi Bhogars, Pattidars and Sub-Pattidars system. The Mayurbhanj district was also under the Zamindari system of land administration. In Sundargarh district, the whole tenure system of land was based on Zamindari, Praganadari, Debottor, Brahmottar, Nuakaran, Head Ganjuani, Gonjuani, Sikmi Gaontiahi were varying from region to region. Looking at the variegated situations of land tenure system towards the last part of the British, the Orissa Land Revenue and Land Tenure Committee was established in 1946 to recommend legislative measures to make an uniform, equitable and elastic form of land administration.

Historically the land system of tribal region varies from region to region and community to community. Reformulation of various small States particularly in tribal area has also largely influenced the land-related laws of the tribal communities. An attempt in following section is made to highlight a few major dominant land systems prevalent in various parts of tribal Orissa. Since Koraput (undivided) and Mayurbhanj districts have been declared as full Scheduled districts in post-independence era, therefore, tribal dominance in both the districts has influenced to form exclusive patterns compared to many other tribal regions.

In Koraput (undivided) district, the land administration started with the Silabansi Kings of Nandapur in 14th century AD and subsequently handed over to the Rajas of Jaypore. However, the Gajapati King of Puri had also partial control over the lands in certain areas during 16th century (District Gazetteer, 1966). The British entered the undivided Koraput district in 1863 and took no interest on land issues of the district. The district followed similar pattern of land policy as was prevalent in Madras Presidency. As a result, Saheed Laxman Naik revolted and organised a local agitation against the British. The Madras Estate Land Act 1908, largely influenced it. The record of right in the district by the government started only during 1940s. The tribal people of the Koraput (undivided) district being induced by the moneylenders and other non-tribal people alienated from their landholdings in cheaper prices (Orissa District Gazetteer, 1966). In spite of the promulgation of Agency Tracts Interests and Land Transfer Act in 1917, its effect in Agency tract area of the State was not satisfactory and the extent of land alienation of the tribal people were not reduced. It was largely because this law was an incomplete one, not clear in several respects and was amended from time to time by the Government of Orissa in 1943 and by the Government of Madras in 1918, 1927, 1931, and 1932. Thus, any transfer of tribal land to non-tribal in undivided Koraput district in early 1918 was not considered as illegal.

The Angul District Regulation, 1894 was in operation in the Kandhamal and Angul sector till 1913 was also incomplete in several respects. In later periods, during 1902, the Deputy Commissioner issued an order regarding the mortgage, gift and sale of land to outsiders and non-agriculturists. This law became a part of Angul District Regulation in 1913. After the State formation, Kandhamal was separated and attached to the system, which was in practice in Ganjam district, and similarly Angul was attached to the system prevalent in Cuttack district with two distinct laws separately for Angul and Kandhamal. Finally, the Angul Laws Regulation of 1912 and Kandhamal Laws Regulation of 1936 were in operation till independence.

During 1918, it was felt through a survey that in spite of the laws to restrict land alienation from tribal people to non-tribal people a good quantity of land of Kandh people have been lost through different means like mortgage, sale, gift, lease, to the non-Kandhs. This clearly indicates that alienation of tribal land to non-tribal people is an age-old phenomenon. In spite of the laws, though inadequate to prevent the interests of the tribal people, the alienation process was operating silently and slowly.

Before formation of the State of Orissa, Sambalpur was under the Central Provinces Act. Under the Central Provinces Land

Revenue Act, 1881 and 1917 and the C.P. Tenancy Act, 1898 and 1920 the transfer of land from tribal hand to non-tribal people was regulated. These laws were also implemented in Bargarh. Later on, during 1953, the Orissa Act XIII of 1953, however, amended the then laws and provisioned the transfer of land through various means imposing restrictions on the tribal communities on transfer of land to non-tribal people. During 1950, when the Scheduled Area of the State was declared, Sambalpur district was not included under it. This led to the withdrawal of all earlier provisions, which were protecting the interest of the tribal people living in this district. Understanding the tribal concentration in certain pockets that demands special provisions, Kuchinda a tehsil of the district was declared as Scheduled Area during 1977.

While realising the differences at the grass-root, the Government of India Act 1919 categorically divided the area as Partial and Fully Scheduled Area and Non-Scheduled Area. The basic objective was to bring certain socio-economic reforms among the tribal people as well as in the regions. The Simon Commission Report of 1930 also mentioned "there were two dangers to which tribal people would have specially exposed. These people are primitive, simple, unsophisticated and frequently, un-provident. There was a risk of their agricultural land passing to the more civilised section of the population, and secondly, they were likely to get into the viles of the moneylenders". The primary aim of the government policy then was to protect them from these two dangers and preserve their tribal customs and this was achieved by prescribing special procedures applicable to these backward areas.

During State formation in 1936, the State of Orissa had a very skewed system of land control, widespread tenancy situation, and un-speculative *debitor* and creditor relations. A good number of tenancy regulations have been formulated in the State in different time periods. They are as follows:

- The Orissa Tenancy Act (Amendment) of 1946 as regards the homestead lands confers the occupancy to *royats*, under *royats* and services tenure holders;

- The Orissa Tenancy (Amendment) Act of 1947 enforces the division of land bounds;
- The Madras Estate Land (Orissa Second Amendments) Act 1946 conferred the occupancy rights in *inam* villages;
- The Orissa Command Forest and Private Lands (Prohibition of Alienation) Act 1948 prevented landlords alienating certain classes of lands without the permission of Collector;
- The Orissa Tenants Protection Act 1948 temporarily protected the tenants against eviction and also assured a fixed rent for produce; and
- The Orissa Tenant Relief of 1955 repealing the Orissa Tenants Protection Act of 1948 prevented large-scale eviction of tenants from actual cultivation of land and conferred certain rights on them.

Prior to the promulgation of Orissa Regulation 2 of 1956, the position existing in the ex-States before merger of Orissa, occupancy tenants belonging to certain castes and tribes could transfer their lands only with the permission of the *Durbar* competent Revenue authority. Administration of Orissa States Order 1948 (Paragraph 10) which came into force in all the ex-States excluding Mayurbhanj on 1 January, 1948, mentioned that an occupancy tenant would be entitled to freely transfer his holding. This is subject to the restriction that no transfer of any holding of a member of the aboriginal tribe shall be valid unless such transfer is made with the previous permission of the Administrator or the Sub-Divisional Magistrate. The term 'Aboriginal Tribe' was defined in the said order to mean any "tribe that may from time to time be notified as such by the provincial government for the purpose of this order". Till the integration of ex-State Mayurbhanj though the similar provision was made in Paragraph–II of the Administration of Mayurbhanj State Order 1949 notification was however, issued by government defining the term 'Aboriginals Tribe' which continued up to the 22 May, 1962.

Again a person belonging to Scheduled Tribe needs prior permission of a competent authority to transfer his/her immovable property put in 1956 was only confined to the

Scheduled Area of the State. In respect to the ex-State areas other than the district of Mayurbhanj and Sundargarh, the restrictions contained in the Orissa Merged States (Laws) Act, 1950 came into force with effect from 22 May, 1962.

In the ex-State areas the position prior to 1956 was as follows:

- Prior to merger, i.e., 1 January, 1948 in all ex-States except Mayurbhanj, ex-State law of restriction in respect of transfer of lands (by an aboriginal Tribe in favour of a non-aboriginal Tribe) were applicable.
- Prior to merger, i.e., before 1 January, 1949 in ex-States of Mayurbhanj, ex-State law was applicable.
- In the ex-State of Sundargarh and Mayurbhanj up to 3 October, 1956 there was no restriction on transfer of land by occupancy tenant whether or not he belonged to a Scheduled Tribe.
- In other ex-States from merger till 21 May, 1962 there was no restriction on transfer of land by occupancy tenant whether or not belonging to a Scheduled Tribe.
- In other ex-States from 21 May, 1962 the merged States (Laws) Act is applicable and operative in other merged States from 21 May, 1962.

Agency Tracts of Ex-Madras Area

Prior to the enforcement of the Regulation 2 of 1956 in Koraput (excluding Kashipur) Agency portion of Ganjam district and Balliguda Sub-Division of Boudh Kandhamal district, the Agency Tracts Interest and Land Transfer Act, 1917 (Madras Act I of 1917) was applicable. Up till the enforcement of Regulation 2 of 1956, in Kandhamal Sub-Division of Boudh-Kandhamal district, the Kandhamal Laws Regulation, 1936 was applicable. Proviso to Clause (b) of Section (2), Section 46 of the C.P. Tenancy Act 1998 as amended by the Orissa Act XIII of 1953 applies to Bargarh and Sambalpur Sub-Divisions. Nuapada Sub-Division of Kalahandi district also put restrictions regarding transfer of land by Scheduled Tribes to others which continued to be in force in the respective areas till 1 October, 1965, when the Orissa Land Reforms Act 1960 was brought into force. In the remaining areas, there were no such laws and hence there was no restriction on transfer of land by an Adivasi to a non-Adivasi till the date of enforcement of the Orissa Land Reform Act 1960, i.e., 1 October, 1965.

For the first time in 1879, the Land Revenue Code of Bombay Presidency prohibited the transfer of land from a tribal to non-tribal. Similar laws were also passed in Gujarat during 1901 in which permission was sought from the Collector for the transfer of tribal land to the non-tribal people, whereas, the Deputy Commissioner was the sanctioning authority in Bihar under Chotanagpur Tenancy Act of 1908 and also in Karnataka in 1978. The Santhal Pragana Tenancy (Supplementary Provisions) Act of 1949 and the Bihar Scheduled Area Regulations, 1969 also prohibits the alienation of land of the tribal people. The Rajasthan Tenancy Act, 1955 as amended in 1956 and Madhya Pradesh Land Alienation Procedure Code 1959 both prohibit the alienation of tribal land. In the State of Andhra Pradesh, Scheduled Area Land Transfer Regulation 1959 and subsequent amendment in 1970 provides both for restriction for land alienation and restoration of alienated land. Apart from this, in various States like Tripura (1960), Assam (1964), Himachal Pradesh (1968), Manipur (1970) Sikkim (1977) different laws relating to the land reform, alienation and restoration in different forms have also been effected to protect the interests of the tribal people against the non-tribal.

Maintenance of Strong Corporate Social Ties

The tribal communities of Orissa are socio-economically backward which is reflected in their economy, technology, polity, level of skill, worldview and knowledge, etc. They largely adhere to food gathering, hunting and shifting cultivation with rudimentary technologies, gender-based division of labour and pre-capitalist modes of production, consumption, distribution and exchange. Their entire social organisation and structural arrangements are largely characterised by strong corporate social ties. These are guided by various norms, customary laws and social sanctions, enforced through traditional functional structures known as Mutha, Pirha, Mandal, and Pragana. This system has been often interpreted as an expression of the social-backwardness of the tribals.

The advent of mining, industries, and hydro-electric mega-projects have influenced some tribal communities to merge with the dominant stream, but many continue to live in the transitional stage, not finding in the dominant stream the appropriate reference group for their sustainable development. The dilemma of this development is evident in Sundargarh, Koraput, Keonjhar and Mayurbhanj (Panda 1982; Pathy, 1987 and 1982; Behura and Panigrahi, 2001; Panigrahi, 2001). Shifting cultivation still continues to dominate the life of many tribal groups of Orissa. However, partial departure from this practice is observed due to the result of State intervention, population growth, and the imposition of the legal system of individual holdings. Many tribal groups such as the Juanga, Bhuiyan, Kondh of all categories, Saura, Paraja, Didayi, Bonda and Koya, etc., continue to be engaged in shifting cultivation. The authority for the distribution of shifting patches vested in the hands of the village elders with no property rights on land except in those areas where rayatwari tenure was imposed on the tribal people along with taxes and tributes, by the local chiefs (Mahapatra, 1968; Pathy, ibid.).

Roy Burman while talking on the corporate tribal rights on land viewed that the formal status of ownership may be with an individual or family, but customarily the other members of the lineage or clan or local group may have defined rights to access or share of the resources. On the other hand, while at the ideological level the land may be owned by the community, the decision-making authority and effective possession may pertain to certain categories of individuals and families only. He therefore, emphasises that it is more important to examine the pattern of access, rather than the formal status of ownership (Roy Burman 1986: 6, quoted in Mahapatra, 1993:87). F.G. Bailey while referring to the Kondhs of Orissa differentiated tribe from caste in India on the principle that as member of the tribal community each tribesman had equal and inalienable access to land, whereas, a member of a caste has differential and unequal access to land, as there was an unequal division of land, based on social hierarchy:

the higher the position in the caste hierarchy, the greater to the access the land, the lowest being landless (*cf.* Bailey, 1960:7-10). With the predatory role of the State imposed over time the welfare state attacked on the customary rights of the tribal people. He asserts that, 'ownership in the land rests with the State, but the right of the occupancy rests with the actual cultivator, who so long as he pays his rents, is left in undisturbed possession'. He commented that the norms are the bedrocks of the British revenue system, though in the ancient statecraft of India the kings never owned lands of the kingdom. While talking on the tribal rights in the pre-colonial periods (ibid.) referred to the situation among the Bhuiyans and Juangas of Keonjhar district. He wrote that 'the Bhuiyans had no settled land, but in Bhuiyan Pirha they had imposed plough tax and house tax, while among the Juangas, produce rents were imposed for the village as a whole and the distribution of the rent among the villagers is left to the village headman.

Secondary data and study findings have been used to analyse the landholding and land ownership pattern among the tribals. Out of 7,31,403 tribal households surveyed by the Scheduled Castes and Scheduled Tribes Research and Training Institute (SCSTRTI) during 1978-80 in the entire Tribal Sub-Plan regions of the State, it was observed that almost 22.84 per cent had no land and 40.46 per cent owned an average of 2.5 acres each (SCSTRTI, 1978-80). The study again established the fact that Lodha (37.41%), Kondha (30.49%), Saura (31.11%), Paraja (36.65%), Munda (25.32%), Bhumija (25.18%), and Kharia (25.97%), were reported as landless. The tribal communities of southern Orissa had a higher percentage of land less households. The average landholding was 1.55 acres among the Bhumija (lowest). The data also show that farmers holding more than 5.1 acres were less among such tribal groups as Kondha, Gond, Munda, Paraja, Oraon, Kharia, and Kissan. (Mohanty, et al., 1993).

Decline of Tribal Operational Holding

The effects of decline of landholding among the SCs and STs are very much pronounced (Beteille, 1972; Diwakar, 1999; Mungekar,

1999). Around 77 per cent of the Scheduled Castes and 90 per cent of the Scheduled Tribes are landless without any productive assets and sustainable employment opportunities (GoI, 1997-2002). The Census of India 1991 reflects that 64 per cent of the SCs and 36 per cent of the STs are agriculture labourers as against 31 per cent among the other categories. It also reveals that 25 per cent of the SCs and 55 per cent of the STs are cultivators compared to 40 per cent of others. As per the Planning Commission, 48 per cent of the population of SCs and 51 per cent of STs are below the poverty line (ibid.). In spite of this, the issue of control and use of land among SCs and STs has not been left entirely out of scientific inquiry; it has received only occasional attention (Patel, 1974). It is observed that inequality and domination are treated as the basis of social relationship of Indian society, which influences the land distribution and land ownership pattern (Nair, 1961; Beteille, 1974; Parry, 1979; Lieten and Srivastava, 1999). The tribals who were initially within a relatively egalitarian and homogeneous social order with a separate socio-cultural and ecological milieu of their own, came under the subservience and dominance of the rich non-tribals in due course through 'civilising' and 'modernising' effects of 'colonialism' and 'planning'.

Land distribution in India largely follows social hierarchy. While the large landowners invariably belong to the upper castes, the cultivators belong to the middle castes and the agricultural workers largely belong to the scheduled castes and tribes (Beteille, 1972; Sankaran, 1996). Land being the important socially valued asset, its unequal distribution helps to maintain the hierarchical structure and strengthen the basis of dominance of the privileged groups by perpetuating inequality and deprivation in various socio-economic spheres. Looking at this basic structure of Indian society, though legislative measures for the redistribution of land have been made in India, the upper caste interest groups of the society have opposed it (Joshi, 1975; Hiro, 1976; Omvedt, 1993; Judge, 1999). Though land reforms in India have been launched in response to compelling demands expressed through agitation, struggle, and movements (Dhanagare, 1983; Radhakrishnan, 1989), but land reform policy being fundamentally a political issue, the

State passes the legislations only to pacify and neutralise the agrarian tensions.

This justifies when one see the empirical situations from Orissa. The Agriculture Census Report for the years of 1980-81 and 1985-86 reported a fall in the size of holdings (for all sizes) of the Scheduled Tribes during the period. More specifically the average size of ST holding of marginal and small farmers had increased over time, while medium and large holdings have declined both in absolute numbers and the area covered. While the number of ST households working on land increased from 9.18 lakh to 9.65 lakh, the total operational area declined from 15.79 lakh hectares to 15.47 lakh hectares. This clearly indicates a decline in ST holdings by 32,000 hectares.

The Board of Revenue conducted another study during 1990-91 to ascertain the operational holdings of tribals in Orissa with special reference to different social groups. Of the 39,48,000 holdings, small and marginal farmers accounted for 79.86 per cent, which included 20.49 per cent Scheduled Tribes. It is assumed that the number of small and marginal farmers must have declined because of the distribution of ceiling surplus and agricultural land by the State. The study also shows that of the total (21,18,800) marginal holdings of the State covering an area of 10,45,000 hectares, ST households (5,14,000) controlled 2,75,000 hectares. Similarly, of the total 10,35,000 small holders who own 14,26,000 hectares of land, 2,95,000 ST households owned 4,14,000 hectares (Revenue Department, 1992).

II

Implementation and Impact of Policies

The Scheduled Areas Transfer of Immovable Property (by Scheduled Tribes) Regulation 2 of 1956 in Orissa

The Government of Orissa has passed two regulations to restrict the alienation of tribal land. They are the Orissa Scheduled Areas Transfer of Immovable Property (by Scheduled Tribes) Regulation, 1956 and the Orissa Land Reform Act, 1960, to distribute surplus government wasteland among landless tribals.

The Orissa Scheduled Areas Transfer of Immovable Property (by Scheduled Tribes) Regulation 1956 is promulgated by the Governor of Orissa with immediate effect in exercise of powers conferred by sub-paragraph 2 of paragraph 5 of the Fifth Scheduled in the Constitution of India. The Regulation received the assent of the President of India on 21 September, 1956 and was first published in Orissa Gazette, Extra Ordinary dated 4 October, 1956. It repealed the Agency Tracts and Land Transfer Act of 1917, the first law to protect the interest of the tribal people during the British period, restricting the transfer of lands situated within the Agency Tracts, i.e., the Scheduled Areas of the State, owned by a hill tribe to a non-tribal without the previous permission of the prescribed officers [Section-4 (1)]. This law clearly defines the concept of Scheduled Area transfer of immovable property, eviction of persons from unauthorised occupation of property, surrender or relinquishment not valid unless settled by the land lord, inadmissibility of a deed for the purpose of registration, bar to attachment of immovable property, burden of proof and power of court to ignore admission, consideration money not refundable in case of invalid transfer, attachment of immovable property, general control of Collector, sale of timbers by Scheduled Tribe and Scheduled Caste persons standing on their Gharbari Rayati lands, etc. The detail of the provision is mentioned in Annexure-1.

The analysis of the data on the functioning of Orissa Scheduled Areas Transfer of Immovable Property (Scheduled Tribe) or the Regulation 2 of 1956, from the period 1980-81 to 1999-2000 on the registration, dispersal of land alienation cases, extent of land restored and distributed among the tribal people shows the government does not have any time planning in its approach to handle the problem of tribal land alienation and its restoration; the achievements as regards the Regulation 2 of 1956 is not satisfactory.

The review reveals that during this period, there were 46,811 land alienation cases instituted officially, and 45,862 cases were dispersed benefiting a total of 33,718 households during that period. An extent of 36,147 acres of land have been restored to the tribal households (Annual Administrative Report of concerned years). The distribution of registration of land alienation cases by the local government officials according to the Regulation 2 of 1956 reflect that more number of cases were registered in years of 1980-81, 1982-83, 1994-95 and 1995-96. There were almost 5,850 cases registered during 1995-96, which account for to one-fifth of the total cases compared several years. Since all the cases registered during the year do not disperse, ultimately the pending cases go to the next reporting year for accumulation (Table 6.2). The table reflects that the pending cases when reported in subsequent years sometimes do not correlate with the figures pending during previous years. This is observed in respect of the years of 1982-83, and in all the years from 1989-90 to 1995-96. Looking at the inconsistencies in the data maintained by the government, one obviously gives a second thought to its accuracy. In such a process, the data inconsistencies seem to be the major cause for the gaps pointed out in reporting of the cases. However, the discrepancies of the data have never been clarified or questioned by the ST and SC Development Department of the State.

The accuracy of the data maintained at government level is doubted by many scholars for not reflecting the extent of the problem of land alienation. It is because the tribal people due to their secluded habitation and illiteracy are largely ignorant of these preventive regulations. Secondly, because of their long experiences of harassment and exploitation in various forms caused both by government and private agencies they feel safe not to disclose to others the facts of their land alienation which normally takes place through *benami* transfers by way of oral agreements and unregistered deeds.

As regards the disposal of land alienation cases and number of households benefited out of the distributed land, it is observed that out of 45,862 cases almost 73.52 per cent of HHs has been allotted an average of 1.07 acres per household. The average distribution of land per HH was to the maximum tune of 2.52 acres during 1980-81, while this was only 0.51 acres in the following years. The data is inconsistantly distributed in various years and do not reflect any trend of positive State effort to restore more land for distribution to the affected tribal HHs, rather it seems as if the State has taken up this activity as a routine work of the department (Panigrahi, 2001).

Table 6.2

Functioning of Orissa Scheduled Areas Transfer of Immovable Property (ST) Regulation 2 of 1956 (Land in Acres)

Year	No. of cases			Cases dispersed	Cases pending till end of the year	Extent of land restored	No. of HH benefited	Avg. land distributed per HH
	Instituted	Pending	Total					
1980-81	4551	3149	7690	3385 (44.00)	4305 (56.00)	7106	2810	2.52
1981-82	2914	4305	7219	2379 (33.00)	4840 (77.00)	1399	2707	0.51
1982-83	5083	4632	9715	7980 (77.00)	2235 (33.00)	4473	4120	1.08
1983-84	1414	2235	3649	1550 (42.47)	2099 (57.53)	689	443	1.53
1984-85	1007	2099	3106	954 (30.42)	2152 (69.58)	239	292	0.81
1985-86	1003	2152	3152	1288 (40.86)	1864 (59.14)	316	186	1.69
1986-87	1203	1864	3067	360 (11.73)	2707 (88.27)	143	114	1.25
1987-88	1480	2707	4187	1381 (33.00)	2886 (77.00)	464	509	0.91
1988-89	2465	2886	5351	3207 (60.00)	2144 (40.00)	2166	2129	1.01
1989-90	2144	1190	3334	458 (13.73)	2876 (86.27)	277	308	0.89
1990-91	1018	2150	3168	1467 (46..30)	1696 (53.70)	1120	1237	0.90
1991-92	1486	3168	4654	871 (18.71)	3783 (81.29)	548	550	0.99
1992-93	3061	650	3711	781 (21.04)	2930 (78.96)	327	465	0.70
1993-94	1398	2223	3621	1866 (51.53)	1755 (48.47)	1034	1238	0.83
1994-95	5343	1840	7183	3944 (54.90)	3239 (45.10)	1801	3150	0.57
1995-96	5850	10752	16422	10050 (61.19)	6366 (38.81)	10379	10066	1.03
1996-97	NA							
1997-98	659	4148	4807	1806	3001	1346	1244	1.08
1998-99	1593	3001	4594	2135	2459	2320	2140	1.10
Total	46811		50828	45862		36147	33718	1.07

Note: Figures in brackets are percentage to total.

Source: Annual Administration Report of Scheduled Areas of concerned years. ST and SC Development Department, Government of Orissa.

Here, an attempt has been made to highlight few facts on the number of cases and extent of land legally alienated during 1956-1997 as recorded in the District Collector's Office. It has been observed that districts such as Nawarangpur, Mayurbhanj, Koraput and Rayagada have lost more land than other districts. As regards reporting of cases, there are more such cases reported in the district of Mayurbhanj followed by Nawarangpur. The details of the (Table 6.3) reflect that there were 9,743 cases of tribal households who are legally permitted to transfer their 3,550 areas of land.

Table 6.3

Distribution of Cases and Extent of Land Alienated Under Section 3 (I) of Regulation 2 of 1956 in Orissa during 1956-97

Districts	*No. of Tribals Legally Permitted to Transfer Land*	*Extent of Land Alienated with Permission from Competent Authority (in acres)*	*Per Cent to the Total Land Lost*
Balasore	124	51.69	0.60
Mayurbhanj	2681	1463.53	17.11
Koraput	34	1298.53	15.18
Rayagada	708	1251.45	14.63
Malkangiri	318	423.10	0.95
Nawarangpur	010	1558.71	18.23
Kalahandi	107	236.65	0.76
Gajapati	70	57.02	0.67
Phulbani	724	196.70	0.30
Keonjhar	963	587.55	0.87
Sambalpur	506	528.39	0.18
Sundargarh	1493	896.49	0.52
Total	9743	3550.00	100.00

Source: Office of the District Collectors of the respective districts.

The Orissa Land Reforms Act, 1960

The Orissa Land Reform Act, 1960 came into force in the State of Orissa from 1 October, 1965, vide Sections 22, 22-A, 23, 23-A and

23-B. The importance of such a law is to cover the interest of the Scheduled Castes and Scheduled Tribes living in non-Scheduled Areas of the State. In response to the National Guidelines suggested by the Planning Commission of Government of India to introduce a comprehensive Land Reform Plan, the Government of Orissa appointed a committee during December 1957. The recommendations of such a committee subsequently came into a statute book known as the Orissa Land Reform (OLR) Act of 1960 and practically unified all the tenancy systems of the State (Annexure-2). While protecting the interest of the SCs and STs, OLR Act 1960 emphasises that any illegal transfer of land without permission from competent authority from these Scheduled groups residing outside the Scheduled Areas will be cancelled by law. The 12 year rule regarding adverse possession of the Limitation Act 1963 was modified to 30 years for the SCs and STs. Again the payment of *salami* was also waived out since 1985 for the SCs and STs during the allotment of Ceiling Surplus Land against them. OLR Act 1960 again provides that during the settlement of surplus land, it will be settled in favour of SC and ST groups according to their population strength. These settled lands could not be transferred within ten years of its settlement.

The law provides that in case of the settlements of surplus lands, seventy per cent of the surplus lands vested in the government under Section 45 shall be settled with persons belonging to the Scheduled Castes or Scheduled Tribes. This will be distributed in proportion to their respective populations in the villages and the remaining lands shall be settled with persons not belonging to the aforesaid categories. It is provided that where the population of the Scheduled Caste and Scheduled Tribe in a village exceeds seventy per cent of the total population of that village, the percentage of lands to be reserved for persons of the said communities shall be equal to the percentage of their population.

If sufficient number of persons belonging to ST categories are not available in the village, in which the lands are situated or being available, are not willing to accept settlement of land, so much of the lands reserved for the said persons as cannot be settled with them, may be settled with other persons. The land so settled cannot be transferred (disposed of) by sale or otherwise within the period of ten years following such settlement. The State Government in Revenue Department Order has exempted from payment of court fee in all cases of application from persons belonging to Scheduled Castes, Scheduled Tribes and other landless persons for the settlement of ceiling surplus lands.

Under Orissa Prevention of Land Encroachment Act, 1972, where any land is in the unauthorised occupation of a landless person, the Tehasildar may, instead of evicting such persons from the land in his unauthorised occupation, settle the same with him so. However, the land so settled with him together with the land excluding homestead, if any, owned by him and the lands owned by all the members of his family who are living with him in common mess, shall on no account exceed one standard acre.

The State Government has taken a decision to amend the Orissa Scheduled Areas Transfer of Immovable Property (by Scheduled Tribes) Regulation, 1956 (Regulation 2 of 1956). It is required further to empower the Gram Panchayat and Gram Sasan in the prevention of land alienation in Scheduled Areas as envisaged under Section 4(m) (iii) of the provisions of the Panchayats (Extension to the Scheduled Areas) Act, 1996. It has also been decided to amend the Regulation for total prohibition or transfer of tribal land in the Scheduled Areas from members of Scheduled Tribes to others, for enhancement of penalty conferment of powers on Executive Magistrate powers of Judicial Magistrates. It also aims to ban alienation of tribal land where someone has less than two acres of irrigated land or five acres of unirrigated land. The Tribes Advisory Council and the State Cabinet have approved the amendment. It is being processed for approval by the Governor of Orissa before being sent to Government of India to obtain the assent of the President, as required under Sub-paragraph 5 of the Fifth Schedule of the Constitution of India. The data on the distribution of various types of land by the government to the scheduled groups of Orissa have also been quantified for 19 years from 1980-81 to 1998-99.

Distribution of Waste Land for Agriculture

As regards the distribution of wasteland among the ST households for agricultural purposes, data (Table 6.4) explain that till 1998-99 almost 32,932 ST beneficiaries have been distributed with a total of 44,195 acres of wasteland. The average land distributed per each HH comes to around 1.34 acres. The number of beneficiaries in the years from 1986 to 1989 and again from 1990 to 1993 and in 1994-95 were so meager that this does not justify the adoption of

Table 6.4

Distribution of Wasteland to both ST and SC Households for Agriculture under OLR Act 1960 (Land in Acres)

Years	*Beneficiaries and Distribution of Waste Land*					
	ST	*Extent of Land*	*Average Land*	*SC*	*Extent of Land*	*Average Land*
1980-81	5343	8352	1.56	1008	1414	1.40
1981-82	3346	5380	1.60	149	2209	1.52
1982-83	2884	4718	1.63	1790	2800	1.56
1983-84	2632	4170	1.58	2526	7505	2.97
1984-85	1846	2412	1.30	2855	13662	4.78
1985-86	1437	2085	1.45	741	1068	1.44
1986-87	1291	1331	1.03	531	500	0.94
1987-88	1192	1180	0.98	478	474	0.99
1988-89	897	1054	1.17	464	495	1.09
1989-90	1058	1149	1.08	422	457	1.08
1990-91	950	794	0.83	498	613	0.76
1991-92	543	525	0.96	314	306	0.97
1992-93	389	411	1.05	343	314	0.91
1993-94	1957	3506	1.79	937	1640	1.79
1994-95	971	1104	1.13	262	347	1.32
1995-96	2942	3085	1.04	442	653	1.47
1996-97	NA					
1997-98	1365	1271	0.93	772	606	0.78
1998-99	1889	1661	0.88	974	950	1.00
Total	32932	44195	1.34	17106	36021	2.10

Source: Annual Administration Report of Scheduled Areas of concerned years. ST and SC Development Department, Government of Orissa.

any time bound programme ever taken by the government to distribute waste land for promotion of agriculture. Similar is also the situation observed in case of SC beneficiaries. During the period, a total of 17,106 number of SC HHs have benefited who have been allotted a total wasteland of 36,021 acres and the average land distributed per HH is 2.210 acres. A look into the data across years from 1985-86 to 1998-99 the programme of distribution of wasteland among the SC groups for agricultural purposes has been so meagre that it seems to have been a routine work on the part of the government.

Distribution of Waste Land for Homestead

The data on the distribution of wasteland across various years from 1980-81 to 1998-99 reflect that there were almost a total of 2,04,954 numbers of ST HHs who have been benefited to the extent of 8,714 acres of land. Quite a sizeable number of ST HHs have been benefited, particularly in the years of 1983-94 (12,529), 1985-86 (21,030 HHs) and during the year 1987-88 (16,993 HHs) which seems to be an exceptional achievement throughout the years. Almost an extent of 7,172 acres of land have been distributed among 1,48,676 SC HH during the 19 years distributed with an average of 0.05 acres, while it was only 0.04 acre among the ST HHs (Table 6.5). The distribution of wasteland for homestead purpose in certain years has no doubt benefited a good number of ST and SC HHs. However, State attempt to distribute land for this purpose has to be done through a planned way to cover more number of beneficiaries in a time bound period. Apart from, reoccupation by the beneficiaries of the distributed land is also an important aspect for better functioning, which however has not been reflected in the report.

Distribution of Ceiling Surplus Land under OLR Act 1960

Distribution of ceiling surplus land is also one of the objectives of OLR Act, 1960. The achievements regarding this have been analysed differently for SCs and STs (Table 6.6) while taking the data from the year of 1980-81 to 1998-99. There were a total of 17,193 ST household beneficiaries who have been distributed with

Table 6.5

Distribution of Wasteland to both ST and SC Households for Homestead under OLR Act 1960

Years	*Beneficiaries and Distribution of Waste Land*					
	ST	*Extent of Land*	*Average Land*	*SC*	*Extent of Land*	*Average Land*
1980-81	1654	113	0.06	863	35	0.04
1981-82	1608	138	0.08	678	30	0.04
1982-83	2465	132	0.05	1943	78	0.04
1983-84	12529	554	0.04	10871	1156	0.10
1984-85	6315	295	0.04	7101	1232	0.17
1985-86	21030	882	0.04	14228	210	0.01
1986-87	7429	310	0.04	6110	214	0.03
1987-88	16993	718	0.04	12159	431	0.03
1988-89	4182	192	0.04	3142	118	0.03
1989-90	5356	216	0.04	3842	114	0.03
1990-91	4732	194	0.04	2937	105	0.03
1991-92	5647	205	0.03	46	163	3.54
1992-93	2728	106	0.03	1394	58	0.04
1993-94	2057	84	0.04	1041	43	0.04
1994-95	2881	122	0.04	1047	42	0.04
1995-96	8504	555	0.06	4025	424	0.01
1996-97	NA					
1997-98	12470	501	0.04	9402	395	0.04
1998-99	86374	3388	0.04	63215	2294	0.04
Total	204954	8714		148676	7172	0.04

Source: Annual Administration Report of Scheduled Areas of concerned years. ST and SC Development Department, Government of Orissa.

17,801 acres of total ceiling surplus land during the period. The average distribution of ceiling surplus land was 1.03 acres that varies from 1.56 acres to ST HH during the years of 1984-85 (as the highest) and 0.57 acres (as the lowest) during the year, 1982-83. Among the Scheduled Caste groups, almost 14,892 households have been benefited during the periods distributed with a total extent of 14,029 acres. The average land distributed to each SC household was 0.94 acres during the period, which varies from a maximum of 1.46 acres during the year of 1980-81, to 0.55 acre (as the lowest) during the year 1990-91.

Table 6.6

Distribution of Ceiling Surplus Land to both ST and SC Households under OLR Act 1960

Years	*Beneficiaries and Distribution of Waste Land*					
	ST	*Extent of Land*	*Average Land*	*SC*	*Extent of Land*	*Average Land*
1980-81	594	619	1.04	161	236	1.46
1981-82	587	337	0.57	354	363	1.02
1982-83	1877	1760	0.93	2118	2318	1.09
1983-84	2910	3326	1.14	26543	2620	0.99
1984-85	536	839	1.56	411	489	1.18
1985-86	2658	2882	1.08	2622	2415	0.92
1986-87	1358	1572	1.15	978	1132	1.15
1987-88	671	576	0.85	537	499	0.92
1988-89	783	578	0.74	550	474	0.86
1989-90	508	543	1.06	361	276	0.76
1990-91	52	45	0.86	177	98	0.55
1991-92	774	839	1.08	867	771	0.88
1992-93	681	515	0.75	699	568	0.81
1993-94	1064	1048	0.98	969	771	0.79
1994-95	965	1267	1.31	415	450	1.08
1995-96	469	476	1.01	204	158	0.77
1996-97	NA					
1997-98	304	242	0.79	254	179	0.70
1998-99	402	256	0.63	572	212	0.37
Total	17193	17801	1.03	14892	14029	0.94

Source: Annual Administration Report of Scheduled Areas of concerned years. ST and SC Development Department, Government of Orissa.

Displacement

The establishment of mega-projects in tribal regions have encroached tribal land and displaced them from their age-old habitation. These projects have immense adverse impact on the life and livelihood of these tribals. Those are hydroelectric-cum-irrigation projects, like Hirakud (1948), Machkund (1949), Balimela (1963), Upper Kolab (1978), Indravati (1978), Rengali (1973) and the Subarnarekha; Mineral based industries like Rourkela Steel Plant (1950), Hindustan Aeronautics Limited (1962), Bauxite Mining Project at Koraput (1981), National Aluminium Company at Angul (1985), and projects on cement, iron, dolomite and lime stone, etc. A cursory calculation reflects that since independence, Orissa has 190 such projects, which have deforested 24,124 hectares of forestland, the basic source of livelihood for the tribal people (PCCF Office, Government of Orissa, 1999). The estimate on the magnitude of displacement of human population in Orissa due to the establishment of various mega-projects during the period 1951-95 reflects that hydro-electric multi-purpose projects have displaced around 3,25,000 people of which only 90,000 oustees (27.69%) have been rehabilitated. Similarly, due to industrial projects a total of 71,794 persons have been displaced in Orissa. Only 27,300 (38.03%) oustees have been rehabilitated. While mining projects have displaced around 1,00,000 people of which almost 60 per cent oustees have been rehabilitated; and due to the declaration of sanctuary around 50,000 people have been displaced of which only 15,540 (31.08%) have been rehabilitated (Fernandes, 1994; Mahapatra, 1999). The details of displacement in different development projects in Orissa calculated in different decadal gaps can be viewed from Tables 6.7 and 6.8. All these projects have immense impact on the village economy, family life, and village power structure of the tribal people, which have been shown in various empirical studies in the State (Panda and Panigrahi, 1986; Behura and Nayak, 1993; Mohapatra 1998; Patnaik, 2000; Swain and Panigrahi, 1999).

Table 6.7

Extent of Displacement of Households in Different Development Projects in Orissa

Sectors of the Project	*No. of Families Displaced*				*Total*
	1950-60	*1961-70*	*1971-80*	*1981-90*	
Power project	22144	1357	19769	443	43713
Irrigation project	1015	578	2883	3607	8083
Industrial project	4251	468	-	5794	10513
Total	4251	2403	22652	9844	62309

Source: Different published documents.

Table 6.8

Displacement Due to Development Projects in Orissa till 1990

Categories of Projects	*No. of Families Affected*	*% of Total Displacement*
Mines	3134	3.37
Industries	10704	11.47
Thermal Power	2426	2.60
Dam Projects	64903	69.55
Wildlife Sanctuary	142	0.15
Urban Slums	12000 (Approximately)	12.86
Total	93318	100.00

Source: Different published documents.

Extent of Land Alienation in Koraput District (undivided)

Here, an attempt has been made to show the extent of land alienation in a tribal dominated district of Orissa, i.e., undivided Koraput. This analysis at certain level reflects the degree of this problem, which has its origin in pre-independence period. However, the problem became acute in post-independence period when the State in the name of development became another legal agent to alienate tribal people from their age-old community ownership over land. Soon after the formation of the new State of Orissa, the first survey was initiated in Koraput district (undivided) in 1938 where it was undertaken in different phases and completed after 20 years excluding the Bonda hill area, where the land survey has not been completed even by middle of 2005. The delay is largely due to frequent changes in the measurement methods, possibly made keeping in mind the interest of the upper class non-tribal landholders of the district. In this process, substantial quantity of land transferred from tribals to non-tribals in Koraput (Patnaik, ibid.; Yunus, 1977; Jha, 1977). The study conducted by SCSTRTI in Sunabeda a thickly tribal dominated pocket of Koraput shows that between January 1961 to February 1968 around 145.41 acres of tribal lands were purchased by the non-tribals. Even during the year 1973-74 alone, more than 7,700 cases of land alienation had been filed in the District Collector's Office (Commissioners Report, 1973-74). In Bissam, Cuttack Tehasil more than 3,000 acres of land belonging to tribals has been handed over to the businessmen of Andhra Pradesh with the help of middle men and revenue officials (*Indian Express*, 1996). Under Bhoodan Movement up to 1955, around 1,65,268 acres of land in 600 villages had been donated. The Assistant Settlement Officers justified that many of the persons who were alleged to have donated lands refused to part with the same later on (Vyasulu, 1985). The lands, which had been donated, were of inferior types (Mahapatra, 1987).

The extent of land alienation in undivided Koraput district between 1956 and 1997 reflects that in Koraput, Jaypore, Rayagada, Gunupur, Malkangiri, and Nawarangapur sub-divisions 2,289 tribal households had been permitted to transfer their land legally to non-tribals. This has alienated 4,111.406 acres land. In Gunupur sub-division, the extent of land alienated was 1,206.24 acres (highest) followed by Nawarangpur which has lost 997.650 acres, Koraput sub-division has lost 699.866 acres of land (District Revenue Sections, 1998).

During 1937, Koraput district was not having any land settlement records by the time it was transferred to Orissa. It was decided that as per the system of record of right in Bihar and Orissa the land settlement would also be carried out in Koraput district. During the settlement operations in undivided Koraput district that took place from 1938 to 1964, almost 604 cases of land alienation were reported which have alienated 1,790.43 acres of land in different tehasils of these districts (Final Report, 1938-64). Another example of alienation of tribal land reflects that in Bisamacuttack tehasil of Gunupur sub-division tribal people have lost their fertile lands to the non-tribal Telugu farmers who have migrated into the area either through illegal or benami or legal transactions (*Dharitri Oriya Daily*, 2 July, 1998). Revenue Divisional Commissioner (IRDC) of Southern Division had an inquiry of the matter who found that almost 604 tribal households had lost 1,790.43 acres of agriculture land. This type of illegal transfer of tribal land to non-tribal Telugu farmers has also taken place in Dashamantapur block of Koraput district.

In post-independence period, the mechanisms of land alienation from tribal people to non-tribals has changed. Apart from this, individual companies/trusts, in the name of commercial plantations, have entered into the district and acquired thousands of acres of tribal land and government wasteland. The State had also acquired thousands of acres of tribal households in the name of development through mega-projects.

Koraput (undivided) district is adjacent to some trade centres like Raipur of Madhya Pradesh and Vishakhapatnam of Andhra Pradesh, The non-tribal business groups while migrating into Koraput district (undivided) before the construction of mega-development projects have found their place in the market economy, government bureaucracy and also in local agriculture. Commercial plantation for paper industries by Mangalam Timber in Nawarangpur and by Ballarpur Industries in Jeypore has practically grabbed a lot of tribal lands, which was used for their subsistence. Cultivation of commercial crops like sal, nilgiri, sisal, coffee, cashew, tea, rubber, and varieties of grasses have taken place in Gunupur, Umarkote, Laxhmipur regions; ethnic conflicts have taken place between the poor tribal people and the resettled refugee Bengalis. A cursory account in respect of undivided Koraput district reflects that there are 181 large development projects/schemes which have occupied 50,000 acres of land or 7.42 per cent of the total district area, depriving around 10 per cent of the tribals from their livelihood (Fernandes, 1996: 442). In spite of so many development projects operating in the district for the last five decades it is unfortunate that the tribal people of Koraput district are by and large in similar socio-economic conditions or in a more distressed state and do not get two square meals per day. Perhaps this is one of the reasons for which the tribal people of Kashipur have been influenced by outside forces. Local people opposed the proposed bauxite mining by Utkal Aumina International Ltd. at Kashipur region, and the BALCO for bauxite mining at Nrusighnath of Bargarh district.

The discussion in the context of Koraput district (undivided) proves that all efforts made to check alienation of tribal land in Orissa have largely failed. The nexus between the middlemen, moneylenders, traders and the State authorities who tried to legitimise the alienation process, and the tribal people on other hand have been protesting for their deprivation. Protest of the tribals against the State policy proves from the recent agitation in Kashipur against the Bauxite mining lease. The data on landholding while reviewed from the Statistical Abstracts reflect a decreasing trend in the average landholding of the marginal holders, while it is increasing rapidly in case of large holders (Mohanty, 1997). Similarly, the percentage of cultivators is decreasing which is accompanied by an increase of agricultural labourers (ibid.).

Tribal people in Orissa by and large are victims of a systematic process of exploitation, which has marginalised and impoverished them. They are hard pressed in the triangular attack of moneylenders at local level, public sector industrial companies and State administration at the higher level. The State policies on land and land-based resources instead of encouraging the tribals have depressed them and opened up tribal economy for others to exploit.

Agony of Tribal People Against Land Acquisition in Orissa

The State of Orissa, particularly the southern belt, i.e., undivided Koraput, Balangir and Kalahandi (KBK) districts are endowed with 1,733 million tonnes (70%) of the total bauxite of the nation. In post-liberalisation period, this mineral resource has attracted foreign investment, which brought the State into the international arena. During the period between 1992-97, bauxite has pulled foreign investment to the tune of Rs. 97,300 crores (US $20.5 billion).

Since 1986, a number of attempts have been made in KBK districts to explore bauxite ores. The major deposits of bauxite in different regions of these districts include 21.30 lakh tonnes in Gandhamardan in Balangir and Bargarh region, 1,957.3 lakh tonnes in Baphali Mali hill range, 810 lakh tonnes in Sasubohu Mali in Kashipur block of Rayagada district, 860 lakh tonnes in the Siju Mali region and 400 lakh tonnes in Kutru Mali region of Rayagada and Kalahandi districts, and 914 lakh tonnes in Kodinga Mali in Laxmipur block of Koraput district. The major companies which have tried to explore bauxite in Orissa at different points of time, failed, and are, also still trying to explore this ore by Balco during 1986; Utkal Alumina, INDAL, TATA, Hydro (Norway), and ALCAN (Canada), HINDALCO (Table 6.9).

The estimation of losses incurred due to these mining projects varies according to organisations and period of calculation. For example, the UAIL calculates that the Bauxite mining at Kashipur would displace only 147 families in three villages; another calculation tells that it affects more than 2,100 families in about 24 villages. A calculation by Norsk Hydro estimates that this would affect 750 families, and Norwegian Development Corporation estimates this to be of 60,000. However, estimation by PSSP says that the plant site would directly affect 2,500 people living in 24 villages and the open caste mining would affect 42 villages.

In all these mining project areas forest resources, hill slopes and the natural water bodies constitute the major livelihood system of tribal people. Due to paucity of suitable land, wet cultivation is not feasible. Depletion of forest resources would be the biggest threat for the tribal people. This has been the sad experience of the tribal people in many hydro-projects established in the State. These mining projects would result in piling up of solid effluents such as red mud, tonnes of sodium hydroxide, high phospate (pH) level in the soil, loss of vegetation and natural habitats.

Table 6.9
A Brief Profile of Bauxite and Alumina Projects in Orissa

District/Area	*Company*	*Nature of Work*	*Work Progress*
Rayagada Kucheipadar, Kashipur	UAIL	Proposed Aluminium plant	Resistance under Prakrutika Sampad Surakha Parishad (PSSP)
Baphlimali, Kashipur	UAIL	Proposed Bauxite mines	Resistance under PSSP
Siju Mali and Kutri Mali, Kashipur	MOU & L&T & GoO	Proposed Bauxite mines	Resistance under PSSP
Sasubohu Mali & Indrajitmali bauxite hill range, Kashipur	MOY of Sterlite with GoO	Proposed Bauxite mines	Resistance under PSSP
Kalahandi Khandual Mali Thuamul Rampur Block	MOU & L&T & GoO	Proposed Bauxite mines	Resistance under Khandual Mali Surakhya Samiti
Lanjigarh	Sterlite	Proposed Aluminium plant	Resistance under the Niyamgiri Surakhya Samiti, work not started
Niyamgiri	MOU or Sterite with GoO	Proposed Bauxite mines	Resistance under the Niyamgiri Surakhya Samiti, work not started
Koraput Ghusuli Mali Dasmantapur	MOU & L&T & GoO	Proposed Bauxite mines	Resistance started
Kodinga Mali Laxmipur	MOU of HINDALCO (Aditya Birla) with GoO	Proposed Bauxite mines	Resistance under PSSP
Deomali, Samiliguda	MOU being negotiated	Proposed Bauxite mines	Under negotiation
Damanjodi	NALCO	Aluminium plant	In operation since 1986
Panchaput Mali Semiliguda	NALCO	Bauxite mines	In operation since 1986
Bolangir Gandhamardan bauxite mining	MOU of BALCO with GoO	Proposed for Bauxite mining in 1986	BALCO was forced to withdraw due to people's agitation

Source: The Struggle against Bauxite Mining in Orissa, 2002, (2nd Edition) KVR, KNPVO, Manasa, PDF and PUCL-K.

The establishment of bauxite mining by NALCO at Damanjodi only 100 kms away from Kashipur has ravaged the tribal people and their livelihood. The tribal people have been pushed out to the level of wage labour in informal sector. Similar situations have resulted in the tribal dominated Mayurbhanj, Sundargarh and Keonjhar districts in northern parts where iron ore mining operations have taken place.

The tribal people in Orissa have raised their voice against such mega development interventions. They have questioned the development process by saying "Development for whom and at whose cost", which basically affects tribal people and their non-renewable livelihood resources. This is the reason why the tribal people of the State have raised their agony against the bauxite mining. In 1985 the tribal people including other peasants under the banner of Gandhamardan Surakhya Parishad launched agitation against BALCO in Gandhamardan Hill ranges in Sambalpur (old) and Balangir, which stopped the implementation of the project. In 1996 tribal people in Kashipur have come together under the banner of Prakrutika Sampad Surakha Parishad (PSSP). Similar processes at Lanjigarh of Kalahandi district have stopped the survey work being carried out by Sterlite Company. In all, these movements women groups took active part through *dharanas*, picketing, processions and public hearings. The emergence of indigenous leadership made all these movements more widespread. The government and political forces left no space for the people, rather made all strenuous efforts to overcome people's resistance by recognising these movements purely as a problem of law and order. In fact, in this process of micro movements, the forest dependent communities are trying to re-establish the functional importance of their indigenous institutions as a part of the political process and in determining the regional needs of the people.

In all these movements, the modernisation process launched by BALCO and UAIL could not establish faith among local people. It could not establish a dialogue process with common people on the issues of century old relation with natural livelihood resources and with local ecosystem. These movements reinforced people's belief on community strength, women's abilities, and environmental consciousness. The villagers could protect their indigenous productive forces. These agitations have proved that people's movement against the global forces can make a meaningful development path to preserve the indigenous sources of livelihood.

III

Study Findings

In order to understand the impact of State policies regarding the tribal people in the villages with respect to the problem of land alienation, the present study focussed on various aspects. They are: the level of awareness of the tribal people regarding the State policies, provisions there-in and procedures followed to prevent land alienation and restore their alienated land from the non-tribal people; extent of land alienation which took place in the form of both land leased-in and leased-out during last five years; sale and purchase of land by tribal households during last 5 years and the knowledge of members of Panchayati Raj Institutions (PRIs) regarding the structural arrangements for the functioning of the government machinery and their access into such provisions to restore back the alienated land.

Knowledge of Tribal People About State Policies

In order to assess the knowledge base of the tribal people on the prevalent State policies with regard to prevention of land alienation, restore back the alienated land and procedure of ventilating grievances some questions were put to each respondent. The analysis of the findings reflects that out of 417 ST households, 264 (63.31%) had the knowledge that tribal land cannot be sold to or purchased by a non-tribal person without the permission of the government. A district-wise look into the situation shows that in the study village of Penaposi Pangara of Kandhamal, the knowledge level among the ST households was almost 96.46 per cent while it was very low in Malkangiri (36.89%) and Kalahandi

(26.84%). Possibly the level of knowledge of tribal people in respect to this issue is related to various socio-economic factors. In Kandhamal district because of frequent ethnic conflicts between Pana, a Scheduled Caste community and the Kandha, a Scheudled Tribe community, the awareness level regarding the restriction of transfer is high, whereas, in Malkangiri district the Bengali refugees play a major role in the life of the Koya tribal people. Similarly, in Kalahandi district the Doma, a SC community and many other caste groups belonging to Other Backward Classes, play a major role in the economic life as well as in rendering a helping hand to the tribal people during emergencies. The non-tribal groups, both in Kalahandi and Malkangiri, maintain a suppressive relation towards the tribal people. Possibly, this is one of the major reasons for which the tribal people acquire knowledge on the rules and regulations, etc.

Tribal Land Leased-In and Leased-Out

Attempt was made to highlight separately the leased-in and leased-out situation of agricultural land of the tribal people. A total of 18 (3.72%) households reported who have taken 19 acres of land on leased-in basis of which only 9 (2.17%) households belonged to tribal communities who have taken 9 acres of land on lease basis. The study observed that 16 (88.88%) households have taken land on lease from within the village. ST households who have taken land on lease basis reflect that land transactions are confined to their village only. This was reported by 33.33 per cent in Kalahandi, 22.22 per cent in Koraput and 80 per cent in Malkangiri district. A total of 49 cases have been reported, who had leased-out 44.5 acres of land. A district wise analysis reflects that 18 (36.73%) households had leased their 14.4 acres of land in the study village of Kandhamal district (highest), which was followed by Kalahandi district having 12 households (24.48%) who had leased-out 12 acres and in Malkangiri district 11 households (22.44%) had also leased-out 10.5 acres of land. The study shows that all the 49 households (11.75%) who had leased-out their land belong to Scheduled Tribe communities. Data on the leased-out cases when analysed according to the source where the lands were mortgaged shows that of the total households, almost 16 (32.65%) households have leased-out their land to their co-villagers and the rest 67.35 per cent households had leased their land to outsiders.

Various reasons for land mortgage assigned by the concerned households have raised a couple of dimension, which can be categorised as social, economic, and health related. All the 49 (100%) households, who had mortgaged 44.5 acres of their land, belong to different tribal communities. The land mortgage situation in different study villages reflects that in Penaposi Pangara village of Kandhamal district, 18 (36.73%) tribal households had mortgaged 14.5 acres of their land, followed by village Kendubaradihi in Kalahandi district where 12 (24.48%) households had mortgaged 12 acres of their land. In Lachipetta village of Malkangiri district, 11 (22.44%) households had mortgaged 10.5 acres of their land. The major reasons for mortgaging land, as said by 17 (34.69%) households is the pressing social needs like marriage ceremony of their children and performance of death ceremonies. Around 23 (46.93%) households linked their problems to health related factors as the major cause for mortgaging their land, whereas, the rest 9 (18.38%) households had linked it to the economic cause as the major factor.

Procedures of Land Mortgage

Procedures adopted for land mortgage vary from region to region. However, methodologically there are certain commonalties found in the transaction. The tribal people give away both their *patta* and the non-*patta* land on certain conditions in lieu of financial assistance, which are primarily required to meet the exigencies like children's marriage, performance of death rituals and to meet the medical expenses. In all these processes, land, one of the major sources of livelihood, goes out of tribal control. Therefore, practically they become landless, which affects their basic livelihood requirements. The non-tribal households, who keep the land through mortgage not only get back their principal loan amount after 3 to 5 years, but also get all produces every year as alternative to the payment of interests. These non-tribal households, who keep tribal land under mortgage, use the low paid labour services of the tribal people in all their agricultural operations and use the tribal people as labourers in their own land. The rate of land mortgage varies depending upon the type/quality of land and period of mortgage.

Coming to specific situations in different regions one finds a standardised rate for both *kuda* (upland) and *khal* (low land) variety as reported in Tungurubahal village of Keonjhar district. Around Rs. 1,500 has been paid towards mortgage of 1 acre of low land for three years, while only Rs. 800 rupees has been paid for mortgage of one acre of upland for a three year period. This type of land mortgage in the village is known as Tankudi mortgage.

In Lachipetta village of Malkangiri district, the practice of *bhaga chasa* is very popular. The Bengali community who have been settled in special colonies in and around the Koya villages have engulfed the Koya villages. During the settlement, Bengalis had been given forest land (with all developmental support) for agriculture purposes. During the last three decades many studies in Malkangiri district have justified the exploitative linkages between those two communities, where the Bengalis dictate terms and exercise control over the production and circulation of livelihood resources among the Koyas. The magnitude of alienation of Koya land by the Bengali people in this district has become a headache for the State administration. The Bengalis always keep an eye on Koya land and with all inducements they try to take the use-right over these lands. When the Koyas get fed up with the labour intensive land development processes that they feel relaxed to handover the use-right over these lands to the Bengalis with a condition to get 50 per cent of the produces even without paying any concurrent inputs for the purpose. The Koyas due to their simplicity feel happy to get whatever unaccountable crops given by the Bengalis to them. Since the status of these lands are basically encroached by nature so Bengalis enjoys the use-rights over these lands and gradually make their position stronger; because of their knowledge and awareness about the revenue administration the Bengalis are able to make use of the local Revenue Inspector to get an encroachment case in his/her name. In this process the poor Koyas never dare to assert their use-right over those lands.

Understanding the magnitude of this problem the Commissioner in charge of Kalahandi, Balangir and Koraput (KBK) districts during 1998 adventurously issued an administrative order to District Collectors of Malkangiri district and other administrative revenue officials like Sub-Collectors, Tehasildar and BDOs, that no non-tribal can cultivate the land of Koya people. The order also emphasised identification of such cases and fine of Rs. 1,000 to 3,000 to the deviants. During the year 1999, no Bengali could dare to cultivate tribal land. While discussing with different government officials and members of local Panchayati Raj Institutions (PRIs) it was found that there was almost a vacuum created during the period and since Koyas were not mentally ready to cultivate all their agricultural land. Therefore, a lot of agricultural land were left uncultivated. Since Koyas largely depend on the Bengalis even for seeds for cultivation, they were unprepared to take over cultivation of left out lands.

In Penaposi Pangara village of Kandhamal district, two major types of practices are followed for land mortgage. They are Kada Bandhak and Karati Bandhak. In Kada Bandhak system the land is mortgaged for one year against a specific amount. Normally for one acre of paddy land, an amount of Rs. 500 to Rs. 1000 is paid to the landowner. However, this amount is normally calculated according to the average paddy produces from that land during preceeding year. In this process after one year, the landowner need not return the principal amount to the lessee. The second system of land mortgage reported by the villagers is Karati Bandhak. In this system, the landowner gets an amount of Rs. 3,000 to Rs. 5,000 for mortgaging one acre of land. Under this practice, the mortgage period normally continues for a period of 3 to 5 years. At the end of the period, the landowner only returns the principal and not the interest. The land mortgage period may be extended until and unless the landowner does not return the principal amount. The data on land mortgaged reflects that in the study village almost 12 (66.66%) Kandha households had not repaid the principal loan amount within the stipulated period. As a result, they were unable to get back their land from the *sahookar*. This affects the life and livelihood system of the tribal households.

Sale and Purchase of Land

The study also wanted to know whether the villagers have legally sold and/or purchased their land during the last five years, i.e., from 1995-2000. As regards purchase of land, the households were asked to indicate the source of purchase and the extent of land purchased. The data reflect that in Lachipetta village of Malkangiri district only one tribal household has purchased 0.5 acres of agriculture land from another tribal households from the same village. Similarly, the study also enquired about the sale of land in the study villages, which took place during 1995-2000. The focus was to know the number of households (ethnic groupwise) sold their land, where they had sold and total amount of land sold during the period. A look into the situation reflects that in Lachipetta village 3 ST households had given their land-use rights over 2.5 acres of their land in lieu of a substantial amount received from the lessee. Similarly, except one case of land purchase in Lachipetta of Malkangiri district no other case was reported.

However, in Penaposi Pangara village of Kandhamal district, the situation was different. In this village, 46 (92%) Kandha households had given their crops under advance mortgage to Sundhi households of the village who are engaged in business. These traders sell various items of daily consumption, and provide seasonal/occasional consumption on credit, which is repaid during the harvest time of turmeric, the major cash crop of the area. The tribal households enter into a forward trading contract while borrowing for production and consumption purposes, and this has become a normal practice in the area. Such advance transactions through borrowings for production and consumption purposes are also, observed in case of Kendubaradihi village of Kalahandi district where the tribal households mortgage their crops to the Kumuti *sahookars*. The sahookars with the help of their agents ensure by using various social channels for 100 per cent recovery of their loans paid both in the form of cash and kind. In both the cases, during the process the sahookars, who are non-tribals, try to recover the loan without sympathy. Even the produces are immediately collected in the cropland itself. In Lachipetta village of Malkangiri district, tribal economy was largely determined through barter, forward trading, and partly through money payments in which the traders dictate the terms to the tribal people. Similar economic transactions have also been reported in tribal dominated districts of Mayurbhanj and Rayagada (Mishra, 1996). Under the situation, advance mortgaging of agricultural produces (main crop) as observed in Kandhamal district through borrowing for production and consumption purposes seem to be more serious then physical alienation of a piece of land. In this process, the caste group traders not only use the local tribal labour force but also appropriate profit out of production by dictating terms as per their whims.

Knowledge of PRI Members

The PRI members were asked a couple of questions regarding the knowledge on the policies, functioning of the government departments and procedure of reporting land alienation cases. Out of the 38 total ST PRI members interviewed, 26 (68.42%) could express their simple knowledge on the policy while 4 (15.38%) could speak about the procedures of reporting such cases and the department, which deals with this issue. The analysis of the finding reflects that the members of the local PRI bodies do not know about the policy so expecting their role (though the policy does not say anything about their role) in this regard will be of little use. This poor situation was reported in almost all the study villages of four different districts of Orissa.

7 Role of Government Agencies in Tribal Development

This chapter reviews the functioning of different agencies responsible for the protection, welfare and development of the Scheduled Tribes and Scheduled Areas of the State. They are to ensure good governance by way of implementing various provisions of the Fifth Schedule of the Constitution. A few of these agencies have been playing major roles in establishing peaceful governance in Scheduled Areas of the State. The agencies are the ST and SC Development Department, Tribes Advisory Council (TAC), National Commission for Scheduled Castes and Scheduled Tribes, Scheduled Castes and Scheduled Tribes Research and Training Institute (SCSTRTI), Orissa Forest Development Corporation Ltd. (OFDC), Tribal Development Cooperative Corporation Ltd. (TDCC), Orissa State Finance Development Corporation Ltd. (OSFDC) and Panchayati Raj Institutions. While reviewing each of these agencies an attempt has been made to highlight some of their achievements, their strength and constraints encountered by them.

ST and SC Development Department

As regards the administration and control of Scheduled Areas and Scheduled Tribes, Article 244 (1) of the Constitution of India elaborates the provisions. For ensuring peace and good governance in the tribal areas, government can institute different committees and commissions for specific issues on temporary and/or on permanent basis. The Scheduled Tribes and Scheduled Castes Development Department which acts as the nodal agency for tribal development in Orissa has constituted different committees at district level as well as at state level from time to time. The first section describes about a retrospective account of tribal welfare programme in Orissa, and various committees and commissions, their structure and functions; while the second section, more particularly, analyses the structure and function of TAC.

I

Tribal Welfare Programme in Orissa

Considering the backwardness of the tribal people and the tribal regions of Orissa, the Partial Excluded Areas Enquiry Committee under the Chairmanship of A.V. Thakkar visited Orissa in 1938 and submitted its report, which was reviewed during 1946 by the Backward Classes Welfare Section. Finally, the Government of Orissa formed a separate department in 1948 known as Backward Class Welfare Department. Not finding the functional appropriateness of the name of the department, Government of Orissa thought of changing the name from time to time as Rural Welfare Department, Welfare Department and presently known as ST and SC Development Department. In spite of the Constitutional provision (Article 164) for a separate Minister in charge of the welfare of SCs, STs and Backward Classes, (though the state of Bihar and Madhya Pradesh have already made the provision separately for the development of STs), the State of Orissa is yet to have such provision. The Tribes Advisory Council (TAC) formed in Orissa since 24 June, 1950 have been advising the Government of Orissa from time to time on the matters of the welfare of tribal communities of Orissa. The Scheduled Areas Order of 1950 first issued in Orissa by the Government of India again revised during 1977 added two full administrative districts as Fully Scheduled Areas and many areas of few districts as Partial Scheduled Areas. The recent reformulation of the districts in Orissa includes six full districts and seven partial districts as Scheduled Areas of the State.

In initial days of Community Development programmes, special projects known as Multi-Purpose Tribal Blocks were started in Orissa during 1956 on experimental basis. The major objectives of those experiments were to develop the tribal people in line with their culture and to safeguard their interest in land, forest and forest-based resources. Being pilot by nature such experiments with financial and administrative functional autonomy were aiming at developing model development programmes for the tribal people. However, these experiments could not be methodologically and contextually sound for the purpose. Considering the recommendations of Elwin Committee regarding the implementation of the structure of Tribal Development Blocks (where more than 50 per cent of the population are numerically represented by the tribals) the State of Orissa initially opened up 62 numbers of Tribal Development Blocks, which were later on increased to 74.

Later on considering the dispersed nature of tribal population, the concept of Tribal Sub-Plan approach was also introduced in Orissa in 1979 where Integrated Tribal Development Projects (ITDP) were launched. Thus, presently Orissa has 118 Tribal Development Blocks distributed over 19 ITDPs and Tribal Development Agencies both for planning and execution of tribal development programmes. Besides, Special Micro-Projects for development of Primitive Tribal Groups (PTGs) were being implemented from time to time. Presently. Orissa has 17 micro-projects for 11 Primitive Tribal Groups (PTGs) to bring the PTGs into the mainstream. Of them, one micro-project was started in 1976-77, five micro-projects were started during 1978-79, one each during 1984-85 and 1985-86, three each during 1986-87, 1988-89 and 1997-98 and the rest two were started during 1993-94.

Over the years, it has been felt that apart from giving financial support to the tribals for their economic development, enactment of certain regulations have become necessary as part of the process to safeguard the interests of the tribal people. A few of such regulations include the Orissa Scheduled Areas Transfer of Immovable Property Act (by Scheduled Tribes) Regulation 2 of 1956 and the Orissa Land Reforms Act (OLR) of 1960, which restricts the alienation of tribal land both in Scheduled Areas and non-Scheduled Areas respectively. The Orissa Scheduled Areas Debt Relief Regulation 1967 provides scaling down of debts through Debt Relief Committees. Similarly, licensing of money-lenders and regulation of interest rates in the tribal areas are there in order to protect them from the clutches of greedy moneylenders for which the Orissa Money Lenders Act of 1993 have been enacted. The Bonded Labour System (Abolition) Act of 1967 is also in operation to free and rehabilitate bonded labourers in tribal areas. The Orissa Reservation of Vacancies in Posts and Services (for SCs and STs) Act of 1975 has been made for the proper representation of the tribals in various public and private sector services and lastly as a part of the decentralization process the State has extended the Panchayati Raj Act to Scheduled Areas (PESA) of the State and decentralized certain developmental arenas for their involvement.

Fund Flow for Tribal Development Programmes

This section provides an understanding of the role so far performed by the State as regards tribal development in Orissa. More specifically, it highlights the financial allocations and the actual investment so far made for the tribal development programmes undertaken in general during different plan periods from various sources like: allocations from SCA to ITDAs, MADAs, Micro-Projects and Clusters since their inceptions in the ST and SC Development Department.

The financial support for tribal development in the State generally comes from three different sources, viz., State Plan, Special Central Assistance (SCA) and Central and Centrally Sponsored Schemes (CCSP). Allotment of funds for tribal development operates on two premises: firstly, for speedier achievement of development of the tribal funds will not be a hindrance for the accomplishment of physical targets; secondly, the budget provisions earmarked for tribal development will neither be felt short nor can be diverted to other purposes if not provisioned in the plan.

The outlays in the State Plan for tribal development is normally decided on the basis of the strength of the tribal people and their levels of development. The State Department allocates separate and special funds for the Tribal Sub-Plan (TSP) areas, which cannot be diverted for other purposes. The source of funding for various development programmes is normally decided by the nature of the project. While the Centrally sponsored projects are totally funded by Central Government, the State Plans are funded by block grants and loans from Central Government. The Centrally Sponsored Schemes cover, viz., Tribal Development Blocks, Cooperatives, Girls Hostel, Research, Post-Matric Scholarships, Coaching and Pre-examination Training to Tribal Youths. The State Plan schemes may be broadly classified as Educational, Economic, Health and Housing. The Ministry of Welfare of Government of India now known as Ministry of Social Justice and Empowerment gives the Special Central Assistance (SCA). The SCA is meant for family-oriented income generating schemes in various sectors like Agriculture, Horticulture, Minor Irrigation, Soil Conservation, Cooperation, Fisheries, Small Industries, Women Issues, Ecology, Environment and Minimum Need Programmes. There are different criteria to decide the budget allocation for ITDAs, MADA Pockets, Clusters, Primitive Tribal Groups (PTGs) and Dispersed Tribal Groups.

The Scheduled Tribe and Scheduled Caste Development Department of Government of Orissa normally acts as the nodal department for the tribal development and provides grant to the Integrated Tribal Development Agencies (ITDAs), MADA, Cluster, DTDPs and Special Micro-Projects. The financial allocations for Tribal Sub-Plan areas of Orissa from different sources like State Plan, Special Central Assistance (SCA) and flow from Central and Centrally Sponsored Schemes have been analysed taking data from the financial year 1974-75 to 1997-98. More specifically, the data on the flow from State Plan to Tribal Sub-Plan (TSP) areas reflect a steady growth of allocation with sudden rise of funds in the year 1990-91. Similarly, the data on the flow of funds from Central and Centrally Sponsored Schemes to TSP areas has increased only since the year 1984-85. However, it has negative growth trend in the allocation during the years 1991-92, 1996-97 and also in 1997-98 (Annual Administration

Report of Scheduled Areas of concerned years). The data on the flow of fund from SCA to the TSP areas of Orissa show that the fund has always been less thought it has marginally increased over time.

An examination of the decadal growth of fund allocations in nominal terms from various sources to the TSP areas of Orissa reveals that the flow from State Plan which was Rs. 1,761.05 lakh during 1974-75 rose to Rs. 11,311.28 lakh in 1984-85, registering an increase of 642.30 per cent. This was further increased to Rs. 33,570.26 lakh in 1994-95, registering an increase of 296.78 per cent over the period 1984-85 to 1994-95 and to Rs. 57,662 lakh during 1997-98. Similarly, the flow of fund from Central and Centrally Sponsored Schemes to TSP areas of Orissa was Rs. 213 lakh during the year 1974-75. This increased to Rs. 6,282 lakh during 1984-85 registering an increase of 29.50 times at the current nominal prices over the period 1974-75 to 1984-85. This further rose of Rs. 27,583 lakh during 1994-95 and diminished to Rs. 13,414 lakh during 1997-98. The amount of flow of fund under Special Central Assistance (Scheduled Caste) also shows an increasing trend. This increased from Rs. 81 lakh in 1984-85 to Rs. 4,312 lakh in 1997-98 at current nominal prices.

From the allocations of State Plan funds in TSP during various Five-Year Plan periods in Orissa, we observe that in between 5th and 6th Five-Year Plans, the growth of total fund for tribal development was 332.46 per cent. This increased by 212.02 per cent during 7th Five-Year Plan and 137.96 per cent during 8th Five-Year Plan. However, this amount has increased further by 212.50 per cent in 9th Five-Year Plan period (TSP Document of concerned Five-Year Plans). The allocation of funds under Special Central Assistance (SCA) similarly increased by 219.65 per cent in 6th Five-Year Plan, 154.93 per cent in 7th Five-Year Plan and 117.79 per cent during 8th Five-Year Plan. The SCA has increased to 154.53 per cent in the proposed 9th Five-Year Plan. The fund under Central and Centrally Sponsored Schemes has however shown a declined trend of growth in terms of percentage increase over 7th, 8th and proposed 9th Five-Year Plan period. Thus, the actual investment from various sources for tribal development in

Orissa when calculated between different Five-Year Plan periods, it is found that the total outlays of the 6th Five-Year Plan compared to 5th Five-Year Plan increased by 319.78 per cent, whereas, during the 7th and 8th Five-Year Plan periods this amount when compared with the previous plan periods increased by 222.83 per cent and 144.34 per cent respectively. However, the total investment for tribal development proposed during 9th Five-Year Plan has increased by 186.71 per cent as compared to the 8th Five-Year Plan period.

Distribution of Special Central Assistance (SCA)

The data on the distribution of SCA since its beginning in 1974-75 invested in different programme components like ITDAs, Micro-Projects, MADAs, Cluster Pockets and DTDPs are taken into analysis. The investment of SCA in various programmes of ITDAs during the year of 1974-75 was only as 81.61 lakh. This was after a decade raised by 119 per cent during the year 1984-85 and by 199.72 per cent during next decade in 1994-95. Similarly, in case of Micro-Project for the PTGs the allocation was only Rs. 5 lakh for one Micro-Project and this has been raised by almost 15 times in the year 1986-87 for 11 of Micro- Projects (75 lakhs), which was again raised by 218.94 per cent during the year of 1996-97 for 17 Micro-Projects (166.18 lakhs). In the case of MADA the total allotment was 86.10 lakhs of rupees during the first year of 1980-81 and was raised by 260.62 per cent during the year of 1990-91, however, reduced to 118.80 lakhs during 1997-98. Similarly, the allotment for different Clusters and Dispersed Tribal Groups has also increased over time. The state has also received amount of 5222.95 lakhs as grants released under First Provision to Article 275 (1) of the Constitution for the year 1992-93 to 1997-98 towards the development of the tribal people (GoI 1997-98).

Allotment and Expenditure for the Development of Primitive Tribal Groups

Till the end of 4th Five-Year Plan of India, there was a special allocation for the tribal development in general implemented irrespective of their level of backwardness or development. As a result, it was observed that quite a good number of tribal groups who were in interior pockets were not properly served. This forced the planners to frame special programmes for specific development of the specific tribal groups. In 5th Five-Year Plan special Micro-Projects were started for those Primitive Tribal Groups popularly known as PTGs uniformly identified on the basis of certain characteristics like their primitive agricultural technology, low level of literacy, stagnant or diminishing population, etc. In Orissa, at present, we have 17 such Micro-Projects being operated for development of 11 PTGs. Of which, one project was established in 1976, 8 Micro-Projects in 1978-79, 3 Micro-Projects during 1986-87 and one Micro-Project each during 1984-85, 1985-86, 1993-94 and 1994-95 covering various Primitive Tribal Groups (PTGs) like Lodha, Mankiridia, Khadia, Juanga, Didayi, Gond, Bonda, Chuktia, Bhunjia, Dangaria Kondha, Kutia Knodh, Lanjia Saora and Paudi Bhuiyan. District-wise distribution of these Micro-Projects reflects that two of these projects are in Mayurbhanj, one each in Keonjhar, Phulbani, Dhenkanal and Sundargarh, 3 in Ganjam, 5 in Koraput and 3 in Kalahandi. Except two Micro-Projects named as Paudi Bhuiyan Development Agency at Jamardihi, and Thumba Development Agency at Thumba, all other 15 Micro-Projects are located within the TSP areas of the State.

A review of the funds allotted to these Micro-Projects shows that almost all the Micro-Projects though started with limited funds, later on received sufficient funds depending upon the type of the programme adopted. However, presently there are certain Micro-Projects like Kutia Kondha Development Agency, Lanjia Saora Development Agency, Paudi Bhuiyan Development Agency at Khuntagaon, have started declining due to lack of funds from Central Government, whereas, Micro-Projects like Juanga Development Agency, Paudi Bhuiyan Development Agency at Jamardihi, Dangaria Kondha Development Agency at Chatikana, Kutia Kandha Development Agency and Didayi Development Agency continues to maintain almost similar trend of getting funds from the Central Government for last couple of years. However, it is not possible to compare the allotment and the expenditure made in development programmes carried out every year in these Micro-Projects, due to the paucity of data in many of the Annual Administration Reports of the Scheduled Areas of the Government of Orissa. While comparing the allotment and expenditure of Micro-Projects during two specific years of 1990-91 and 1995-96, it was observed that the expenditure levels were lagging behind the allotment in almost all the Micro-Projects owing to the fact of delay in release of funds, lack of technical expertise at project level for implementing programmes, etc.

The state of Orissa has formed few committees, for the promotion and welfare of STs and SCs of the State and to advise the government on these matters. Some of them are Tribes Advisory Committee, Standing Committee on Employment of SCs and STs, and the Committee on Welfare of SCs and STs which have been constituted by the Orissa Legislative Assembly. The District Welfare Committees and Sub-Divisional Harijan Welfare Boards constituted at the district and sub-divisional levels respectively review the progress of welfare schemes meant for SCs and STs within their respective jurisdictions.

State Level Committee

In pursuance of the guidelines of the Government of India and the Planning Commission, a Tribal Sub-Plan Committee for the state of Orissa has been constituted to monitor the progress of development of backward tribal regions of the State. Government has constituted 21 Integrated Tribal Development Project level sub-committees for 21 ITDAs in the Sub-Plan area.

For effective and expeditious implementation of different programmes and to discharge various responsibilities, the State Government has set up a Committee for Sub-Plan area programmes. The composition of the committee includes the Chief Minister as Chairman; Minister, Tribal and Rural Welfare (T&RW) as Vice-Chairman; Development Commissioner-cum-Chief Secretary, Agricultural Production Commissioner, Additional Development Commissioner, Secretary, Finance Department, Secretary, Revenue Department, Secretary, C.D. Department as Members, and Secretary, SC and ST Development

Department as Member-Secretary. The Secretaries of other departments may be co-opted or invited to meetings as and when required.

This Committee shall have the powers to examine and approve project reports of ITDPs; scrutinise funds earmarked by the concerned departments for sub-plan areas; approve annual plans and programmes; place funds with ITDAs if necessary after effecting inter-sectoral re-appropriations; liaison with sectoral authorities at the state level as also with public sector and semi-autonomous organisations like K&VI Board, Commercial Banks, NABARD, Reserve Bank of India and the Union Ministries; undertake continuous evaluation of programmes and analyse feedback to solve problems; oversee the pace of development in the tribal areas; ensure implementation of Special Acts; examine problems arising from extension of general laws to the tribal areas; oversees the working of non-developmental organisations in so far as they affect tribal interests. The headquarters of the Committee is fixed at Bhubaneswar and the Committee meets once in every quarter or more often, if necessary.

The State Level Evaluation Committee

The State Level Evaluation Committee is constituted with official and non-official members of which the Director, ST and SC Development Department is the Member-Secretary. The Committee evaluates (qualitative and quantitative) the achievements made during previous plan periods and the benefits derived by the ST and SC people out of the special schemes executed for their welfare; advises the government for formulation and implementation of schemes best suited to the ST and SC people; reviews the benefits derived by ST and SC people out of the general sector programmes implemented in the past; advises government as to what portion of the provision to general development sector can suitably be earmarked for exclusive benefit of backward classes people, particularly for ST and SCs; draws up a programme of their work, meets from time to time according to their convenience and submit their report on a particular scheme as soon as the study is completed.

Atrocity Enquiry Committee

The State Government has constituted a high level committee, known as the Atrocity Enquiry Committee consisting of six members to enquire into cases of atrocity committed on Harijans and Adivasis. According to the terms of reference, the Committee is required to enquire into the allegations of harassment and atrocity on Harijans and Adivasis, to enquire into allegations connected with unlawful eviction or dispossession from land where the matter is not subjudice and to report to the government about the administrative and other lapses on the part of the State Government officials and other individuals, which has resulted in such atrocity or harassment. The Committee may also recommend to the State Government for suitable remedial action against recurrence of such incidents, extending legal aid in appropriate cases and sanctioning exgratia grants to the Scheduled Castes and Scheduled Tribes to mitigate their hardships resulting from harassment and atrocities.

By the end of 1979-80, the Committee made spot enquiries into 18 cases and submitted its reports in respect of 15 cases. It has observed that after 10 years, i.e., 1989-90 the Committee met thrice and a total amount of Rs. 9,659 was provided as monetary relief to 33 persons and Rs. 13,488 sanctioned as relief to 19 ST persons. By the end of 2000, the Committee had met only four times. This at one level reflects the nature of functioning of the Atrocity Committee.

Standing Committee on Employment of Scheduled Castes and Scheduled Tribes

In pursuance of Section 15 of the Orissa Reservation of Vacancies in Posts and Services (for Scheduled Castes and Scheduled Tribes) Act, 1975, the State Government has constituted a Standing Committee on Employment of Scheduled Castes and Scheduled Tribes consisting of 9 members. The Minister, Tribal and Rural Welfare, Orissa is the Chairman of the Standing Committee. The Committee is to review implementation of the provisions of the Reservation Act and the rules framed thereunder, suggest measures for removal of difficulties in such implementation or for improvement thereof and to discharge such other functions as the State Government, may from time to time assign to the Committee.

This Committee organises pre-recruitment camps for SC and ST candidates in a phased manner for their appointment in the Armed Forces of our country. It also expedites verification of roster register by the authorised officer for ensuring filling of reserved vacancies by SC and ST communities in various offices. This committee has made few recommendations. They are: the inspecting officers are to be empowered to file prosecution for violation of the provisions of the ORV Act, under Section-12 (B) of the Act for violation of the reservation policies, and to ensure strict application of ORV Act in fully aided educational institutions, and the provision which has been made to enhance the maximum penalty from Rs. 1,000 to Rs. 5,000. The meeting of the Committee held on 15 September, 1995 stressed that special drive should be made to clear the backlog of reserved vacancies by different appointing authorities for SC and ST candidates. Decision was also taken to undertake test inspection for ascertaining the implementation of the revised 80-point model roster by the authorised Inspecting Officers. The ST and SC Development Department has started the process of reviewing the progress initially in medical colleges and government owned technical institutions. However, it should be completed in all departments within a time frame.

District Welfare Committee

District Welfare Committees have been constituted in all the 14 districts with the objective of making regular review of progress of execution of different schemes. The concerned District Magistrate is the Chairman of the Committee and the DWO functions as the Member-Secretary. Local Scheduled Caste and Scheduled Tribe MLAs and MPs, some leading non-officials interested in the welfare of SCs and STs (who need not necessarily be the MLAs/MPs) and other officers of government or non-government (voluntary) organisations belonging to SCs and STs, interested in the welfare of SCs and STs are included as members. The Committee may also co-opt official members of the District

Development Committee as its members. This Committee at district level meets twice a year.

II

Tribes Advisory Council

There shall be a Tribes Advisory Council (TAC) established in each State having Scheduled Areas therein and, if the President so directs, also in any State having Scheduled Tribes but not Scheduled Areas therein, a TAC consisting of not more than twenty members of whom, three-fourth shall be the representatives of the Scheduled Tribes in the Legislative Assembly of the State: provided that the number of representatives of the Scheduled Tribes in the Legislative Assembly of the State is less than the number of seats in the TAC to be filled up by such representatives, the remaining seats shall be filled by other members of those tribes. The TAC to advise on matters pertaining to the welfare and advancement of the Scheduled Tribes in the State as may be referred to them by the Governor*. The Governor** may make rules prescribing or regulating, as the case may be – (i) the number of members of the Council, the mode of their appointment and the appointment of the Chairman of the Council and of the officers and servants thereof; (ii) the conduct of its meetings and its procedure in general; and (iii) all other incidental matters.

Functioning of TAC in Orissa

The TAC in Orissa was constituted on 24 June, 1950 in keeping with the Constitutional obligation. The council consists of 20 members of whom as many as three-fourths shall be the representatives of Scheduled Tribes in the State Legislative Assembly including the Chairman. The Chief Minister of Orissa and the Minister in-charge of Tribal Welfare acts as the chairman and Deputy Chairman respectively. As regards the membership in

---

* The words "or Rajpramukh, as the case may be" omitted by the Constitution (Seventh Amendment) Act, 1956, S 29 and Sch.

** The words "or Rajpramukh" omitted by S 29 and Sch Ibid.

TAC, the Orissa Tribes Advisory Council (Amendment) Rules 1983 says that of the total TAC members, three-fourths, i.e., 15 members from State Legislative Assembly shall be nominated annually on rotation basis, so that all the representatives of STs in the State Legislature may represent in the Council during their term period. However, the Chairman and Deputy Chairman shall not be affected by such rotation. Remaining 3 members shall be the persons nominated annually by rotation from among the representatives of STs of Orissa in the Parliament.

Again Rule 5 of the said rule amended that unless sooner dissolved by the Governor or with the dissolution of the Legislative Assembly, the Council shall continue for a period of one year from the date of its constitution and shall be reconstituted in such a manner so that there may not be any gap intervening between the date of expiry of the term and the date of reconstitution of the Council (TAC Meeting, 1987). The business transacted in the TAC meetings is according to the provisions, contained in the Orissa Tribes Advisory Council Rules, 1950. As per the guidelines issued by the Ministry of Welfare, the TAC should meet at least twice a year to implement the agenda effectively. In order to study the structure and functions of the TAC, here an attempt has been made to analyse the frequency of TAC meetings organised, ethnic background of the members, representations from different districts, gender distribution, frequency of membership, and frequency of participation in the TAC meetings. Data have been collected from ST and SC Development Department by reviewing TAC related documents and proceedings of TAC meetings, from the year 1987 to 1998. However, data could not be available for the year 1991.

Frequency of Organising TAC Meeting

As per the guidelines of Ministry of Social Justice and Empowerment, TACs are to sit twice a year. It has been conceived that with an effective agenda if the TAC sits for twice a year then the TAC as a body in the State can be more functional. It is only then the TAC can become a meaningful and important forum representing the interests of the tribal people in the State. Ministry of

Social Justice and Empowerment of Government of India in its Annual Report for the year 1997-98 has commented that despite repeated requests by the Ministry, no State Government has reported about the TAC meetings held during 1996-97. Similarly, State office at Bhubaneswar of the National Commission for SCs and STs while submitting a note to its Chairman during his visit to the State in 1998 has also noted rightly that TAC meetings in Orissa are not held at regular intervals. While reviewing the data, it is observed that from 1996-97 to 1998-99 no TAC meeting was held in the State. It was also reported from the ST and SC Development Department that the Annual Administration Report for the Scheduled Areas is released up to the year 1999-2000 only. This sufficiently indicates violation of the provisions of the Fifth Schedule of the Constitution of India by the State.

Ethnic Background of the TAC Members

In order to find out the ethnic background, a total of 88 TAC members represented from different districts from 1987 to 1998 are randomly analysed according to their district and ethnic background. The distribution of data in different districts show that, of the total of 88 TAC members, 30 (34.09%) members represented Mayurbhanj district, followed by 12 from Koraput district (13.63%), 12 from Keonjhar district (13.63%), 9 from Rayagada (10.22%), 8 from Kandhamal (9.09%), 8 from Sundargarh (9.09%) etc. Among the ethnic groups, it is observed that the tribal communities, which have represented frequently are Santhal, Kandha, Bhuiyan, Oraon, Munda and Saora. In total, the analysis shows that during 1987 to 1998 the TAC members represented from 17 different tribal groups. They are Santhal, Ho/Koi, Bathudi, Mahali, Bhuiyan, Munda, Oraon, Kissan, Khadia, Bhatada, Omanatya, Kandha, Gadaba, Koya, Saora and Sabar. Districtwise data reflect that during the above period few dominant tribal communities of Orissa have frequently represented in TAC meeting of the State. They are: Santhals of Mayurbhanj, Oraons of Sundargarh, Kandhas of Koraput, Nuapada and Kandhamal, Saoras of Rayagada, Bhuiyans of Keonjhar, Saoras of Gajapati, and Kissans of Sambalpur district.

Since the tribal representatives of numerically dominant ethnic communities are elected to the State Assembly or to the Parliament, and only people's representatives can be the members of TAC, under the existing rules numerically small tribal communities are rarely nominated to the TAC. Details of distribution of TAC members according to different ethnic groups and different districts have been given in Table 7.1.

Table 7.1

Distribution of TAC Members According to their District and Ethnic Background in Orissa who Participated in TAC Meetings from 1987 to 1998 (except 1991)

Name of the District	*Name of the Tribal Community*	*Members Represented in TAC*	*Total Members*	*Percentage to Total*
Mayurbhanj	Santal	14	30	30.49
	Ho/Kol	8		
	Bathudi	1		
	Mahali	1		
	Bhumij	1		
	Munda	5		
Sundargarh	Oraon	6	8	9.09
	Kissan	1		
	Khadia	1		
Nawarangpur	Bhatada	1	2	2.27
	Omanatya	1		
Koraput	Kandha	11	12	13.63
	Gadaba	1		
Rayagada	Saora	6	9	10.22
	Kandha	3		
Malkangiri	Koya	1	1	1.13
Kandhamal	Kandha	8	8	9.09
Keonjhar	Munda	4	12	13.63
	Bhuiyan	6		
	Santal	1		
	Oraon	1		
Gajapati	Saora	2	2	2.27
Sambalpur	Kissan	2	2	2.27
Dhenkanal	Sabar	1	1	1.13
Nuapada	Kandha	1	1	1.13
	TOTAL	88	88	100

Source: ST and SC Development Department, Government of Orissa.

Frequency of Representation of Members in TAC

Representatives of a few tribal communities have often represented in the TAC of Orissa. Since membership in TAC is always linked with the Membership of Parliament and State Legislative Assembly, it is observed that only few political leaders (peoples' representative) who have often represented in the State Legislature and Parliament have been nominated as members of TAC. It is interesting to note the frequency of membership of a member in the TAC. For the purpose of analysis, 88 TAC members were randomly taken from 1987 to 1998 (except 1991). The frequency of membership in TAC is measured through a seven-point scale differently for the Members in State Assembly and in Parliament. It has been observed that out of 13 members of Parliament who represented in TAC, 5 (38.46%) members have represented in TAC more than four times, while 4 (30.76%) members represented two times and 4 (30.76%) members represented the TAC only once. Similarly, among the Members of Legislative Assembly who have represented in TAC the analysis shows that, out of a total of 75 TAC members, 16 (21.33%) have represented only once, 29 (38.66%) have represented twice, and 6 (21.33%) have represented

Table 7.2

Distribution of Frequency of Membership of MLAs and MPs in TAC from 1987 to 1998 (except 1991)

Frequency of Membership in TAC	*Members*		*Total*
	MP	*MLA*	
Once	4(30.76)	16(21.33)	20(22.72)
Twice	4(30.76)	29(38.66)	33(34.50)
Thrice	Nil	16(21.33)	16(18.18)
Four times	2(15.38)	4(5.33)	6(6.81)
Five times	1(7.69)	3(4.00)	4(4.54)
Six times	1(7.69)	5(6.66)	6(6.81)
Seven times	1(7.69)	2(2.66)	3(4.00)
Total	13(100)	75(100)	88(100)

Note: Figures in the bracket are percentage to total.

Source: ST and SC Development Department, Government of Orissa.

thrice, while 14 (18.66%) have represented for more than four times. The details of frequency of membership in TAC of the Members of Parliament and Members of Legislative Assembly have been given in Table 7.2. Some members have frequently represented in the TAC. Sometimes because of political affiliations few members have been frequently represented in the TAC.

Preparation of Agenda

Soon after the date for the TAC meeting is decided, SC and ST Development Department invites individual agenda notes from TAC members. On receipt of information, the department incorporates them in the main agenda or prepares additional agenda notes for the TAC meeting. It has been observed that few MLAs and MPs who are the regular members of the TAC normally submit their agenda notes. The review reflects that a few TAC members who have actively participated in different meetings are Balabhadra Majhi, Raghunath Hembram, Haladhar Karji, Chaitanya Prasad Majhi, Ulaka Ramachandra, Mangala Kissan, Khelaram Mahali, Chotarai Majhi, Chandra Mohan Singh, Nagarjuna Pradhan, Khagapati Pradhani, Parama Pujari, Frida Topno, Mauris Kujur and Giridhari Gamango. All are either continuing or ex-MLAs or MPs.

Participation of TAC Members in TAC Meetings

In order to understand the functioning of TAC in Orissa, an attempt has been made to find out the attendance of the TAC members in different TAC meetings. For the purpose, data have been collected from 1987-88 to 1995-96 and attendance of TAC members has been analysed. Data could not be made available regarding the attendance of TAC members for the years 1991-92 and 1993-94. The details of the membership and their attendance in TAC meetings during different years have been given in Table 7.3. The data shows that in none of the TAC meeting all the TAC members were present. The attendance of TAC members in the meetings was almost less than 50 per cent. In all the TAC meetings almost 50 per cent participants were government officials representing different departments who have attended TAC meetings.

Table 7.3

Distribution of TAC Members and their Participation in TAC Meetings Organised from 1987 to 1998 in Orissa

Years	Members of TAC						TAC members attended meeting						Other Officers including CM attended
	Male		Female		Total		Male		Female		Total		
	MLA	MP	MLA	MP	MLA	MP	MLA	MP	MLA	MP	MLA	MP	
1987-88	15	2	3	-	18	2	13	1	1	-	14	1	16
1988-89	15	2	2	1	17	3	12	1	2	-	14	1	15
1989-90	15	2	3	-	18	2	8	2	2	-	10	2	16
							6	1	1	-	7	1	23
1990-91	17	3	-	-	17	3	15	1	-	-	15	1	22
1991-92	Not Available												
1992-93	17	2	-	1	17	3	13	-	-	1	13	1	15
							12	-	-	-	12	-	13
1993-94	17	1	-	1	17	3	-	-	-	-	-	-	-
1994-95	16	2	1	1	17	3	11	-	-	-	11	-	19
							7	-	-	-	7	-	16
1995-96	15	1	2	2	17	3	11	1	1	1	12	2	20
1996-97	17	3	-	-	17	3	NA						
1997-98	15	1	2	2	17	3	NA						
1998-99	7	3	-	-	17	3	NA						

NA: Not Available.

Source: ST and SC Development Department, Government of Orissa

In the meetings where the numerical participation of TAC members are less and the government officials are more. It might have so happened that official views have been represented more in TAC meetings than that of the people's representatives, which obviously influences the decision-making processes on tribal welfare. When we analyse the level of participation of the TAC members in TAC meetings it has been observed that quite a few members because of their regular representation in TAC, raise certain issues in all the meetings and many TAC members remain silent observers in the process. Logically, this affects the whole discussion in presenting various acute problems of different tribal communities by some TAC members.

Common Issues Discussed in TAC Meetings

An attempt has been made to review the agenda notes of TAC meetings for the period from 1987 to 1998. The common issues discussed in almost all the TAC meetings were: Orissa (Scheduled Areas) Money Lenders Regulation 1967 (Orissa Regulation 2 of 1968); Orissa Scheduled Areas Transfer of Immovable Property (By Scheduled Tribes) Regulation 2 of 1956; (Orissa Regulation 2 of 1956); the Orissa Debt Bondage Abolition Regulation, 1948 (Orissa Regulation No. 1 of 1948); the Bonded Labour System (Abolition) Act 1976; the Inter-State Migrant Workmen Regulation (Employment and Conditions of Services) Act 1979; the Orissa Dadan Labour (Control and Regulation Act 1975); the Protection of Civil Rights Act 1955 against social offences like untouchability; proposal on inclusion and exclusion of Scheduled Tribes in the list of Scheduled Tribes of Orissa; Single Line Administration in Scheduled Areas of the State; Excise Policy in Tribal Areas; education/residential schools in tribal areas and reservation of seats, rights of tribal people on Minor Forest Produces; and alternative sources of livelihood for the Shifting cultivators. As regards the finalisation of the proceedings of the TAC meeting some members strongly expressed their views that the issues discussed in TAC meetings should be elaborately covered in the proceedings and the draft of the proceedings be circulated among the members much before its finalisation. Secondly, the ST and SC

Development Department should establish a system of feedback flow so that the members can be informed (within their tenure) about the actions taken by the government on the suggestions made by them. This will make the system more dynamic and effective.

The outcome of TAC meetings on different issues from time to time have been incorporated through amendments of existing Regulations and/or Acts, which have also been implemented in tribal areas. A few of such recommendations and amendments have been explained in Chapters 4, 5 and 6 of this book while dealing with excise policy, indebtedness, and land alienation respectively.

Some former TAC members said that the decisions taken by TAC in order to be made operational needs the concurrence of concerned departments. The responses of some departments in this regard, particularly of Law Department, Forest and Environment Department are not satisfactory. As a result, various issues raised by TAC members are not implemented fully. In subsequent years, if the same TAC members do not continue in TAC, then by and large many of the issues raised by the old members do not get due importance. Under this situation, some TAC members have suggested that the ST and SC Development Department should ensure specific actions on the suggestions made by members within a specified time period.

Submission of Governor's Report on the Annual Administration of Scheduled Areas

As per the provision of Para 3 of the Fifth Schedule, the Governor of a State having Scheduled Areas has to submit an objective evaluation report to the President of India on the developments of both Scheduled Tribes and Scheduled Castes and of Scheduled Areas of the concerned State. The report is supposed to be an unbiased assessment of the Scheduled Areas, highlighting various measures taken by the State Government for upgradation of administration of such areas, implementation of the protective laws, matters discussed by the TAC and its recommendations, etc. Various committees, commissions and working groups which went into the problems of STs, particularly in the Scheduled Areas, such as, the Dheber Commission in 1961, Shilu Ao Study Team in 1969 and the Working Group on the development of STs during Seventh Plan, 1984 have observed that no instructions had been issued by the Union government about the format and contents of annual administration report of the Governors. According to the Dheber Commission, it was finally accepted that preparation of Governor's Report should be the responsibility of the State Secretariat. It was also agreed that views of TACs would also be incorporated in the Governor's report.

It has been generally observed that the report of the Governor normally prepared by the ST and SC Development Department of State and basically provides information on the physical achievements of the State Government. It does not provide any information on the sufferings of the tribal people who struggle for a bare living.

The format of the Annual Administration Report is prepared by Government of India, which includes guidelines to prepare an objective assessment on the administration of Scheduled Areas, explain about the exploitative elements, State Legislations/Acts/Regulations, and to provide a complete sketch of the development programmes undertaken by all departments emphasising more on ITDA/ITDP, Micro-Projects, MADA, Cluster and Dispersed Tribal group Development Programmes, etc. Basing on the facts gathered by the department, the Commissioner-cum-Secretary, SC and ST Development Department, prepares Annual Administration Report on Scheduled Areas and obtains approval of the Chief Secretary. After the approval of TAC, the report is sent to the Governor of the State for approval. The Governor provides his comments and may return back the report to the department. After the final approval of the Governor, the report is submitted to the President of India through the Ministry of Social Justice and Empowerment.

It has been provisioned that the states having Scheduled Areas have to submit the Governor's Report within six months of the closing date, i.e., by 30 September of each year. Ministry of Social Justice and Empowerment in its Annual Report has observed that the Governor's Reports have not been received in time during the year 1997-98. The State of Orissa had also not submitted the Governor's Reports by due date for the years of 1995-96, 1996-97 and 1998-99. This is a common problem still observed in ST and SC Development Department. It has been found during the discussion in the ST and SC Development Department that during 1996-97 no annual report was released (till the end of March 2001). The report from 2000-01 and onwards till 2003-04 was also not released till the end of 2005. The reasons for delay in conducting TAC meetings and publishing the annual reports are multiple. However, a query into the process shows that the department has to be vigilant enough to adhere to the provisions of the Fifth Schedule of the Constitution. It is a fact that Government of India during 1997-98 has highlighted the common irregularities by some states (having Scheduled Areas) in submitting the Governor's Report on time and the State of Orissa is no exception to it. Under the situation, the State has to be abided by the Constitutional provisions while dealing with the administration of Scheduled Areas, and the Government of India has to find out alternative methods for streamlining these reporting system.

Conclusion

The above analysis with regard to various committees and commissions, particularly the structure and functions of the Tribes Advisory Council does not present a very healthy picture. The TAC as an important constitutional agency needs streamlining in operation and be more alert and sensitive to the problems of STs and SCs as per the provisions of the Fifth Schedule of the Constitution of India. It has been observed that there is a big gap in the recommendations of the TAC and implementation of the decisions. There lies a big gap in policy formulation and implementation in Orissa with regard to providing protection to the tribal people. At certain level, it also justifies that monitoring authorities are yet to be sufficiently vigilant in the whole process of formulation and implementation of different welfare policies of the State directed towards the tribal people and Scheduled Areas.

National Commission for Scheduled Castes and Scheduled Tribes

Looking at the economic and social backwardness of different ethnic groups, the framers of the Constitution had felt the need for making certain special provisions for tribals in the Constitution. The basic objectives behind this are to upgrade the position of most backward communities in the economic, educational and social fronts of the society. In order to streamline the development, the founders of Indian Constitution have rightly built up few supervisory bodies to look after effective implementation of development programmes carried out for weaker sections, particularly for Scheduled Tribes and Scheduled Castes. One such supervisory body looking after the implementation of Constitutional provisions is popularly known as 'eyes and ears' of Central government, created on 18 November, 1950, named as the National Commission for Scheduled Castes and Scheduled Tribes. The first section explains about the origin, growth and functions of National Commission; while the second section more specifically elaborates about the functioning of National Commission in Orissa in general and its achievements in the light of the provisions of Fifth Schedule in particular.

Origin and Growth

The Constitution of India under Article 338 (1) has made the provision for a Special Officer to investigate all matters relating to Constitutional safeguards provided for the SCs and STs. The Special Officer will report to the President of India as and when required on the status of STs and SCs. Again during 1967 the office of Special Officer was redesignated as the Commissioner for Scheduled Castes and Scheduled Tribes. As a result of which 17 Regional Field Offices were created to perform similar roles in all States of India. During that time the Central government was of the view that instead of the Special Officer, the task should be entrusted to a high level commission consisting of persons of eminence and status in public life. Later on, again all these 17 Field Offices were regrouped under five Zonal Offices known as Backward Classes Welfare which was headed by a newly created post of Director General, Backward Classes Welfare, under the Union Department of Social Welfare. As per the Resolution of Ministry of Home Affairs, the first Multi-Member Commission was set up in August, 1978, and the Field Offices of the earlier Commissioner for SC and ST were put under the control of the new Commissioner. The objective was to establish a closer supervision over the states as regards their adherence to the Constitutional provisions for SCs and STs.

Functions

It is necessary to examine various functions of the National Commission which are clearly laid down in Clauses 5, 6, 7, 8 and 9 of Article 338 (Amended) of the Constitution of India. They are: (i) to investigate and monitor all matters relating to the safeguards provided for the Scheduled Castes and Scheduled Tribes under the Constitution, and to evaluate the administration of such safeguards, (ii) to inquire into specific complaints raised by SCs and STs with regard to the deprivation of rights and safeguards, (iii) to participate in the planning process of development and to advise the government for the socio-economic development of the SCs and STs, and to evaluate the progress of their development, (iv) to present reports to the President of India on the working of those safeguards either annually or at such times, as National Commission may deem fit, (v) to give recommendations to the Union and states to take measures for effective implementation of those Constitutional safeguards, welfare and socio-economic development of the SCs and STs, and (vi) to discharge such other functions for the protection, welfare, development and advancement of the SCs and STs as the President of India wants and as per the provisions of any law made by the Parliament.

The President of India shall cause all such reports to be laid before each house of the Parliament along with a memorandum explaining the action taken or proposed to be taken or not taken and the reasons thereof. In case of a report concerning any State Government a copy will be sent to the Governor of that State who shall cause it to be laid before the Legislature of the State along with the memorandum explaining the action taken or proposed or not taken and reasons thereof on particular recommendation.

Monitoring of Constitutional Safeguards

National Commission is committed to safeguard the interests of tribal people in various respects of their life way processes. They are: (i) the abolition of untouchability provided under Article 17; (ii) prohibition of traffic in human beings and forced labour provided under Article 23; (iii) prohibition of child labour under Article 24; (iv) provision of economic safeguards under Article 244 working of Fifth and Sixth Schedules; and release of grants for raising the level of administration in tribal areas; (v) educational safeguards under Article 15 (4) with regard to the reservation of seats in educational institutions; (vi) to safeguard distinct language, script or culture provisioned under Article 29 (i); (vii) to provide adequate facilities for teaching in mother tongue at primary level for various linguistic groups provided under Article 350 (A); and (viii) working of service safeguards provided under Articles 16 (4), 16 (4) A and 335 providing for adequate representation for SCs and STs in appointments or posts.

The National Commission also deals with various statutes and legislations which reflect the interest of the SCs and STs. These legislations are: the Protection of Civil Rights Act 1955; The Bonded Labour System (Abolition) Act, 1976; The Forest Conservation Act, 1980; The Child Labour (Prohibition and Regulation) Act, 1986; The SCs and the STs (Prevention of Atrocities) Act, 1989; Acts and Regulations in force in different states to prevent alienation of land belonging to SCs and STs; and Acts prevalent in different states for restoration of alienated land to SCs and STs.

The National Commission both at state and national level is actively involved in watch and ward function as regards implementation of Constitutional safeguards for protection of the interests of SC and ST people. Besides, the National Commission also issues directives for extending various facilities and concessions to SC and ST employees. The Constitution of India in Section 9 under the Article 338 has made it mandatory for the Union and every State Government to consult the National Commission on all major policy matters, which affect SCs and STs. One of its important functions is to keep track of all the major policy decisions taken by both the State Governments and Central Government. The National Commission is also required to participate in the planning process of SCs and STs and evaluate the progress of their development in any State or Union Territory. Thus, the National Commission plays an important role in the activities of the Planning Commission, Central Ministries and State Governments in respect of the welfare and development of Scheduled Caste and Scheduled Tribe population of the country.

Procedure for Inquiry

On receipt of any complaint from a member of SC and ST on the deprivation of the benefits provisioned under the safeguards of the Constitution of India, the National Commission is supposed to take up the case for providing justice to aggrieved person. It may visit any spot to enquire and console the victims, review the records, and actions taken by law and order authorities. The victims are provided with relief and protection and compensations for their loss. The Commission initiates close monitoring of the situation. It also keeps close contact with the Chief Secretaries and senior officials of the concerned State and Ministry of Social Justice and Empowerment.

The National Commission while investigating any matter referring to Sub-clause (b) of Clause (5), enjoys all the powers of a civil court and can sue in respect of summoning and enforcing the attendance of any person from any part of India and examines on oath; requiring the recovery and production of any document; receiving evidence on affidavits; requisitioning any public record or copy thereof from any court or office; issuing notice for examination of witnesses and documents; and any other matter which the President may determine.

According to Clause (d) and (e) of Section 5 of Article 338 of the Constitution of India, the National Commission is supposed to present a report to the President of India on the states working of Constitutional safeguards meant for SCs and STs with suggestions and recommendations on various aspects which can be considered for policy decisions. This report on the wish of the President shall be placed before each House of the Parliament along with the memorandum explaining the actions taken or proposed to be taken. The copy of the report or part thereof if relates to the matter of State Government, then a copy shall be forwarded to the Governor of the State who shall cause it to present before the legislature of the State along with a memorandum explaining the actions taken or proposed to be taken as per the recommendation relating to the State and the reasons for non-acceptance, if any.

II

Functioning of National Commission in Orissa

The office of the National Commission for SCs and STs in Orissa carries a long history behind it. The state of Orissa including West Bengal and the Union Territory of Andaman and Nicobar Islands was being supervised by the Deputy Director, Backward Classes Welfare, Patna Zone. In the year 1980, the Office of Deputy Director Backward Classes Welfare in Orissa was upgraded to the post of Director for SCs and STs which is still continuing in Orissa in the name of National Commission for SCs and STs and since 2004 a separate National Commission for SCs has been established at Bhubaneswar. Presently the Orissa Field Office of National Commission for STs is headed by a senior IAS officer acting as the Director who is assisted by one Research Officer (RO), one Senior Research Investigator, one Junior Research Investigator, one Office Superintendent, one PA to Director, one Upper Division Clerk, two Lower Division Clerks, two Peons, one *Daphtari* and one Choukidar. The Orissa Field Office of National Commission is now functioning exclusively for the State of Orissa, It looks after the interests of the SCs and STs residing in the Scheduled areas, partially Scheduled Areas and also in non-Scheduled Areas of the State.

As per the Fifth Schedule of the Constitution, the Governor of the State has been vested with powers to modify and screen the State and Central laws for peace and good governance of the

Scheduled Areas of the State and to protect the interests of STs and to curb their exploitation. The following protective regulations have been promulgated and enforced in the Scheduled Areas of the State, which are being watched by the National Commission for their effective implementation. These regulations are: the Orissa (Scheduled areas) Transfer of Immovable Property (By Scheduled Tribes) Regulation, 1956 (Regulation 2 of 1956); the Orissa (Scheduled Areas) Money Lenders Regulation, 1967 (Regulation 2 of 1868); the Orissa (Scheduled Areas) Debt Relief Regulation, 1967 (Regulation 1 of 1968). Apart from these, they also supervise the implementation of the Orissa Land Reforms Act, 1960; the Orissa Money Lenders, Act, 1939; the Orissa Debt-Relief Act, 1980; the Orissa Protection of SCs and STs (Interest in Trees) Act, 1981; the Bonded Labour System (Abolition Act, 1976); the Minimum Wages Act, 1948; the Protection of Civil Rights Act, 1955; the Orissa Reservation of Vacancies in Posts and Services (for SCs & STs) Act, 1975 in the Scheduled Areas and Rules framed thereunder have been operational in the State since 1 July, 1976.

In light of the above regulations and laws enacted in Orissa, the State office of National Commission performs multiple functions. It investigates and monitors the implementation of Constitutional safeguards, which are meant for the protection of SCs and STs. It inquires into specific complaints as regards the deprivation of rights and safeguards of the SCs and STs. It also participates and advises in the planning process linked to the development of SCs and STs. It compiles data in respect of the status of SCs and STs and informs the New Delhi office of the National Commission, and discharges all other duties in relation to the protection, welfare and development of the tribal people as assigned by the National Commission, New Delhi. Here an attempt has been made to highlight the implementation of one Act, i.e., Prevention of Atrocity Act of 1989 with regard to the role the National Commission has played in the matter.

Collection of Information and Reporting Atrocity on STs and SCs

The Prevention of Atrocity Act of 1989 came into force in Orissa on 30 January, 1990 with an aim to prevent atrocities on SCs and STs. Following this one Atrocity Enquiry Committee has been set up at state level for field level enquiry and to suggest preventive and corrective measures to check various forms of atrocities taking place on the Scheduled groups. In addition to these, the Government of Orissa has also established a Harijan Atrocity and Dowry Death Cell at state level. Later on, this State Level Cell has been upgraded and renamed as Human Rights Protection Cell (HRPC) headed by one Director-cum-IG of Police operating with headquarters at Cuttack.

Atrocity on tribals are mainly committed by police and the local landlords, traders, and moneylenders who basically belong to non-scheduled communities. In a sense atrocity on the tribal people by the non-tribals is historical by nature and revolves around the concept of exploitation of the tribals. Atrocities taking place on SCs and STs in Orissa are basically on account of land disputes, claims for minimum wages, restriction to fetch water from public ponds and wells and to enter into the temple.

According to Section 14 of the Prevention of Atrocity Act of 1989, the state of Orissa has 23 courts, which function as Special Courts on the level of District and Session Judge. Before discussing atrocity on the Scheduled Tribe, it is necessary to describe the status of atrocity cases registered and disposed of by the special courts during last ten years, that is, from 1990 to 1999 (Table 7.4). The data show that disposal of cases is around 4 per cent, which seem to be very negligible. The poor disposal of the registered cases indicates that apart from other reasons, the government has insufficient infrastructure for early disposal of such cases.

In order to know the extent of atrocity on STs, according to its nature, an attempt has been made to analyse the data for six consecutive years, i.e., from 1992 to 1997 (Table 7.5). It has been observed that of the total number of registered atrocity cases (1,313) almost 11 per cent are due to rape of tribal women, while other type of atrocity cases like murder, grievous hurt, arson are very negligible, but other IPC offences share almost 82.78 per cent. Similarly, when one compares the frequency of atrocities on the tribal people across the years the data reflect that occurrence of atrocity on STs is increasing day by day (National Commission for SCs and STs, 1997). Of the total cases of atrocity made on the tribal

Table 7.4

Distribution of Registered Cases under Schedule Castes and Scheduled Tribes Prevention of Atrocity (POA) Act, 1989

Year	*No. of offences registered*	*Investigation completed*	*Percentage of investigation completed*	*Investigation completed within stipulated time (out of Col. 3)*	*Cases decided by the court*	*Cases acquitted*	*Cases convicted*	*Percentage of conviction*	*Cases pending in the courts*	*Percentage cases pending to cases registered*
1	*2*	*3*	*4*	*5*	*6*	*7*	*8*	*9*	*10*	*11*
1990	400	400	100	—	132	118	14	4.20	196	49.00
1991	499	499	100	—	252	234	18	4.10	187	37.47
1992	473	473	100	—	240	224	16	3.90	169	35.73
1993	662	662	100	—	348	335	13	2.30	212	32.02
1994	764	764	100	—	259	248	11	1.70	353	46.20
1995	930	930	100	—	368	354	14	1.80	392	42.15
1996	1138	1138	100	—	342	330	12	1.20	638	56.06
1997	1180	1178	99.83	1118 (94.74)	68	64	4	0.40	878	74.41
1998	1332	1267	95.12	749 (56.23)	18	18	0	0.00	1023	76.80
1999	1449	1136	78.40	701 (48.38)	3	3	0	0.00	906	62.53

Note: Figures in parentheses are percentage of total.

Source: Home Department, Government of Orissa.

people from 1992 to 1997, it is observed that during 1992 it was only 8.22 per cent, which have increased to more than three times, i.e., 26.04 per cent during 1996 and however, reduced a little to 21.78 per cent during 1997.

Table 7.5

Distribution of Atrocity Cases on STs by Nature of Crimes Registered with Police in Orissa during 1992-1997

Name of Crime	*No. of Cases of Atrocities on STs*						
	1992	*1993*	*1994*	*1995*	*1996*	*1997*	*Total*
Murder	00	3	00	07	05	03	18 (1.37)
Grievous Hurt	01	2	04	05	16	09	37 (2.81)
Rape	11	20	17	27	43	25	143 (10.89)
Arson	04	03	06	05	02	—	20 (1.52)
Other IPC Offences	89	139	175	159	276	249	1087 (82.78)
PCR Act 1955	03	03	02	—	—	—	08 (0.60)
Total Cases	108 (8.22)	170 (12.94)	204 (15.53)	203 (15.46)	342 (26.04)	286 (21.78)	1313 (100.00)

Note: Figures in parentheses are percentage of total.

Source: Home Department, Government of Orissa, 2000.

As regards registration of the cases according to Protection of Civil Rights Act 1955 and their disposal by the special courts (Table 7.6), it is observed that, out the total of 20,640 cases reported during the period from 1989 to 1997, only 4.91 per cent of cases are disposed, whereas, almost 95.08 per cent of cases are left unsolved. Of the total of 8,014 cases disposed, only 11.73 per cent of the cases the accused were convicted while in 88.26 per cent of cases the accused were acquitted. As regards disposal of the cases by the Special Courts the position is not satisfactory. Apart from this, the State Government is not paying cash compensation to the victims of atrocity, which has not been provisioned in the POA Rules of 1995 (National Commission for SCs and STs, 1997).

Table 7.6

Distribution of Cases Registered under Protection of Civil Rights Act, 1955 in Orissa

Year	*No. of offences registered*	*Investigation completed*	*Investigation completed within stipulated time (out of Col. 3)*	*Cases decided by the court*	*Cases acquitted*	*Cases convicted*	*Cases pending in the courts*	*Percentage of cases pending to cases registered*
1990	55	55	Nil	14	14	Nil	31	68.89
1991	46	46	Nil	9	9	Nil	30	76.92
1992	32	32	Nil	4	4	Nil	21	84.00
1993	33	33	Nil	2	2	Nil	24	92.31
1994	14	14	Nil	1	1	Nil	11	91.66
1995	6	6	Nil	Nil	Nil	Nil	5	100.00
1996	4	4	Nil	Nil	Nil	Nil	2	100.00
1997	7	7	6	Nil	Nil	Nil	7	100.00
1998	4	4	3	Nil	Nil	Nil	4	100.00
1999	4	3	2	Nil	Nil	Nil	3	100.00

Source: Home Department, Government of Orissa.

There are also inordinate delays in conducting joint enquiry. This has deprived the victims to get cash relief in time.

Looking at the extent of atrocity taking place on the tribal people, it is felt necessary to have timely review of the atrocity situation on regular basis chaired by the Chief Minister of the State. Since the delivery of services through the existing judicial structure is very slow and unsatisfactory, appropriate measures are needed to establish more number of special courts and appoint adequate special public prosecutors specifically for the tribal people. It has been observed that several cases of atrocity on SCs and STs have been registered which are mainly due to confrontation with the police functionaries, which could have been avoided. Police personnel need to be oriented through training so as to bring a change in their behaviour towards these scheduled groups (Acharya et al., 2000).

A recent study was conducted by a team of scholars of the NKC Centre for Development Studies, Bhubaneswar, on the constraints faced during the implementation of the Protection of the Civil Rights Act, 1955 and Prevention of Atrocity Act, 1989 in tribal regions of Orissa and the report has been submitted to the Committee of Governors (ibid.). As regards prevention of atrocities is concerned the study found that provision of complaint box at block offices is not functional due to multiple reasons. They are: (i) victims prefer to inform appropriate police authorities directly; (ii) ignorance of the victim about the complaint box; and (iii) victims do not have faith on the functioning of the complaint box. The delay in investigation of the registered cases (as discussed with the district police personnel) is due to inadequate number of investigating staff; engagement of investigating staff in other law and order duties and lack of proper coordination between the executive magistrate and the police officer to conduct the joint inquiries. As a result, large number of cases is pending unsolved in court of law

As regards Protection of Civil Rights Act 1955, the data show that there is a drastic reduction in the number of registration of cases. The major reasons for non-registration may be due to low rate of disposal of cases, non-availability of justice in favour of the victims and delay in getting justice. One of the most important aspects of atrocity is the need of post-atrocity measures for the victims. Normally, the government has observed that it is necessary to have a package for the rehabilitation of the victims during post-atrocity period, which will help them in restoring the earning capacity of the family.

National Commission also collects other information from government departments on problems like land alienation, restoration of alienated land, distribution of waste land among the SC and ST people; budget provisions and allotments made from various sources for the development of these groups; implementation of excise policy in tribal areas; exploitation of tribals by the moneylenders, functioning of Tribes Advisory Council (TAC) and other aspects which directly and/or indirectly protect the interests of the SC and ST people.

Collection of Representations

The National Commission also receives quite a good number of representations from SC and ST employees seeking redressal of their grievances. These grievances cover various aspects like recruitment, appointment, promotion, regularisation, confirmation, reinstatement in services, fixation of seniority, allotment of residential accommodation, provision of in-service training, transfer and posting, and other matters like problem in the fixation of salary, non-payment of dues, appointment of non-Scheduled Castes/STs on production of false caste certificate, entry of adverse remark in the CCRs, suspension and termination of services of employees belonging to Scheduled groups.

During data collection from the National Commission's Field Office at Bhubaneswar, attempt was made to find out the type of representations received by the office.

While reviewing the General File Register in the Field Office at Bhubaneswar of National Commission for STs and SCs which deals with the details of representations received from SC and ST people for different years, data could be made available only for five years, i.e., from the year 1990 to 1992 and from 1997 to 1998. While analysing the data a couple of observations have been made.

The representations made by SCs and STs to the National Commission centre around certain specific issues. This proves that there are only 15 (1990) cases of harassment registered against SCs and STs, which vary in number from year to year, i.e., 28 (1991), 21 (1992), 26 (1997) and 14 (1998).

Similarly, representations in respect of land and agriculture which have been received by the National Commission are four in number during 1990, whereas, the same has been reported as 9 cases during 1991, 4 cases during 1992, 3 cases during 1997 and no case has been received during 1998. The National Commission has not received a single case of representation on problems relating to housing and house-site except 3 cases during 1991 only.

As regards service matters, the National Commission has received quite a good number of representations from SC and ST employees belonging to State Government, Central Government, Central Government Undertakings and State Government Undertakings. During 1998, the representations received by National Commission from ST and SC employees on various issues were reduced by 50 per cent than what was reported during the previous years (Table 7.7). At certain level, one can say that even SC and ST

Table 7.7

Distribution of Representations Received from SCs and STs by National Commission for SCs and STs, Bhubaneswar, on various issues in Orissa

Issues	*1990*	*1991*	*1992*	*1997*	*1998*
Untouchability	1	1	3	4	Nil
Harassment & Atrocities	15	28	21	26	14
Land & Agriculture	4	9	4	3	Nil
Education	2	6	3	4	2
Housing & House Site	Nil	3	—	Nil	Nil
Central Government	17	28	21	24	6
State Government	32	40	30	23	13
Central Government Undertaking	27	30	22	25	13
State Government Undertaking	2	7	6	7	5
Misc.	14	11	—	—	4

Source: General File Register, 1997-1999, National Commission for SC & ST, Bhubaneswar.

educated employees working in various government and semi-government agencies, if denied justice, report the same to the National Commission, but, the poor tribal people who inhabit the remote villages, by and large, do not approach the National Commission even to ventilate their genuine grievances, and the National Commission too has no mechanism to reach these poor victims unless the illiterate, shy and poor tribal people come with a piece of paper called, 'representation'.

Conclusion

- The National Commission performs multiple functions. One of its most important functions is the compilation of achievements of various State Government departments in respect of their concerned areas over SCs and STs of Orissa.
- In order to protect the interest of SCs and STs one of the major mechanisms adopted by National Commission is to undertake investigations only when they receive representations from the people. Practically in Orissan situation, cases of exploitation of tribal people are very common which are even reported by local newspapers. It is a fact that uneducated tribal people living in Malkangiri district which is situated around 700 kms away from the state capital as well as from the office of the National Commissions at Bhubaneswar may not reach the National Commission to get justice. The National Commission can *suo motto* take up the cases of tribal exploitation for investigation. It has been observed that Orissa Field Office of the National Commission has one Research Officer, one Senior Research Investigator and one Research Investigator. With only three field staff it is impossible to say that the National Commission is reaching every nook and corner of the inaccessible tribal pockets of Orissa. Therefore, it is suggested that more number of field staff may be posted in the State office of ST and SC Commission. An independent network for the flow of feedback may be established from districts to the State office of the National Commission. This will reduce over-dependency of the National Commission on State Government and will help to

maintain the independent role of becoming the eyes and ears of the Central government.

- It is said that the National Commission is the eyes and ears of the Government of India, who reports to the President of India about the exploitation of tribal people. The field office of National Commission practically exercises less power and undertakes limited activities except to see and listen to the problems of the tribal people basically from secondary sources and suggest to the State Government as and when required. In this regard, some TAC members expressed their views that ST and SC Commission only reviews the reports collected from various departments of the government. It has insufficient monitoring mechanisms to review field situations, which sufficiently justifies that it is yet to be the ears and eyes of Government of India to look after the implementation of Constitutional provisions in the Scheduled Areas of the State. They suggested that ST and SC Commission in order to get first hand knowledge should undertake various primary surveys, reviews, and impact assessments of various Constitutional provisions and development programmes implemented in the Scheduled Areas of the State.
- During the visit of the Chairman of the National Commission for SCs and STs, Shri Dillip Singh Bhuria, during August 2000 and October, 2001, the local newspapers while quoting the Chairman, highlighted several issues affecting tribal people of Orissa. Perhaps, the limited structural base of the Field office of the National Commission at the state level does not allow them to present tribal issues in a dynamic manner as the Chairman highlighted various issues during his short visit to Orissa.

Scheduled Caste and Scheduled Tribe Research and Training Institute

Origin of the Institute

Scheduled Caste and Scheduled Tribe Research and Training Institute (SCSTRTI) is one of the state level agencies working for tribal development. This institute started as a semi-official organisation during 1952 and then, was known as Tribal Research Bureau. The objective of this Bureau was to collect, and process basic data on various aspects of life-way processes of scheduled groups in Orissa, and perform advisory services to the government on matters of their socio-economic development. During 1967, an Orientation Training Institute was set up by Government of Orissa at Machakund (presently in Malkangiri district). The objective behind this was to impart training to different categories of government officials working in tribal regions of Orissa.

Government of Orissa in 1972, finally, merged both Research Bureau and the Orientation Training Institute and formed a state level new institute known as Tribal and Harijan Research-cum-Training Institute (THRTI) which is kept under the administrative control of the Secretary, T&RW Department. With the rise of a controversy over the issue of the term 'Harijan' during 1980 (GoI, Home Ministry, 1980), Government of Orissa again redesignated this institute as Scheduled Castes and Scheduled Tribes Research and Training Institute (SCSTRTI) on 31 December, 1994.

Objectives of SCSTRTI

The prime objectives of the institute are multiple by nature. It formulates action plan for SCs and STs and undertakes ethnographic and monographic studies on various SC and ST communities of Orissa; it evaluates the development programmes meant for the Scheduled groups of Orissa and organises training programme for those who are working in Scheduled Areas on tribal related issues; and finally, the institute documents various aspect of socio-cultural and politico-economic life of the tribal and Scheduled Caste people of Orissa.

An Advisory Board is constituted for a period of 3 years, under the Chief Minister of the State as Chairman, and Minister, ST and SC Development Department as Vice-Chairman, which meets twice a year. The Advisory Board advises the institute on various policy matters relating to the development of SCs and STs of Orissa.

Functioning of SCSTRTI

The functioning of the SCSTRTI has been assessed depending on the availability of data from various sources of office records. However, an attempt has been made to trace back its performance at least for last ten to fifteen years. The performance of the institute is presented according to different activities with special reference to the specifications enshrined in the Fifth Schedule of the Constitution of India.

Research and Evaluation

Undertaking of Research and evaluation is the major focus of SCSTRTI. Various research and evaluation studies carried out by the institute are basically decided and entrusted by three different expert and policy bodies. They are: SCSTRTI Advisory Board; SC and ST Development Department of Government of Orissa, and the Director SC and SCSTRTI. Apart from these, special studies on tribal communities are also assigned from other departments of both Government of India and Government of Orissa.

The institute carries out research on Scheduled Castes and Scheduled Tribes covering various aspects of their life-way processes is one of its important functions. While scanning the records available from 1977 to 1998, it has been observed that there are 85 research studies enlisted which have been undertaken by SCSTRTI on various issues like ethnographic and monographic studies, welfare activities, ethno-linguistics, health and nutrition and land problems. A few other studies have also been undertaken on ethnic issues, literacy, migration, forest, and the problem of shifting cultivation (Table 7.8).

With special reference to the provisions of Fifth Schedule of the Constitution of India, it is observed that the institute has undertaken a couple of studies on specific issues like, excise policy, indebtedness and land alienation. An attempt has been made to find out the district-wise distribution of different research studies so far undertaken by SCSTRTI which reflects that more numbers of research studies have been carried out in the districts of

Table 7.8

Distribution of Research Studies according to the Issues Covered by SCSTRTI during 1977 to 1998

Sl. No.	*Major Study Issues*	*Frequency*	*Per cent*
1	Ethnographic Studies	28	32.94
2	Studies on Welfare Schemes	10	11.76
3	Tribal Language Dialect	10	11.76
4	Health and Nutrition	7	8.23
5	Land Problems	5	5.88
6	Living Conditions of Tribals	5	7.05
7	Educational Problems	4	4.70
8	Forest Issues	4	4.70
9	Shifting Cultivation	3	3.52
10	Migration	2	2.35
11	Employment	2	2.35
12	Gender Issues	1	1.17
13	Natural Calamity	1	1.17
14	Indebtedness	1	1.17
15	Displacement	1	1.17
16	Bonded Labour	1	1.17
	Total	85	100.00

Source: SCSTRTI, Government of Orissa, Bhubaneswar.

Koraput, Rayagada, Kondhmal, Mayurbhanj, Sundargarh, Keonjhar, Nawarangpur, Malkangiri, Gajapati, Boudha, Kalahandi, Angul and Jharsuguda (Table 7.9). More than thirty reports on different project areas of ITDAs and ITDPs have been prepared out of the data collected during the Universal Benchmark Survey which was conducted by the institute in Scheduled Areas of Orissa during 1978-80. Similarly, 17 individual documents have been prepared out of the baseline survey and need assessments made for Tenth Five-Year Action Plan Period (2002-2007) covering all the 17 Special Micro-Project areas which have been implemented for the development of the Primitive Tribal Groups (2001).

Table 7.9

Distribution of Various Research Programmes Undertaken by SCSTRTI in the Districts of Orissa

Sl. No.	Districts	No. of Socio-Economic Surveys	Preparation of Action Plan	Evaluation and Impact Assessment	Research Studies	Report in UBMS	Total
	Scheduled Area						
1	Koraput	2	6	2	9	2	21
2	Rayagada	6	3	4	5	2	20
3	Malkanagiri	2	4	2	3	2	13
4	Nawarangapur	2	1	1	0	1	5
5	Kandhamal	3	7	2	10	3	25
6	Gajapati	5	5	3	2	2	17
7	Mayurbhanj	4	9	5	11	6	35
8	Keonjhar	3	6	7	3	3	22
9	Sundargarh	4	4	2	5	2	17
10	Kalahandi	3	3	4	3	0	13
11	Balasore	2	2	2	1	2	9
12	Sambalpur	0	6	1	1	0	8
13	Ganjam	1	2	0	2	0	5
	Total	37	58	35	55	25	210
	% of Total	17.62	27.62	16.67	26.19	11.9	100.00
	Non-Scheduled Area						
1	Nayagarh	2	1	1	1	0	5
2	Puri	0	6	1	0	0	7
3	Khurda	0	2	1	1	0	4
4	Cuttack	0	4	0	0	0	4
5	Jajpur	0	0	1	1	0	2
6	Jagatsinghpur	0	0	0	1	0	1
7	Kendrapada	0	1	0	0	0	1
8	Bhadrakh	0	1	0	0	0	1
9	Nuapada	0	9	1	2	0	12
10	Deogarh	1	3	2	1	2	9
11	Bargarh	0	1	0	0	0	1

Contd...

Contd...

12	Balangir (Old)	0	1	0	1	0	2
13	Dhenkanal	0	3	0	1	0	4
14	Angul	0	1	1	0	0	2
15	Jharsuguda	0	2	0	2	0	4
16	Boudh	2	2	2	2	0	8
17	Orissa (General)	3	1	0	30	0	34
	Total	8	38	10	43	2	101
	% of Total	7.92	37.62	9.9	42.57	1.98	100.00
	Grand Total	45	96	45	98	27	311
	% of Grand Total	14.47	30.87	14.47	31.51	8.68	100.00

UBMS: Universal Bench Mark Survey.

Source: SCSTRTI, Government of Orissa, Bhubaneswar.

Determination of Caste Status

Determination of caste status of various tribal and non-tribal communities has been carried out by SCSTRTI. Studies on such caste categories for determination of status has been referred to either by the field level government functionaries or has been recommended by the Welfare Department. The data show that various communities belonging to Scheduled Tribes and Scheduled Castes have been recommended by Tribes Advisory Council to Government of Orissa for inclusion and/or exclusion in different time periods of 1978, 1981, 1985 and 1989. During 1978, as regards the determination of ethnic status, the institute has recommended almost 77 tribal sub-groups for merger with existing 16 tribal communities. Out of that, only one tribal community was identified for inclusion in the list of Scheduled Tribes of the State. Again during 1981, about 116 tribal groups and sub-groups have been recommended for merger with 22 existing Scheduled Tribal groups, whereas, only one community has been recommended for new entry in each Scheduled Tribe and in Scheduled Caste List of the State. Similarly, during 1985 a total of 22 tribal sub-groups have been recommended for merger by the institute with seven Scheduled Tribal communities. Apart from that, 4 new tribal communities and one caste group have also been recommended for entry into the Scheduled List.

Data on the determination of caste status collected from 1990 to 1994 have also been analysed. Almost 26 per cent and 20 per cent of proposed sub-communities have been finally recommended for their merger in Scheduled Tribes and Scheduled Caste categories respectively, whereas, almost 18 per cent STs and 28 per cent SCs are not found included in any of the list. Only 2 per cent from each scheduled category have been found to be suitable for inclusion in scheduled groups who are already in the list. Another analysis relating to the determination of caste status shows that more number of representations claiming independent scheduled status have come from existing tribal communities like Saora and Savar, Khond, Bondo Paraja, Paraja, Kharia, Bagata, Gadaba, Luhara, Koya, Bhattoda/Dhatoda, etc., who have already been listed as Scheduled Tribe during 1950. This at certain level indicates that there are various sub-sections of tribal communities who are still claiming for independent recognition in the Scheduled List of the State. However, they do not fit in as per the criteria adopted by the State to classify them as independent Scheduled category.

As regards the determination of caste status it is observed that while the minimum time period taken by the institute to complete a study for determining the caste status of a community was 3 months, the maximum time taken to complete a study for this purpose was 10 years. The reasons for delay to complete such studies, as informed, are beyond the control of SCSTRTI. However, adoption of a time-bound planning may help SCSTRTI to complete such studies within the stipulated time period. In this regard, some TAC members of the State expressed their dissatisfaction saying that SCSTRTI while undertaking the studies for the determination of caste status is unable to complete them within the stipulated time period. They suggested that any assignment entrusted by TAC to SCSTRTI should be accomplished in time. This will help TAC to take policy decisions on various issues within a time frame.

Socio-Economic Survey

The socio-economic benchmark survey, which was undertaken during 1978 in the entire Scheduled Areas, is one of the major research activities of the institute. The data generated out of such a massive survey provides a database for preparation of various schemes implemented for the development of different tribal communities. A second mega baseline survey and need assessment was carried out in all the Special Micro-Projects covering all households. This need assessment was prepared for the Tenth Five-Year Action Plan Period (2002-2007) for different primitive tribal communities. The institute has prepared 17 individual reports for 17 Special Micro-Projects.

A total of 374 listed titles of different reports carried out up to 2002 have been taken into consideration for analysis. While looking at the total number of socio-economic surveys so far carried out by the institute in various districts of Orissa, it is observed that socio-economic survey as a component in the entire research work constitutes 12.03 per cent (Table 7.9).

Specially in connection with the provisions enshrined in the Fifth Schedule of the Constitution as regards land alienation, regulation of allotment of land among Scheduled Tribes and regulation of moneylending by private creditors, a few studies have been conducted by the institute. A study on indebtedness carried out among the Scheduled Tribes of Paralakhemundi Sub-Division seems to have contributed substantially to the understanding of the mechanisms of moneylending going on in tribal areas. However, many socio-economic benchmark surveys have covered the issues relating to land alienation and indebtedness among the tribal people of Orissa.

While reviewing various dimensions of research activities so far undertaken by SCSTRTI, it is found that a couple of studies have been carried out on the problem of prohibition, and restrictions on the transfer of land by or among the members of the Scheduled Tribes; regulation of the allotment of land to the members of the scheduled groups and regulation of business of moneylending in tribal areas.

The SCSTRTI is also taking active role in the preparation of Tribal Sub-Plan (TSP) document, project reports, action plans for Integrated Tribal Development Agencies (ITDAs). Several studies have been undertaken on identification of MADA, Cluster pockets, and Primitive Tribal Groups. The institute has played an important role as a support organisation of the State as regards the development of the weaker sections.

Training

Sources of Fund Support

Organisation of Training programmes as one of the major activities of the institute aims at catering to the needs of government departments, universities and NGOs. Various departments of Government of Orissa and Government of India fund these training programmes. The 'Training Division of the Department of Personnel and Training', New Delhi; Ministry of Environment Forest and Wild Life; Ministry of Social Justice and Women Empowerment, and Ministry of Welfare of Government of India financially support SCSTRTI to organise various training programmes and workshops. These training programmes are organised by the Training Division of the institute.

The training programmes sponsored by Government of India and Government of Orissa during last 15 years (i.e., the period from 1983-84 to 1997-98) have been analysed for the present purpose. The analysis is made according to the sources of funding; age group, education and ethnic background of the participants; their distribution according to various departments they represent, the positions they held; and various training issues covered and the background of the resource persons.

Frequency of Training Programme

As regards the total number of training programmes organised and total number of training days covered during last 15 years under both the state and national sponsored training programmes, the data reveal that, a total of 82 state level training programmes have been carried out from 1983-84 to 1997-98. These training programmes have covered a total of 623 training days. The average training days per each programme is 7.89 days. There are 251 (19.57%) female and 1,031 (80.42%) male trainees have participated in the training programmes. Almost 55 (67.07%) number of programmes are meant for the male participants, 17 (20.93%) number of programmes meant for female participants only, whereas, 10 (12.19%) programmes are meant for both male and female participants. Similarly, when one looks at the programmes sponsored by Government of India, it is reported that only 36 programmes have been organised by SCSTRTI during the above period (1983-84 to 1997-98). These programmes have covered a total of 474 training days, with an average of 13.16 man-days covered per each training programme. Out of the total of 891 trainee participants, 393 (44.10%) have been invited from outside the State, whereas, 498 (55.89%) participants are from within the State.

Gender Composition

As regards the sex composition of the participants, one finds that the share of female participants in the state level training programmes is less (16.23%) compared to the national level training programmes. There was only one national level training programme specially meant for women, whereas, 12 (33.33%) training programmes were organised only for the male and the rest 23 training programmes were kept open for both male and female participants. At a certain level, this justifies that the institute has not given adequate attention to include more numbers of women participants. This could have justified the gender component of the training to a large extent.

Ethnic Background of the Trainees

The ethnic composition of the trainees is very important. The institute is meant for undertaking training programmes for SCs and STs on priority basis and also to train both tribals and non-tribals on various development issues. The data regarding ethnic composition of the trainees reflect that out of 1,282 participants covered under the state level training programmes, almost

150 (11.70%), 314(24.49%) and 818 (63.80%) belonged to Scheduled Castes, Scheduled Tribes and Other Caste groups respectively. The ethnic composition of the trainees in the national level training programmes indicate that participants belonging to Scheduled Castes (6.60%) and Scheduled Tribes (8.15%) are less compared to state level training programmes. This at certain level proves that SCSTRTI have not taken much care to include SC and ST participants in the training programmes proportionately. In order to encourage their participation, more number of special training programmes could have been organised for the STs and SCs.

Trainees' Age

The age factor of the trainees is important. If the trainees are younger in age, the knowledge gained through training is more useful for a longer period; and if the trainees are senior persons, who are about to retire, then the knowledge gained out of training may be less useful. The state level training programmes reflect that around 35.91 per cent trainees, are below 30 years of age, whereas, 22.46 per cent and 25.50 per cent are within the age group of 31 to 40 years and 41 to 50 years respectively. Similarly, in national level training programmes around 17.58 per cent trainees are below the age of 30 years, whereas, 34.71 per cent and 26.65 per cent of trainees are within the age group of 31 to 40 and 41 to 50 years respectively. This clearly indicates that the institute while selecting the trainees has purposefully laid emphasis on utilisation of the training skill for a longer duration.

Trainees' Official Position

Other dimensions of trainees, which have been taken for our analysis are their official positions and disciplines to which they belonged. This at one level throws light on the importance of training inputs relevant for government employees posted in tribal areas. In state level training programmes more number of officers from Welfare Department, such as, DWO, ADWO, WEO, SO, CDPO, have participated (35.72%). Participation of Panchayati Raj functionaries (7.72%), Scheduled Caste and Scheduled Tribe

Youths (7.33%), Ashram School Teachers (16.14%), OAS Officers (5.38%) is satisfactory. Data regarding the departments of the trainee participants (as shown in Table 7.10) explain that, out of the total participants, almost 58.59 per cent were from the Welfare Department, and 10.45 per cent are from Panchayati Raj Department.

Table 7.10

Distribution of Departments Representing in Various State Level Training Programmes Conducted by SCSTRTI from 1983-84 to 1997-98

Sl. No.	*Name of the Department*	*No. of Participants*	
		Frequency	*Percentage*
1	SC and ST Development Department	755	58.89
2	Panchayati Raj	134	10.45
3	Industries	67	5.22
4	General Administration	61	4.75
5	Agriculture-Soil Conservation-Horticulture	60	4.63
6	Women and Child Development	54	4.21
7	Forest and Environment	47	3.66
8	Revenue and Excise	46	3.58
9	Rural Development	27	2.10
10	Tourism and Culture	15	1.17
11	Cooperation	15	1.17
12	Fisheries and Animal Resource Development Department	1	0.07
	Total	1282	100.00

Source: Training Registration Records, SCSTRTI, Government of Orissa, Bhubaneswar.

Training Issues

Major issues covered in State sponsored training programmes and their frequency have been described under (Table 7.11). Issues like the 'Constitutional Protective Measures' and 'Development Programmes'; 'Tribe, Society, Culture and Development'; 'Scheduled Caste and Tribal Welfare'; 'ORV Act and Rules' are some of the programmes which have been covered by SCSTRTI.

Table 7.11

Distribution of Major Issues Covered under State Level Training Programmes Organised by SCSTRTI during 1983-1984 to 1997-98

Sl. No.	*Major Issues*	*Frequency*	*Percentage*
1	Constitutional Protective Measures and Development Programmes	22	26.51
2	Tribal Society, Culture and Development	16	19.28
3	Scheduled Caste Welfare	8	9.64
4	ORV Act and Rules	6	7.23
5	Training of Trainers of Beneficiary at ITDA Levels	5	6.02
6	Environment Management on Tribal Development	5	6.02
7	Tribal Development Programmes in Orissa	5	6.02
8	Primitive Tribes and Development	5	6.02
9	Reservation Act in Orissa	5	6.02
10	Tribal Development Administration, Monitoring and Evaluation	3	3.61
11	Role of Tribal Women in Tribal Welfare	3	3.61
	Total	83	100.00

Source: Training Registration Records SCSTRTI, Government of Orissa, Bhubaneswar.

Table 7.12

Distribution of Major Issues Covered under Central Government Training Programmes Organised by SCSTRTI during 1983-84 to 1997-98

Sl. No.	*Major Issues Covered*	*Frequency*	*Percentage*
1	Planning, Monitoring and Evaluations of Tribal Development Programmes	9	25.00
2	Tribal Women and Development	7	19.44
3	Tribal Development Administration, Health and Culture	6	16.67
4	Forest and Tribal Development	5	13.89
5	Implementation of Tribal Development Programmes	4	11.11
6	Environmental Management and Tribal Development	3	8.33
7	Society, Culture, Education and Development	2	5.56
	Total	36	100.00

Source: Training Registration Record, SCSTRTI, Government of Orissa, Bhubaneswar.

Similarly, there are almost 7 different issues, which have been covered under 36 training programmes sponsored by various ministries of Government of India. This has covered issues like Development Planning, Monitoring and Evaluation Methodologies, etc. The details of such issues so far covered are given in Table 7.12.

Resource Persons

As regards participation of Resource Persons in both national and state level training programmes is concerned, one observes that the resource persons invited for providing training belong to two categories. They are in-house trainers, and outside or external trainers. The in-house resource persons who have provided training are the Director, ex-Director, Research Officers, Research Assistants, and Officer on Special Duty (OSD). Similarly, the resource persons who came from outside are either academicians (basically anthropologists) and/or administrators. Attempt has been made to distribute the training classes among different resource persons from 1983-84 to 1997-98 as per their expertise. Data reflect that out of the total of 1,448 classes, resource persons from outside have undertaken 49.72 per cent classes in which academicians have taken 19.61 per cent and administrators have taken 30.11 per cent of classes. The data reflect that the Director who is by position an anthropologist has taken 8.63 per cent of the classes, Deputy Directors who belong to social science faculties have taken 7.52 per cent of the classes. The Research Officers, Research Assistants and Officer on Special Duty (who is also an anthropologist) have covered 15.74, 11.09, and 3.03 per cent of classes respectively. At certain level, SCSTRTI has tried to bring a balance while identifying resource persons, however, anthropologists have played a major role in providing training in SCSTRTI. While discussing with the staff of Training Unit it is confirmed that training need and resource persons' expertise are taken into account while identifying resource persons for different training programmes.

Course Contents and Supply of Reading Materials

As regards course contents and supply of reading materials to the trainees of various training programmes, an attempt has been made here to analyse them. For example, the reading materials supplied during a national training programme on 'Environment Management and Tribal Development' organised from 11 to 18 December, 1995 show that it is of high standard, more academic and research oriented. The materials are informative and written by experienced authors. However, the reading materials could have also included various modern methodological tools like Participatory Rural Appraisal (PRA), Rapid Rural Appraisal (RRA), Strength, Weakness, Opportunity and Threat (SWOT) analysis, etc., for environmental management which are largely used by bilateral implementing agencies, NGOs and funding agencies like World Bank, SIDA, DANIDA, ODA, etc. The reading materials provided during training programmes are useful for the trainees.

Different Ministries of Government of India sponsor training programmes. It is difficult to find out the priority of the institute to select the issues. Certain training programmes like Tribal Development Administration, Health and Culture, etc., though do not focus specific dimensions, and nonetheless it is felt that these issues are appropriate since the tribal societies are backward.

Release of Funds from Government of India

The paper tries to find out the extent of fund support provided by Government of India during the period 1990-91 to 1997-98 to different Tribal Research Institutes (TRIs) of India. The objective is to know whether the funding pattern of Government of India follows any principles as regards allocation of funds to the studies on the basis of size of tribal population or backwardness or both. The ST population in Orissa shares 22.21 per cent, is little less than Madhya Pradesh (old) (23.27%), Manipur (34.41%), and Tripura (30.95%), who also have TRIs (1991 Census Report). Similarly, the literacy status of the STs in Orissa was 22.31 per cent which was the third lowest among the states who have TRIs (Andhra Pradesh

Table 7.13

Release of Funds from Government of India to Different Tribal Research Institutes in India

Sl. No.	States Having TRI	ST Population 1991*	ST Literacy 1991	Release of Funds (in Lakhs)								
				90-91	91-92	92-93	93-94	94-95	95-96	96-97	97-98	Total
1	Andhra Pradesh	6.31	17.16	11.50	5.00	4.81	5.66	15.98	25.54	25.00	20.47	113.96
2	Assam	12.82	49.16	14.76	16.00	10.70	12.10	12.55	17.77	13.01	22.40	119.29
3	Bihar	7.66	26.78	—	9.25	9.82	12.71	10.63	14.73	0.00	—	57.14
4	Gujarat	14.92	36.45	1.18	2.25	2.19	0.55	6.15	0.14	0.00	8.90	21.18
5	Kerala	1.10	57.22	10.00	12.00	8.00	7.85	10.00	11.25	13.50	20.00	92.60
6	Madhya Pradesh (old)	23.27	21.54	13.80	13.20	28.28	23.35	13.09	22.21	22.02	47.74	182.90
7	Maharashtra	9.27	36.79	4.34	5.80	11.27	23.75	24.30	0.00	22.70	49.45	141.61
8	Manipur	34.41	53.63	9.00	10.00	6.60	3.50	2.00	0.49	10.35	9.00	50.94
9	Orissa	22.21	22.31	1.60	2.60	3.22	3.73	8.59	12.90	6.70	5.85	45.19
10	Rajasthan	12.44	19.44	1.00	5.00	4.58	5.57	6.14	7.93	5.66	12.82	47.70
11	Tamil Nadu	1.03	27.89	25.00	11.54	9.44	7.39	7.12	16.54	9.30	30.50	116.83
12	Tripura	30.95	40.37	—	—	0.69	6.80	10.41	8.27	11.21	10.95	48.24
13	Uttar Pradesh	0.21	35.70	10.00	5.00	3.46	4.98	0.00	1.12	4.27	—	28.83
14	West Bengal	5.59	27.78	—	5.48	1.03	0.93	1.19	10.83	6.06	21.80	47.32
15	Himachal Pradesh	4.22	47.09	—	—	0.31	0.27	0.21	0.28	0.22	—	1.29
16	Arunachal Pradesh		34.45	—	—	0.00	0.57	0.00	0.00	0.00	—	0.57
17	Karnataka		36.01	—	—	0.00	0.29	0.63	0.00	0.00	—	0.92

*Per cent to the total population of the State.

Source: Annual Report 1997-98, 1998-99, Ministry of Social Justice and Empowerment, Government of India, New Delhi.

had 17.16%, Rajasthan had 19.44%). These two indicators sufficiently establish that the state of Orissa has a substantial tribal population, and is much below the average development indices. This situation when compared with other states having TRIs at one level demands the flow of more funds from GoI to Orissa (Table 7.13).

The data indicate that the states like Assam, Andhra Pradesh, Bihar, Kerala, Maharashtra, Rajasthan, Tamil Nadu and West Bengal, who have less tribal population and higher literacy status, have received more funds than Orissa. This low level of fund flow to Orissa may be due to multiple reasons. It may be that the TRI of Orissa is unable to highlight tribal problems of the State, may be due to poor leadership projection, both at bureaucratic and political levels. Is it that Government of India while allocating funds discriminates among the states and does not follow a realistic approach. The fact remains that the state of Orissa with higher tribal concentration is backward in all respects and has received less funds compared to many other states. This has grossly affected the functioning of TRI of the State of Orissa. Under the situation, the TRI of the State with appropriate leadership has to focus tribal problems in a more realistic manner. Simultaneously, Government of India while sanctioning allotment should aim to minimise regional imbalances and backwardness of tribal people as well as tribal dominated region.

Conclusion

The institute has contributed substantially in the field of research on tribal society, culture, and has provided training to the personnel engaged in tribal development. But one hardly finds more than one or two studies/evaluations/training programmes on any of the issues of land alienation, indebtedness and prohibition. Moreover, no study has been undertaken on the functioning of Tribes Advisory Council (TAC) in the State of Orissa. Such a study would have helped reminding TAC members about their role and responsibilities and helped in streamlining the functioning of TAC in Orissa. When discussed with some senior professionals of SCSTRTI, it transpired that the assignment in respect of research, training, evaluation, etc., are normally decided at higher levels, namely by the Administrative Department and Advisory Board of SCSTRTI. The fact is that sufficient attention is needed to work on the core issues of the SC and ST communities of the State. Since the government has established SCSTRTI for looking into the interest of these deprived ethnic/minority groups (SCs and STs), it is expected that the State and the researchers of SCSTRTI have to play a strong, dynamic and vibrant role in days to come. The institute is a part of the government machinery. It should be given certain autonomy to carry out research activities. Government control will curtail its efficiency.

Orissa Forest Development Corporation Ltd.

Here an attempt has been made to explain the role played by Orissa Forest Development Corporation Ltd. (OFDCL) in the protection of tribal livelihood with special reference to kenduleaf, timber and sal seed trading in Orissa. It also justifies that in spite of planned attempt made by the State to protect the interest of forest dwellers, the tribals are largely deprived of their rights over forest resources and to present their grievances before the State.

With the fast depletion of forest resources one observes changes in the symbiotic relationship that have been long existing between the tribal people and forest. The decline of forest resources in Orissa merely cannot be attributed to the loss of forest resources due to the construction of mega-projects which accounts for two lakh hectares. The bulk of these resources have been lost prior to 1960, and the major portion of the loss is due to over exploitation through both legal and illegal means. The progressive decline in forest coverage indicates that it was 45.5 per cent in 1971, reduced to 38 per cent in 1981, and to 35.24 per cent in 1991 and subsequent periods (Government of Orissa, 1998). The data on the conversion of forest land for non-forest use (Table 7.14) explains that a lot of forest areas have been diverted for various non-forest purposes like irrigation, industries, mining, transmission of electric line, roads and bridges, railway line, defence, human habitations and for other purposes. This loss is

Table 7.14

Distribution of Forest Areas Released for Non-Forest use Under Forest (Conservation) Act 1980 up to 01.06.2001

Name of the Sector	*Proposals Finally Approved by Government*		*No. of Proposal in Pipeline at Various Stages of Compliance*	*Total No. of Proposals*
	No. of Proposals	*Forest Area Diverted in Hect.*		
Irrigation	51 (23.50)	5739.98 (22.64)	59 (28.22)	110 25.82)
Industries	4 (1.84)	2403 (9.48)	9 (4.30)	13 (3.05)
Mining	74 (34.10)	8228.94 (32.46)	82 (39.23)	156 (36.61)
Transmission Lines	37 (17.05)	2488.71 (9.82)	13 (6.22)	50 (11.73)
Roads and Bridges	21 (9.67)	221.83 (0.87)	9 (4.30)	30 ((7.04)
Railway Lines	4 (1.84)	1909.95 ((7.53)	2 (0.95)	6 (1.40)
Defence	4 (1.84)	3865.25 (15.29)	Nil	4 (0.93)
Miscellaneous	19 (8.75)	163.43 (0.64)	9 (4.30)	28 (6.57)
Human Habitations	3 (1.38)	322.09 (1.27)	26 (12.44)	29 (6.80)
Total	217 (100)	25343.26 (100.00)	209 (100)	426 (100)

Note: Figures in parentheses are percentage to the total.

Source: Office of the Principal Chief Conservator of Forests, Orissa, Bhubaneswar.

also partly due to the duality in administration of forest resources between Revenue Department and Forest Department that still prevails in the State. This has highly affected the potentiality of forest resources. Attitude of the government and the people, lack of appropriate, market, value addition, etc., of the forest produces in Orissa compounds the problem. Convention of 'privileges' (1894 Act) into 'concessions' (1952 Act) has highlighted the encroachment on the rights of the forest dwellers in the Scheduled

Areas (Scheduled Tribes Commission, 1961). The National Committee on Development of Backward Areas in its first report highlighted expropriation of rights which were envisaged as an outcome of development, while in its second report these were considered as the precondition of development. The Forest Conservation Act 1980 and its amendment during 1988 clarified that various agencies engaged in the management of forest resources, particularly in their production, regeneration, and development have to look into the interest of forest dwellers in general and tribal people in particular.

In Orissan context, understanding the copious availability of forest resources in general and minor forest produces in particular, a couple of organisational structures in different names for procurement and marketing of various forest produces have been formed, which are functioning. A few of them are named as Orissa Forest Development Corporation Ltd. (OFDC), Tribal Development Cooperative Corporation Ltd. (TDCC), Utkal Forest Products Ltd. (UFPL), and Orissa Rural Marketing Society (ORMAS). A good number of Mahila Mandals under DWCRA scheme, has also been linked in the process of collection, processing and marketing of forest resources. Looking at the commercial viability of forest produces the State at different points of time has nationalised almost all the major forest produces like kenduleaf, timber, sal seed and bamboo. In reality, it has been observed that nationalisation of forest produces has by and large deprived in providing a fair-price to the primary gatherers. Such an arrangement in Orissa, where private industries/parties have been encouraged to trade over, has resulted in a situation worst than the system of appointing labour contractors which was abolished in late 1960s (Das, 1996).

The Orissa Forest Produce (Control of Trade) Act 1981 provides the scope for State monopoly over certain forest products, which the State may notify about the specific forest produce from time to time. This enables the State to exercise monopoly over the trade of almost all NTFPs. This is done through the practice of granting exclusive rights to TDCC,

OFDC, Joint Sector Companies and even to private parties. Only recently (during 2000) Government of Orissa has handed over seventy NTFPs to the Gram Panchayats for their collection, processing and marketing exclusively through granting license by the concerned Gram Panchayats.

Kenduleaves, sal seeds, timber and bamboo are the major forest produces in terms of earning revenue by the State, which have been nationalised at different points of time. The Kenduleaf Department and OFDC procure kenduleaf while sal seeds are being collected by TDCC and also by OFDC. The Kenduleaf (Control of Trade) Act 1962, controls its trade with an aim to eliminate private trading and to keep its transactions under the control of government.

Orissa Forest Development Corporation (OFDC) of the Department of Forest and Environment was established during the year 1979. The OFDC has been allotted kenduleaves and sal seeds, silai leaves, harida, bahada, amla, hill brooms, sabai grass in Athagarh, Athamallik, Dhenkanal, Angul and Puri Forest Divisions of Orissa. The OFDC also collects honey, sal resins and arrowroot in Karanjia, Baripada and Keonjhar Forest Divisions. However, currently it is largely engaged in marketing of kenduleaves and few NTFPs. OFDC has been entrusted with various nationalised products to trade over. The objective of purchase is to generate good revenue for the State and to provide a sustainable livelihood to the forest dwellers, particularly to save the tribal people from the exploitation of private traders and moneylenders.

The discussion tries to unveil a few dimensions of trading carried out by OFDC on kenduleaf, bamboo, sal seed, and mahua flower. In the analysis, an attempt has been made to highlight the role of OFDC in protecting the State interest, i.e., to earn more and more revenue, protecting the livelihood interest of tribal people, eliminating the role of middlemen, traders and sub-agents, and establishing confidence of tribal people on such organisational arrangements which have been created by the State to protect their interest.

Kenduleaf Trading

Among various forest produces kenduleaf plays a dominant role in contributing to the household economy of the poor tribal people as well as to the State exchequer. Kenduleaf popularly known as 'beedi leaves', has also played an important role in shaping the political economy of the State. Looking at its market value, both for rural people as well as for the urbanities and its copious availability in Orissa, the non-Oriya communities particularly Gujuratis have played an important role in the management of the kenduleaves in Orissa. The free and natural growth of kenduleaf in both deciduous as well as in uplands of Orissa, along with the locally available cheap labour, always have been the points of attraction for the traders to trade on kenduleaves. The quality of kenduleaves depends on the practice of regular pruning, which is mainly carried out by the Kenduleaf Division of the Forest Department, Orissa, and by Gram Panchayats, which helps for the healthy growth of the tree. However, poor pruning of kenduleaf bushes carried out by the Kenduleaf Division affects the healthy growth of kenduleaves and the total produce in the State. Apart from its use for 'bidipata' the fruits, barks and flower of kendu tree are used for multiple purposes both for the rural people and for the State to enrich State exchequer.

State control over kenduleaves started with the introduction of Orissa Kenduleaves (Control of Trade) Act 1961. The basic objective of this Act was to control kenduleaf trading by the State without entering directly into the trade. Considering the revenue potentiality and in order to eliminate private trading the State during 1973 nationalised kenduleaves. Kenduleaf Division undertook the production and procurement of kenduleaves, while OFDC was solely given the responsibility of marketing of kenduleaves. Due to various technical and legal implications government decided to nationalise kenduleaf trade in 1972. Since one of the objectives of nationalisation of kenduleaves is to streamline trading and generate more revenue, later on such a joint approach to trade kenduleaves helped the State to increase the production from 3.52 lakh quintals in 1973 which earned Rs, 3.52 crores to 5 lakh quintals in 1997 which earned Rs. 84.16 crores

(1994-95). However, in subsequent years the revenue from kenduleaf has fluctuated and largely reflected a negative trend for the State. This is proved when one sees the revenue statistics during 1996-97 (Rs. 47.86 crores) and 1997-98 (Rs. 40.60 crores). The revenue contribution from different major forest produces (Table 7.15) also justifies the potentiality of forest produces in terms of quantity, quality and income generation strength. But the

Table 7.15

Distribution of Revenue Receipt from Different Forest Produces

Years	*Items*				
	Timber and Firewood	*Bamboo*	*Kenduleaf*	*Others*	*Total*
1990-91	21.10 (19.34)	6.45 (5.91)	76.45 (70.45)	4.68 (4.29)	109.08 (100.00)
1991-92	18.15 (21.42)	7.00 (8.26)	51.57 (60.87)	8.00 (9.44)	84.72 (100.00)
1992-93	10.40 (10.00)	10.00 (9.62)	78.26 (72.25)	5.34 (5.13)	104.00 (100.00)
1993-94	8.33 (8.39)	9.65 (9.72)	75.35 (75.88)	5.97 (06.01)	99.30 100.00
1994-95	17.39 (14.65)	8.91 (7.51)	84.16 (70.92)	8.21 (6.92)	118.67 (100.00)
1995-96	7.95 (11.65)	10.02 (14.68)	43.58 (63.84)	6.71 (9.83)	68.26 (100.00)
1996-97	11.74 (15.32)	8.74 (11.41)	47.86 (62.46)	8.28 (10.81)	76.62 (100.00)
1997-98	10.24 (14.01)	9.06 (12.39)	40.60 (55.53)	13.21 (18.07)	73.11 (100.00)
1998-99	6.47 (7.45)	8.52 (9.81)	63.50 (73.15)	8.32 (9.58)	86.81 (100.00)
1999-2000	5.21 (5.46)	5.50 (5.77)	74.50 (78.10)	10.18 (10.67)	95.39 (100.00)
2000-01	14.23 (16.89)	5.11 (6.85)	55.00 (65.28)	9.91 (11.76)	84.25 (100.00)
2001-02*	12.60 (12.98)	2.01 (2.07)	69.00 (71.06)	13.44 (13.89)	97.10 (100.00)

* *Provisional.*

Source: Forest and Environment Department, Bhubaneswar. Presented in the Economic Survey (Government of Orissa) of different years.

situation also raises certain basic questions that whether collection of kenduleaves and marketing have been reduced over the years? Whether a parallel trading of kenduleaves by the private traders siphons a major portion of kenduleaves through black market? Whether there is a nexus between the private traders and the Kenduleaf Division of the government, which helps in the draining out of kenduleaves? The functioning of a couple of parallel organisations for trade over kenduleaves definitely reflects the potentiality of kenduleaf in the State. In spite of the restrictions imposed by the Territorial Wings of the Forest Department to break the vicious nexus of the smugglers, the department fails due to lack of amendments in the Orissa Forest Act 1972, Orissa Timber and other Forest Produce, Transit Rules 1980 and Kenduleaf (Control of Trade) Act 1961. Apart from these problems, low official prices paid for kenduleaf by the government to the kenduleaves pluckers, differential mode of disposal by the pluckers at the collection centres, maintenance of 'phadies', (procedure of drying, storage, etc.) have created difficulties for the government to secure official targets fixed from time to time (Mallik, 1997).

A look into the collection, processing and marketing of kenduleaves in Orissa shows that OFDC only provides working capital for a joint scheme of management of kenduleaf trade. Kenduleaf Division procures and processes kenduleaves, and auctions are made by OFDC at different nodal points within the State and outside the State. While discussing with the managerial staff of OFDC, it transpired that the commercial and market friendly strategies of OFDC are open to receive and modify according to national and international demand of kenduleaves. Thus, one finds changes in mechanisms of procurement, marketing and utilisation of kenduleaves in different time periods.

When one looks at the ground realities of Orissa in respect of the status of kenduleaf pluckers, their wage pattern, mode of payment, and life support system, it is pathetic that the profit accrued by OFDC/TDCC and other private traders out of trading kenduleaves is largely due to suppression and exploitation of the poor kenduleaf pluckers. The delay in the payment of dues of the kenduleaf pluckers (mostly tribals) forces them to take distress loan from the moneylenders (sahookars) who not only exploit them by charging high interest, but also, after sometime when the loan accumulates to a big amount they force tribal people to mortgage their small patches of land against the payment of interest of the loan. Since a large chunk of kenduleaf trees are found under private ownership and the primary sellers (owner of the trees) do not get their dues compared to the traders and government corporation, there is a tendency among many to cut their trees and sell them in the form of logs which fetches more price though it is for one time. Such instances have been observed in Keonjhar district during the field-study.

The provision of life support system with regard to medical services has become a daydream even for the registered kenduleaf pluckers and binders, though a small amount is always deducted as premium towards medical services. Similar situations are also observed in respect of the payment of bonus as per the Bonus Act. Such welfare services, as provisioned, are more or less confined to the files of government. The implementation of these provisions needs qualitative improvement as rightly shared by the pluckers and observed in Keonjhar district.

Trading of Bamboo

Bamboos (*Salia bansua*) are plentifully available in Orissa, which equally contributes to the State exchequer as well as to the rural artisans who earn their day-to-day livelihood by making various household appliances out of bamboo. Apart from private paper mills some companies are also given right to collect bamboos. OFDC also collects and markets bamboo. The major paper mills working in Orissa and collecting bamboo are M/s Orient Paper Mills and M/s Straw Products Ltd., M/s Titlagarh Paper Mills, M/s Sewa Paper Mills and M/s BILT. A look into the collection of bamboo by these paper mills from the State controlled agency from 1984-85 to 1986-87 reflects that Orient Paper Mill has collected 299.09 MTs, while Straw Products Ltd. has extracted 309.3 MTs, and Titlagarh Paper Mill has extracted 104.652 MTs of bamboo. In total these paper mills have pulled out 713.042 MTs of bamboo with an average of 237.680 MTs per annum. Apart from this, they also collect bamboos directly from the people who grow bamboos on commercial basis. The requirement of bamboo in Orissa as calculated in lakh MTs by the department shows that it was 4.68 during 1991, and 4.89 during 1996 and 5.09 during 2001. However, the average turn out of bamboo is 2.50 lakh tons as per 1996-97 which is worth Rs. 8.28 crores (Forest and Environment Department, Government of Orissa, 2001).

The revenue generated from bamboo extraction, when analysed from the data during last five decades, one finds that during 1950-51 it was Rs. 6.2 lakh which had increased to Rs. 6.32 crores during 1988-90, and to Rs. 10 crores during 1992-93 and to Rs. 10.06 crores during 1995-96. However, revenue generated from bamboo extraction during certain periods, namely, 1993-94 and 1994-95 shows a negative trend due to multiple reasons. With the nationalisation of bamboo during 1988 OFDC and paper mills became the agent and sub-agent for procurement and disposal of bamboo. Payment of royalty for the collection of bamboo by the sub-agents varies according to the quality of bamboo. However, since 1995 these paper mills have been given authority to procure bamboo directly from the forest. This not only breached the provision of Forest Conservation Act of 1980 and Forest Policy of 1988, but led to reckless exploitation of bamboo resources of Orissa. As a result, the purpose of generating revenue by the State exchequer and helping the poor tribals in increasing their economic level became a daydream. Unplanned over-exploitation of bamboo resources by OFDC as well as by the paper mills ignoring their sustainable growth as well as peoples interest became a major setback for the State.

Trade of Sal Seed

Sal seed is one of the major forest produces of Orissa. The tribal people extract oil from sal seed through crude techniques. Up till its nationalisation in 1983 the traders largely dominated the procurement, processing and its final use. In spite of nationalisation, earning from the sale of sal seeds was supplementing the household economy of the tribal people. Since 1983, OFDC and TDCC have been trading on sal seeds and TRIFED plays a vital role in the marketing of sal seeds in Orissa. Though there is an opportunity for value addition in respect of sal seeds in Orissa, in reality nothing has been done. Five industries have been established in the private sector, which are now sick and unable to make use of the total produces of sal seeds. Though OFDC and TDCC operate in the market, due to multiple factors they are not able to offer remunerative prices to the tribal people. However, collection of sal seed provides a lot of under-paid employment to the tribal people. Since the government agencies like OFDC and TDCC suffer from certain limitations, such as, lack of working capital, lack of scope for taking policy decisions in time and lack of having an efficient organisational network at grass-root level. Hence they are unable to procure sal seeds directly from the primary collectors. As a result, not withstanding such situations, the poor tribal people, in order to meet their livelihood requirements, always make distress sale to the local traders and agents who maintain a nexus with the staff of OFDC and TDCC and sell them later on at the support price. The mechanisms adopted by the agents to collect sal seeds at village level at a cheaper price are often dubious. They sometimes forcefully take away the stocks kept for household consumption. Since tribal people do not have an assured mechanism and price to dispose their produces they are inclined to sell their produces as early as possible at their doorstep even at lower rates. Here, OFDC by and large has failed to protect the interest of the tribal people as well as that of the government; rather it indirectly supports the middlemen to extract profit out of circulation.

Trading of Mahua Flower

Mahua flower and mahua seed (tola) are two important forest produces which generate revenue for the State and also influence the livelihood status of tribal people. Apart from the collection of mahua flower and seeds from mahua trees owned by private persons, tribal people also collect these produces from community owned plants as well as from the forest. These forest produces are normally available for a very short duration, but their collection influences the household economy of tribal people. Before nationalisation of mahua flower in 1991, the private traders were primarily controlling procurement and marketing of mahua flower as well as its fruits in Orissa. Under the regulation of Orissa Excise (Mahua Flower) Rules, 1976 tribal people are made a medium in the process. From the time of nationalisation of mahua flower till date, TDCC and OFDC enjoy the procurement right throughout the State with differential jurisdictions. Use of mahua flower and mahua seeds by the tribal people are multiple by nature. Not only they collect mahua flower for consumption during the lean season when there is shortage of food, but also they extract oil from the mahua seeds for use in day-to-day life.

Sometimes inter-state variations in the price of mahua flower leads to transport of these produces from Bihar to Orissa, and vice versa depending on the pricing. As a result, the agencies engaged in the procurement and marketing of mahua flower in Orissa are unable to purchase the local produces at government fixed rates. Conversely if the prevailing market price is lower, then they cannot dispose of their stock. In both ways, this affects the revenue of the State as well as the livelihood system of the tribal people.

Both the Orissa Forest Act and The Orissa Forest Produce (Control of Trade) Act, 1981 have vested immense power on the State to exercise control over the trading of forest produces. The State from time to time may control or open the procurement, marketing of any forest produces. There are certain principles, which always guide the State as regards the procurement and marketing of these produces. Still the principle of earning more revenue for the State exchequer has always been the influencing force (Table 7.15). Many backdoor forces operate while selecting the forest items and leasing out forest areas in favour of private traders, corporate bodies/companies and government corporations. It is a fact that the prices of nationalised produces like kenduleaf, bamboo, sal seed, and mahua flower are decided by an Advisory Committee at state level, and for other minor forest produces the prices are determined by a Price Fixation Committee which functions at the district level, consisting of DFO, Cooperative Society, the District Collector and the specific lease holder of the district, but in all the cases the stipulated price never reaches the primary pluckers/collectors. There always remains a communication gap and a difference between the decisions and the practices. It has been observed that the attitude of both private and government agencies has always been exploitative, suppressive and apathetic. The hierarchical procurement networks adopted by these agencies adopt, create scope for exploitation of the poor pluckers/primary collectors who are mostly tribal people. By this, the State does not get appropriate revenue, so also people do not receive their legitimate dues. It is the private traders and private leaseholders who siphon the benefits out of the trade in forest produces. For the government corporations, acting as leaseholder of nationalised as well as other forest produces, the alternatives are limited unlike that of private leaseholders. Though the procurement and supply channels are open to all the stakeholders, government owned corporations/agencies fail to compete with the private stakeholders in grabbing the business due to various constraints. These constraints are: lack of ready availability of working capital for investment, lack of immediate and flexible policy decisions, lack of accessible organisational and managerial processes which hinder them to fetch a good business and profit. Even the private traders, private agencies dictate terms of references for several produces, whereas, the government owned corporations/agencies feel handicapped to compete in a fast changing open market system. In spite of the growing complex market situation and its unhealthy impact on the forest dwellers in general, and tribal people in particular, one finds that the social and economic life-way processes of the tribal people are intertwined with the forest economy. They have been depending on forest resources for generations.

The revenue potentiality in percentage of NTFP (including kenduleaf) to total revenue from forest in Orissa reflects that it was 7.8 during 1985-86, reduced to 5.1 in 1987-88, again to 4.3 in 1990-91, however, increased little to the tune of 4.8 in 1995-96, but this again was reduced to 9.6 in 1998-99. This indicates that the State income from forest sources is fluctuating, which is not maintained consistently by the State.

The cultural practices, belief systems and social taboos influence the relation of the tribal people with the forest. Perhaps, this is the reason for which many scholars have called this relationship as symbiotic with nature. However, in this process a group of tribal people is always exposed to organised trade/market economy, which could not assure and ensure them of a minimum price support. Rather, such exploitative attitude has created parallel exploitative channels. As a result, tribal people have become easy haunts in the hands of non-tribal traders. The lucrative mechanisms adopted by the traders never allowed some tribal people to be away from them. Many times, it so happened that a section of tribal people (very few) overexploit the forest resources with the hope to get more income; while another section (majority) always lives in a marginalised condition. The attitude and behaviour of tribal people towards forest which are the product of various cultural forces, have been influencing forest resources. Since tribal economies are mixed in nature which encompasses several type of economic activities such as collection and gathering of various edible items, hunting and catching games, herding, shifting cultivation, settled agriculture, etc., most of which centres around forest and forest resources, so the tribal people always try to adopt various culturally influenced coping mechanisms while extracting their livelihood for day-to-day living.

Conclusion

The strategies adopted by OFDC over the years have mostly considered forest resources as a source of generating revenue. This has, by and large kept tribal communities who live in the forest as an integrated society. By treating tribal people as individuals, but not as persons of the larger society, helped OFDC to exploit forest resources as and when desired by the government and also by the traders and private companies, who basically played various exploitative roles with regard to the poor tribal people and the forest resources. The personnel of the corporation at ground level often become a part of the exploitative process, as a result, the tribal people go through more marginalised conditions.

The functioning of OFDC and its impact on the tribal people when compared in the light of the provisions of the Fifth Schedule of the Constitution, one can say that OFDC by and large has fulfilled the goal of enriching government revenue. As regards protecting the livelihood interest of the tribal people it does not seem to have fulfilled that goal convincingly. The organisation has played an important role in mobilising forest produces from tribal people to non-tribals. Being deprived of forest resources, tribals are mortgaging their small landholdings to the moneylenders (who are non-tribals) for incurring distress loans, which keeps them permanently indebted. This is a paradoxical situation. When the State and private traders are enriched by the procurement of forest produces, the poor tribals, who are basically primary collectors, are impoverished by being eliminated from the centre of the operation. Perhaps, OFDC attaches more importance to the interest of the State exchequer and traders and less to the interest of the poor tribals, the traditional managers of forest produces.

Tribal Development Cooperative Corporation Ltd. (TDCC)

The Tribal Development Cooperative Corporation of Orissa Ltd. (TDCC) is an apex cooperative society, which has been registered under Orissa Cooperative Societies Act of 1962. Since 1972, it is functioning as an apex Cooperative organisation for the development of tribal communities of Orissa. The basic objectives of TDCC are: (i) to procure Surplus Agricultural Produces (SAPs) and Minor Forest Produces (MFPs) from tribal people on payment of remunerative prices through proper market arrangements; (ii) to supply essential commodities and other consumer goods to the tribal people at a fair price; (iii) to process the procured SAPs and MFPs through value addition with a view to increase profit and provide employment to the tribal people; and (iv) to provide advance consumption-cum-production credit to the tribal people which helps them to raise crops and also to meet their consumption needs.

TDCC has been created by the merger of several forest marketing cooperative societies, credit institutions, purchase, sale and fair price shops of the Welfare Department of the Government of Orissa. The Managing Committee of TDCC includes members from various government departments; they are: the Principal Secretary of Forests and Environment Department, and the Secretary of Finance Department as the nominees of the government, apart from, the Commissioner-cum-Secretaries to government of various Departments of Welfare, Cooperative, Food Supply; Chief Conservator of Forest, Registrar of Cooperatives, Director of SCSTRTI, representative of State Cooperative Bank, President of Tikabali Agency Marketing Cooperative Society, Govindapalli Forest Marketing Cooperative Society, MLA of Gunupur and one woman representative.

The corporation presently has 240 LAMPS and other Primary Societies, 47 Panchayat Samitis and 3 individuals as members. TDCC comprises 3 divisions and 15 branches (2002). The distribution of all LAMPS and permanent procurement centres are grouped in different districts of Orissa, and the details of branches, procurement centres, fair price shops, etc., of TDCC in Orissa are given in Table 7.15. There are 130 number of permanent procurement centres, 66 godowns located at different places of Orissa, having a storage capacity of 35,998 MTs.

Apart from these, there are also 47 Panchayat Samitis which have been associated with their share capital invested in TDCC. These Panchayat Samitis are mostly distributed in the districts of Koraput, Nawarangpur, Malkangiri, Rayagada, Kalahandi, Mayurbhanj, Phulbani, Gajapati, Sundargarh and Sambalpur. TDCC is making all endeavours to maximise the collection of SAPs and MFPs from all the interior areas of tribal regions of Orissa. The produces are procured through LAMPS with the help of local agents, as well as in certain areas TDCC directly procures from weekly markets and villages. In respect of certain forest produce commodities, the government fixes the minimum support price and TDCC offers that rate depending upon the quality of the stock.

The major forest produces procured by TDCC are tamarind, sal seed, myrobalan, siali leaves and hill brooms. Apart from the fair price shops, TDCC also opens quite a good number of temporary procurement centres (800) to procure SAPs and MFPs. LAMPS also help in the procurement of these Minor Forest Produces. A look into the involvement of LAMPS for procurement of MFPs for TDCC from 1985-86 to 1993-94 reflects that because of their past default the LAMPS are unable to collect more MFPs for TDCC. Table 7.16 describes the functioning of LAMPS and their procurement of MFPs. Data show that TDCC has fetched a good business during the year 1990-91 and 1991-92, but in subsequent years the turnover of TDCC has fallen due to multifarious reasons.

Table 7.16

Distribution of Procurement Centres and Fair Price Shops under Various TDCC Branches of Orissa

Name of the TDCC Division/Branches	*No. of Procurement Centres of TDCC*	*No. of Fair Price Shops of TDCC*	*No. of TDCC Godowns*
Berhampur Division			
Paralakhemundi	10	8	18
R. Udayagiri	10	5	11
Balliguda	8	7	8
Nayagarh	7	7	2
Keonjhar Division			
Keonjhar	14	11	2
Lahunipada	6	4	-
Udala	7	2	2
Sundargarh	10	3	6
Sunabeda Division			
Rayagada	5	2	1
Muniguda	6	3	1
Bhawanipatna	6	3	4
Kashipur	5	3	3
Jeypore	15	2	2
Umarkote	12	3	1
Sunabeda	9	5	4
Head Office Bhubaneswar	-	1	1
Total	130	69	66

Source: TDCC Office Records, (2000), Orissa, Bhubaneswar.

The major shareholders of TDCC are the Welfare Department, P&C Department, Cooperative Societies of Government of Orissa and Panchayat Samitis. The major sources of barrowings for TDCC are the Welfare Department (which provides margin money), Food and Civil Supplies Department, (which provides ways and means advanced by government, from NCDC through OSCB and RCS (O) for construction of storage godown and purchase of transport vehicles), the DRI loan from Andhra Bank, and cash credit (highest) against fixed deposits from the State Bank of India. The financial assistance received by TDCC in shape of share capital, grants-in-aid, subsidy and managerial assistance from the State Government from 1971-72 till 1995-96 is given in Table 7.17.

Table 7.17

Distribution of LAMPS Procuring MFPs for TDCC during 1985-86 to 1993-94

Years	*No. of LAMPS*	*Procurement Values of MFPs (in lakhs)*
1985-86	33	22.18
1986-87	29	21.58
1987-88	63	52.34
1988-89	54	81.00
1989-90	22	19.28
1990-91	31	62.68
1991-92	50	96.71
1992-93	36	25.55
1993-94	8	36.87

Source: TDCC Office Records, 1998, Orissa, Bhubaneswar.

Prior to the nationalisation of kenduleaf, TDCC was in-charge of its collection in the entire state of Orissa, enjoying exclusive rights and later on, the operational area was divided between OFDC and TDCC to collect kenduleaves. OFDC was given the charge to collect kenduleaves in 13 Forest Divisions and TDCC in 14 Forest Divisions in the state of Orissa. Since 1991, soon after kenduleaf was nationalised, TDCC became the agent to collect kenduleaf in 11 Forest Divisions. It is observed that because of price variation of mahua flower in border areas of Chhattisgarh the traders purchase mahua from Chhattisgarh and sell to TDCC and OFDC in Orissa market. However, in later periods TDCC could not dispose those kenduleaves due to lower price in the local market and was forced to make distress sale at a lower price. This led to the loss of almost Rs. 9 crores for TDCC during 1992-93. This clearly indicates the inability of TDCC to forecast the market potentiality of kenduleaves. Perhaps, it is due to lack of necessary expertise among the employees of TDCC. The procurement planning of TDCC should include certain prerequisites, like storage facilities, transport facilities, and marketing and the organisational set-up at various levels. Compared to many other states, the state of Orissa though has a sizeable forest area and tribal population who live basically on procurement of MFPs and SAPs, the State has received less amount as grant-in-aid from Government of India.

In spite of the losses, TDCC has been endeavouring to increase the procurement of SAPs and MFPs. Data on procurement of SAPs and MFPs collected from 1984-85 to 1997-98 reflect that there is an inconsistency in the procurement trend, that is, the total procurement has decreased since 1993-94 (except 1995-96). Similarly, procurement of MFPs so far carried out by TDCC in different years is unpredictable. It is basically due to unplanned efforts made by the organisation. For example, since 1984-85, procurement of MFPs during the year 1991-92 was a record-breaking incidence, which may be rare in the history of TDCC, in subsequent years it slashed to one-fifth. The details of business turnover of TDCC on SAPs and MFPs during the period from 1983-84 to 1997-98 are explained in Table 7.18. When one looks at profit and loss of TDCC it is found that till date TDCC has not so far been able to generate any net profit (Table 7.19).

Table 7.18

Distribution of Business Turnover of TDCC during the Year 1983-84 to 1997-98

(Rs. in lakhs)

Years	*Procurement*		*Consumer Business*	*Total*
	SAP	*MFP*		
1983-84	101.39	79.04	137.28	317.71
1984-85	117.97	189.16	168.87	530.00
1985-86	204.26	176.83	237.38	618.47
1986-87	151.88	120.81	200.65	473.34
1987-88	256.42	135.51	190.78	582.68
1988-89	134.02	417.88	185.33	737.23
1989-90	163.39	64.28	133.83	361.50
1990-91	573.08	361.23	187.18	1061.49
1991-92	55.50	1013.99	145.26	1214.75
1992-93	429.68	221.00	141.18	791.86
1993-94	90.69	321.83	187.51	599.26
1994-95	38.18	330.52	276.85	645.55
1995-96	318.02	338.24	-	-
1996-97	45.64	255.43	-	-
1997-98	149.33	126.86	-	-

Source: TDCC Office Records, 1998, Orissa, Bhubaneswar.

Various reasons have been put forward by TDCC for incurring such losses. They are: low turnover, high overhead cost, heavy interest burden, payment of heavy amount as royalty to Forest Department for MFPs and continuance of government employees of erstwhile PSFS scheme in the corporation. The annual interest paid by TDCC to Commercial Banks in different years when analysed reflects that TDCC has paid an amount of Rs. 180.47 lakh during 1991-92, Rs. 285.64 lakh during 1992-93, Rs. 248.66 lakh during 1993-94, Rs. 196.03 lakh during 1994-95, Rs. 194.91 lakh during 1995-96 and Rs. 214.41 lakh during the year 1996-97. Similarly, the TDCC also suffers from high overhead costs towards the existing staff strength of 495 (out of total 619) towards which an amount of about Rs. 1.81 crores is spent per annum. Government of Orissa releases a subsidy of Rs. 20 lakh

Table 7.19

Distribution of Profit and Loss of TDCC during the Year 1972-73 to1993-94

(Rs. in lakhs)

Years	*Gross Profit/Loss Trade Account*	*Net Profit/Loss*	*Cumulative Loss*
1972-73	+6.44	-1.80	2.92
1973-74	+30.58	+2.17	0.75
1974-75	+15.49	-4.61	5.36
1975-76	+45.20	+0.05	5.31
1976-77	+55.90	+0.04	5.27
1977-78	+34.62	-21.01	26.28
1978-79	-18.72	-122.61	148.89
1979-80	-17.70	-83.34	232.23
1980-81	+24.83	-45.64	277.87
1981-82	+90.31	+0.15	277.72
1982-83	+39.37	-61.01	338.73
1983-84	+82.91	-9.98	348.71
1984-85	+67.39	-30.01	378.72
1985-86	+68.20	-53.77	432.49
1986-87	+31.40	-87.16	519.65
1987-88	+78.01	-70.51	590.16
1988-89	NA	NA	NA
1989-90	-27.17	-153.21	NA
1990-91	-126.71	-74.60	NA
1991-92	+645.92	-964.84	NA
1992-93	+39.15	-506.81	NA
1993-94	+81.12	-340.25	NA

Source: TDCC Office Record, 1995, Orissa, Bhubaneswar.

towards managerial subsidy seems to be insufficient to meet the minimum requirements of TDCC. Again payment of royalty by TDCC to the Department of Forest and Environment seems to be another major factor for incurring loss.

A recent study carried out by TDCC clearly has identified certain limitations long prevailing in the structural and operational frontiers of the organisation. First, the shortage of working capital has reduced the procurement capacity of TDCC to around 58 per cent only. The barrowings by TDCC from commercial banks even at a high rate of interest do not meet the requirements to explore the potentialities of SAPs and MFPs to full extent. Second, though one of the objectives of TDCC is to purchase, process MFPs and provide short-term loans to the tribals for their production-cum-consumption requirements, but the corporation is yet to achieve these objectives to a desirable extent. TDCC is largely depending on loans from commercial banks who are not coming forward to provide loans, along with inadequate managerial subsidy received from the government. Apart from, the heavy royalty paid to the Forest and Environment Department and regular fluctuations of the market price has largely affected and is one of the important reasons for TDCC for not achieving its objectives. Other reasons responsible for the present position of TDCC as reported are mainly due to high price of SAPs/MFPs, inadequate working capital, and inability of TDCC to fetch more loans from commercial banks for the purpose. TDCC in many respects is handicapped to implement various programmes for the fulfilment of its objectives.

Here an attempt has been made to present a comparative analysis of TDCC of Orissa with the functioning of TDCC in Maharashtra, West Bengal and with such a structure known as GCC of Andhra Pradesh. The nature of assistance in the form of subsidy, royalty and payment of tax received from the government is taken for the present analysis. When TDCC of Orissa receives only Rs. 20 lakhs as grant from the government, other State Governments fully reimburse the total expenditures. Again, the royalty on MFP is also fully reimbursed in case of Andhra Pradesh and West Bengal, TDCC of Maharashtra compensates this trading loss, whereas, in case of Orissa, TDCC pays heavy royalty to the Forest Department. Similarly, purchase tax and sales tax is fully exempted in case of other states, while in case of Orissa it is paid by TDCC which affects the sales rate. It is true that in many respects TDCC in Orissa is functioning in a suffocated climate, whereas, such organisations in other states are functioning in a free climate with all responsibility shouldered by their respective governments.

SCSTRTI carried out evaluation on the functioning of Balliguda Branch of TDCC in Phulbani district, during November 1994. The study has assessed various programmes implemented, and the benefits accrued out of the programmes to the tribal people, procurement arrangements made to collect SAPs and MFPs and the operational bottlenecks experienced by the officials. Data have been collected through interview schedules covering 128 beneficiaries from 3 selected sales centres of the Balliguda Branch.

The study finds that in Balliguda branch, eight godowns are operating with a capacity of 3.151 MTs. They are partially procuring various SAP items like niger, turmeric, kating, mustard, maize, black grams and horse grams. Collection of these items is meagre mainly due to lack of sufficient funds. The branch also collects mahua, sal seeds and hill brooms. Around 5 fair price shops were functioning under this branch. The study found out that lack of sufficient funds is one of the major causes for not purchasing the available SAPs and MFPs to the fullest extent.

The study suggested that: (i) TDCC sales centres due to their dealing with controlled items earned less profit, and therefore, it has been suggested that they may deal with non-controlled items; (ii) the operational area of TDCC branch covers a large area and it seems to be quite difficult to cover the entire area due to geo-physical and communication constraints; (iii) loss of TDCC is mainly due to payment of sales tax, income tax and royalty towards the procurement of MFPs; (iv) lack of processing units for MFPs and SAPs at branch level which fetched less return; and (v) lack of sufficient funds has resulted in malfunctioning of their fair price shops, and incentives may be paid to the employees to boost their interests.

In three different meetings held in October 1992, January 1993 and July 1994, it has been decided by the Government of Orissa that TDCC should procure different MFPs through tie up arrangements only. The interest burden is kept to a minimum. As regards the collection of various MFP items, so far collected by TDCC over last 10 years, it is observed that 17 MFPs seem to be important in terms of quantity of collection and revenue generation. MFP items like amla, bahada, mahua flower, nox vomica, hill brooms, tamarind, sal seeds, marketing nut, kusum seed, mango kernel, char gum, mahua seeds, sunari bark and siali leaf are procured by TDCC in good quantity. These MFPs are procured regionally in different districts. A few MFP items like mahua seeds, kusum seeds, neem seeds, karanja seeds have been taken out from the purview of TDCC and handed over to joint sector company like Utkal Forest Products Ltd. Many MFPs like broom grass, tamarind seeds, gums, mushrooms, thorn brooms, bahada, curry leafs not collected earlier are now being collected by TDCC.

TDCC had the total collection right over tamarind in the undivided Koraput district, but government decision to hand over this to a private entrepreneur Doki Satyanarayana of Koraput district till 2001 has created fear of exploitation not only in the minds of TDCC employees, but also in the minds of tribal people. The MLA while opposing during that time alleged that the deal was the outcome of a nexus between Forest Minister and the private entrepreneur. He again commented that handing over of tamarind without minimum support price will definitely be a problem for six lakh tribal collectors (Patnaik, 1995-96).

The study of Mallik and Panigrahi (1998: 176) on the NTFP: Collection, Benefits and Management in Orissa found that TDCC in Bhuiyan and Juanga Pirha of Keonjhar district is entitled to procure 19 MFP items against 27 available products, but practically they collect only 2 items, i.e., harida and tamarind. As a result, *de facto* agents of TDCC or middlemen collect many NTFP items available in the region. The reasons for not collecting NTFP items in this region as explained by TDCC are jurisdiction conflict. TDCC does not collect from the interior pockets and even the primary collectors fail to move to TDCC for sale since they live in distant places. TDCC often leases out a portion of its operational area allotted to it due to varied reasons. This has resulted in direct involvement of the middlemen/private agents in the purchase of available NTFPs at lower than the market price. Middlemen and traders often reach the forest dwellers at the time of harvest to which TDCC does not. The price of many MFPs and

SAPs is fixed by the government, which is often not known to the forest dwellers (often it is declared late). In such situations, the tribal people accept any price offered by TDCC. Whatever quantity of produces (SAPs and MFPs) is purchased by TDCC it is stored and after a couple of months NTFPs are disposed through auction sales. Due to the nexus between the auction-holder and middlemen turned buyers, often a lower price is fixed at the auction centres, which sometimes even comes below the procurement price.

NTFP market is a buyer's market where the sellers play almost no role in deciding the price of the products and do not get a minimum price. Lack of any effective support mechanism always result in losses by the primary collectors. The sellers always complain that often the price fixed by the Price Fixation Committee is not realistic because the government agencies like TDCC and OFDC are either unable to understand the factors which influence the NTFP price or do not take into account these factors while the price of these produces are fixed. The issue of 'fair price' of the NTFP should take into the local factors including the cost rendered by the community who protects the forest from the forward and backward values of the produces (up to a certain level), may also be taken into account while fixing the price of NTFPs.

Under the situation scholars, activists, and the NTFP collectors often raise certain basic questions: who will fix NTFP price at what level? Is it Gram Panchayat, or Panchayat Samiti and/or Zilla Parishad? Since Gram Panchayats and Panchayat Samitis are not equipped with technical knowledge with regard to the fixation of NTFP prices and if they do that then what support mechanisms they need from government agencies? NGOs and people at large? Whether the existing rules and regulations are sufficient or need amendment to decentralise the process?

Recommendations of Working Group on Minor Forest Produce

Recommendation in Sixth Five-Year Plan (1980-85)

Minor Forest Produces (MFPs) play an important role in tribal economy. All the states should confer the rights of the tribal people over it. For the marketing of MFPs, which are collected by tribal people, LAMPS at ground level should function as purchase centres. Apart from this, a state level agency along with TRIFED at the national level should operate for smooth procurement, processing and marketing of SAPs and MFPs. Processing of MFPs should be undertaken through cooperatives formed by primary collectors.

Recommendations in the Seventh Five-Year Plan (1985-90)

The Seventh Five-Year Plan has highlighted the development of MFPs through regeneration and plantation; and its collection, processing, and marketing through cooperatives and corporate sector, which should receive high priority under the Plan programmes. Specific thrust has to be given to organisation of MFPs through cooperatives to cover all Gram Panchayats in tribal areas. In order to provide support to TDCC, and Orissa Forest Development Corporation who are handling trade on MFPs at state level, an organisation called as TRIFED (Tribal Marketing Federation) should be set up at the national level.

Recommendations in the Eighth Five-Year Plan (1985-90)

The Eighth Five-Year Plan has suggested that private contractors should be replaced by tribal cooperatives in matters of collection of forest produces. The tribals should be associated with such works for protection, regeneration and optimum collection of MFPs along with institutional arrangements for marketing the produces. Since MFPs are a major source of earning for the tribal households, institutional arrangements are needed in the form of TDCC/Federation/cooperatives which will serve the purpose. Collection of certain items of MFPs has to be organised either through State Departments or State Federations.

Revamping and Strengthening of TDCC

Presently the Corporation has 15 branches, and 3 sub-branches, which are operating with a staff strength of 465 employees. The total annual establishment cost of the corporation is Rs. 300 lakh. Almost 54 number of the staff have applied for voluntary retirement, but only 11 of them have availed of the benefit till the time of data collection. The department has drawn up 237 proceedings against 132 members of the staff involving financial irregularities to the extent of Rs. 186.5 lakh (TDCC, 2001).

Among the major infrastructure facilities available with the TDCC one finds that there are 14 office buildings, 23 residential buildings, 101 godowns, 9 trucks, 14 jeeps, 1 car and 6 motor bikes which have functional values. Around 20 godowns with a capacity of 13,000 MT have been rented only for Rs. 70,000 and major portion of the main building has been given on rent to different governments and government undertakings. In spite of all hurdles, TDCC still deals on minor forest produces, surplus agricultural produces and consumer commodities (ibid.).

The financial position of the organisation is very weak. The equity base has been completely eroded due to bad fiscal and administrative measures in the past and the organisation is now bereft of any working capital. Since 1972, the corporation never earned any profit except during 1983-84. The current loan liability of TDCC is Rs. 25.25 crores (Rs. 16.88 crores of loan amount and accrued interest of Rs. 8.37 crores). In addition, TDCC has got other liabilities of Rs. 616 lakh as on 30 June, 2000.

Though decisions have been taken to exempt TDCC from payment of forest royalty and purchase tax, so far no progress has been made in this respect. Another decision has been taken in the said meeting to raise the share capital of TDCC from the existing Rs. 20 crores to Rs. 25 crores, which has been approved by Government of India. It has been decided to verify branch-wise analysis of profitability and deployment/retrenchment of staff accordingly. However, this work is yet to be completed (ibid., 2002). It is seen that the paid-up capital of Rs. 21.92 crores has been totally eroded. The accumulated loss, loan and other liabilities taken together come to Rs. 7,227 lakh. Due to such deplorable financial condition, the Corporation is not able to function properly to achieve its objective of rendering social services to the most vulnerable group of the society. As revamping strategies TDCC has suggested for the sale of some of its fixed assets, reduction of its staff strength, branch-wise analysis of performance, value addition to non-perishable commodities, closing down consumer business/fair-price shops, increasing annual turnover and tapping of women Self-Help Groups.

Conclusion

The above description reflects that TDCC at present seems to be handicapped when it is compared with its objectives, i.e., to look after the interest of the tribal people. As a result, the government has greater responsibility to restructure TDCC more efficiently. Government may sanction a handsome amount against all outstanding loans and interest on 100 per cent grant-in-aid basis. Government of Orissa may also provide full managerial expenses of the TDCC as subsidy. Royalty paid by TDCC to the Forest Department may be waived out and the tax paid for purchase and sale may also be reduced. One possible solution may be to grant one-time procurement advance in favour of TDCC so as to pull it out from its present financial crisis.

Instead of insisting TDCC to deposit the forest royalty taxes and subsequently reimbursing the same, the State Government may make such a system so as to facilitate forest royalty and taxes to be paid by the Welfare Department to the Forest and Environment Department. With this, the TDCC may be able to collect the MFPs from the tribals during the commencement of the procurement season. In the structural and administrative front TDCC has to be revamped. In order to fetch a good market and to generate good return, value addition of certain MFPs has to be carried out on priority basis. Since the availability of MFPs has region specific potentiality, a regional planning for its exploration, utilisation, value addition and marketing, is of utmost importance. Development of community skill through providing training to tribal people is required to enhance their potentiality, purchasing and bargaining power. With little modifications in the organisational and functional structure TDCC can be revamped to meet the changing demand and requirement of both the tribal people and the government.

As regards the processing of MFPs at the ground level Tribal Primary Cooperative Societies for primary processing unit be established at Panchayat level under TDCC. Proper interaction, grading and packaging training may be part of the processing and value addition package. Since most of the MFPs are seasonal, an efficient procurement system and a dynamic monitoring mechanism should be established. Technical inputs should be provided for scientific preservation and storage of the value added MFP produces. The micro-credit plans introduced by NABARD since 1988 for the development of Tribal Areas in Orissa through an integrated approach which provides realistic credit requirements for MFP processing can be taken as a guideline for the development of MFPs in tribal areas of the State.

The Orissa State Finance Development Corporation Ltd.

The Orissa State Finance Development Corporation Ltd. (OSFDC) was established during the year 1979-80. It is a state level organisation working for the welfare of both SCs and STs who are below the poverty line. Assistance is provided through various bankable schemes and non-bankable fully subsidised schemes. Economic programmes are being adopted for the development of dispersed tribal people living outside the ITDAs, MADA pockets, clusters and special micro-project areas, rehabilitation of scavengers and their dependants. The high cost schemes with term loan from the NSFDC are incorporated and are being implemented by OFDC for the benefit of SCs and STs. The corporation has also been declared as a state level agency for implementation of economic development programmes for the backward sections among the minority groups of the State.

OSFDC has its own branch offices in all the 13 district headquarters of the undivided districts and also in newly formed Rayagada district. District Branch Managers coordinate all the welfare activities implemented under the district level branch offices of OSFDC. In newly created 17 districts, the District Welfare Officers (DWOs) act as the District Manger of OSFDC. The absence of Branch Managers in the District level offices as observed, in the districts of Kalahandi, Dhenkanal, Kandhamal and Rayagada, not only affects the quality of work, but also timely completion of the target oriented development programmes.

Schemes and Programmes

All the schemes and programmes of OSFDC can be categorised as: (a) bankable schemes, and (b) fully subsidised schemes. The bankable schemes include various income-generating schemes (IGP) under Margin Money Loan (MML) programme in agriculture development, minor irrigation, animal husbandry, fishery, horticulture, small and village industries, vocational trades and small business sectors. The fully subsidised schemes include community minor irrigation projects, self-employment and wage-employment-oriented training programmes, construction of shop-rooms for taking up small business, handloom programmes for SC weavers, construction of rearing-house under sericulture programme, scavengers training programme, implementation of high cost schemes in agriculture, transport and allied sectors.

While the bankable schemes are implemented with the tie-up participation of banks, the non-bankable schemes are implemented through the line departments and agencies like Orissa Lift Irrigation Corporation (OLIC), Soil Conservation Department, Directorate of Textile, AH & VS, fisheries and others. The high cost schemes are being implemented since 1997-98 with term loan from OSFDC without the involvement of banks. These programmes aim for accrual of the economic benefits to the poor SCs and STs.

Sources of Fund

The economic development programmes meant for the poor SCs and STs of the State are implemented with the funds out of the share capital, special central assistance and grant-in-aid received from the government. The high cost schemes with unit cost exceeding Rs. 35,000 in agriculture and allied sector, transport and services and industries are implemented with term loan from the NSFDC. The high cost schemes (term loan) are implemented with the financial support received from institutions like National SC Finance and Development Corporation (NSFDC), National ST Finance Development Corporation (NSTFDC), National State Karmacharis Finance Development Corporation (NSKDC),

Table 7.20

Distribution of Various Activities and Programmes of OSFDC

Name of the Programme	*Objectives of the Programme*	*Sources of Fund*	*Name of the Scheme*	*Scheme Details*
Special Central Assistance to Special Component Plan	Upliftment of specially vulnerable groups among SCs by filling up the critical gaps in the family-based employment-cum-income generation activities.	Government of India	1. Bankable IGS. It covers schemes like: (i) Animal Husbandary, (ii) Fishery, (iii) Agriculture, (iv) Minor Irrigation (v) SVI, and (vi) Small Business.	Rs. 10,000.00 subsidy (maximum) is provided to each beneficiary in addition to bank loan.
			2. Non-Bankable IGS	
			(i) Minor Irrigation	Community Irrigation Projects such as Lift Irrigation Points, Water Harvesting Structures and Shallow Tube-wells are provided to SC/ST Small and Marginal Farmers at 100% subsidy basis.
			(ii) Dev. of SC (women)	Training of SC women to improve their family earning. Assistance is also provided to the SC women for setting up production units and marketing of consumer goods.
			(iii) Cooperative	Rs. 40 per person is given as share capital to each SC member of any cooperative society.

Contd...

Contd...

Name of the Programme	*Objectives of the Programme*	*Sources of Fund*	*Name of the Scheme*	*Scheme Details*
			(iv) Handloom, Sericulture, Horticulture, Social Forestry, etc.	Rs. 10,000.00 subsidy (maximum) is provided to each beneficiary through Director Handloom, Sericulture, Horticulture and Social Forestry.
Special Central Assistance to Tribal Sub-Plan (SCA to TSP)	Upliftment of specially vulnerable groups among STs by filling up the critical gaps in the family-based employment-cum-income generation activities.	Government of India	(i) Bankable IGS	Rs. 10,000.00 subsidy (maximum) is provided to each beneficiary in addition to Bank loan.
National Scheme for Liberation and Rehabilitation of Scavengers (NSLRS)	Literate persons engaged in manual scavenging and assisting them for taking up alternate dignified activities.	Government of India	(i) Bankable IGS	Maximum unit cost is up to Rs.50,000 Rs.10,000 subsidy is being provided by OSFDC and the rest is Bank loan.
			(ii) Training for Self-employment	TRYSEM pattern training in trades such as TV and Radio repairing, Tailoring, Toy making, Auto repairing and other trades are provided to scavenger beneficiaries with 100% subsidy.

Contd...

Contd...

Name of the Programme	*Objectives of the Programme*	*Sources of Fund*	*Name of the Scheme*	*Scheme Details*
Term Loan (High Cost) Schemes for SCs	To provide loan at concessional value of interval for undertaking viable economic activities.	National SC Finance Development Corporation (NSFDC)	High cost loan to SCs	High cost loan with unit cost exceeding Rs.35,000 are being provided by OSFDC to SC beneficiaries with Term Loan from NSFDC and NSTFDC schemes such as Tractor-cum-Trolly, Comm. Jeep, Mini Truck, Diesel Car, Poultry, Diary, Xerox Machine, Auto Rickshaw, etc., are financed with 6% interest per annum.
Term Loan (High Cost) Schemes for STs	Providing loan (institutional finance) to STs at concessional rate of interest.	National ST Finance Development Corporation (NSTFDC)	High cost loan to STs	High cost loan with unit cost exceeding Rs.35,000 are being provided by OSFDC to ST beneficiaries with Term Loan from NSFDC and NSTFDC schemes such as Tractor-cum-Trolly, Comm. Jeep, Mini Truck, Diesel Car, Poultry, Diary, Xerox Machine, Auto Rickshaw, etc., are financed with 6% interest per annum.
Term Loan (High Cost) Schemes for Scavengers/Safai Karmacharis	Providing loan (institutional finance) to Scavengers.	National Safai Karmacharis Finance and Dev. Corporation (NSKDC)	(i) Sanitary Mart	25 Scavengers are formed into groups and Rs.5.00 lakhs are provided to each group for setting up a production-cum-marketing centre/shop sanitary items.

Contd...

Contd...

Name of the Programme	*Objectives of the Programme*	*Sources of Fund*	*Name of the Scheme*	*Scheme Details*
			(ii) Term loan from NSKFDC.	High cost units not exceeding Rs.1.00 Lakh such as Band Party, Auto Rickshaw, Electrical Decoration shop, two and three wheeler repairing shops are being financed with 7% interest per annum.
Term loan schemes for minorities (Sikhs, Christians, Muslims, Buddhists and Parsis)	Providing loan (institutional finance) to Minorities.	National Minorities Finance and Dev. Corporation (NMDFC)	Tatkal Yojana with finance assistance from NMDFC.	Small business and artisan and allied establishments are financed with unit cost not exceeding Rs.50,000 with 6% interest per annum.

Source: OSFDC, Orissa, Bhubaneswar.

National Minorities Finance Development Corporation (NMFDC), etc. These institutions provide loan indirectly through OSFDC to the beneficiaries. The details of the fund supported to the beneficiaries from different sources under various schemes is given in Table 7.20.

Special Central Assistance to Special Component Plan

Special Central Assistance (SCA) to Special Component Plan (SCP) has been receiving special attention since its introduction in the year 1979-80. This is a central scheme based on 100 per cent grant-in-aid which acts as support towards the effort made by the State Government for the development of SCs who are below the poverty line through family based income generating programmes. It basically aims for increasing the productivity and income out of their limited resources of the poor SC households based on their local occupational pattern. The flexibility of utilising this fund is given to the State Government who can make use of this fund in conjunction with corporations, financial institutions, etc. It is mandatory that 10 per cent of the total grant released to the State Government be utilised for the development of infrastructure in these areas, 15 per cent be utilised for the development of viable income generating economic development schemes and programmes for SC women, 5 per cent of the total released fund be utilised for the economic development of the SC disabled persons. The details of amount of SCA to SCP received and utilised by the OSFDC with the beneficiaries covered during the Eighth and Ninth Five-Year Plan periods is given in Table 7.21, 7.22 and 7.23. The table reflects that the fund allocated from SCA to SCP has been enhanced from 5,799.9 lakhs in the Eighth Five-Year Plan to Rs. 8,681.7 lakhs in Ninth Five-Year Plan, indicating therein an increase of 49.7 per cent. Similarly, the amount released by the OSFDC for the implementation of different schemes and programmes has increased from Rs. 5,013.9 lakhs in the Eighth Plan to Rs. 9,544.5 lakh in the Ninth plan, implying an increase of 90.4 per cent. However, the coverage of beneficiaries under the SCA to SCP was 2.1 lakhs in the Eighth Plan, which declined to 2 lakhs.

Table 7.21

Distribution of Flow of Funds to OSFDC under SCA to SCP with the Beneficiaries Coverage for SCs during the Eighth and Ninth Plan (1997-2002)

Year	*Amount of SCA Receipt*	*Amount of SCA Utilised*	*No. of Beneficiaries Covered*
1992-93	836.04	400.27	35429
1993-94	776.46	978.63	74971
1994-95	596.73	970.01	29998
1995-96	1536.03	1186.19	37829
1996-97	2054.68	1578.76	38766
1997-98	1920.25	2074.14	66713
1998-99	707.96	1863	44222
1999-2000	3431.55	1688.47	30746
2000-01	1921.96	2022.03	29854
2001-02	700	1898.88	25026
During 8th Plan	5799.94	5013.86	216993
During 9th Plan	8681.72	9544.52	196561

Source: OSFDC, Bhubaneswar, Orissa.

For high cost schemes, the District Managers of OSFDC collect the loan applications from SC and ST candidates through the BDOs in pursuant to the advertisement issued by OSFDC. It scrutinises and examines the capability of the candidate as in the matters of providing promoter's contribution, security, guarantee and then place the valid application before the district selection committee for final selection keeping in view sector-wise notional allocation of funds which the head office communicates to each district for this purpose.

Proposals in respect of other non-bankable schemes are formulated by different Line Departments and agencies, BDOs, Executive Officers of Urban bodies for implementing the programmes for the benefit of eligible and deserving SC and ST beneficiaries. These proposals are then forwarded to the District Managers of OSFDC who in their turn examine and send them to the head office of the corporation with the approval of District Collectors for sanction and release of funds.

Table 7.22

Utilisation of Special Central Assistance by OSFDC

(Rs. in Lakhs)

Sl. No	*Name of the Sector*	*Funds Allotted*	*Expenditure Incurred*	*Physical Achievement (No. of Families Assisted)*
	1997-98			
1	Scheduled Caste Sector	2303.02	2303.02	66293
2	National Scheme of Liberation and Rehabilitation of Scavengers	137.11	137.11	2310
3	High Cost Schemes with term loan assistance from NSFDC	217.34	217.34	93
	1998-99			
1	Scheduled Caste Sector	2134.47	2134.47	43350
2	National Scheme of Liberation and Rehabilitation of Scavengers	167.78	167.78	1898
3	High Cost Schemes with term loan assistance from NSFDC	73.79	73.79	37
	1999-2000			
1	Scheduled Caste Sector	1571.18	1571.18	29221
2	National Scheme of Liberation and Rehabilitation of Scavengers	226.16	226.16	2197
3	High Cost Schemes with term loan assistance from NSFDC	931.14	931.14	351

Source: Orissa State Finance Development Finance Corporation Ltd., Bhubaneswar, Orissa.

The banks and financial institutions play a major role in the promotion of OSFDC schemes. The financial institutions involved in the implementation of OSFDC bankable IGPs are: Commercial Banks, Central Cooperative Banks, Urban Cooperative Banks and Regional Rural Banks.

Table 7.23

Distribution of Cumulative Achievements Made by OSFDC Under Different Programmes Since Inception Till End of 1998-99

Sl. No.	Scheme/ Programme	Total Achievement by 1998-99		
		Physical	Financial (Rs. in Lakhs)	
			Margin Money Loan	Subsidy
1	Bankable IGS	261746	1500.67	6047.66
2	Community Irrigation Projects	57357	—	3571.11
3	Training Programme	13687	—	254.39
4	Housing for SVGs among SCs	1405	—	170.92
5	Shopping Complex	339	—	33.07
6	Construction of Shop Room	1562	—	173.49
7	Handloom Programme	3363	—	157.31
8	Sericulture Programme	1614	—	36.40
9	Share Capital for enrolment of SCs as member of Cooperatives	204838	—	74.84
10	Renewable Energy Programme	4304	—	21.97
11	Payment for SC houses under Kutir Jyoti Programme	78768	—	51.32
12	Completion of Hostel Building	14	—	39.74
	ST (DTDP Sector)			
1	Bankable IGS	77792	377.84	1883.70
2	Community Irrigation Project under CLBS	5981	-	322.53
3	Training Programme	454	-	8.03
4	Share Capital for enrolment of STs as member in Cooperatives	6739	-	3.51
5	Construction of Hostel Building	25	-	2.50
6	Special Repair of Educational Building	150	-	23.21
	National Scheme of Liberation & Rehabilitation of Scavengers and their dependents			
1	Rehabilitation under bankable scheme	6284	84.98	315.46
2	Training Programme	4663	-	203.67
3	Construction of Shop Room	350	-	49.19

Source: Annual Action Plan – 2000-2001, OSFDC, Bhubaneswar, Orissa.

Fund Allocation, Utilisation and Slippage

Under the Dispersed Tribal Development programme, various income-generation schemes are implemented for the Scheduled Tribes settled outside the areas covered under Integrated Tribal Development Agency, Special Micro-Project, Modified Area Development Approach and Cluster. The required funds for implementation of these schemes are released from the Special Central Assistance grants. The Scheduled Tribe and Scheduled Caste Development Department of Orissa releases the grants to the Scheduled Tribe and Scheduled Caste Development Finance Cooperative Corporation Limited. The funds received by OSFDC is given to the dispersed tribal people in the shape of economic assistance under bankable schemes comprising 5 per cent subsidy and 15 per cent Margin Money Loan subject to a limit of Rs. 10,000 and Rs. 5,000 per beneficiary respectively. Besides, out of this fund, some amount is also utilised for community irrigation programmes, training programmes, renewable energy programmes, land reclamation and development, construction of hostel building, etc. However, the grants sanctioned to the Corporation for implementing the Dispersed Tribal Development programmes appear to be very less when compared with the budget provision in the annual action plans. It is stated by the sample official data of OSFDC that due to non-receipt of sufficient funds, the corporation is running with minus balance of Rs. 3.10 crores (till the end of 1999-2000), and hence, programmes for the dispersed tribes are not implemented up to the desired extent. This clearly indicates that the corporation is unable to implement all its programmes as planned out during the beginning of the year. The staffs have not received their salary for months together. As a result of this, the corporation has started reducing its organisational structure throughout the State. In addition to the shortfall of grant, it is observed that the sanctioned funds are not released on time. During the year 2000-2001, OSFDC had not received the grants even after 9 months of the stipulated time. Owing to this, implementation of programmes as per the approved annual action plans becomes impossible. As far as the Margin Money Loan is concerned, the Government of India and the Government of Orissa have released the loan component on an equity ratio of 49:51 under the Centrally Sponsored Scheme. It is marked during enquiry that the Government of India has been releasing its share of Margin Money Loan on time, but Government of Orissa, because of financial constraints, has been unable to release its share of the Margin Money Loan from 1997-98 to 1999-2000. Under this situation, the corporation fails to implement the development programmes efficiently and adequately.

OSFDC undertakes development programmes for both the Scheduled Tribes and Scheduled Castes. For the Scheduled Tribes, the programmes are operated under the Dispersed Tribal Development programme and for the Scheduled Castes similar programmes are implemented under the Special Component Plan. Its district level branch offices in collaboration with the nodal banks, block offices and district level line departments, carry out the programmes. The analysis of its functioning indicates that the corporation had undertaken bankable income generation schemes under Margin Money Loan programme for the dispersed tribal households. Tribal beneficiaries have been provided with development facilities related to different sectors such as animal husbandry, fishery, agriculture, land reform, minor irrigation, horticulture, small and village industries, vocational trade and small business. The Block Development Officer selects the beneficiaries in rural areas and the Executive Officer in urban areas. Applications are sponsored and endorsed to the nodal banks for sanction and release of loan money and to the District Managers for release of subsidy. Apart from individual benefit-oriented schemes, OSFDC has also taken up community benefit-oriented programmes relating to irrigation, hostel building, vocational training, common worksheet, etc.

The guidelines of Government of India on utilisation of funds under SCA to SCP the corporation also earmarks 15 per cent of the total funds for the development of women. Among various schemes skill upgradation, training, and handloom programmes are some of the most successful ones for the corporation. However, specific schemes should be strengthened relating to income generation programmes (IGPs) centring on the production and marketing of agro-based and forest-based resources. The concept of Self-Help Groups and Micro Credit should be largely adopted as an approach for women development through a sustainable manner. Presently, the schemes for them seem more to be target oriented. The schemes for the rehabilitation of scavengers also suffer from lack of similar approach.

For the upliftment of the Scheduled Castes, OSFDC apart from implementing the National Schemes for Liberation and Rehabilitation of Scavengers and their dependants, has also undertaken several bankable schemes and infrastructure development programmes. While implementing the development programmes, OSFDC face the following constraints. First, OSFDC suffers from inadequate staff strength at its district level offices. Because of this, verification of loan applications and sanction of loan as well as subsidy are delayed. Second, the staff of the district level branch offices of the corporation is not its core staff. They have come under deputation, as a result of which, the corporation had no effective control over these staff. Since these staff is not the core staff of the corporation, their involvement in development activities are half-hearted. Third, initially OSFDC had the responsibility of undertaking development programmes for the Scheduled Castes under Special Component Plan and the staff strength was adequate for that. But subsequently, the task of implementing development programmes for the dispersed tribes, scavengers and minority population was also assigned without any increase in the staff strength. With large number of schemes and programmes under different sectors, which are spread over 20 zones, it has become very difficult to manage the office with the same staff strength. Fourth, shortfall and delay in sanction of grants have also affected the development administration of Dispersed Tribal Development programmes. The Orissa Scheduled Castes and Scheduled Tribes Development Finance Cooperative Limited, which is undertaking this programme, finds difficulty to implement the Margin Money Loan schemes because of non-release of equity by the State Government. Fifth, compared to Tribal Sub-Plan, the Development Departments have allocated funds for Special Component Plan more close to the national principle. However, the Scheduled Tribe and Scheduled Caste Development Department does not carry the mandate to ensure that the line departments earmark funds for Special Component Plan as per the national principle and, therefore, the occasional shortfall of fund allocation is not controlled. Sixth, the OSFDC provides funds to the line departments and agencies to implement development programmes for the Scheduled Castes but is unable to collect the progress report as well as utilisation certificates on time since it does not have any administrative control over them.

Conclusion

The above discussion has attempted to find out the structural and functional strength and weaknesses of OSFDC. It is observed that OSFDC is not directly performing any role in respect of the provisions of the Fifth Schedule of the Constitution of India. However, OSFDC basically aims at improving the economic status of the tribal people through different income generating schemes. It is expected that once tribal people become stronger in their economic base, they need not run from pillar to post for taking small loans on high interest, and later on, they are compelled either to mortgage their tangible properties for redemption of the loan with the moneylenders who are basically non-tribals and are exploitative by nature. In spite of the achievements over the years, it has been observed that OSFDC is suffering from a number of structural and functional impediments. This affects its achievements both in terms of quality and quantity. The evaluation study of Mishra (2004) of the OSFDC IGP bankable schemes for the year 1999 to 2002 shows that the impact on the generation of income reveals that the total income between pre- and post-assistance period increased by 21.9 per cent. The study has also found out the schemes have generated 28,500 man-days of employment during the pre-assistance period and this has increased to 38,100 man-days of employment during the post-assistance period, showing variations of 33.6 per cent over the periods which stretched from 137 man-days to 183 man-days per beneficiary per annum during both the periods respectively. This indicates the net incremental generation of employment of 46 man-days, i.e., 1.5 man-days. The impact of the schemes is more visualised with reference beneficiaries crossing poverty line. The study justifies that around 18.3 per cent of the total beneficiaries have crossed the poverty line (ibid.). The study undertaken by Acharya et al., (2001) suggest that OSFDC is handicapped in several ways for delivering its services to its target groups on time. This at one level justifies that OSFDC need be revamped to implement various income generating schemes which will strengthen their livelihood resources so that they will not be victimised by the unscrupulous traders and moneylenders who are exploiting them day and night.

Panchayati Raj Institutions

The Cripps Mission of 1942, the Cabinet Mission of 1946 and the Government of India Act 1947, had enormous influence on the formulation of special policies for the tribal people. The Constituent Assembly framed two-way strategies for tribal development: providing protection from exploitation and simultaneously assisting them through economic activities. In this regard Thakkar Bapa and Jaipal Singh, two Indian proponents of tribal interests, had enormous influence to prepare the draft of the Constitution. It was presumed that provision of various protective measures were the only prerequisite for the development of tribal people. However, Gandhiji was of the view that the true foundation of civil revolt will be possible through networking of rural organisations (i.e., Panchayats) functioning in the villages which will help in restructuring the government machinery and welfare economic activities. This philosophy of Panchayati Raj Institutions has been highly neglected in the post-independence period. As a part of Directive Principles of State Policy, Panchayati Raj Institutions have been treated more with concessional approaches in which the "State shall take steps to organise village panchayats and endow them with such powers and authorities as may be necessary to enable them to function as units of self-government."

Panchayati Raj Institutions from time to time have been revived with the recommendations of the Balawantrai Mehta

Committee (1952); Ashok Mehta Committee (1977); CAARD Commission (1985); Singhui Committee (1986); Sarkaria Commission (1988); Thungon Committee (1985); Sixty-Fourth Amendment Bill (1989), and lastly by Seventy-Third Constitutional Amendment Act (1992). However, the major setback came to PRIs during the period of 1960-80 due to irregular elections, and less flow of financial resources to these organisations (Mathew, 1994). This has substantially affected the growth of Panchayati Raj Institutions.

Emerging Concept of Governance

Much late the issue of governance has caught the attention of the researchers, policy makers, NGOs and international agencies. In the discourse of development, the term 'governance' occupies a central position. Quite sizeable theoretical constructions have been made over the time opening the gamut of governance. The democratic institutions and welfare strategies of the State have been underestimated because of the failure of the State machinery to ensure good governance. Wide range of growth and welfare policies adopted over the time, aiming at attaining growth yielded low result. The expectations on the trickle down effects through both natural man made processes to overcome poverty and deprivations have not been materialised (Dandekar and Rath, 1971). The poverty alleviation programmes adopted since Fourth Five-Year Plan period seems to have achieved limited result due to some structural and operational problems at programme level and human factors at implementation level (Rao, 1990). Lack of people's participation in the development programmes created a major hurdle for the qualitative and significant improvement in the poverty situation of the poor.

Differences in defining the concept of governance carry a lot of divergent views, which have incorporated and recognised the role of private sector and civil society. This has redefined the role of State and people from an inter-dependant syndrome to a partnership one. The scope of political contract theory based on the agreement between the State and the people through a legal document popularly known as the Constitution, now has been much widened, aiming at establishing a development ideology behind the state-man relation on a sustainable basis. The conceptualisation and operationalisation of the new phenomenon of dismantling the welfare state though started during 1980s in the West, but much later the complexity of the phenomenon came to developing countries. The new governance paradigm is being seen and analysed both in the descriptive and prescriptive sense (Chandhoke, 2003). The State has now widened the attributes encompassing the horizon of accountability, transparency, efficiency, empowerment, participation, sustainability, equity and justice which are the creation of and imposed by the world bodies on individual states who are basically the fund providers and reform initiators across different countries. This paradigm shift has admitted the fact of development failures of yester-years and widened the scope of governance with more specific people-centric approaches. Under this new process, the roles of state (multilateral agencies, UN, WB, WTO, national and regional government, local self-government, etc.,), market (multinational companies, domestic companies/MNCs local traders and businessmen) and civil societies (INGOs, NGOs at national and regional levels and local level CBOs) at global, national and local levels cannot be ignored. This is proved when one finds that the World Bank, which for the first time tried to define and link up governance issues to development through four major areas, they propagate mutual functioning for good governance in a contextual manner. They are: improving the public sector management; ensuring accountability; creating appropriate legal framework; promoting transparency; and disseminating information (World Bank, 1994). This has been reflected in the governance paradigm of Government of India adopted in the Tenth Five-Year Plan (2002-07) of the country. In order to bring human development GoI has adopted the plurality of agencies functioning in a harmonious manner. The three parameters GoI has emphasised are the institutions (both formal and informal), the delivery mechanisms (law courts, hospitals, schools and police stations), and legal framework (laws, rules and procedures). In order to contextualise governance by way of effective people's participation, decentralisation through local self-governance, and involve civil society and voluntary agencies, ensure right to information, improve accountability and efficiency, the fiscal health of the State, reform the judicial system, coordinate through better synergy and efficiency are required (Government of India, 2002a). At operational level, this has influenced the delivery of development programmes and even the strategies of implementation of rural development programmes like road, education, sanitation, drinking water, etc.

Panchayati Raj Institutions in Orissa

Unlike many other states of India, Orissa has also passed the Gram Panchayat Act of 1948, to form local authorities like District Boards or Joint Committees. Similarly, the Zilla Parishad and Panchayat Samiti Act of 1959 had led to the foundation of Orissa Panchayat Samitis at block level and Zilla Parishads at district level. Since then, both Panchayat Samitis and Gram Panchayats are facing elections frequently at different times which were held during 1967, 1970, 1975, 1985, 1992, 1997 and recently during 2002. Irregular elections for the formation of Panchayati Raj Institutions in Orissa have been influenced by the sweet political interest of various parties in power. For example, various alternative structural arrangements have been experimented for Zilla Parishads, at different points of time which are named as District Advisory Council, and District Development and Planning Board. These newly formed bodies are replicas of Zilla Parishads. And they led to concentration of power either in the hands of Ministers or the District Collectors. Over politicisation and bureaucratisation of panchayat bodies over the time have encouraged malpractice and malfunctioning of the system as desired by the vested interest groups. Gradually, it was felt that in order to avoid the uncertainties and irregularities in the formation of Panchayat bodies, the Panchayati Raj system should have Constitutional bindings. Perhaps this has become one of the important factors, which had influenced the then Prime Minister during 1989 who gave a new shape to PRIs. It was a kind of 'controlled decentralisation'. Later on, this bill received

Constitutional recognition, through 73rd Amendment from the date of its inception, i.e., 24 April, 1992.

The 73rd Amendment of the Constitution of India has empowered Gram Sabha at village level, Panchayat Samiti at block level and Zilla Parishad at district level. During 2002 in Orissa there were 5,261 GPs with 93,781 elected representatives, 314 intermediary tiers, i.e., Panchayat Samitis with 6,541 elected representatives and 30 Zilla Parishads having 884 elected representatives (State Election Commission, 2002) (Tables 7.24 and 7.25). As regards participation of women in Panchayati Raj bodies, Orissa has introduced 33 per cent reservation for them and the achievements with regard to the participation of women have become more spectacular when it is seen against the backdrop of a low literacy level of women in the State (Mathew, 1994).

Table 7.24

Restructuring of Panchayati Raj Institutions in Orissa

Offices of PRIs	*Panchayat Election Year*		
	1997	*2002*	*Change*
Wards	81077	87547	+6470
Gram Panchayats	5261	6234	+973
PS Constituencies	5260	6227	+967
PS Chairman	314	314	-
ZP Constituencies	854	854	-
ZP President	30	30	-

Note: PS: Panchayat Samiti, ZP: Zilla Parishad.

Source: State Election Office, Bhubaneswar, Orissa, 2002.

An attempt has been made to know the status of both male and female candidates elected unopposed for different posts of PRIs during the year 2002. As regards the representatives elected as Ward members, it is found that of the total of 87,543 Ward members, around 38,150 (43.57%) have been nominated unopposed in the State, while it is 3.88 per cent in case of Sarpanch and 5.44 per cent in case of Panchayat Samiti members. The data when compared with few coastal districts and Scheduled Districts

Table 7.25

Social Group and Genderwise Distribution of PRI Representatives in Orissa as per 2002 Panchayat Election (in Nos.)

Orissa	*SC Total*	*ST Total*	*BCC Total*	*UR Total*	*Total*
GP Level					
(a) Ward Member	14930	23049	22686	26882	87547
(b) Sarpanch	816	2404	1231	1782	6234
Sub-Total	15746	25453	23917	28664	93781
Block Level					
(a) Samiti Member	1025	1704	1623	1875	6227
(b) Chairperson	38	139	54	83	314
Sub-Total	1063	1843	1677	1958	6541
ZP Level					
(a) ZP Member	139	219	232	264	854
(b) ZP President	4	10	6	10	30
Sub-Total	143	229	238	274	884

Note: ZP: Zilla Parishad, GP: Gram Panchayat.

Source: Government of Orissa, Information on Three-Tier Panchayat General Election 2002, State Election Commission, Bhubaneswar, Orissa.

reflect that the unopposed elected candidates for the post of Ward members are 1,020 in case of Jagatsinghpur, 791 in case of Balasore, 1,008 in case of Khurda and 984 in case of Puri district, is much less than the Scheduled districts of Koraput (1,818), and Sundargarh (1,703). Similarly, the status of women members who have been elected unopposed is 378, 347, 304, 320 in the districts of Jagatsinghpur, Khurda, Balasore, and Puri respectively, while in Scheduled districts their share is 671, 914, 485, 504 and 718 in the districts of Koraput, Mayurbhanj, Nawarangpur, Rayagada, and Sundargarh respectively. This at one level indicates that in comparison to many coastal districts where the development indices are much high, the villagers in scheduled districts have shown their higher degree of village unity and unanimously elected their Ward members unopposed. As regards women contestants for the post of Ward members in coastal districts their participation is much above the line of women reservation of 30 per cent. In case of scheduled districts their share is 21.17 per cent,

26.53 per cent, 23.14 per cent, 27.87 per cent, and 28.49 per cent in Koraput, Malkangiri, Nawarangpur, Rayagada and Sundargarh respectively. This indicates that in spite of the reservation, tribal women are yet to come forward to participate in decentralisation of administration through PRIs.

Similarly for the post of Sarpanch the data reflect that 19, 11, 18 and 24 Sarpanchs have been unopposedly elected in tribal districts of Koraput, Malkangiri, Rayagada, and Gajapati. This also partly justifies that the villagers have usual faith and unanimity in accepting their leaders. A good number of women for the post of Sarpanch have also been elected unopposed in the districts of Koraput (12), Malkangiri (5), Rayagada (9), and Gajapati (5) Similar is the situation in tribal districts while the people elected their Panchayat Samiti Member unopposed, both in case of male and female candidates. In case of contest for the post of Panchayat Samiti Members and Sarpanchs, tribal women have just fought as per their reservation requirements.

A Critical Comparison of Central Act 40 and the Orissa Gram Panchayat (Amendment) Act 1997

The Scheduled Areas, where more than 50 per cent tribal communities reside, are different in many respects. It was felt that the introduction of formal panchayats might not be suitable to these areas where community organisations and authority of traditional tribal councils still prevail and play a significant role for various purposes. This led Government of India to appoint a political committee, chaired by Dillip Singh Bhuria, to suggest necessary modifications as may be considered suitable, which would be approved by the Parliament. The New Panchayati Raj Act of 1996 of Orissa, draws its spirit from the Panchayat Samiti Act of 1959, the Orissa Gram Panchayat Act of 1969 and The Orissa Zilla Parishad Act of 1991 with suitable modifications. But it is yet to cope with the traditional pattern of governance of Tribal Communities. With the 73rd Constitutional Amendment, Government of Orissa enacted the Extension of Panchayati Raj Act (Amendment) of 1997 for the Scheduled Areas of Orissa. Since its inception Government of Orissa has been trying to make various structural arrangements for participatory economic development of the tribal communities. The Central Act 40 for the Panchayat Raj in Scheduled Area, which is popularly known as Panchayat Extension to the Scheduled Area Act (PESA) 1996, whereas, the State Act in Orissa for the Scheduled Area is known as Gram Panchayat (Amendment) Act 1997, produced out of the Amendment of Orissa Gram Panchayat Act 1964. A comparative picture of the Central Act and the State Act has been given in Table 7.26.

Table 7.26

A Comparative Status of the Powers in the PESA Act

Items	*Central Act*	*Orissa*
Definition of village	A village consists of a habitation or a group of habitations or a hamlet or a group of hamlets comprising a community and managing its affairs in accordance with traditions and customs	Adopted this definition.
Status and functions of Gram Sabha	Every village will have a Gram Sabha which will be competent to safeguard and preserve the traditions and customs of the people, their cultural identity	The State Act follows the Central Act. However, Orissa Act adds that it should be consistent with the relevant laws in force and in harmony with the tenets of the Constitution and human rights.
Constitution of Panchayat	Panchayats will be constituted at the village level with reservation for Scheduled Tribes in the manner prescribed in Part IX of the Constitution	Extended the reservation of elective seats and chairpersons to both Gram Panchayats and Mandal/intermediate panchayats.
Acquisition of land for development projects and of displaced persons	Prior consultation with Gram Sabha or panchayats at the appropriate level shall be made mandatory.	Assigned the power to Zilla Parishad with no role for the Gram Sabha/Gram Panchayat.
Planning and Management of minor water bodies	Entrusted to panchayats at the appropriate level.	Assigned power to Zilla Parishad instead of Gram Sabha/Gram Panchayat.

Contd...

Contd...

Grant of prospecting license or mining license or mining minerals	Prior recommendation of the Gram Sabha or the panchayats at the appropriate level shall be made mandatory	Gives powers to Zilla Parishad.
Grant of concession for exploitation of minor minerals by auction	Prior recommendation of Gram Sabha or panchayats at appropriate level shall be made mandatory.	Assigned the power to Zilla Parishad.
Enforce prohibition/ regulate or restrict sale & consumption of any intoxicant	Panchayats at the appropriate level and the Gram Sabha to be endowed with the power.	Gram Panchayat or Gram Sabha shall exercise the power
Ownership of minor Forest produce (MFP)	Panchayats at the appropriate level and the Gram Sabha endowed with the powers of ownership.	Followed the Central Act
Prevention & Restoration of Tribal Alienated Land	Panchayats at appropriate level and the Gram Sabha to be endowed with this power.	Subject to the control and supervision of Gram Sasan. Gram Panchayat will look into the matter.
Manage Village Market	Panchayats at appropriate level and the Gram Sabha to be endowed with this power.	The gram panchayat, subject to control and supervision of the Gram Sasan, shall have the power to manage the village market.
Moneylending to the Scheduled Tribes	Panchayats at the appropriate level and the Gram Sabha to be endowed with this power.	Followed the Central Act.
Exercise control over institutions & functionaries in all social sectors	Panchayats at the appropriate level or the Gram Sabha to be endowed with this power.	The Panchayat Samiti shall exercise the power in consultation with the Gram Sasan.
Control over local plans and resources including tribal sub-plans	Panchayats at appropriate level and the Gram Sabha to be endowed with this power.	Assigned the power to Panchayat Samiti.

Source: Various Sources.

- The Central Act of Panchayati Raj for the Scheduled Area of 1996 envisages community as the basic unit of self-governing system. Section 4 (b) of this law defines that a village shall consist of one or more habitations or hamlets comprising a community and managing its affairs in accordance with its traditions and customs. To understand, a community in tribal areas is to take into consideration a functioning collectivity, and face-to-face relationship. The essence of the community is social cohesiveness. Under the new Scheduled Area Act the formal recognition of the 'Community' and the 'Gram Sabha' is the most significant achievement in the history of democratic institutions so far built up. This has led to the foundation for participatory democracy in real sense. The significance of community command over natural resources has been recognised in this new Act not in isolation or as merely an economic issue, but in relation to the cultural identity of the people. Since community in the form of 'Gram Sabha', as a functional unit, enjoys the Constitutional recognition; its authority shall not be questioned, henceforth. Gram Sabha shall act as the supremo in matters of decision-making, implementation of the programmes, etc., under the extended Panchayat Act in Scheduled Area, whereas, according to Section 4 (iii) in the context of the state of Orissa, Gram Sasan has been conferred with this power to plan and approve the programmes in various matters of socio-economic development. Here powers have been conferred on the Gram Sasan which comprises all the voters of a Gram consisting of all communities having distinct socio-cultural practices, who elect a formal body known as Gram Panchayat, which is practically known as the executive council of the Gram Sasan.

- As regards the traditional rights of the tribal people are concerned, in Section 4 (iv) the state of Orissa provides right to the Gram Sasan and makes it competent to safeguard and preserve the traditions and customs of the people, their cultural identity, community resources and customary mode of dispute resolution consistent with the relevant laws which are in force (this is not in Central law) and in harmony with basic tenets of the Constitution. In practice in case of any dispute the rules of Cr PC, and IPC will prevail instead of customary laws of these communities. By this the State practically does not give any right to the tribal people to safeguard, exercise and preserve their traditional rights. These laws in true sense are not implemented mainly due to the non-demarcation of functional areas in development activities, which creates confusion as regards their jurisdiction and authority.

- The power to frame rules by the Gram Panchayat as per Section 6 (ii), that the State Government has handed over the power to Gram Panchayats to enforce restrictions for the prohibition or sale and consumption of any intoxicant; enjoy ownership and to provide licences for the use of minor forest resources, and finally, to control the practice of money-lending by amending the existing regulations like Orissa Bihar Excise Act, 1915, Orissa Forest Act 1980 and Money Lenders Regulation 1967. This power has been vested with Gram Panchayats in 2000 by amending the Orissa Land Reforms Act 1960, Regulation 2 of 1956 regarding the distribution of wasteland and transfer of immovable properties in Scheduled Areas.
- The Central Act, Clause 4 (1) provides scope for consultation with Gram Sabha while acquiring land in the Scheduled Areas, but the State law in Orissa, under Section 3 (6) of Orissa Zilla Parishad (Amendment Act 1997) confers this right on Zilla Parishad who even without the knowledge of Gram Panchayat can lease out land for mining, resettle the displaced people and manage the minor water bodies. In this context, the State practically curtails the power of the Gram Panchayats which is a matter of concern and needs attention for revision by the State in the days to come.
- The State Government during July 2003 has empowered Gram Panchayats with various development activities of 11 different departments of the government, like agriculture, cooperatives, schools and mass education, SC and ST Development Department, Women and Child Development Department, Panchayati Raj Department, Water Resource Development Department. The power to plan, implement,

monitor development activities has been conferred upon the Panchayati Raj Institutions at various levels.

- The Orissa Gram Panchayati Raj Bill 2003, has amended the Orissa Gram Panchayat Act 1964. It covers the provisions for a minimum presence of one tenth of the members in Palli Sabha or else the Palli Sabha will be dissolved. Secondly, the proposal for setting up industries within the geographical area of Gram Panchayat has to be approved by Gram Panchayat within 60 days and then sent to District Collector for approval where the decision of District Collector will stand and in case of any dispute at district level, the decision of the government will be final.

The issue of decentralisation and devolution of power among different tiers of Panchayati Raj system has been specially analysed. Different policies adopted by the State for the procurement and trade of non-timber forest produces, which are one of the major livelihood sources of the tribals in the State have been discussed. The State is yet to demarcate the jurisdiction over various functions or activities among different tiers of the Panchayat system. Structurally all the tiers starting from Gram Sabha (Palli Sabha) at lower level, Panchayat Samiti at the middle level and Zilla Parishad at the higher level have been formed in the State recently. Till date all these tiers suffer from overlapping of exercise of power in respect of financial and administrative matters. Lack of demarcation of socio-economic functions of PRIs at various levels initially created doubts (due to lack of accountability) about their success owing to overlapping of functions, which are reflected in the absence of clear-cut demarcation of responsibilities. As a result, the issue of trade offs between economics of scale and inter-jurisdictional externalities were overlooked, leading to overlapping of multiple functions among the official agencies like District Rural Development Agency (DRDA), District level Council and District Planning Committee (Mallik, 1989). Since panchayats are the vibrant institutions, the nexus between administrative and financial functions of the panchayats have become indispensable. Though the 11th Finance Commission has spelt out the processes of financial devolution

(Government of Orissa, 1998), degree of dependence, level of self-reliance and also the level of raising the financial resources for development activities at the grass-roots level. In practice, it has so happened that panchayats instead of becoming institutions of self-governance, have turned into mere agencies with delegated power by the ruling party in power at the State. However, over the time a lot of changes have been introduced in the devolution of power and areas of working in few departments of the Government of Orissa. This clearly shows that the Government of Orissa has started the processes of decentralisation in financial and administrative arenas among different tiers.

Decentralisation of Power in Vouge

The Non-Timber Forest Produces (NTFPs) have traditionally been perceived as an important source of forest revenue. As a result, the approach of the government towards NTFP resources has always been to maximise the revenue out of it. Simultaneously, NTFPs have been important sources of livelihood for the tribal and rural people. The prevailing systems do not provide scope to the tribal people to get a fair price over these produces. At the same time, it is of importance that collection of NTFPs must be non-destructive to sustain the long-term livelihood of the people (Government of Orissa, 2000) (Table 7.27).

While formulating the policies in respect of NTFPs and role of PRIs, the Forest and Environment Department of Government of Orissa (2000) has duly considered the provisions of the Panchayat (Extension to Scheduled area) Act 1996. The government has not defined the term 'Monitor Forest Produces' under Joint Forest Management (JFM) system. The local communities are being closely involved as partners of the Forest Department for the management of degraded forests, and the members of the Vana Surakhya Samiti (VSS) are entitled to share the usufructs. Considering these dimensions Government of Orissa has approved certain policies for streamlining the system of collection and disposal of various NTFP items in tribal dominated Scheduled Areas of the State.

In Clause 3 (a) of the said rule Government of Orissa has clearly mentioned seventy NTFP items as Minor Forest Produces. However, the list of NTFPs can be modified by the government from time to time depending upon various factors not linked with peoples' interest. The Gram Panchayat and Gram Sabha in the Scheduled Areas will have the ownership over these seventy NTFPs within its territories, i.e., in and around government land and forest lands within the limits of a revenue village under the said Gram Panchayat. In non-Scheduled Areas, the GP is not vested with powers of ownership over NTFPs, but can have the authority to regulate the purchase, procurement and trade of NTFPs.

Clause 3 (b) explains that no GP within and outside the Scheduled Area will have ownership over NTFPs produced in Reserve Forests, wild life sanctuaries and national parks, which are outside the jurisdiction of the revenue villages; thus, the GPs do not enjoy the rights to grant, lease or issue licence to individuals or agencies for collection of NTFPs from the restricted zones. However, members of VSS and tribal artisans as part of their customary right will be free to collect NTFPs from forest areas excluding sanctuaries, national parks and reserve forests and once these NTFPs are brought into the jurisdiction of the GPs it will be controlled by the GPs who enjoy power to regulate procurement and trading. But where VSS functions, its members will have the priority in the matter of collection and disposal of NTFPs in the respective forest areas.

As per Clause 3 (C) of the said policy any person desirous of purchasing NTFPs from primary gatherers or trading in NTFPs have to register in specific GPs for a season (October 1 to September 30) on payment for the individual NTFPs and on payment of registration fee to the concerned Range Officer along with the royalty of minimum 10 per cent. In Scheduled Areas of the State the exploitative role of some Scheduled Castes like Pano, Dom, Ganda, and of other caste groups like Gouda, Sundhi, Teli, etc., towards the innocent tribal communities is well established. Under this situation in the Scheduled Areas priority should be given to the persons of Scheduled Tribes to trade in NTFPs within the GP. In case of any trader found to be cheating the primary collectors by not paying the prices fixed by the government for each NTFP then his/her license should be forfeited after an enquiry. It has been stated that the local DFO will endeavour to promote competition among the traders and dealers by registering as many dealers as reasonably practicable for a specified area. Besides, the VSS, Mahila Samiti, recognised groups of primary gatherers may also be registered for the purpose. By opening NTFP market at primary level the State wants to have free trade in NTFPs. The question is, as to what extent the tribal dealer will be competent enough to work as per the rules of the OFDC and TDCC, which are supported by the State. Here, the State has to ensure the interest of the tribal dealers and offer more registrations to local level tribal dealers to compete in the open market.

Clause 3 (e) allows government agencies like OFDC, TDCC, etc., which may also register themselves to procure one or more NTFP items in one or more GPs after registration. This may create problems for the tribal people engaged as dealers or traders at the primary level. By this, the tribal agents who collect NTFPs from the primary collectors can easily dispose of their collections to higher level organisations.

The study focuses on the frequency of representation of PRI members, their educational background, landholding, knowledge on Constitutional provisions particularly on reservation, and bonded labour, functioning of different government departments for tribal development. It also throws some light on the knowledge of the PRI members regarding organisational arrangements meant for the implementation of development programmes for tribals.

Frequency of Representation of Members in PRIs

As regards the frequency of representation of PRI members, data have been collected separately for Ward members, Naib Sarpanchs and Sarpanchs. The frequency of representation has been calculated as 'first time', 'second time', and 'third time'. The analysis of the data across different ethnic groups shows that in total out of 30 ST PRI members represented as Ward members almost 22

(57.89%) of them have represented for the 'first time' while 7 (18.42%) are representing for 'second time'. Similarly, out of 7 ST Sarpanchs 5 (71.42%) members have represented for the 'first time', while 28.58 per cent have represented for 'third time' and none of them have represented for 'second time'. The analysis of above data reflects that a new generation of leadership is representing the local PRI structure. In other words, one can say that the intervention of new party based political system has encouraged leadership among younger generation. By this, in many situations neither the new generation coped with the older traditional leadership prevalent in villages, nor are they even able to bargain with the party based new political system. The reasons for not coping with the new system lie with their educational and mental backwardness, when they are compared with other non-tribal PRI members. As a result, in many villages the authority of traditional leaders is more effective in village internal administration. In this regard, some TAC members expressed their views that in spite of devolution of power to the Gram Sabha in Scheduled Areas, the bureaucrats have influenced the members of Panchayati Raj Institutions. This is largely due to over bureaucratisation of government functioning, lack of or less education, and poor awareness among the members.

Educational Status of Members of PRIs

During the study, an attempt was made to find out the educational background of the PRI members. It has been observed that among the ST members almost 15.78 per cent are illiterate, 55.26 per cent are educated up to primary level, who actually do not know anything about PRI except putting their signatures. There are 15.78 per cent ST members educated up to the middle level while little less than 13.75 per cent are educated up to high school level. First, because of the educational backwardness the elected tribal PRI members are unable to participate in a formal structure of Panchayati Raj system. For example, Motum Buchi, the Ward member of Pendulibai under Malkangiri Potteru village and 54 of Tandabai GP, even does not understand Oriya language. Similarly, Dule Naik, the Ward member of Ranapalli GP under Padia Block is just a literate to put his signature on official papers and unable to understand the functioning of Panchayati Raj system. As a result, many of the PRI members remain silent observers in Panchayat meetings and seem to be more interested for their daily allowances. Sumitra Pradhan, Ward member of Bhramarbadi village under Bhramarbadi GP comments that because of their low level of consciousness about the organisational and operational system, they are not able to participate in the proceedings of Gram Panchayats. Some PRI members also commented that they have not received any orientation training in this regard. This has made the system less dynamic, as a result, tribal PRI members are largely non-influential.

Knowledge of PRI Members on Reservation Policy

In order to assess the level of knowledge of the PRI members, an attempt has been made to find out their knowledge with regard to reservation policy, bonded labour system and organisational set-up functioning for the implementation of Constitutional provisions. As regards the policy of reservation for tribals some queries were made to ascertain the level of knowledge of PRI members on reservation provisions for Parliament, State Assembly, in educational institutions and employment. Specific questions were also asked about the period of commencement of this policy. Few more questions were also asked relating to the continuity of the policy and accrual of benefits to them. A straight question was asked to all PRI members regarding their knowledge on Indian Constitution. It was found that almost 39 (79.59%) PRI members knew that there is a Constitution in India, but they do not know much about the Constitution for governance of the country. As regards the reservation policy for the Scheduled Tribes in different sectors, about 47 (95.91%) members could not tell the year of commencement of this policy, and the provisions therein and 41 (83.67%) viewed that the reservation policy should continue further. When PRI members were asked to mention about the special provisions made in the reservation policy many PRI members expressed that except reservation in the State Assembly,

Parliament and in employment, they do not know other privileges available for the STs under reservation policy. Provision of reservation in employment and educational institutions has little meaning to them, because very few of them have availed these facilities in their life time. Provision of stipend, scholarship and other special facilities for the tribal children in Ashram Schools do not carry much importance because of their irregular release. The most interesting fact was that 5 (10.21%) PRI members said that they did not like that reservation policy should be made open to all ST families. They suggested that a family once benefited under this provision should be deleted, to present them from getting this benefit again and again. This will give scope for covering all the uncovered ST households and de-list the covered households.

The study also highlights that many ST PRI members ventilated their grievances against the continuity of reservation for them who have once benefited out of this facility. They suggested that there are certain posts for employment of Scheduled Tribes and Scheduled Castes, which can be covered under 'qualification relaxation' provisions. These posts at district level includes constables, home guards, excise constables, hospital and dispensary attendants, mid-wives, watchmen, forest guards, deputy surveyor, chainmen, record assistants, balwadi teachers, anganwadi workers, cooks, etc. These posts in Scheduled Areas should be exclusively reserved for the local tribal people. This will ensure representation of tribals under the reservation policy and will minimise the manipulations made by administrators who by and large belong to non-tribal categories.

PRI Members and their Awareness about Bonded Labour

Four different questions were asked to each PRI member covering various aspects of bonded labour practice. They are: whether the bonded labour system is still practised in tribal societies? In order to eradicate such a system in tribal areas what major steps have been taken by the government? It is strange to know that all the PRI (49) members confessed that such a practice is going on in tribal villages which varies only in magnitude. Even it is found that not a single PRI member knows about the functioning of Bonded Labour Abolition Act in the State. For many the economic reasons is the important factors (77.55%), while 22.45 per cent commented that the tribal children were lured to adhere to such an obnoxious practice. In all the study villages, it is observed that the functioning of Ashram Schools at Primary and Secondary levels for educating tribal children are operating outside the village. In Penaposi Pangara village of Kandhamal district, there is a primary school in the village, which attracts both tribal and non-tribal children. As a result, the focus of Ashram Schools for the tribal children is lost. In this school, the tribal children are not getting special attention by the teacher. So, in the process, they became easy haunts by the non-tribal landholders. The economic pressure of the family forces parents of such children to keep their children away from schooling who are normally engaged in despicable vocations. This denies tribal children the right to education. This is also observed in Kendubardihi village of Kalahandi district where tribal children work in hotels, shops, etc., in nearby urban centres like Lanjigarh and Biswanathpur. The details of the frequency distribution on the knowledge of the PRI members regarding this policy is explained in Table 5.27. In all the sample villages, the PRI members said that quite a sizeable number of tribal households are landless and because of limited livelihood opportunities they are forced to adopt bonded labour system as a source of income for them.

Knowledge about Implementation of Constitutional Provisions

PRI members have been asked about their knowledge on different organisational arrangements and the involvement of these organisations for tribal development. For example, whether the PRI members know about the functioning of the Joint Forest Management, OFDC, TDCC, District Level Government Departments, District Planning Board, Government Departments and TAC. The objective was to know the spectrum of knowledge base of the tribal PRI members. The analysis of the data reflect that except one member (2.04%) almost 97.96 per cent of PRI members showed ignorance about the Tribes Advisory Council (TAC).

Table 7.27

Status of Devolution of Powers to PRIs in Orissa

Name of Department and Subjects Transferred	*Designation of Functionaries who will be Accountable to PRIs*	*Sanction of Casual Leave*
1	*2*	*3*
Agriculture Department (1) Kharif, Rabi (2) Soil Conservation, Horticulture (3)Watershed	(i) District Agriculture Officer (ii) District Soil Conservation Officer (iii) District Horticulture Officer (iv) Junior Agriculture Officer	President Zilla Parishad Chairman, Panchayat Samiti
Cooperation Department Credit Plan	Dy. Registrar Asst. Registrar of Cooperative Society	President Zilla Parishad
School & Mass Education Department (4) Primary Education. (5) Non-Formal Education & Adult Education	C.I/D.I of School Headmaster of Primary School	President, Zilla Parishad A committee comprising of Chairman, BDO and DI of School will make transfer of Primary teachers within the Panchayat Samiti and limits of educational district Recommendation of the Sarpanch will be given due weightage for transfer within the Panchayat Samiti Sarpanch

Contd...

Contd...

Name of Department and Subjects Transferred	*Designation of Functionaries who will be Accountable to PRIs*	*Sanction of Casual Leave*
1	*2*	*3*
		If it is considered to transfer a teacher from one Panchayat Samiti to another Panchayat Samiti, the above-mentioned committee will recommend the same to the Zilla Parishad. A committee comprising of President, Executive Officer, Zilla Parishad and D.I. of Schools/C.I. of Schools will take decision regarding inter-block transfer of Primary school teachers within educational district.
Food Supplies & C.W. Department (6)Public Distribution System	Civil Supplies Officer	President, Zilla Parishad
ST&SC Development Department (7) Primary Education	District Welfare Officer Headmaster of Sevashram	President Zilla Parishad Sarpanch
H&F.W. Department (8) Health (9)Family Welfare Schemes	Chief District Medical Officer Medical Officer In Charge of PHC/Hospital Village Level Health Workers/ANM	President Zilla Parishad Chairman Panchayat Samiti Sarpanch or Naib Sarpanch whoever is a woman
W& C.D. Department (10) Social Security Schemes/Mid-Day Meal Programme	District Social Welfare Officer CPDO, ICDS/Anganbadi Workers	President Zilla Parishad Chairman/Vice Chairman, whoever is a woman Sarpanch or Naib Sarpanch whoever is a woman

Contd...

Contd...

Name of Department and Subjects Transferred	*Designation of Functionaries who will be Accountable to PRIs*	*Sanction of Casual Leave*
1	*2*	*3*
F& A.R.D. Department (11) Diary (12) Fishery	District Fisheries Officer Asst. Director. Fisheries Chief District Veterinary Officer Veterinary Asst. Surgeon Livestock Inspector	President Zilla Parishad President Zilla Parishad Chairman Panchayat Samiti Sarpanch will report attendance of livestock Inspector to Chairman and Veterinary Assistant Surgeon
R.D. Department (13) Drinking Water and Sanitation	Executive Engineer R.W.S.S.	President Zilla Parishad
P.R. Department (14) Poverty Alleviation (15) Road, Culvert, Bridges and Ferries (16) Minor Forest Produces (17) Rural Housing (18) Markets (19) Non-Conventional Energy (20) Maintenance of Community Assets	BDO	Chairman Panchayat Samiti
Water Resources (21) Minor Irrigation up to 100 acres	Executive Engineer, MI Asst. Engineer	President, Zilla Parishad Chairman, Panchayat Samiti

Regarding the state level departments and district level departments, which are implementing development programmes, more or less, 95.91 per cent of members, seemed to have possessed the knowledge. When the members were asked more specifically about the functioning of District Planning Board/Zilla Parishad, around 67.34 per cent members could tell and the rest could not conceptualise about their functions. Similarly, when the members were asked specifically about the functions of OFDC and TDCC around 35 per cent and 40 per cent respectively expressed their ignorance. This at certain level shows that the members do not have specific knowledge about the functioning of specific department and agency operating for Tribal Development. The PRI members told different reasons for the poor level of knowledge they have on the functioning of different organisations floated for tribal development. Firstly, the knowledge of PRI members is highly influenced by their range of interaction with various agencies and participation in day-to-day political issues. It is observed during the study that except few PRI members, others are docile, isolative, and indifferent to active politics. Under the situation their interaction with block and district level agencies are very casual and non-enistent. They suggested that the PRI members be given sufficient training regarding the organisational and functional efficacies of the departments engaged directly with tribal development.

Influence of Traditional Polity on Tribals

Many scholars have pointed out the importance of traditional tribal polity in the context of tribal societies from time to time. It has been observed that in spite of changes introduced through the establishment of modern democratic institutions and set-up in tribal areas, the importance of tribal political system has not changed completely. Various village functionaries, designate differently among different tribal communities which still perform their role as regards village administration, maintenance of socio-cultural life and award of punishment to the social deviants. These functionaries are hereditary, who by and large enjoy the community village support.

Here, an attempt has been made to understand the importance of traditional tribal polity by way of analysing the findings of few studies, which have been carried out, by various scholars in different tribal communities of the State. Behura and Sahu (1970-71) while studying the Mutha: the political organisation of the Kondh with special reference to Pusungia Mutha in the Phulbani district of Orissa have highlighted its various aspects. They pointed out that the Mutha was exercising effective group control, looking after the welfare of the community, general administration of the village, collection of land revenue or *mamuls*, maintain the customary laws of the Kondh tribe and ensures safety of life and security of property by resolving all disputes, domestic or otherwise, delivering judgement, inflicting punishment and imposing fines on miscreants and culprits and redressing the grievances in consonance with the Kondh traditional rules. Over the time, Mutha political organisation has dwindled away and the functions of its functionaries have either been attenuated or have ceased to exist altogether. It is largely due to the imposition of police administration, introduction of statutory panchayat system, extension of Criminal Procedure Code and Indian Penal Code in the tribal areas. However, among these functionaries particularly the religious head and administrative head of the village still enjoy certain control and authority in the village.

The traditional leadership pattern in Koya village centres around Peda: the political head; Perma: the priest; Wadde: the Shaman; and the Katual or messenger. The Peda: the headman of the Koya tribal community along with other traditional village leaders (which are hereditary by nature) play a major role in the political and social life of the village and even in the panchayat of other Kulas and Muthas. They settle various problems, like adultery, rape, witchcraft and divorce, etc., which takes place in the village. Though the traditional political system of the Koya for settlement of disputes cannot be said to be perfectly in harmony with the statutory panchayat system, its functions have been largely confined to social life even today; however, the entry of the non-tribals like Dom, Telgu traders and Bengali resettlers into the modern statutory political system has partially disturbed the processes and control mechanisms (Behura and Panigrahi, 2001).

The study of Elections and Pattern of Leadership in two Lanjia Saora villages of Gumma Panchayat Samiti of Ganjam district (Patnaik and Mishra, 1976) have highlighted the types of new tribal leadership which have entered into the political arena of statutory local government, election campaigning and voting behaviour of the Saoras. The study pointed out that the Muthas among the Saora were headed by the Mutha head, who was assisted by Paiks, Dandasena, Majhi, Dalpati, Pradhan, Dalai and Gamango (Baral and Sahu, 1989). However, over the time, a lot of changes have taken place in their leadership pattern. It is largely due to their growing exposure to systems of modern education, communication and new authority pattern. Now, the modern young, educated Saora leaders play a major role in the conflict resolution processes and are also more influential in the village in relation to outside agencies. However, they lack courage, confidence and articulation like that of their traditional leaders to raise voice against injustice both within and outside the village.

Choudhury's study (1976) among the Oraon of Sundargarh district of Orissa highlights the processes of change in the traditional leadership that is popularly known as Gountia system which was based on heredity, custom, wealth and wisdom;, which has given way to a dynamic and revolutionary leadership based on education, enlightenment, and political consciousness. The paper explains that the new leadership has proved to become ineffective in the recent past and few traditional leaders like the priest still has command over the masses. However, this is confined only to the arena of performing religious rites. The disintegration of the traditional Oraon leadership is mainly due to the spread of Christianity, influence of caste Hindu social institutions, introduction of modern education, implementation of socio-economic development programmes, and introduction of statutory panchayat system in tribal regions. Panda (2004) studied the political system of the Binjal of Orissa and has reported that in spite of the political intervention over the decades, the Binjhal are able to maintain their own political system who still plays a very dynamic role both within and outside their village.

In accordance with the implementation of the Panchayati Raj Act (Amendment) of 1997 in the Scheduled Areas of the State, it is necessary that all Regulations, Acts, and laws operating in Scheduled Areas, such as IPC, CrPC, and Land Alienation, etc., be suitably amended within a stipulated time for decentralising power among different tiers of the Panchayati Raj system. This will facilitate all the tiers of Panchayati Raj Institutions to work more efficiently. It is essential to impart training to the functionaries of Panchayati Raj Institutions in the Scheduled Areas. This will enhance the skill, knowledge and functional efficiency of PRI members belonging to Scheduled categories. This will also help PRI members in preparing development programmes and in reviewing the technicalities of various programmes implemented in their operational areas. Another aspect of the successful implementation of decentralisation of powers rests on the selection of right kind of PRI members. It should be based not merely on political interventions; rather their selection should be guided by non-political and development-oriented approaches. Building small political coteries in the PRI structures will never be a blessing for fulfilling the pious objectives of 73rd Amendment of Panchayati Raj system.

Major Challenges Ahead

The emerging governance system has posed many challenges before the stakeholders. It is time to see the operational feasibility of the new paradigm of governance and its contribution to overcome the poverty cycle of the tribal poor. Whether the gradual withdrawal of the State from its Constitutional welfare responsibilities by handing over the scope and opportunities to the market players and civil societies will ensure the dignity and empower the tribals in the long run? Whether the tribal people and their institutions will cope with the changing demand of the governance partners like market, state and dominant civil society? In spite of the fact that the tribal people have developed interest in their own welfare and development, but by and large the governance mechanisms the State has adopted so far for tribal development has failed to fulfil the Constitutional obligation of the welfare State. Under this situation whether the present governance mechanisms are not sufficient enough to meet the expected goals of development The issue is whether decentralisation so far made under the garb of participatory governance system is sufficient enough to fulfil the objectives, has to be carefully analysed by the stakeholders?

8 Summary and Policy Recommendation

Summary

India is one of the nation states having hundreds of ethnic minorities in general and tribal communities in particular. Understanding the historical reasons for the backwardness of these communities, the founding fathers, while framing the Constitution of India, have made special provisions for the development of these groups. Thus, there are twenty Articles, two Special Schedules and many protective provisions in the Constitution of India, specifically in Part III, IV, X, XI and XVI. These protective provisions have been contained in the Constitution under Articles: 14, 15 (I, II), 15 (4), 16 (1, 4, 4A),17, 19 (4), 23, 24, 25, 29, 38, 39, 39 (A), 41, 46, 47, 48, and 48 (A), 164 (II), 244, 275, 330, 332, 334, 335, 338, 339 (I), 340, 341, 342, 366, 371, (A, B, C). All these Constitutional provisions can be classified into four categories such as: (i) Social Safeguards, (ii) Educational and Economic Safeguards, (iii) Political Safeguards, and (iv) Safeguards for the Administration of Scheduled Areas. In addition to these, there are also a good number of Regulations, Acts, Government Orders, specifically made by the State at different points of time to protect the culture and livelihood interests of the tribal communities.

In order to assess the impact of these special protective Constitutional provisions on the life and livelihood system of the tribal people, quite a good number of issue-based evaluative studies have been undertaken by various scholars at different points of time. These studies have found out the uneven impact of such provisions and the reasons thereof. The development efforts made by the State during the last half century have raised certain basic issues before the nation. One of such issue popularly raised is the rights of the tribal people over the natural resources such as land, water, forests, and minerals.

The present exercise has tried to find out the manner of functioning of the Fifth Schedule of the Constitution in the State of Orissa through various State level agencies in respect of the welfare and development of the weaker sections, particularly the Scheduled Tribes. The objectives of the academic exercise have guided the entire process of data collection and analysis. They are: (i) to review the jurisdiction of Scheduled Areas and the list of Scheduled Tribes, and the processes of inclusion and exclusion therein over the years in Orissa, (ii) to review the magnitude of few problems like prohibition, indebtedness and land alienation pertaining to protection, welfare and development of the Scheduled Tribes, and the Scheduled Areas in Orissa, and (iii) to review the functioning of various State level agencies meant for the welfare of the tribal communities in the context of the provisions of Fifth Schedule with special reference to the functioning of the Tribes Advisory Council (TAC); National Commission for Scheduled Castes and Scheduled Tribes, Bhubaneswar, (NCSC & ST), Tribal Development Cooperative Corporation (TDCC), Bhubaneswar, Scheduled Castes and Scheduled Tribes Research and Training Institute, Bhubaneswar (SCSTRTI), Orissa Forest Development Corporation Ltd. (OFDC); and State actions relating to the assessment of prohibition policy of Government of Orissa in tribal regions of the State; regulation of moneylending business by private operators and agencies in tribal areas of Orissa and regulation of allotment of land among the members of the Scheduled Tribes.

The study while selecting villages has adopted multi-stage-sampling method keeping districts at higher level and the villages at lower level. In each stage while selecting the districts, blocks and villages, the study has emphasised more on the concentration of tribal population, various indicators of backwardness and geographical representation. In total, four villages have been selected, one from each of the four geographically representative districts in Scheduled Areas of the State. The sample districts are Kandhamal in central part, Kalahandi in western part, Keonjhar in northern part and Malkangiri in southern part of Orissa.

Both primary and secondary data as well as qualitative and quantitative data have been used. It has adopted various research methods, such as: household survey, case study, and focus-group discussion, largely to explore primary data in the study-villages. Quite a good number of functionaries of different agencies like Panchayati Raj Institutions, Tribal Development Cooperative Corporation Ltd., Orissa Forest Development Corporation Ltd., Nationalised Banks, have been personally interviewed. Furthermore, data have been collected from various secondary sources like published reports, records, registers, and proceedings of meetings of various government departments and agencies.

The findings of the study have been incorporated in seven chapters. Analysis of data has been made according to ethnic groups and different districts. By using both the criteria, the study has presented the data through two-way tables and has emphasised the analysis more on ethnic group index.

Major Findings

The State of Orissa is harbouring 62 different Scheduled Tribes. Basing on their socio-economic backwardness 11 tribal communities have been categorised as Primitive Tribal Groups (PTG). Almost 44.21 per cent of the total land area of the State have been declared as Scheduled Area, which covers six districts as fully, and seven districts as partially scheduled. Thus, out of 314 Community Development Blocks in Orissa, 118 (37.3%) blocks are popularly known as Tribal Sub-Plan (TSP) area blocks, which are preponderantly inhabited by the tribal communities. Tribal population in Orissa is 22.21 per cent of the population of the State, who more or less, posses common characteristics, such as, primitive technology, and pre-industrial economy, segmentary social structure, homogenous culture, non-literate language, educational backwardness, etc. They are relatively autonomous. The economy of the tribals in Orissa by and large centres around land and forest produces. The non-tribal communities, particularly the Scheduled Caste communities, maintain a symbiotic relationship with the tribal communities.

The founding fathers of Indian Constitution have adopted a two-way strategy of tribal development, i.e., providing protection to the tribal people against exploitation and simultaneously assisting them through planned development so as to bring them above the poverty level.

The framers of Indian Constitution, have conferred power on the Governor of a State, under Para 5 of the Fifth Schedule so as to: (a) prohibit or restrict transfer of land by or among members of the Scheduled Tribes; (b) regulate allotment of land among members of Scheduled Tribes in Scheduled Areas; and (c) regulate carrying on of moneylending business among the members of Scheduled Tribes in Scheduled Areas.

Alcoholism and Excise Policy

- As regards the growth of excise policy of the State is concerned, it has been observed that Bihar and Orissa Act on Prohibition constituted a benchmark guideline in Orissa which was followed by Opium (Orissa Amendment) Bill, 1939 and Orissa Prohibition Bill, 1939. Both of these policies aimed at bringing about a total prohibition in the entire province of Orissa. Later on, the Bihar and Orissa Excise (Orissa Amendment) Bill, 1947 was introduced by establishing a separate Excise Department in the State. Only during 1975, the Scheduled Areas and Scheduled Tribe Commission reviewed the excise policy which became effective in the Scheduled Areas thereafter. Following the National Policy on Prohibition, Government of Orissa during 1974 closed down vending of liquor in the tribal inhabited areas of the State. In order to make total prohibition effective, Government of Orissa took various steps. Following this, the State Government during 1977, abolished the contract system of vending liquor in the Scheduled areas except the District, Sub-Division, and Tehasil headquarters, industrial areas, NACs and Municipal Areas. During 1992, Government of India Tribal Division made effective the excise policy in the Scheduled Areas of India on two basic principles of discontinuing commercial vending of alcoholic beverages in Scheduled areas and permitting Scheduled Tribes to brew their traditional beverages for consumption at home, and on religious and social occasions. In spite of repeated recommendations of the Tribes Advisory Council for unconditional withdrawal of excise cases pending against STs, and repeated requests by the Parliamentary Committee to the State Government to implement the Central Excise Policy for the Scheduled Areas, that is to make a complete ban of distillation and vending of liquor in Scheduled Areas of the State, the State Government interested in the revenue potential of the Out-Still (OS) based on mahua flower at different points of time has introduced and reintroduced the circulation of liquor in the Scheduled Areas of the State.

- Magnitude of the problem of alcoholism in the study villages can be seen from the data, which show that almost 28.29 per cent tribal households produce mahua liquor and only 10. 17 per cent per cent produce handia on commercial basis. The average production of mahua liquor per tribal household per annum was 182 litres, while production of handia per household was 638 litres. It is observed that the tribal people consume around 30 to 40 per cent of the total liquor produced by them.
- The non-tribals who trade on liquor also use tribal people to produce liquor by supplying them mahua flowers on certain conditions of handing over of the liquor at pre-decided rates to the traders for sale. For this, everybody blames the tribal people as liquor producers. However, by this, tribal people get more opportunities for consumption of liquor.
- Use of alcohol in tribal society has a strong bearing on the livelihood of the poor tribal people. The study shows that for the weakness of the tribals for liquor, non-tribals push liquor

into the tribal society through various manipulative means. Tribal people purchase liquor on credit; if they do not have ready cash to buy, they assure the liquor vendors to clear all dues during the harvest period. In such situations, liquor vendors sell liquor at higher prices, which they collect during the harvest period. As a result, the stock of agricultural produces and NTFPs of several tribal households get highly depleted.

- It has been observed that if the tribals are denied liquor from the vendors on credit they do not hesitate even to sell or mortgage their assets like watch, bicycle, torch, radio and utensils once for all. Excess drinking of liquor also results in wife-beating and drop-outs of their children from schools.
- As regards the extent of liquor consumption in tribal society, 91.38 per cent PRI members have said that consumption of mahuli by the tribal people has increased overtime, and 81.63 per cent have said that the control of tribals over the production, distribution, and consumption of liquor has decreased. In order to substantiate their viewpoints, they have put forth some justifications by saying that government restriction on liquor preparation has marginal impact on the tribal people which has contributed very little to refrain them from preparing liquor which was freely prepared during 1950s and 1960s.
- The educational and awareness programmes carried out by the NGOs in certain parts of tribal areas have immense impact on restricting the free production and consumption of liquor.
- The excise policies of the government have marginal impact on the illegal liquor trading in tribal areas. The non-tribal liquor brewers and traders have reflected this through the frequent occurrence of hooch tragedies, which have been the result of spurious liquor preparation by the non-tribal liquor brewers and traders. It is alleged that there is an illicit trade of country liquor and Indian make Foreign brands in the State, which is beyond the knowledge of Excise authorities.

Indebtedness

- Surveys and studies undertaken by Reserve Bank of India and National Sample Survey Organisation at different points of time on the debt and investment position, both in rural and urban areas of the State of Orissa, show that the proportion of households reporting debt has increased, whereas, there is a decline in the share of institutional agencies in the total amount of debt of rural households which show that non-institutional agencies like moneylenders, traders, relatives, friends, have played a dominant role in rural areas. Another study carried out by Government of India among the tribal people shows that indebtedness has increased from 14.47 per cent in 1975-76 to 33.77 per cent in 1982-83 and the debt liability has increased from Rs. 419 to Rs. 819 during the above period.
- The State of Orissa at different times enacted various laws, passed regulations and issued administrative orders, which basically aim at saving tribal people from the clutches of moneylenders and minimise the burden of indebtedness on the tribals. These policies are: Agriculturists Loan Act, 1884; Orissa Small Holders Relief Act, 1938; Orissa Money Lenders Bill 1938; Money Lenders (Second Amendment) Bill 1947; the Money Lenders Regulations, 1967 (Regulation 2 of 1968) and the Orissa Debt Relief Act 1980.
- The findings of the study show that 28.77 per cent tribal households have taken loan from unregistered private sources, out of which 71.66 per cent have received loan from persons belonging to the general caste categories. The money-lenders do not always belong to SC caste groups. Some of them are also government employees like Revenue Inspectors and School Teachers. The Sundhis in Kandhamal maintain relationships of credit with the turmeric growing Kandhas, who fulfil their commitment to sell their produces at pre-determined rates.
- Around 97.36 per cent tribal households expressed their ignorance about the Orissa Scheduled Areas Moneylenders

Policy of 1967 and Orissa Regulation 2 of 1998. This reflects the marginal impact of the policy.

- The terms and conditions of hand-loans vary from community to community and district to district. While some prefer to provide loans against the mortgage of standing turmeric crops, others prefer land as a form of mortgage during such loan transactions. Since both the creditors and debtors maintain a face-to-face relationship and even ritual relations, the need for guarantor does not arise. Land mortgage under certain conditions is the most important mode of security in the process of moneylending, and in this process tribal people lose the right of use over their valuable lands.
- The study has found out that tribal people always live in marginalised conditions and are unable to meet their basic requirements, which force them to go in for borrowing from private sources even at the cost of mortgaging their productive lands, the only assured source of their livelihood.
- It has been observed that illiteracy, limited world view, simplicity, trustworthy-nature, and the influence of their traditional culture on the belief pattern of tribal people, etc., help the non-tribal moneylenders to maintain a durable ritual relation with the tribal debtors.
- The tribal people over generations have felt that the local moneylenders are easily accessible, who come to their help during crisis situations, which is not possible in any formal organisations like Credit Cooperatives and Rural Banks, Nationalised Banks, LAMPS, TDCC, etc. The loan procedures of these formal organisations are cumbersome which, also include other factors, which force the tribal people not to opt for loan facilities from these institutions.
- The provisions of various time-bound loan schemes, which have been implemented through Cooperatives, Banks, TDCC and LAMPS, have by and large failed to meet the timely requirements of the tribal people. As a result, tribals are forced to become victims of non-tribal moneylenders.

Land Alienation

- Land tenure system in modern Orissa has a complex legacy. Due to some historical factors land tenure system in tribal regions of Orissa vary from region to region. Prior to the formation of Orissa as a State, transfer of land to the non-tribals was not considered as illegal in various parts of the State. As a result of this, in early days, the tribals had lost their valuable land through mortgage, sale, gift and lease to non-tribals.
- In post-independence period two major policies were adopted to check alienation of land from tribals to non-tribals. First, the Scheduled Areas Transfer of Immovable Property (by Scheduled Tribes) Regulation 2 of 1956 defines the meaning of transfer of immovable property, competent authority to permit transfer of land from tribal people to non-tribals, eviction of unauthorised occupants, etc. A couple of amendments to these policies have been made with regard to the procedure of transfer, control of District Collector, on land transactions, sale of timbers by Scheduled Tribes, etc. Second, Orissa Land Reforms Act 1960, i.e., OLR Act 1960, protects the interests of the SCs and STs by distributing surplus land for homestead and agricultural purposes. The experiences gained over time have prompted the State Government to make the law more effective with a number of amendments, which have been incorporated in the Act.
- From a review of the Annual Administration Report of Scheduled areas of Orissa from 1979-80 to 1998-99, it has been found that 4,6811 cases of land alienation have been instituted, of which 45,862 cases have been disposed which have benefited a total of 33,718 tribal households. By this, a total of 36,147 acres of land have been restored and distributed among the tribal households. It has been observed that all the cases instituted during a year, if could not be disposed during that year, then the cases accumulate for the next reporting year. The data show that the carry-over of cases to subsequent years, sometimes do not correlate when compared with the

pending cases of the previous years. Inconsistencies in data maintained in government records obviously raise doubts on the accuracy of these figures. It has been found that tribal people due to lack of awareness and illiteracy are largely ignorant of the prevailing preventive regulations of land alienation.

- Review of data with regard to the distribution of various types of land by the State Government among the Scheduled Groups in Orissa from 1980-81 to 1998-99 shows that, though there is a provision for distribution of wasteland both for agriculture and homestead purposes according to the proportion of SC and ST population, in fact STs have received less land compared to SCs. However, STs have been allotted more of ceiling surplus land as compared to SCs. Taking of possession of such land by them is still a problem for multiple reasons.

Role of Welfare Agencies

Tribes Advisory Council (TAC)

- The TAC meeting is to be held twice a year, but in Orissa it is not organised at regular intervals. This has affected the role, which is supposed to be played by the TAC in respect of tribal welfare in the State.
- The principle of representation in the State Assembly and Parliament, as well as political party affiliations have always influenced the membership in TAC. It is found that a little less than fifty per cent of the tribal members in the TAC are frequently represented. As a result, many new MLAs are deprived of becoming members of the TAC and ventilate their views in TAC meetings as regards welfare of the tribal people.
- As regards the participation of members in TAC the data reflect that only 50 per cent or a little more of the total members participate in TAC meetings. It has been observed that equal number of government employees also participate in such meetings. In this process, only few TAC members

who are continuing members of the State Assembly and Parliament participate actively in the meetings, whereas, many TAC members remain as silent observers in the meetings. This does not contribute much to the strengthening of the role of TAC in tribal development affairs of the State.

- The ST and SC Development Department, provides information on the physical achievements of the State Government on tribal development, and prepares the Governor's Report on the 'Annual Administration of Scheduled Areas' as per the provision of Para 3 of the Fifth Schedule. This report does not reflect the sufferings of tribal people who struggle for a bare living. It has been observed that often the ST and SC Development Department is unable to submit the Governor's Report in time. Such deviation of the Constitutional provisions by the State has already been pointed out by Government of India and by the State office of the National Commission for STs and SCs.

National Commission for SCs and STs

- The monitoring mechanisms adopted by the National Commission are inadequate to cover the entire Schedule Areas of the State. The poor tribals who inhabit the remote villages, rarely come to the office of the National Commission at Bhubaneswar to ventilate their genuine grievances. As a result, the Commission receives only few representations from SCs and STs, and the employees of scheduled groups seeking reddressal of their grievances.

Scheduled Caste and Scheduled Tribe Research and Training Institute (SCSTRTI)

- In the context of the provisions of Fifth Schedule of the Constitution of India, one hardly finds more than one or two studies/evaluation/training programmes on any one of the issues of land alienation, moneylending, prohibition policy and functioning of Tribes Advisory Council in Orissa. Since SCSTRTI is the only government research institution dedicated to the study of the problems of the scheduled communities in the State, it is expected that the institute will have to play a more dynamic role to achieve its goal.

Orissa Forest Development Corporation Ltd. (OFDC)

- The OFDC Ltd. aims to protect the livelihood interests of the tribal people while trading over kenduleaves, bamboos, sal seeds, and mahua flowers; and to eliminate the role of middlemen, traders and sub-agents in the transaction of forest produces. The study reflects that OFDC is yet to protect the livelihood interests of the tribals on priority basis. It has to restrain the traders and middlemen in the best interests of the tribal people. Exploitation of tribals can be reduced if traders and middlemen are kept under surveillance and Panchayati Raj Institutions at ground level get involved with true spirit of service.
- The agency has played an important role in mobilising forest resources from tribal people to non-tribal people, and has enriched government revenue to a greater extent. As a result, tribal people are suffering from the problem of mortgaging their productive lands to the private moneylenders while incurring distress loans.

Tribal Development Cooperative Corporation Ltd. (TDCC)

- TDCC as an apex cooperative organisation is to procure SAPs and MFPs from tribal people, by supplying them essential commodities and other consumer goods, and to provide advance consumption-cum-production credits, but practically TDCC has largely failed in delivering the required services to the needy tribals, and has not been able to build up an appropriate strategy to provide sustainable services to the tribals.
- TDCC is suffering from shortage of working capital, burden of heavy royalty (to be paid to the Forest and Environment Department), low turnover, heavy interest burden, etc. Thus, when compared with similar organisations in other States, it is found that the TDCC in Orissa is functioning in a suffocated climate. This has restricted the scope of functioning

capabilities and service delivery mechanisms of the organisation.

Orissa State Finance Development Corporation Ltd. (OSFDC)

- It has been observed that OSFDC, started in the year of 1979-80, suffers from adequate staff requirement in all its district level offices. As a result, the smooth functioning of OSFDC is questioned. This has been found in respect of processing of loan applications for sanction of loans, monitoring of progress of work. Therefore, major load of work of the district offices has been shifted to the central office of OSFDC at Bhubaneswar. This has dwarfed the role of district offices in service delivery system.
- OSFDC also suffers from shortfall in fund allocation and delay in release of funds by the State. Non-release of equity on time by the State Government under Marginal Money Loan schemes affects both qualitative and quantitative functioning of this agency.
- The district level offices of OSFDC do not have control on the line departments so as to streamline the implementation of various schemes funded by them for the development of SCs and STs. The OSFDC sometimes is unable to collect the utilisation certificates in respect of expenditures from the line departments, who have spent the allotted funds on various schemes. Expenditures show that many programmes at district level are not implemented within the stipulated time period and have been carried forward to subsequent years. In this process, the line departments do not feel the importance of implementing tribal development programmes in time.

Panchayati Raj Institutions

- With the 73rd Amendment of the Constitution of India, Government of Orissa has enacted the extension of Panchayati Raj Act (Amendment) of 1997 to the Scheduled Areas of the State. This has empowered Gram Sabha at village level, Panchayat Samiti at block level, and Zilla Parishad at district level.

- Accordingly, power has been decentralised through amendments of laws and regulations and has been handed over to Gram Sabha in respect of NTFPs, moneylending and excise policy prevalent in Scheduled Areas of the State. However, certain experience gained during the implementation needs to be incorporated in these policies. It has been observed that there are some laws like Indian Penal Code (IPC), Criminal Procedures Code (CrPC), Regulation 2 of 1956; Orissa Land Reform Act 1960 etc, which are being implemented in Scheduled Areas need be delegated to Gram Sabhas.
- The data indicate that the awareness level of tribal PRI members about various policies, such as job and seat reservation, bonded labour eradication, and implementation of various Constitutional provisions is very low. As a result, the bureaucratic process controls the implementation of welfare programmes.

Major Suggestions

Excise Policy

- It would be very appropriate if the State Government adopts a people-oriented excise policy. The policy need not solely aim at revenue maximisation. The policy should have a welfare approach.
- The State Government may reduce the number of liquor shops in the tribal areas of the State. Liquor sale may be restricted to two days a week. If it is implemented it may reduce the drinking habits of the tribals.
- The NGOs may be assigned with the task of creating awareness about the maleffects of alcoholism among the tribals. This is likely to have a positive impact.

Indebtedness

- Moneylenders operating in tribal areas be forced to secure licenses from concerned Gram Sabhas for their business.
- Cooperative Banks, Gramya Banks, Nationalised Banks and credit institutions operating in tribal areas be asked by the

government to simplify their operational procedure. If it is done, simple tribals will be in a position to articulate with such institutions as and when they need.

Land Alienation

- Alienation of tribal land in Scheduled Areas is a serious problem. A lot of land of tribal people have been alienated from the owners. The beneficiaries are mostly non-tribals and the State. Stringent measures be taken by the State Government to check this stealthy menace in tribal areas.
- Alienated land of the tribals be restored, wherever possible, to the owners. This will prevent conflicts in tribal areas.
- Restoration of alienated land should be taken up on priority basis to reduce the sufferings of tribal households.

Role of Welfare Agencies

Tribes Advisory Council (TAC)

- The TAC is the foremost Constitutional apparatus as regards tribal development in a State. The Scheduled Caste and Scheduled Tribe Welfare Department of the Government of Orissa should convene meetings of TAC as per the provisions of the Fifth Schedule of the Constitution.
- It will be beneficial if some new members are inducted to the TAC every year while nominating members annually.

National Commission for Scheduled Castes and Scheduled Tribes (NCSC&ST)

- The State office of the NCSC&ST is a monitoring body in respect of Scheduled Castes and Scheduled Tribes welfare and development activities. This office possibly does not undertake *suo motto* field visits to check up welfare activities in the field. Normally its staff go to the field only when there is a complaint by someone. Instead of only reviewing the reports, if the State office of NCSC&ST

makes field visits to monitor ongoing development activities among the SC and ST population on regular basis, it would be very helpful.

Scheduled Castes and Scheduled Tribes Research and Training Institute (SCSTRTI)

- The Scheduled Castes and Scheduled Tribes Research and Training Institute of the State has been undertaking research, training, and preparation of action plans in connection with the welfare and development of Scheduled Caste and Scheduled Tribe population of the State. The institute is engaged in publication of monographs, evaluation reports, project reports and a journal concerned with welfare and development of Scheduled Caste and Scheduled Tribe population. It would be better if the institute also concentrates on the issues enshrined in the Fifth Schedule of the Constitution.

Orissa Forest Development Corporation Ltd. (OFDC)

- The OFDC while trading on NTFPs should adopt a people friendly approach rather than following a revenue generation approach. Under this approach, a tribal will be treated as a part of the larger socio-cultural system of procurement, processing and marketing of NTFPs. As the tribals depend more on these sources for livelihood the traditional system of the tribals should not be disrupted.
- The OFDC Ltd. has to attach more importance to the value addition aspect of NTFPs. This will help the tribal people to get more remuneration while improving the quality of the NTFPs. Tribal Self-Help Groups (SHGs) be promoted to undertake value addition activities of NTFPs.

Tribal Development Cooperative Corporation Ltd. (TDCC)

- Government of Orissa is requested to strengthen the organisational and functional dimensions of TDCC by sanctioning the required amount to put the institution on its rails. TDCC has to strengthen the processes of procurement of SAPs and NTFPs from the tribal households and supply essential commodities and consumer goods to them so as to increase the quality of life of the tribal people. The TDCC has to strengthen its operational channels so as to cater to the needs of the beneficiaries more efficiently.

- The concept of 'green gollas' to store and supply basic grains to the tribal people should be reestablished, operated and monitored by the TDCC in the Scheduled Areas for the benefit of tribal people.
- In order to reduce the control and influence of moneylenders on tribal economy the TDCC should promote micro-credit plans introduced by NABARD as an integrated development approach.

Orissa State Finance Development Corporation Ltd. (OSFDC)

- The OSFDC needs revamping of the total organisational set-up. The State level office of OSFDC seems to be more functional, whereas, the district level offices are dormant.
- The State Government needs to release equity funds under the Margin Money Loan schemes through the OSFDC on time; so that the OSFDC can implement its loan schemes efficiently.

Panchayati Raj Institution (PRIs)

- In accordance with the implementation of the Panchayati Raj Act (Amendment) of 1997 in the Scheduled Areas of the State, it is necessary that all Regulations, Acts, and laws operating in Scheduled Areas, such as IPC, CrPC, etc., be suitably amended within a stipulated time for decentralising power among different tiers of the Panchayati Raj system. This will facilitate all the tiers of PRIs to work more efficiently.

- It is essential to impart training to the functionaries of PRI in the Scheduled Areas. This will enhance the skill, knowledge and functional efficiency of PRI members.

The above suggestions appear to be relevant in view of the operational aspects of the Fifth Schedule of the Constitution of India in the State of Orissa; hence their incorporation.

Annexure

Annexure-1
The Scheduled Areas Transfer of Immovable Property (by Scheduled Tribes) Regulation of 1956

The Orissa Scheduled Areas Transfer of Immovable Property (by Scheduled Tribes) Regulation 1956 has been promulgated by the Governor of Orissa with immediate effect in exercise of powers conferred by Sub-paragraph 2 of paragraph 5 of Fifth Scheduled to the Constitution of India. The Regulation received the assent of the President of India on the 21 September 1956 and was first published in Orissa Gazette; extraordinary dated the 4 October 1956.

Scheduled Area as per Regulation 2 means the Scheduled Areas specified in respect of the State of Orissa in the Scheduled Areas (Part-A States) Order, 1950 and the Scheduled Tribes specified in respect of the State of Orissa in the Constitution (Scheduled Tribes) Order 1950.

(i) Transfer of immovable property means mortgage with or without possession, lease, sale, gift, exchange or any other dealing with such property not being a testamentary deposition and includes a charge or contract relating to such property. The regulation says any transfer of immovable property situated within a Scheduled Area absolutely null and void and of no force or effect what so ever unless made in favour of another member of a Scheduled Tribe or with the previous consent in writing of the competent authority.

Competent authority refers to the District Collector and includes any other Officer or Officers appointed by the State Government under Section 2 (a) of the Regulation by notification to perform all or any of the functions of a competent authority under this Regulation. Under notification No.40955–R dated 1.9.1962, the State Government appointed all Sub-Divisional Officers, Special Officers or Revenue Divisional Officers as the case may be of the areas to which the said Regulation is applicable to perform the functions of a competent authority under Section–3 of the said Regulation within their respective jurisdiction.

Nothing in Sub-section (1) of Section (3) of the Regulation shall apply to any transfer by way of mortgage executed in favour of any public financial institution for securing a loan granted only for agricultural Section 2 (a) by such institution for any agricultural purposes. In execution of any decree for realisation of the mortgage money, no property mortgaged to any public and/or financial institution for securing a loan granted by such institution for any agriculture shall be sold in favour of any person not being a member of the Scheduled Tribe without the previous consent in writing of the competent authority.

Where a transfer of immovable property is made in contravention of Sub-section (1) of Section 3 of the Regulation, the competent authority may, either on application by any one interested there in or on his own motion and after giving the parties an opportunity of being heard, order enactment against any person in possession of the property claiming under the transfer and shall cause restoration of possession of such property to the transferor or his heirs. In causing such restriction of possession; the competent authority may take such steps as may be necessary for securing compliance with the said order or preventing any breach of peace. A proviso has been added to the effect that if the competent authority is of the opinion that restoration of possession of immovable property to the transfer or his heirs is not reasonably practicable, they shall record his reasons, therefore, and shall, subject to the control of State Government, settle the said property with another member of ST or in the absence of any such member, with any other person in accordance with the provisions contained in the Orissa Government Land Settlement Act, 1962.

Section 3 (3) provides that subject to such conditions as may be prescribed an appeal if preferred within thirty days of the date of the order under Sub-section (2) of Section 3 of the Regulation shall, if made by the Collector lie to the Board of Revenue and if made by any other competent authority to the Collector or any other Officer specially empowered by the State Government in this behalf and the decision of the competent authority under Sub-section (2) shall be final and shall not be challenged in Courts of Law.

(ii) Eviction of persons from unauthorised occupation of property: Under Section 3 (A) (1) of the Regulation, where a person is found to be in unauthorised occupation of any immovable property of a member of the ST by way of trespass or otherwise, the competent authority may, either on application by the owner or any person interested there in, or on his own motion, and after giving the parties concerned an opportunity of being heard, order enactment of the person so found to be in unauthorised occupation and shall cause restoration of possession of such property to the said member of the STs or to his heirs.

The provision contained in Sub-section (2), (3) and (4) of Section 3 shall, *mutatis mutandis* apply to the proceedings instituted or initiated under Section (1).

(iii) Inadmissibility of a dead for the purpose of registration: Section 4 states that notwithstanding any thing contained in the Indian Registration Act, 1908 no deed of transfer of any immovable property executed in contravention of the provisions of this Regulation shall be accepted for registration.

(iv) Surrender or Relinquishment not valid unless settled by the Land-lord: As per Section 5: (1) No surrender or Relinquishment of any holding or a part of a holding by a tenant can be to a landlord under any law for the time being in force and applicable to such tenancy, such tenant being a member of a Scheduled Tribe, shall be valid unless after such surrender of relinquishment the landlord there of by whatever name called either settles the said holding or part of the holding as the case may be, with another member of a Scheduled Tribe or else retains it in his possession or settles it was any other person with the approval of the competent authority when such member of a Scheduled Tribe is not available. (2) Any surrender or relinquishment shall be deemed to be a transfer of immovable property within the meaning of this Regulation and except as otherwise provided in Sub-section (1) the other provisions of this Regulation that should, so far as may be applied. (3) Nothing in this Section shall apply to any tenant holding immediately under the State Government.

(v) Bar to attachment of immovable property: Section 6 - in execution of money-decree against a member of a ST, no right, title or interest held by him in any immovable property within any Scheduled Area shall be liable to be attached and sold except as and if prescribed.

Penalty: Section 7 (1) – If, after the commencement of this Regulation, any person who is not a member of a ST is found to be in possession of any immovable property in contravention of the provisions of this Regulation, such person shall, without prejudice to his liability to enactment under Sub-section (2) of Section 3, be also liable to a penalty of an amount not exceeding two hundred rupees per acre of such immovable property for each year of any part therefore, during which his unlawful possession continues. (2) Such penalty may be imposed by the competent authority ordering enactment under Sub-section (2) of Section 3, and shall be recoverable as an arrears of land revenue and such portion of the penalty as the competent authority may order shall be paid to the transferor or his heir.

(vi) Offence: Section 7 (A) – Whoever, after having been evicted under any provision of this regulation from any immovable property of a member of any ST reoccupies the same without a valid transfer made in his favour, shall be punishable with rigorous imprisonment for a term which may extend to two years or with fine which may extend to two thousand rupees, or with both.

(vii) Consideration money not refundable in case of invalid transfer: Section 7 (B) – Notwithstanding anything contained in any law for the time being in force, where a transfer of immovable property is found to have been made in contravention of the provisions of Section 3 and the transferee or any other person in possession of the property has been evicted there from under the said Section, the transferee shall not be entitled to the refund of any amount paid by him to the transferor by way of consideration for the transfer.

(viii) Burden of proof and power of court to ignore admission: Notwithstanding anything contained in any other law for the time being in force:

(a) if in any proceedings under this Regulation the validity of the transfer or relinquishment of any immovable property is called in question or if such proceedings are for the recovery of possession of immovable property, the burden of proving that the transfer or relinquishment was valid shall lie on the transferee.

(b) The Court shall, in any suit or proceeding relating to the transfer of immovable property of a member of the Scheduled Tribes, have power to require any fact expressly or impliedly admitted by such member to be proved otherwise than by mere admission.

(ix) Amendment of the Limitation Act, 1963 in its application to the Scheduled Areas: In the Limitation Act, 1963 in its application to the Scheduled Areas in the Scheduled, the words "twelve years" have been replaced by thirty years in relation to immovable property belonging to a member of a ST specified in respect of the State of Orissa.

(x) The Orissa Scheduled Areas Transfer or Immovable Property (By Scheduled Tribes) Rules, 1959:

(a) Procedure for transfer to non-Scheduled Tribe. The Regulation prescribes procedure as follows:

(1) A member of a ST who intends to transfer any of his immovable property situated with a Scheduled Area to a member of any Non-Scheduled Tribe, shall submit an application for the purpose and obtain the prior consent in writing of the competent authority under Section 3 (1) of the Regulation.

(2) On receipt of such application, the competent authority may cause necessary enquiries of a summary nature to be made by an officer duly authorised by him for the purpose before passing order.

(b) Attachment of immovable property:

(1) There shall be no attachment of sale of immovable property in execution of money decrees against a member of a Scheduled Tribe within any Scheduled Area without the written permission of the competent authority. The property at such sale shall be sold only to members of Scheduled Tribe unless otherwise specifically directed in writing by the competent authority.

(2) Subject to the provision contained in Sub-rule (1), the procedure laid down in the Code of Civil Procedure, 1908 relating to execution of decrees shall apply to the said money decrees.

(c) General control of Collector: All orders except those, against which an appeal lies, passed under these rules by any other competent authority shall be subject to general control of the respective collectors having jurisdiction.

(d) Sale of Timbers by Scheduled Tribe and Scheduled Caste persons standing on their *Gharbari Rayati* lands.

There is no legal bar with regard to sale of trees belonging to Scheduled Tribe/Scheduled Caste at present. The law seeks to regulate cutting of trees belonging to Scheduled Caste/ Scheduled Tribe as in case of transfer of lands belonging to Scheduled Caste/Scheduled Tribe under Regulation 2/1956 or under the Orissa Land Reforms Act. The trees could be cut and sold with prior permission of Divisional Forest Officer on payment of proper market value. But, it does not take into consideration the ecological aspect of the society, which is more important.

(i) Cutting of fruit bearing trees on private lands has been banned under a notification of the Forests, Fisheries and Animal Husbandry Department issued under Section 42 of the Orissa Forest Act in 1979 prohibiting cutting of following species of trees like Mango, Jack fruits, Mahula, Kusum, Palm, Asan, Tamarind and Sandal.

While giving transit transport permission, the Divisional Forest Officer/Tehasildar should see that no such trees are allowed to be cut except those are dead or wind fallen.

(ii) A rigid procedure or issue of transit transport permits has been prescribed under Rule 7 (8) of the Orissa Timber and other Forest Produce Transport Rules, 1980. This involves joint inspection by the Revenue and Forest Authorities. During this joint inspection, it should be ensured that:
   (a) The trees proposed to be cut actually stand on private land and not on any government land.
   (b) That the tribal is not exploited and proper market value is paid to the tribal. The market value will be the prevailing market price on the date of contract between the Trader and Tribal.
   (c) The tribal is persuaded not to dispose of trees having good ecological value.

Annexure 2
Orissa Land Reforms Act, 1960 – Orissa Act 16 of 1960 (A 2)

There are some special provisions enshrined in this legislation to safeguard the interests of Scheduled Caste and Scheduled Tribe people on the economic front. They are illustrated below to show how far the legislative measures have advanced to safeguard the interests of Scheduled Tribes on land.

(a) Surrender/abandonment by *Raiyat* Tenant

Section 22-A (4) reads that where the surrender or abandonment of any holding or part thereof is approved by the Revenue Officer under this Section, the holding or part thereof so surrendered or abandoned shall be settled by the government. Section 6-A (1) provides that any transfer by a raiyat of any land which has been settled with him for agricultural purposes under a permanent lease from government shall, if such transfer is made within a period of ten years from the date of such settlement without obtaining the previous permission in writing of the Revenue Officer, be void. This is also a general provision applicable to all the *raiyats* whether a Scheduled Caste, Scheduled Tribe or general.

The Act protects the interests of the Scheduled Caste and Scheduled Tribes as follows: where any person is found to be in unauthorised occupation of the whole or part of a holding of a holding of a *raiyat* belonging to a Scheduled Tribe within any part of the State other than a Scheduled Area, by way of trespass or otherwise, the Revenue Officer may, either on application by the owner or any person interested therein, or on his own motion, and after giving the parties concerned an opportunity of being heard, order eviction of the person so found to be in unauthorised occupation and shall cause restoration of the property to the said *raiyat* or to his heir.

If in any proceedings, the validity of the transfer of any holding or any part thereof is called in question or if such proceedings are for the recovery of possession of such holding or part thereof, the burden of proving that the transfer was valid shall, notwithstanding anything contained in any other laws for the time being in force, lie on the transferee. In the Limitation Act, 1963 in its application to proceeding 30 years have been granted instead of 12 years applicable to the general cases.

Some other special privileges for Scheduled Tribe and Scheduled Caste people on land have been given. Some of these are indicated in the following pages:

The Orissa Land Reforms Act, 1960 provides that in case of the settlements of surplus lands, seventy per cent of the surplus lands vested in the government under Section 45 shall be settled with persons belonging to the Scheduled Castes or Scheduled Tribes in proportion to their respective populations in the villages in which the land are situated and the remaining lands shall be settled with persons not belonging to the aforesaid categories.

It is provided that where the population of the Scheduled Caste and Scheduled Tribe in a village exceeds seventy per cent of the total population of that village, the percentage of lands to be reserved for persons of the said communities shall be equal to the percentage of their population.

It is provided further that if sufficient number of persons belonging to the aforesaid categories are not available in the village in which the land are situated or being available, are not willing to accept settlement of land, so much of the lands reserved for the said persons as cannot be settled with them may be settled with other persons. The land so settled cannot be transferred (disposed of) by sale or otherwise within the period of ten years following such settlement. The State Government in Revenue Department Order has exempted from payment of Court fee in all cases of application from persons belonging to Scheduled Castes, Scheduled Tribes and other landless persons for the settlement of ceiling surplus lands.

In the Orissa Prevention of Land Encroachment Act, 1972, it has been provided that where any land is in the unauthorised occupation of a landless person, the Tehasildar may, instead of evicting such person from the land in his unauthorised occupation, settle the same with him so, however, that the land so settle with him together with the land excluding homestead, if any, owned by him and the lands owned by all the members of his family who are living with him in common mess, shall on no account exceed one standard acre. The landless tribal people can avail benefit of this provision if encroached government land by them.

Bibliography

Journals and Books

Abraham, J., 1995, 'Impact of Prohibition on State-Excise Study of Four Southern States', *Economic and Political Weekly*, December 2, pp. 3051-53.

Acharya, P.K., Mishra, R., Panigrahi, N. and Mohanty, R.P., 2001, 'Functioning of Welfare Schemes for the Scheduled Castes and Scheduled Tribes: A Report on Orissa', report submitted to Committee of Governors of India, NKC Centre for Development Studies, Bhubaneswar.

Acharya, P.K. and Mishra, R., 2000, 'Evaluation of Lanjia Saora Development Agency, Puttasing, Rayagada District, Orissa'. Submitted to SC and ST Development Department, by NCDS Bhubaneswar.

Ahmed, I., 1972, 'Perspectives of the Communal Problems,' *ICSSR Research Abstracts Quartely*, II (1).

Bailey, F.G., 1960, *Tribe, Caste and Nation*, Bombay, Oxford University Press.

—, 1961, 'Tribe and Caste in India', *Contributions to Indian Sociology*, No-V, pp. 7-19.

Bandura, A., 1969, *Principles of Behaviour Modification*, New York, Rinehart and Winston.

Behura, N. and Sahu, B.N., 1970-71, 'Mutha: The Traditional Political Organisation of the Kondhs (with specific reference to Pusungia Mutha in the Phulbani District of Orissa)', *Journal of Adivasi*, Vol. XII, No. 1-4, pp. 13-21.

Behura, N.K., 1982, 'Forest and Tribal World View', *Journal of Social Research*, Vol. XXV, No. 1, pp. 1-8.

—, 1983, 'Tribes and the Forest: An Overview', *Journal of Adivasi,* THRTI, Bhubaneswar.

—, 1988-89, 'Tribal Societies in Orissa', *Manav,* Vol. 3, pp. 195-215.

—, 1990, 'The Tribal Development: A Critical Review', *Manav,* Vol. 3, pp. 22-32.

—, 1990, 'Socio-Economic Problems and Social Change', in *The Uprooted,* Sudarshan, V. and Kalyan. M.A. (ed.), New Delhi, Gyan Publishing House.

—, 1996, 'Environment, Displacement and Development: Case Study from Orissa', *Indian Anthropologist,* Soc. 31, pp. 149-159.

Behura, N.K. and Nayak, P.K., 1993, 'Involuntary Displacement and the Changing Frontiers of Kinship: A Study of Settlement in Orissa', in *Anthropological Approach to Resettlement,* Cernea, M. Michael and Scott E., Guggenheim.

Behura, N. and Panigrahi, N., 2001, 'Functioning of the Fifth Schedule of the Constitution of India: The Role of Welfare Agencies in the State of Orissa', report submitted to ICSSR New Delhi, NKC Centre for Development Studies, Bhubaneswar.

Beteille, Andre, 1998, *Inequality and Social Change,* Delhi, Oxford University Press.

—, 1974, *Studies in Agrarian Social Structure,* Delhi, Oxford University Press.

Bose, N.K., 1967, *Culture and Society in India,* Bombay, Asia Publishing House.

—, 1972, 'Anthropology and Some Indian Problems', Institute of Social Research and Applied Anthropology, Calcutta.

Chandhoke, N., 2003, 'Governance and the Pluralisation of the State: Implications for Democratic Citizenship', *Economic and Political Weekly,* Vol. 38(28), pp. 2957-68.

Choudhury, B., 1976, 'Disintegration of Leadership among the Oraons of Sundargarh District of Orissa', *Journal of Adivasi,* Vol. XVI, No. 2 pp. 41-45.

Choudhury, M., 1977, *Tribes of Ancient India,* Calcutta, Indian Museum, Calcutta.

Damodaran, A., 1992, 'The Economics of Forest Conservation and Sustainable Development', paper presented at National Seminar on Socio-economic Research in Forestry, Thrissur, May, pp. 18-20.

Dandekar, V.M. and Rath, N., 1971, *Poverty in India,* Bombay, Sameeksha Trust.

Das, Arvind, N., 1983, *Agrarian Unrest and Socio-Economic Change 1900-1980,* New Delhi, Manohar Publications.

Das, B., 1997, 'Welfare of Weaker Sections: Effective Implementation of Protective Laws and Regulations', Occasional Paper.

Das, B.S., 1978, *Studies in the Economic History of Orissa: From Ancient Times to 1833*, Calcutta, Firma KLM.

Das, V., 1996, 'Minor Forest Produce and Rights of Tribals', *EPW*, Vol. XXXI, No. 50, pp. 3227-3229.

Dhanagare, D.N., 1983, *Peasant Movements in India: 1920-1950*, Delhi, Oxford University Press.

Dhebar, U.N., 1963, 'Report of the Scheduled Areas and Scheduled Tribes Commission', Dhebar Committee Report, New Delhi, Manager Publication.

Diwakar, D.M., 1999, 'Dalit Question of Inequality, Exploitation and Mobilisation: A Micro View of Ground Realities', *Man and Development*, Vol. XXI, No. 3, Population, pp. 62-81.

Dube, S.C., 1977, *Tribal Heritage of India*, Vol. I, New Delhi, Vikas Publishing House.

Elwin, V., 1938, *The Baiga*, London, John Murray.

—, 1948, 'Notes on the Juanga', *Man in India*, Vol. XXVIII, Nos. 1&2.

—, 1948, *The Aboriginal*, Bombay, Oxford University Press.

Encyclopedia Americana, 1981, Grolier Incorporated Library of Congress Catalogoing in Publications, Vol. 1.

Fernades, W. et al., 1984, 'Forest, Environment and Forest Dwellers Economy in Orissa' (mimeo), New Delhi, Indian Social Institute.

—, 1986, 'Forests Environment and Forest Dwellers Economy in Chattishgarh, A Report on Deforestation, Marginalisation, and Search for Alternatives', New Delhi, Indian Social Institute.

Fernades, W., 1988, *Forest Environment and Tribal Economy*, New Delhi, Indian Social Institute (Tribes of India Series).

—, 1994, 'Development, Inducemed Displacement in the Tribal Ares of Eastern India (mimeo), New Delhi, Indian Social Institute.

Fried, M.H., 1966, *On the Concept of Tribe and Tribal Society*, transactions of the New York Academy of Sciences, Series-II, No. 4, pp. 527-540.

Gadgil, M., 1989, 'Deforestation: Problems and Prospects', Foundation Day Lecture, May 12, Society for Promotion of Wastelands' Development, New Delhi, Supplements to *Wastelands News*, Vol. 4, May-July.

Gandhi, M., 1929, 'Harijan', December 21, 1947.

Ghurye, G.S., 1943, The Aboriginals: So-Called and their Future', Poona: Gokhale Institute of Politics and Economy.

Godelier, M., 1977, 'Perspective in Marxist Anthropology', Cambridge: Cambridge University Press.

Government of Orissa, 1937, 'Proceedings of Orissa Legislative Assembly', Government of Orissa, Vol. I, p. 1054.

—, 1938-64, 'Final Report on the Major Settlement Operations in Koraput District of Orissa', Government of Orissa.

—, 1938, 'Proceedings of Orissa Legislative Assembly (OLA)', Government of Orissa, Vol. II, Part I, p. 44 and Vol. III, p. 167.

—, 1947, 'Proceedings of Orissa Legislative Assembly', Government of Orissa, Vol. V, No. 3, p. 93.

—, 1961, 'Shifting Cultivation in Orissa', Agricultural Department of Social Conservation Organisation, Orissa Government Press.

—, 1972-73, 'Report on the Survey on Shifting Cultivation', THRTI, Bhubaneswar.

—, 1980-81 to 1990-91, 'Report on Agricultural Census of Orissa', Government of Orissa.

—, 1983, 'Amendment Rule 3 of Orissa Tribes Advisory Council (Amendment) Rules 1983', Welfare Department, Government of Orissa.

—, 1988, 'Transfer of Land Alienation in Scheduled areas of Orissa', Proceeding of Tribes Advisory Council, ST and SC Development Department, Government of Orissa.

—, 1992, 'Single Line Administration in TSP Areas of Orissa', Proceedings of Tribes Advisory Council, ST and SC Development Department, Government of Orissa.

—, 1995-96, 'Report on the Annual Administration of Scheduled Areas in Orissa', Welfare Department, Government of Orissa, Bhubaneswar.

—, 1999, 'Scheduled Tribes and Scheduled Castes Development Department', Orissa, Bhubaneswar.

—, 2000, 'District Excise Office: Kalahandi Office', Government of Orissa, Bhawanipatana.

—, 2000, 'Conferment of Ownership Rights to Persons Cultivating Land in the Hill Slopes within 30 degrees in Scheduled Caste, Revenue Department, Government of Orissa.

—, 2000, 'Policy on Procurement and Trade of Non-Timber Forest Produces'. Government Resolution No. 5503/F&E, Forest and Environment Department, Government of Orissa,

—, 2002a., 'Tenth Five-Year Plan (2002-2007): Dimensions and Strategies', Vol. 1, New Delhi: Planning Commission.

Government of India, 1954, 'Prohibition Enquiry Committee Report' (Sriman Narayan Committee), New Delhi.

—, 1964, 'Report of the Study Team on Prohibition', Vols. I & II (Tek Chand Committee), Planning Commission, New Delhi.

—, 1985, 'Seventh Five-Year Plan (1985-90)', Socio-Economic Programme for Women', Chapter 17, Planning Documents on Women in India; op. cit. New Delhi, pp. 72-80.

—, 1992, 'Eighth Five-Year Plan (1992-97)', Vol. II, Planning Commission of India, Government of India, New Delhi.

—, 1994, 'Report of the Working Group on Tribal Development during Seventh Plan, 1985-90', Government of India, New Delhi.

—, 1996, 'The Constitution of India', Law Ministry, Government of India, New Delhi.

—, 1997-98, 'Annual Reports'. Social Justice and Empowerment, Government of India, New Delhi.

—, 1997, 'State Election Commissions Office', Orissa, Bhubaneswar.

—, 1997-2002, 'Approach Paper to the Ninth Five-Year Plan', Planning Commission, Government of India, New Delhi.

—, 2000a., 'Statistics at a Glance: 1996-97', Ministry of Agriculture, New Delhi.

Guillet, D., 1983, 'Towards a Cultural Ecology of Mountains', *Current Anthropology*, XXIV (5): pp. 561-574.

Hiro, D., 1976, *Inside India Today*, London, Routledge and Kegan Paul.

Illaiah, K., 1992, 'Andhra Pradesh's Anti-liquor Movement', *Economic and Political Weekly,* November, 7, pp. 2406-8.

Jha, V., 1977, 'Paper in Orissa', in *Land Alienation and Restoration of the Tribal Communities of India* (ed.), S.N. Dubey and Ratna Murdia, Bombay, Himalayan Publishing House.

Joshi, P.C., 1975, *Land Reforms in India: Trends and Perspectives*, New Delhi, Allied Publishers.

Judge, P.S., 1999, *Social Change Through Land Reforms*, Rawat Publications, New Delhi.

Kant, S. et.al., 1970, 'Community Forest Management in Orissa', The Ford Foundation, paper presented in the Workshop on Sustainable Forestry, New Delhi.

Kar, S., 2001, 'Country Liquor Trade and Cottage Industry in Orissa', *Indian Express*, February 25, 2001, Bhubaneswar.

Kulkarni, S.D., 1979, 'Bonded Labour and Illicit Money Lending in Maharashtra: Review of a Report', *EPW*, Vol. XIV (10), pp. 561-564.

Leach, E., 1964, 'Political System of Highland Burma', London, Bell.

Lieten, G.K. and Ravi Srivastava, (1999), *Unequal Partners, Power Relations: Development in Uttar Pradesh*, New Delhi, Sage Publications.

Mahal, A., 2000, 'What Works in Alcohol Policy? Evidences for Rural India, *Economic and Political Weekly*, November, 4-110, Vol. XXXV, No. 45, pp. 3959-3968.

Mahapatra, L.L., 1968, 'Problems and Welfare of Orissa Tribals', *Applied Anthropology in India: Principles, Problems and Case Studies*, Vidyarthy, L.P. (ed.), Allahabad, Kitab Mahal.

—, 1987, *Economic Development of Tribal India*, Ashish Publishing House, New Delhi, p. 137.

—, 1998, 'Participatory Approach in Resettlement and Rehabilitation Implementation', paper presented at Gopabandhu Academy of Administration in the Seminar on 'Resettlement and Rehabilitation'.

—, 1999, 'Participatory Approach in Resettlement and Rehabilitation Implementation', paper presented at Gopabandu Academy of Administration, in the Seminar on 'Resettlement and Rehabilitation'.

—, 1999, 'Tribal Rights to Land and the State in Orissa', in *Contemporary Society Tribal Studies*, Behera, D.K. and Pfeffer, G., New Delhi, Concept Publishing Company.

Mallik, R.M., 1997, 'Procurement and Marketing of Kenduleaves in Orissa: A Study of Economic Deprivation and Benefits to Primary Collectors', report submitted to NKC Centre for Development Studies, Bhubaneswar, Orissa.

Mallik, R.M. and Panigrahi, N., 1998, 'Non-Timber Forest Produce: Collection, Benefits and Management in Orissa', A Study Report of NKC Centre for Development Studies, Bhubaneswar, submitted to The Ford Foundation, New Delhi.

Mandelbaum, D.G., 1956, 'Social Grouping in in Man', in *Culture and Society*, Sapire. H.L. (ed.), New York, Oxford.

Marx, K., 1970, *Capital III*, New York, International Publishers.

Mathew, G., 1994, *Panchayati Raj: From Legislation to Movement*, New Delhi, Concept Publishing House.

Mohanty, B.B., 1997, 'State and Tribal Relationship in Orissa', *Indian Anthropologist*, Vol. 27, No. 1, June, pp. 1-17.

—, 2001, 'Land Distribution among Scheduled Castes and Scheduled Tribes', *EPW*, October 2001.

Mohanty, K.K., et al., 1993, 'Pattern of Land Holding among Major Tribes of the Sub-Plan Area in Orissa (based on Universal Benchmark Survey 1978-80)', *Journal of Adivasi*, Vol. XXXIII, No. 2, pp. 1-16.

Mohanty, M., 1984, 'Social Roots of Backwardness in Orissa', Social Science Probings, 1(2), pp. 184-228.

Mohapatra, L.K., 1960, 'A Hill Bhuiyan Village', Department of Anthropology, Utkal University (mimeo).

—, 1982-83, 'Barriers to Development in Isolated Tribal Areas: Two Case Studies of Most Backward Gram Panchayats in Orissa', *Manav*, Vol. 1, No. 1.

—, 1993, 'Customary Rights in Land and Forest and the State in Continuity and Change', in K.S. Singh (ed.), *Tribal Society*, Shimla, Indian Institute of Advanced Study.

Mohapatra, K. et al., 1973-74, 'Report on the Survey of Indebtedness Among the STs of Paralakhemundi Sub-Division in Ganjam District', *Journal of Adivasi,* Vol. 15, Nos. 1, 2, 3 & 4.

Mohapatra, P.C., 1987, *Economic Development of Tribal India*, New Delhi, Ashish Publishing House.

Mohapatra, P.K., 1970, 'Leadership and Religion of Koya', *Journal of Adivasi,* Vol. XI, No. 4, pp. 53-59.

Moreman, M., 1965, 'Ethnic Identification in a Complex Civilisation: Who are the Luel, *American Anthropologist*, 67(5).

Mungekar, N., 1999, 'State, Market and the Dalits Analytics of the New Economic Policy', in S. Michael (ed.), *Dalits in Modern India*, New Delhi, Vistaar Publications.

Nadkarni, M.V., 1996, 'Forests, People and Economics', *Indian Journal of Agricultural Economics,* Vol. 51, Nos. 1 & 2, January-June.

Nair, Kusum, 1961, *Blossoms at the Dust*, London, Duckworth and Co.

Naroll, R., 1964, 'On Ethnic Unit Classification', *Current Anthropology*, V (4).

Ninan, K.N., 1992, 'Economics of Shifting Cultivation in India', *EPW*, Vol. 27, No. 13, March 28, pp. A.2-A.6.

Omvedt, Gail, 1993, *Dalits and the Democratic Revolution: Dr. Ambedkar and the Dalit Movement in Colonial India*, New Delhi, Sage Publications.

Oklay, Peter et al., 1991, *Projects with People: The Practice of Participation in Rural Development*, Geneva, International Labour Office.

Panda, P., 1982, 'Binjhal: A Royal Tribe of Orissa: A Study of their Traditional Political System', Ph.D. awarded by Sambalpur University.

Panda, P. and Panigrahi, N., 1989, 'The Problem of Displacement of Displaced People: A Study in the Coal Mines of Brajarajnagar, Orissa', in *Tribal Development in India*, Pati, R.N. and Jena, B. (ed.), New Delhi, Ashish Publishing House.

Panigrahi, N., 2001, 'Impact of State Policies on Management of Land Resources in Tribal Areas of Orissa', *Journal of Man and Development*, Vol. XXIII, No. 1, March, 2001.

Parry, J., 1979, *Caste and Kinship in Kangra*, London, Routledge and Kegan Paul.

Patankar, B. and Gail Omvedt, 1979, 'The Dalit Liberation Movement in Colonial Period'. *Economic and Political Weekly*, Vol. XIV, Nos. 7 and 8, pp. 409-24.

Patel, M.L., 1974, *Changing Land Problems of Tribal India*, Progress Publishers, Bhopal.

Pathak, S., 1985, 'Intoxication as a Social Evil: Anti-Alcohol Movement in Uttarakhanda', *EPW*, August 10, pp. 1360-65.

Pathy, J., 1976, 'Political Economy of Kandhaland', *Man in India*, 56(2), 1-36.

—, 1982, 'An Outline of Modes of Production in Tribal India', in *Tribal Development in India: Problems and Prospects*, (ed.) Choudhury, B., New Delhi, Inter-India Publications.

—, 1984, *Tribal Peasantry Dynamics of Development*, New Delhi, Inter-India Publications.

—, 1987, *Ethnic Minorities and Processes of Development,* Jaipur, Rawat Publications.

Pati, S. et al., 1993, 'Community Organisers in Forest Management', Indian Institute of Forest Management, Bhopal (mimeo).

Patnaik, N., 1972, 'Tribes and their Development: A Study of Two Tribal Development Blocks in Orissa', Hyderabad, National Institute of Community Development.

—, 1996, 'Minor Forest Produce in Orissa', Social Science and Development Research Institute, Bhubaneswar, report submitted to NABARD, Bhubaneswar.

Patnaik, N. and Mishra, H.S., 1976, 'Elections and Pattern of Leadership in Two Lanjia Saora Villages of Gumma Panchayat Samit, Ganjam', *Journal of Adivasi*, Vol. XVI, No. 3 pp. 1-16.

Patnaik, S.M., 2000, 'Understanding Involuntary Resettlement: An Anthropological Perspective', *The Eastern Anthropologists,* Vol. 53, 1 and 2.

Pitner and Cappel, 1974, 'Modification of Affective Consequences of Alcohol: A Comparison of Social and Solitary Drinking', *Journal of Abnormal Psychology*, No. 83-84, August.

Prasad, K., 1994, 'Women and Panchayats: Making Success of the New Experiment', *Kurukshetra*, June, pp. 16-18.

Radhakrishnan, P., 1989, *Peasant Struggles, Land Reforms and Social Change: Malabar, 1836-1882*, Sage Publications, New Delhi.

Ramachandra, K. et al., 2000, 'Indebtedness of Households: Changing Characteristics', *EPW*, Vol. XXXVI, No. 19, pp. 1617-1626.

Ramachanadra Rao, K.S. and Tripathy, A.K., 2001, 'Indebtedness of Households: Changing Characterstics', *Economic and Political Weekly*, Vol. XXXVI, No. 19.

Ram, N., 1979, 'Dravida Movement in its Pre-Independence Phases', *Economic and Political Weekly*, Vol. XIV, Nos. 7 and 8, pp. 337-402.

Ranadive, B., 1979, 'The Caste, Class and Property Relations', *Economic and Political Weekly*, Vol. 14, Nos. 7 and 8, pp. 337-48.

Rao, V.M., 1988, 'Sustained Development Through People: The Need for Political, Activisation', *Vikalpa*, Vol. 13, No. 13, July-September.

—, 1990, 'Interventions for the Poor: Critical Dimensions Potentialities and Limitations', in Krishnaswamy, K.S., *Economic Development*, 1990.

Ratha, S.N., 1992, 'The Community Situation in Western Orissa: A Study in Ethos', in *Silver Jubilee Commemorative Volume,* (ed.) Pati, R.N., Sambalpur University.

Reddy, D., Narasimha and Arun Patnaik, 1993, 'Anti-Arrack Agitation of Women in Andhra Pradesh', *Economic and Political Weekly,* May 22, pp. 1059-66.

Reddy, V.R. et al., 1999, 'Impact of Prohibition in Andhra Pradesh: Some Empirical Results', *Journal of Rural Development and Change,* Vol. IV, No. 2, pp. 270-297.

Reserve Bank of India, 1991, 'Report on Trend and Progress of Banking in India', 1989-90, New Delhi.

—, 1991, 'Report on Currency and Finance 1990-91', RBI, Mumbai.

Robert, C. et al., 1989, *To the Hands of the Poor*, New Delhi, Oxford & IBH Co. Pvt. Ltd.

Roth, H.D., 1979, 'Moneylenders Management of Loan Agreements: Report on a Case Study in Dhanbad', *Economic and Political Weekly,* Vol. XIV, No. 28., p. 1166-1170.

Roy Burman, B.K., 1961, *Social Process in the Industrialisation in Rourkela*, Delhi, Census of India.

—, 1982, 'Report of Committee on Forest and Tribals in India'. Tribal Development Division, Ministry of Home Affairs, New Delhi.

—, 1986, 'Historical Ecology of Land Survey and Settlement in Tribal Areas and Challenges of Development', New Delhi, Council for Social Development.

Roy, N., 1972, 'Introductory Address' in *Tribal Situation in India*, K.S. Singh (ed.), Shimla, Institute of Advanced Studies.

Roy, S.C., 1935, 'The Hill Bhuiyans of Orissa', *Man in India*, Ranchi.

Sabu, L.N., 1942, *Hill Tribes of Jeypore*, Cuttack, Mission Press.

Sahlins, M.D., 1968, *Tribesmen*, Foundations of Modern Anthropological Series, Prentice Hall.

Saldanha, I.M., 1995, 'On Drinking and Drunkenness: History of Liquor in Colonial India', *EPW*, September 16, pp. 2323-31.

Sankaran, S.R., 1996, 'Introduction', in B.N. Yugandhar (ed.), *Land Reforms in India*, Vol. 3, New Delhi, Sage Publications, pp. 17-27.

Sarojini, T.K., 1978, 'Prohibition', *Encyclopedia of Social Work in India*, Vol. II, Ministry of Welfare, Government of India.

Satapathy, N., 2000, 'Liquor Sale Touches New High in Koraput', in *The Utkal Age*, April 7, 2000, Bhubaneswar.

Saxena, N.C., 1995, *Forests, People and Profit: New Equations for Sustainability*, Centre for Sustainable Development, Lal Bahadur Shastri National Academy of Administration, Mussorie, Dehradun, Natraj Publishers.

Seeta Prabhu, K. Anadurani and Achuthan, C.U., 1988, 'Rural Credit: Mystery of the Missing Households', *Economic and Political Weekly*, December 10.

Service, E.R., 1962, *Primitive Social Organisation*, New York, Random House Inc.

—, 1975, *The Origins of State and Civilisation*, New York, W.W. Norton.

Sharma, B.D., 1978, *Tribal Development: The Concept and the Frame*, New Delhi, Prachi Prakashan.

—, 1994, *Dalit Betrayed*, New Delhi, Haranand Publications.

—, 1998, *The Little Lights in Tiny Mud Pots Defy 50 Years of Anti-Panchayati Raj*', New Delhi, Sahyog Pustak Kuteer.

Sinha, S., 1962, 'State Formation and Rajput Myths in Tribal Central India', *Man in India*, Vol. XLII, No. 1.

Sitaprabhu, K. et al., 1988, 'Rural Credit: Mystery of the Missing Households', *EPW*, Mumbai, December, pp. 1-10.

Special Representative, 2000, 'Sasstra Spulinga', special report, *Satabdi*, The Oriya Magazine, December 15, Bhubaneswar.

Srichandan, G.K., 1993, *Tribal Development and Welfare Legislation in Orissa (Under Indian Plan Perspective)*, New Delhi, Pratibha Prakashan.

Stanley, W., 1996, 'Machkund, Upper Kolab and NALCO Projects in Koraput Districts, Orissa', *EPW*, Vol. XXXI, No. 24, pp. 1533-38.

Subba Rao, K.G.K. et al., 1997, 'Indebtedness of Rural Households', *EPW*, Mumbai, December, pp. 1-10.

Swain, M. and Panigrahi, N., 1999, Development, Displacement, and Rehabilitation in Orissa: An Overview', *Man in Life*, Vol. 25, No. 3&4, pp. 163-179.

Thakkar, A.V., 1940, *Report of the Partially Excluded Areas Committee*, Government of Orissa, p. 2.

Verma, M.M., 1996, *Tribal Development in India: Programmes and Prospective*, New Delhi, Mittal Publications.

—, 1998, 'On Prohibition: Dangers of a Blanket Solution', *EPW*, Vol. XXXIII, No. 16, pp. 877-879.

Vyasulu, V., 1985, 'Underdeveloping Koraput', *South Asian Anthropologist*, Vol. 6 (I), pp. 63-71.

—, 1998, 'On Prohibition: Dangers of a Blanket Solution', *EPW*, April 18, pp. 877-9.

Yunus, S.A., 1977, 'Paper of Orissa', in *Land Alienation and Restoration in Tribal Communities in India*, (eds.) S.N. Dubey and Ratan Murdia, Bombay, Himalayan Publishing House.

Index